The Great Eight

Memorable Teams in Baseball History

The Great Eight
The 1975 Cincinnati Reds

Edited by **Mark Armour**

Published by the **University of Nebraska Press, Lincoln and London,** and the **Society for American Baseball Research**

Chapter 1, now substantially revised, originally appeared as "Bob Howsam" in *Drama and Pride in the Gateway City: The 1964 St. Louis Cardinals*, edited by John Harry Stahl and Bill Nowlin (University of Nebraska Press, 2013).

Chapters 3 and 5, now substantially revised, originally appeared respectively as "Sparky Anderson" and "Alex Grammas" in *Detroit Tigers 1984: What a Start! What a Finish!*, edited by Mark Pattison and David Raglin (Society for American Baseball Research, 2012).

Chapter 7, now substantially revised, originally appeared as "Ted Kluszewski" in *Go-Go to Glory: The 1959 Chicago White Sox*, edited by Don Zminda (ACTA Publications, 2009).

Chapters 19 and 28, now substantially revised, originally appeared respectively as "Merv Rettenmund" and "Terry Crowley" in *Pitching, Defense, and Three-Run Homers: The 1970 Baltimore Orioles*, edited by Mark Armour and Malcolm Allen (University of Nebraska Press, 2012).

All photographs are courtesy of the National Baseball Hall of Fame Library, Cooperstown, New York.

Player statistics are courtesy of Baseball-Reference.com and Retrosheet.org (information obtained free of charge from and copyrighted by Retrosheet, www.retrosheet.org).

Manufactured in the United States of America

Library of Congress Cataloging-in-Publication Data
The great eight: the 1975 Cincinnati Reds / edited by Mark Armour.
pages cm. — (Memorable teams in baseball history)
Includes bibliographical references.
ISBN 978-0-8032-4586-0 (pbk.: alk. paper)
ISBN 978-0-8032-5345-2 (epub)
ISBN 978-0-8032-5346-9 (mobi)
ISBN 978-0-8032-5340-7 (pdf)
1. Cincinnati Reds (Baseball team)—History. I. Armour, Mark L.
GV875.C65G75 2014
796.357'640977178—dc23
2013037730

Set in Sabon by Laura Wellington.

Contents

Introduction

Mark Armour

When SABR and the University of Nebraska Press agreed to create a Memorable Teams in Baseball History series, one of the first clubs I thought of was the 1975 Cincinnati Reds. Baseball historians have not neglected this team and season, but the stories of the people who made up or led this team have started to fade. Two of the most famous members of the club—Joe Morgan and Pete Rose—have been in the news regularly since they stopped playing, but usually for nothing related to their extraordinary playing careers.

The Reds were quite a team. Besides Morgan and Rose, they also featured Johnny Bench, perhaps the biggest star in the game at the time, behind the plate; Tony Pérez, the veteran leader and a star in his own right; young players like George Foster, Don Gullett, Ken Griffey, and Dave Concepción, excellent players destined to be overshadowed; and the peerless Sparky Anderson managing in the dugout. The Great Eight, the title of this book, comes from the wonderful starting-position players on this club: Bench, Pérez, Morgan, Concepción, Rose, Foster, César Gerónimo, and Griffey. This may have been history's best starting lineup, but the team was even better than that.

Most of this team had been together for the previous few years, and the team had been a favorite to win the World Series more than once but had thus far come up short. This book is a celebration of that great Reds team and the men who played the game so well. Many readers will remember the big events described here, but the stories of how each of these men was prepared for this season, and what came after, will likely be new to all of you.

Putting together such a book took the efforts of many dedicated baseball researchers. I want to thank especially two people who read every word in the book: Russ Lake, our tireless fact-checker, and Len Levin, who reviewed and edited the manuscript from start to finish. The book is so much better for their efforts. The writers not only put together these interesting stories but also had to keep to a schedule and to respond to many queries as the book was nearing completion. I thank all of them for their professionalism.

Enjoy reliving 1975, the year the Big Red Machine finally took home the ultimate prize.

The Great Eight

Chapter 1. **Bob Howsam**

Mark Armour

Bob Howsam would consider himself one of the last of a breed. A protégé of Branch Rickey, who believed in scouting, player development, and the art of making a deal, Howsam built—just before the advent of free agency—one of history's greatest teams, the 1975–76 Cincinnati Reds, a ball club that reflected that same Rickey-like approach. With the introduction of free agency, however, Howsam, who was greatly disturbed by it, believed future champions would be built mostly by having the most money, not through the traditional scouting, player development, and deal making.

Robert Lee Howsam was born on February 28, 1918, in Denver, Colorado, to Lee and Mary Howsam. Lee had emigrated from Canada as a child, and Mary was a native of Colorado. Lee was a partner in a beekeeping business, harvesting and selling honey.

When Howsam was eight years old his family moved to La Jara, a town 250 miles south of Denver in the San Luis Valley, just north of the New Mexico border. He attended high school in La Jara, where he starred on the basketball team. He also played first base for an American Legion baseball team and often told the story of being struck out by Satchel Paige on one of the famed Negro League star's barnstorming trips through the West.

After high school Howsam attended the University of Colorado in Boulder, intending to learn enough to help his father run the family business. In 1936 Howsam ran into Janet Johnson, whom he had met briefly on a double date in high school. The two began dating and a few years later were married, on September 15, 1939. Johnson was the daughter of Edwin "Big Ed" Johnson, who served Colorado

The architect of the Big Red Machine, Bob Howsam made a series of great deals to turn a good team into a great one.

as either governor or U.S. senator for twenty-five years. Big Ed would become one of the most important people in Howsam's life.

After a few years at Boulder, with World War II approaching, Howsam enrolled in a flight-training program in Alamosa, Colorado, and then moved to a more advanced one in Parkersburg, West Virginia. Eventually he became a flight instructor. In 1943 he joined the navy and became a test pilot, checking out new planes before delivering them to naval air stations around the country. During this time Janet lived in La Jara with Howsam's parents. She gave birth to two sons, Robert Jr. in 1942 and Edwin in 1944. After the war, Howsam returned to La Jara to help run the beekeeping business, which became highly profitable in the late 1940s.

Howsam didn't stay with the family business long, though, for in late 1946 he left for Washington DC to be Senator Johnson's administrative assistant. It was while working for Johnson that he got his start in organized baseball. It came about when the Western League, a Single-A circuit disbanded in 1937, was revived in 1947 in Denver, Pueblo, Sioux City, Des Moines, Omaha, and Lincoln, and Senator Johnson was asked to be the unpaid president of the league. He asked Howsam to move to Lincoln to be the league's executive secretary. In this role, Howsam more or less ran the league—he wrote a constitution and bylaws, drafted a schedule, hired an umpiring crew, and worked with local operators in the six league cities. He spent most of the summer of 1947 driving his car throughout this vast area.

After one season the Denver owners wanted to sell out. Howsam approached his brother and father, who agreed to put up the money from their business, recently sold, to buy the Denver team for $75,000. With that, Howsam, at age thirty, became the owner of the Denver Bears. As he still had to run the league, the rest of the family helped run the team. Lee Howsam, his father, was the president, Mary and Janet collected tickets, and even the boys, Robert and Edwin, helped out by raking the field. Howsam later claimed this experience was invaluable—it taught him how to run every aspect of a baseball franchise.

One of Howsam's first moves was to buy an old dump site in the city and build a new stadium, naming it Bears Stadium when it opened in August 1948. It was later to become Mile High Stadium and would be the principal outdoor facility for baseball and football in Denver for more than fifty years. The Bears led the league in attendance in 1948, as they would for the rest of their tenure in the league. In 1949 the Bears drew nearly five hundred thousand fans, more than the St. Louis Browns of the American League and one of the highest attendance totals in Single-A history. In 1951 Howsam was named the *Sporting News* Single-A Executive of the Year. The next season the Bears won their first league championship, and they copped a second in 1954.

After the 1954 season Howsam bought the Kansas City Blues of the American Association and moved them to Denver, where they became the New York Yankees' Triple-A affiliate and replaced the Single-A Bears. The move had been precipitated by the Blues themselves being displaced in Kansas City by the Philadelphia Athletics' move there for the 1955 season. Howsam's great success continued, as the new Bears led the American Association in attendance during their first three years in the league. Howsam won the *Sporting News* Triple-A Executive of the Year Award in 1956, then watched his Bears win the league title and the Little World Series in 1957.

Howsam often credited two men in particular for his baseball success. One was Branch Rickey, whom Howsam got to know when Denver was a Pirates affiliate in the early 1950s. Howsam watched Rickey run tryout camps and team drills in the spring and thought him baseball's greatest talent evaluator. He also considered Rickey a great speaker and motivator. Some of Rickey's lessons—about the importance of speed and the importance of youth—show up in Howsam's own Major League teams later.

Howsam's other main influence was former Yankees president George Weiss, with whom Howsam worked closely when the Bears became the Yankees' top Minor League team. Weiss's roots were similar to Howsam's—he spent years running hugely successful Minor League teams before joining the Yankees in the 1930s as farm director. Weiss was not a baseball man in the sense that Rickey was (Rickey had both played and managed in the Major Leagues), but Weiss knew how to run an organization. He surrounded himself with baseball people he could trust, and he listened to their advice.

By the late 1950s Howsam had reason to feel that

MARK ARMOUR

he had conquered Minor League baseball, with a celebrated ballpark, three championships in eleven years, and two prestigious executive awards. Given that success, he spent a couple of years on two unrelated efforts—bringing professional football and Major League baseball teams to Denver. Howsam was one of the leaders behind the Continental League, a proposed rival to the American and National Leagues that planned to open in 1961 with teams in Denver, New York, Minneapolis, Houston, Dallas–Fort Worth, Toronto, Atlanta, and Buffalo. The league wanted to be part of the established order and attempted to work within the existing Major Leagues for approval. After the Continental League was announced in 1959, the effort fell apart in August 1960 when the two Major Leagues countered, announcing plans to expand.

Howsam got involved in football at the behest of Dallas oil magnate Lamar Hunt, who wanted to own a football team and thought his best option was to start his own league. The National Football League tried to lure away some of Hunt's potential owners with expansion franchises, but Hunt ultimately got the American Football League off the ground in 1960. Howsam's family-owned business, Rocky Mountain Empire Sports, owned the Denver team, called the Broncos, who played in Bears Stadium beginning in September 1960. The club finished just 4-9-1 in its debut season and reportedly lost $1 million for Howsam and his family. At the end of the season Howsam sold his business, which meant he lost not only the Broncos, but the Bears and the stadium as well. He saved his family's finances, but he was now out of work. For the Howsam family it was a heartbreaking time. Howsam and a friend spent the next three years selling mutual funds.

In August 1964 baseball called again. The St. Louis Cardinals were in the midst of a disappointing season and had fired General Manager Bing Devine. August "Gussie" Busch, the chairman of Anheuser-Busch, owned the club, and over the past couple of seasons had employed Branch Rickey as a

senior adviser. Most observers felt that Rickey had undermined Devine, publicly questioning many of the trades he had made. With Devine dismissed, Rickey turned down the job himself and instead recommended Howsam. Busch agreed, and when Rickey called Howsam in Denver to offer him the job, Howsam took it.

Although the club had started the 1964 season poorly, by the time Devine was fired the Cardinals had been playing well for two months, thanks in no small part to Devine's brilliant acquisition of Lou Brock in June. It took a while for the Cardinals to make up any ground on the first-place Philadelphia Phillies, who had opened up a big lead and maintained it late into the season. However, beginning on September 21 the Phillies lost ten consecutive games, and the Cardinals stepped into the void ahead of the Reds, Phillies, and Giants to win their first pennant since 1946. Howsam, who did not change the personnel at all during this time, always credited Devine for building the team. After the season Devine was in fact named the Executive of the Year by the *Sporting News* for his second consecutive season.

The change in general managers was not well-received in St. Louis. Devine was popular with the fans, players, and media, all of whom blamed Rickey for his dismissal. Howsam's style, meanwhile, differed greatly from Devine's. Whereas Devine had been personal friends with many of the players and spent time on the field before games, Howsam mostly stayed away, other than occasionally sending word that someone was not wearing his uniform properly. Soon after firing Devine, however, Busch realized he had made a mistake, so he told Howsam to in turn fire Rickey. Howsam did so, but only after Rickey talked him out of resigning. Howsam stayed to run the defending champions, aware that his position might not be terribly secure.

Although Howsam greatly respected Devine as a player evaluator, and grew to admire Busch as an owner, many things about the Cardinals operation bothered him. He felt his Denver clubs and his own business outside baseball were better run, and he made changes accordingly. Surprised that the Cardinals had no promotions or season-ticket sales, for instance, he implemented a plan to organize those. Also, in 1965 he ordered the resodding of Busch Stadium's playing field, which was a mess, even though the club would move into a new facility in 1966. And as in Denver, Howsam demanded that his ballpark be clean, park employees be friendly, and the field be well tended at all times. There was natural resentment among front-office people and other club employees, many of whom resisted the changes. Faced with their resistance, and having discovered that some had been leaking news to the press while others had been grafting tickets, Howsam replaced many of those employees.

The Cardinals' front office presented a further challenge for Howsam. While Busch spent most of his energies running his brewery, he employed Dick Meyer as his personal representative with the team. All important decisions, including trades, had to first be run past Meyer, who would talk to Busch. Devine, who had been with the Cardinals his entire professional life, did not mind this setup—he figured Busch owned the team and had the right to have final say. In fact, Devine and Meyer became close friends, and Meyer had tried to intervene to save Devine's job. Howsam, used to complete control, chafed under the arrangement and resented Meyer's interference. In his memoirs, Howsam did not point to any particular decision that was ever overruled; he objected to the relationship in principle.

Taking a page from George Weiss, Howsam identified two key assistants to help run the club. Dick Wagner, who had operated the Lincoln club in the Western League when Howsam was in Denver, was hired as Howsam's second in command. Wagner ran the business side, organizing the club's promotions and setting up its season-ticket operation. Howsam also promoted Sheldon "Chief" Bender to farm director. Howsam wanted people who would be loyal to him and his vision. In return, he granted complete trust to his subordinates. These two men would work with Howsam for twenty years.

Howsam was faced with a major decision immediately when Manager Johnny Keane resigned just days after winning the World Series (partly because of the earlier firing of his friend Devine). Busch had wanted to hire Leo Durocher and had talked with him even before the season had ended. Howsam did not approve of Durocher's off-field lifestyle and advised Busch that his best chance to get the fans back on his side (after the unpopular departures of Devine and Keane) was to hire longtime favorite Red Schoendienst to manage the club. Busch agreed.

After the team fell to seventh place in 1965, Howsam made several bold moves. In a style similar to that of his mentor Rickey, he traded his three aging regulars—Bill White, Dick Groat, and Ken Boyer. Although the moves were not popular, Howsam was correct that all three were near the end of the road. In May 1966 he traded pitcher Ray Sadecki to the San Francisco Giants for first baseman Orlando Cepeda, who would win the MVP Award for the Cardinals in 1967. In December 1966 Howsam sent third baseman Charlie Smith to the Yankees for right fielder Roger Maris. These two acquisitions helped transform the team: Maris and Cepeda became the number three and four hitters for the club that would win the next two pennants and the 1967 World Series. But Howsam was not there to see it.

In late 1966 the Cincinnati Reds were sold by Bill DeWitt to an eleven-man group headed by Francis Dale, the publisher of the *Cincinnati Enquirer*. DeWitt was a longtime baseball man, previously the general manager with the Browns, Reds, and Detroit Tigers before buying a majority stake in the Reds in 1962. DeWitt had wanted to build a ballpark in the suburbs, and the group that bought him out did so primarily to save the team for the city. The men did not know baseball and needed someone who did. They contacted Howsam and offered him complete control over the ball club, a substantial raise, and a three-year contract. Howsam was happy with the Cardinals and felt they were moving in the right direction, but he could not turn down either the money or the total freedom.

Once again Howsam found the organization and performance of the front office not to his liking. He again hired Dick Wagner to run the business side of the team and brought Chief Bender from St. Louis to run the Minor League operation. The new owners had much more money than DeWitt had, and Howsam was able to hire more scouts and expand the farm system. He also replaced much of the office staff, focusing more on advance ticket sales and the upkeep of Crosley Field and its environs.

Howsam inherited quite a bit of talent in Cincinnati. After a surprising pennant win in 1961, the Reds had nearly won in 1964, losing on the final day to the team Howsam had taken over in St. Louis. Though the Reds had fallen to 78-84 in 1966, their worst finish since 1960, the farm system had recently produced Pete Rose, Tony Pérez, and Lee May and in 1967 would serve up Johnny Bench. Howsam did not make any big trades until after the season, when he dealt Deron Johnson to the Atlanta Braves for Mack Jones to open up first base for May. In February 1968 he traded starting catcher Johnny Edwards to the Cardinals, creating a spot for Bench.

Later in 1968, Howsam made two of his best deals. In June he traded pitcher Milt Pappas, who Howsam felt was a bad clubhouse influence, and two journeymen to the Braves for shortstop Woody Woodward and pitchers Clay Carroll and Tony Cloninger. All three would be key members of the team for a few years. After the season he dealt center fielder Vada Pinson to the Cardinals for outfielder Bobby Tolan and relief pitcher Wayne Granger. This last deal was classic Howsam. Pinson had been a star for many years, but Howsam saw him as fading and Tolan, seven years younger, as a rising star. He got the Cardinals to throw in Granger, who anchored the Reds' bullpen for three years.

In Howsam's first three years in charge, the Reds won eighty-seven, eighty-three, and eighty-nine games, respectively, finishing only four games out in 1969. After that season Howsam replaced Manager Dave Bristol, whom he had inherited, with thirty-five-year-old Sparky Anderson, who had five years of Minor League experience. The choice was met with derision, but Anderson proved to be one of history's greatest skippers. In his first season the Reds finished 102-60, losing the World Series to the Baltimore Orioles. The Reds had acquired the nickname "The Big Red Machine" and were led by offensive stars Bench, Rose, May, Pérez, and Tolan.

One highlight of the 1970 season for Howsam was the opening on June 30 of Riverfront Stadium, which hosted the All-Star Game just two weeks later. The park was already being planned when Howsam got to Cincinnati, but he had typically insisted upon having a spotless facility, friendly and clean employees, and efficiency everywhere. He also had artificial turf installed, part of the ongoing trend with new facilities. Howsam, like Rickey, believed in team speed—an element that helped on both offense and defense. This would be especially important, Howsam believed, on artificial turf.

In 1971 a number of Reds had off years, and the team fell to 79-83 and a tie for fourth. Bobby Tolan, who had hit .316 with fifty-seven steals in 1970, injured himself playing basketball in the winter and missed the entire season. In Howsam's view, it was the loss of Tolan that hurt the team the most at bat and in the field, and he and Anderson determined that they needed more team speed to return to the top. In December 1971 Howsam pulled off his most famous deal, trading slugging first baseman Lee May, second baseman Tommy Helms, and utility man Jimmy Stewart to the Astros for second baseman Joe Morgan, infielder Denis Menke, outfielders César Gerónimo and Ed Armbrister, and pitcher Jack Billingham. Billingham and Gerónimo were key members of the upcoming teams, while Morgan, an unappreciated star in Houston, became the best player in the game. Howsam also added out-fielder George Foster and pitcher Tom Hall through trades in 1971.

The trades paid dividends, as the 1972 Reds won ninety-five games and returned to the World Series. Tolan's return and Morgan's arrival gave the team even more firepower, and it was a surprise when they lost the Series to the Oakland Athletics. In 1973 pitcher Fred Norman was added, further strengthening the team, but the Reds' season ended in even more of a surprise than did the 1972 team's—the club won ninety-nine games, the best record in baseball, but lost in the NLCS to a Mets team that won just eighty-two. Still, Howsam's achievements were recognized with the *Sporting News* Executive of the Year Award in 1973.

After the 1973 season Howsam traded Tolan, one of his favorite players, to San Diego. Tolan had just suffered a disastrous season, hitting .206, and had sulked and feuded with Anderson and his teammates. The loss of Tolan, however, did not slow the Reds down. In 1974 they won ninety-eight games; they were bettered only by the Dodgers, who kept them from winning their own division and making the playoffs. The Reds seemed destined to be a great team that could not quite take the final step.

During this time, an era when facial hair was increasingly prevalent in the culture and in baseball, the Reds stood out for their short hair and lack of facial hair. Howsam had very conservative views about the image of the game and his players. He was insistent that they wear their uniform a certain way—not too baggy, socks visible up nearly to the knee, low stirrups, black shoes—and the uniforms were cleaned and pressed each day. While the Cardinals players had chafed at Howsam's old-fashioned sensibilities, the Reds players, starting with leaders like Rose and Bench, went along. One notable exception was Ross Grimsley, a young star pitcher, who was traded to the Orioles in 1973 for very little. To Howsam, looking and performing as a team was part of the formula for success.

Ultimate success finally came to the Reds in 1975 and 1976. They won World Series titles both years and those teams are considered among the greatest baseball teams ever. The 1976 team swept the Yankees in the World Series, the crowning achievement of Howsam's career. He later said that he felt some sadness knowing that no team would ever be put together the way his team had been. Howsam was referring to the onset of free agency in baseball, which would take place in the upcoming off-season for the first time. Howsam was one of baseball's most vocal hawks on labor matters, speaking out for holding the line during the 1972 strike and the 1976 lockout. Howsam had more power than most general managers, as both Francis Dale and later Louis Nippert (who bought controlling interest in 1973) let him represent the club at ownership meetings.

Howsam and the Reds did not adjust well to the changing landscape. They lost star pitcher Don Gullett to free agency that fall and lost several other free agents in the coming years, foremost among them Rose and Morgan. After a slow start in 1977, Howsam acquired pitcher Tom Seaver from the Mets. Despite Seaver's great second half, the Reds could not catch the Dodgers. After the season Howsam resigned, taking a position as vice chairman of the board while appointing Dick Wagner as his successor. Wagner's regime was contentious, as he became the scapegoat with the fans and the press for the loss of the well-known players and for the deteriorating performance of the team. The club contended for a few years before falling to last place in 1982.

Midway through the 1983 season Howsam returned as general manager, a position he held for two years. Howsam's biggest move was to reacquire Rose in August 1984 and make him player-manager. Rose helped turn the team around—beginning in 1985, it finished second for four straight seasons. Howsam retired, as planned, effective July 1, 1985. His insistence on keeping to his retirement date was solidified by the sale of the team in late 1984 to

Marge Schott, with whom Howsam did not get along. While Howsam had stayed busy with the team during his five years as vice chairman, this parting was a real retirement. Howsam's baseball career had ended.

He and Janet split their retirement years between their homes in Glenwood City, Colorado, and Sun City, Arizona. The Howsams were a devoted baseball couple—Howsam had it written into his contract that Janet could travel with him on any of his business trips, and she often had. The entire family remained very close. Howsam's parents lived long enough to attend the World Series in 1970. His children, Edwin and Robert Jr., each had success in other pursuits before finding work with the Reds while their father ran the team—Edwin as a scout, Robert Jr. in marketing.

Howsam was named to the Cincinnati Reds Hall of Fame in 2004. He has been a perennial candidate for the Baseball Hall of Fame, but as of 2013 had not yet attained that honor. He died of heart failure on February 19, 2008, in Sun City, just nine days shy of his ninetieth birthday. He was survived by Janet, his wife of sixty-nine years, and their two sons.

Chapter 2. Scouting and Player Development

Jim Sandoval

When forty-eight-year-old Bob Howsam was hired by new team president Francis L. Dale as general manager of the Cincinnati Reds in January 1967, he analyzed the organization top to bottom, looking for ways to improve the team on the field and at the box office. Two areas Howsam quickly addressed were the scouting and player-development departments.

Howsam had brought Sheldon "Chief" Bender with him from the St. Louis Cardinals to run the player-development department. Bender, a World War II veteran, had played in the Cardinals' Minor League organization for thirteen years and had managed for five seasons before becoming a scout and then moving into management. He ran the Cardinals' Minor League system for a couple of years before moving to the Reds. Bender's task with the Reds was to oversee the development of the players the scouting department would provide.

Howsam soon realized that the scouting department could be improved. The Reds had a core group of good scouts but he knew they needed more. As a source he turned to Branch Rickey disciples still working for the Pittsburgh Pirates organization. Late in 1967 he persuaded the Bowen brothers to leave the Pirates, Rex becoming a special assistant to Howsam with many scouting duties and his younger brother Joe taking the position of scouting director. The Bowens, both of whom had master's degrees and had worked as teachers, had developed a strong scouting staff in their years with the Pirates. They moved quickly to bring their best scouts with them to Cincinnati in 1968, among them Bill Clark, Elmer Gray, and George Zuraw. The Reds under the Howsam-Bowen regime also expanded their bird-

The Reds owed much of their success to scouting and player development, as exemplified by catcher Johnny Bench.

dog network, having as many as three hundred men reporting to the paid area scouts.

The pre-Howsam Reds scouting department had already starting building the foundation of the Big Red Machine. Infielder Pete Rose (signed by Buddy Bloebaum, Ralph "Buzz" Boyle, and Gene Bennett) and infielder Tony Pérez (Tony Pacheco) were both signed in 1960. Catcher Johnny Bench (Tony

Robello) was selected in the second round of the draft in 1965 behind first-round infielder turned outfielder Bernie Carbo. Pitcher Gary Nolan (Reno DeBenedetti, Dale McReynolds, and Tony Robello) was the first-round pick in 1966 and shortstop Darrel Chaney (Dale McReynolds, Bob Thurman, and Tony Robello) followed him in the second.

In 1967 Wayne Simpson was taken in the first round and pitcher Dave Tomlin in the twenty-ninth. Shortstop Dave Concepción was signed by Wilfredo Calvino as an international free agent. In the secondary phase of the draft that June, the Reds acquired shortstop Frank Duffy in the first round and shortstop Greg Riddoch in the third. Riddoch never played for the Reds but served an important role with the Big Red Machine by managing in their Minor League system for eight seasons.

The 1968 draft saw the Reds select pitcher Ross Grimsley in the first round of the January secondary phase and acquire pitcher Milt Wilcox in the second round of the June draft. The changes and improvements in the scouting staff began to pay major dividends beginning with the 1969 draft. Pitcher Don Gullett (Gene Bennett and Cliff Alexander) was selected in the first round, pitcher Rawly Eastwick (Joe Caputo and Joe Bowen) in the third, and outfielder Ken Griffey (Elmer Gray) was nabbed in the twenty-ninth round. First baseman Dan Driessen (Bill Jamison) was signed as a nondrafted free agent that year as well.

In 1970 the Reds drafted catcher turned utility man Joel Youngblood in the first round of the January draft, and in June they obtained pitcher Tom Carroll (Elmer Gray) in the sixth round, pitcher Will McEnaney (Warren Barnett and Cliff Alexander) in the eighth, pitcher turned third baseman Ray Knight in the tenth, and pitcher Pat Zachry in the nineteenth round. Catcher Don Werner (Bill Clark) was grabbed in the fifth round in 1971. Pitcher Tom Hume was selected in the first round of the January secondary phase draft. Infielder Doug Flynn (Chet Montgomery) was signed as a nondrafted free agent in 1971.

Of the twenty-nine players who appeared in a game for the 1975 Cincinnati club, fourteen were originally signed by the Reds. One was acquired for cash (utility man Terry Crowley) and the remaining fourteen were acquired through trades. Organizations that try to build a championship team through scouting and player development will often use prospects in trades to fill roster holes. Howsam's Reds utilized this philosophy to help build the 1975 club. Using the scouting talents of Rex Bowen and Ray Shore, along with those of area scouts, the Reds were able to acquire missing parts for the great team. The most important instance of this was "The Trade," an eight-player deal with the Houston Astros in which the Reds acquired key parts of the club.

Howsam, knowing that Riverfront Stadium, which opened on June 30, 1970, required a different type of winning player than Crosley Field needed, had set out in the off-season between the 1970 and 1971 campaigns to remake the club. Although the Reds won the NL pennant in 1970, Howsam knew that for sustained success he would need a more balanced squad, well-rounded players with speed who could play defense on an artificial-turf field rather than a team of one-dimensional sluggers who could thrive in small Crosley Field.

"The Trade," which many think made the ensuing championships possible, was consummated on November 29, 1971, and sent second baseman Tommy Helms, slugging first baseman Lee May, and utility man Jimmy Stewart to the Astros for second baseman Joe Morgan, pitcher Jack Billingham, outfielder César Gerónimo, infielder Denis Menke, and outfielder Ed Armbrister. Helms (Paul Campbell and Phil Seghi) in 1959 and May (Jimmy Bragan) were both Reds signees.

Billingham went on to be the workhorse of the Reds pitching staff. Menke was later dealt back to the Astros for pitcher Pat Darcy. Gerónimo, with his nine-foot-long strides in the outfield, went on to be a four-time Gold Glove winner in center field, stabilizing the Reds' outfield and eventually hitting better than even the scouts suspected he might. Armbrister proved to be an important bench player.

But the key to the trade was Morgan, who became simply the best player in baseball for the next five years, winning back-to-back MVP Awards in the world championship seasons. Grapevine gossip had suggested that he might have a bad character. Howsam sent Shore to investigate the rumors and scout the Astros. Shore's report said Morgan was a stand-up guy. Howsam made the deal.

Future MVP outfielder George Foster was acquired in a trade for former Reds first-round pick Frank Duffy and pitcher Vern Geishert, while backup outfielder Merv Rettenmund was obtained in a trade for former Reds first-rounder Ross Grimsley and catcher Wallace Williams (Reds third-rounder in 1973). Third baseman John Vukovich was acquired in a trade for pitcher Pat Osburn (Reds first-rounder, 1970 June secondary draft) and pitcher Clay Kirby in a trade for outfielder Bobby Tolan and Dave Tomlin (Reds 1967 draft).

Relief pitcher Pedro Borbon, along with starter Jim McGlothlin, was obtained in a trade with the Angels for outfielder Alex Johnson and infielder Chico Ruiz (Reds international free agent in 1958). Pitcher Clay Carroll was acquired in a trade with Atlanta for pitcher Milt Pappas, pitcher Ted Davidson (Reds signee, 1960), and infielder Bob Johnson. Pitcher Fred Norman came to the Reds in a trade with the Padres for outfielder Gene Locklear (Reds nondrafted free agent, 1969) and pitcher Mike Johnson (Reds nondrafted free agent, 1969).

Backup catcher Bill Plummer and pitcher Tom Hall were acquired in trades that did not involve a player originally signed by the Reds but both were scouted by the Reds prior to the transactions.

The Reds also began to use advance scouting of their opponents, something previously done rarely during the regular season. Former Major League pitcher Ray Shore did most of this work and also was an adviser to Howsam on trades involving Ma-

jor Leaguers. Shore would travel ahead of the team, sending back reports on their next opponents. He looked for tendencies, who would run and when, who liked or didn't like certain types of pitches—anything that could help the Reds defeat an opponent.

Shore also worked as what today would be called a special-assignment scout. He would be sent to scout specific players in another organization if Howsam was interested in making a trade. Howsam could not always see each of the players he might be interested in, especially those in the American League or still in the Minors. He would use Shore and sometimes an area scout to give him reports on the players he might ask for in a deal. As an example, Bill Clark scouted and gave a favorable report on Hall before the Reds acquired him from the Minnesota Twins in 1971.

Perhaps showing how strong the scouting department was, many of the Reds scouts went on to higher-level positions in their baseball careers. Among them, Bill Clark set up the international scouting departments for the Braves and then the San Diego Padres. Larry Doughty became the general manager of the Pirates. Chet Montgomery became the director of scouting for the Cleveland Indians, while Julian Mock did the same with the Reds and Fred Uhlman with the Baltimore Orioles. George Zuraw held many front-office positions, including assistant to the vice president of baseball operations with the Seattle Mariners. Greg Riddoch was the manager of the Padres during the 1990–92 seasons.

The Reds scouting department, 1975
Rex Bowen, special assistant to the GM
Joe Bowen, director of scouting
Ray Shore, advance scout/special-assignment scout

Scouting supervisors
Cliff Alexander (Ohio, Indiana, Michigan)
Larry Barton Sr. (Southern California)

Larry Barton Jr. (Southern California; later his son Jeff became a scout with the Reds, creating what was, to the author's knowledge, baseball's first three-generation scouting team. For three seasons all three were employed by the Reds until Larry Sr. retired.)

Porter Blinn (New England, eastern New York State)

Joe Caputo (eastern Pennsylvania, New Jersey, Delaware, Maryland, eastern Virginia, eastern North Carolina)

Bill Clark (Wisconsin, northern Illinois, Iowa, Minnesota, North Dakota, South Dakota, northern Missouri)

Reno DeBenedetti (Northern California, Washington, Oregon, Nevada, western Idaho)

Larry Doughty (Louisiana, Mississippi, Alabama, South Carolina, northern Georgia, northwestern Florida)

Elmer Gray (western Pennsylvania, western New York, western North Carolina, West Virginia, Virginia)

Edwin Howsam (Arizona, New Mexico)

Chet Montgomery (Kentucky, Tennessee, southern Illinois, southern Missouri)

Tony Robello (Texas, Oklahoma, Arkansas)

Neil Summers (Long Island, New York City)

Fred Uhlman Sr. (Kansas, Nebraska, Colorado, Utah, Wyoming, Montana, eastern Idaho)

George Zuraw (southern Georgia, Florida, Latin America)

Area scouts

Gene Bennett (Ohio)

Ramon Conde (Puerto Rico)

Larry D'Amato (Northern California)

James Davies (New Jersey)

Ed DeBenedetti (Northern California)

Stephen Gruwell (Southern California)

Les Houser (New Mexico)

Julian Mock (Georgia)

Harry Pritikin (Illinois)

Johnny Sierra (Dominican Republic)

Harry Steinriede (Cincinnati)

Gaetan Ste-Marie (Canada)

Jim Vennari (Ohio)

William Weaver (New Jersey)

Don Williams (Texas)

Murray Zuk (Canada)

Chapter 3. **Sparky Anderson**

Cindy Thomson

George Lee "Sparky" Anderson was one of the great baseball men of all time in terms of success, integrity, and personality. He led the Cincinnati Reds to back-to-back world championships in 1975 and 1976 and the Detroit Tigers to a World Series title in 1984, becoming the first manager to win the World Series in both leagues. Four times in his career teams he managed won more than one hundred games, and in six other seasons his teams won at least ninety. In his twenty-six years managing in the Majors Anderson amassed 2,194 victories, five pennants, and three World Series championships.

Born in Bridgewater, South Dakota, on February 22, 1934, to LeRoy and Shirley Anderson, George relocated with his family in 1942 to Southern California, where his father and grandparents found wartime work in the shipyards. LeRoy played some semipro baseball and passed his love of the game on to his son. Young George became a batboy for the University of Southern California's Trojans baseball team, coached by Raoul "Rod" Dedeaux, who was an early influence in his baseball life.

During his childhood Anderson played a lot of sandlot ball. In 1951 his American Legion team won a national championship at Detroit's Briggs Stadium (later renamed Tiger Stadium), where Anderson later managed the Tigers. His Dorsey High School team won forty-two consecutive games, and Anderson was named an all-city player in his junior and senior years. In choosing Dorsey for its baseball program, Anderson passed up a school closer to home and had to take two buses.

While still in high school, Anderson worked a summer job loading lumber onto boxcars. In the evenings he played with a semipro team. He grad-

"Sparky Who?," said the critics when he was hired in 1969. Anderson would go on to be one of history's greatest managers.

uated from Dorsey High in 1953 and Dedeaux offered him a partial baseball scholarship to USC. Anderson never went to college, though, because a Brooklyn Dodgers scout he had met years earlier on the sandlots, Lefty Phillips, offered him $250 a month to play for the Dodgers' Santa Barbara team in the Class C California League. Anderson's parents knew and trusted Phillips, and Anderson called him "the sharpest baseball man I ever met."[1]

Phillips knew Anderson's limitations and told him that to make it in baseball he would have to work very hard. Anderson was only 5 feet 9 and weighed just 170 pounds, but his determination and will to win gave him an edge. Anderson's boyhood friend Billy Consolo signed his first Major League contract that same year, with the Boston Red Sox. Consolo was one of baseball's bonus babies, with the rule at the time requiring the team providing the bonus to keep the player on its Major League roster for two seasons. Anderson's signing gave him a steady income, even if he wasn't a bonus baby, and he bought an engagement ring for his childhood sweetheart, Carol Valle. The two had known each other since the fifth grade and began dating in high school. They married in October 1953, at the end of Anderson's first Minor League season as a shortstop for the Santa Barbara Dodgers. He played in 141 games and hit for a .263 average.

The playing manager at Santa Barbara was George Scherger, a man Anderson would later invite to coach for him in Cincinnati. Anderson described Scherger as a man who wanted to win badly. Whenever the team lost, there would be extra practice the next day. This drive influenced Anderson, who adopted it when he became a manager himself.

Anderson moved around in the Brooklyn Minor League system, playing in Pueblo, Colorado; Fort Worth; Montreal in the International League; and Los Angeles in the Pacific Coast League. In Pueblo he hit .296 in 1954. In 1955 he moved up to Double-A with the Texas League's Fort Worth Cats. Tommy Holmes was the manager. (The team produced several future big league managers: Anderson; Dick Williams, who was Anderson's opposing manager in the 1972 and 1984 World Series, managed in the Majors for twenty-one seasons, and joined Anderson in the Hall of Fame in 2008; Danny Ozark, who managed the Philadelphia Phillies and San Francisco Giants; Norm Sherry, who managed the California Angels and coached on several Major League teams; and Maury Wills, who managed for parts of two years in Seattle.)

Anderson received his nickname in Fort Worth.

A radio announcer dubbed him Sparky because of his feistiness. It was a trait that sometimes got Anderson into trouble. He wanted to win so badly that he could not tolerate anything that got in the way.

In 1958 the Dodgers put Anderson on their forty-man roster. He later remembered, "I had no right to think I could break in with a club that had [Gil] Hodges, [Charlie] Neal, Don Zimmer, Junior Gilliam, Dick Gray, [Carl] Furillo, Duke Snider, Gino Cimoli, Norm Larker, and Johnny Roseboro—and with a pitching staff built around Sandy Koufax, Don Drysdale, and Johnny Podres. I simply didn't belong in that kind of company."[2] Sparky was sent back down to Montreal. Dodgers manager Walter Alston broke the news of his demotion to him, at a time when most managers left this duty to the traveling secretary. This impressed Sparky, who as a manager followed that example. He was told that the Philadelphia Phillies had expressed an interest in him, and since they had an International League farm team in Miami, they would be able to get a look at him.

Sparky played reasonably well in Montreal, batting .269 and stealing twenty-one bases for the Royals. He even hit two home runs. ("That's what's so good about not hitting many. You remember them all," he said.[3]) He was named the club's Most Valuable Player and finished second in the running for the league MVP. He did indeed catch the eye of the Phillies, who traded for him on December 23, 1958, and made him their starting second baseman.

Sparky's first day in the big leagues came on Opening Day of 1959 against Cincinnati at Philadelphia's Connie Mack Stadium. In the eighth inning he singled home what became the winning run in a 2–1 game. He received his first media barrage afterward. In his autobiography, *The Main Spark*, he wrote that there was no more media attention for him until August of that year. He played in 152 games but batted only .218 and drove in only thirty-four runs. It was to be the only year he played in the big leagues.

That year Anderson noticed a difference in the routine compared with the Dodgers' big league spring camp. The Dodgers operated on a set schedule, discipline that Sparky would come to value. In Philadelphia no one kept track of when players rolled in for practice, and often there would be no coaches around, according to Sparky's account. The Phillies that year were a last-place team, as they had been the year before. Sparky said he would never forget the thunderous boos the hometown crowd greeted the Phillies with as they took the field on Opening Day. There was definitely not an attitude of winning in Philadelphia, and Sparky had been raised in an organization with the opposite outlook.

He later said, "I realized you can't be in a game as a professional unless winning and losing are everything, your whole life."[4]

During spring training in 1960, when he didn't make it into many games, Anderson knew he would not stay with the team. He had hoped he would be traded to another Major League team but instead was sold to Toronto. With one child and another on the way, he was about to quit. Toronto's owner, Jack Kent Cooke, offered him $10,000 to play, $2,000 more than he had made in Philadelphia. Because he had bills to pay, he accepted. Cooke told him he planned to sell him to a Major League club, but Anderson did not believe it would happen. He called the 1960 season a turning point in his career. He decided to start observing baseball strategies with the idea of one day becoming a manager. After four more years in the Minors, all with the Maple Leafs, he landed his first managerial job, in Toronto in 1964. He uttered what would be the first of many boasts that he would later regret by saying, "If I can't win with this club, I ought to be fired."[5]

Anderson's temper made him a prophet. He was fired at the end of the season and soon realized that jobs for managers who could not control their emotions during the games were few. By his own admission, he was lucky to get his next job, with the St. Louis Cardinals' farm club in Rock Hill, South

Carolina, in 1965, because the Cardinals were desperate to find a manager just before spring training. Bob Howsam was the Cardinals' general manager; the association proved to be advantageous a few years later. In 1968, when Howsam was the GM of the Cincinnati Reds, Sparky was hired to manage the Reds' Minor League club in Asheville, North Carolina.

Anderson could not make ends meet during his Minor League managing career, so he took various odd jobs, including a factory job, a stocking job at Sears, and some off-season gigs selling used cars.

Then, after five years as a Minor League manager, Anderson landed the third base coaching job with the expansion San Diego Padres in 1969. At the end of the season he resigned to accept a job coaching with the California Angels under his old mentor Lefty Phillips. But he never took that job.

While the ink was still drying on Anderson's contract with the Angels, California GM Dick Walsh received a phone call from Bob Howsam, the Reds' GM, requesting permission to speak with Sparky about managing in Cincinnati. It was Walsh who broke the news to Sparky.

Sparky's hiring prompted Cincinnati newspapers to declare, "Sparky Who?" He was only thirty-five years old and unknown to the public.

One of Anderson's first moves as Reds manager was to make Pete Rose the team's captain. Because Willie Mays was so well received in San Francisco as the Giants' captain, Anderson thought Rose could serve the same role in Cincinnati. Rose was very popular, a hometown boy, and the top player on the team. With Rose delivering the lineup to the umpire before the game, perhaps people would not focus on "Sparky Who?"

Anderson inherited a talented team and remarked to George Scherger, whom he had brought aboard as a coach, that it would win the division by ten games. These types of statements were often seen as exaggerations, and Sparky himself admitted that he was overconfident, but the fact remained that the

1970 Reds were an excellent team. Catcher Johnny Bench was on the verge of a breakout season. Tommy Helms, Lee May, Tony Pérez, Bernie Carbo, and Bobby Tolan joined Rose on the club. The Reds had finished in third place in 1969, winning eighty-nine games under Dave Bristol, and they were primed to be winners. The 1970 team brought in rookie shortstop Dave Concepción and pitchers Don Gullett and Pedro Borbon. On June 30 of that year the team moved from aging Crosley Field into the new Riverfront Stadium and began to play on artificial turf.

The Reds won 102 games in Anderson's Major League managerial debut season, a record that gave them the National League West Division championship over the Los Angeles Dodgers by 14½ games. The Reds swept the Pittsburgh Pirates in the best-of-five NLCS to take the pennant and meet the Baltimore Orioles in the World Series. The Reds fell to the Orioles in five games, but it was a stunning first year for Anderson.

Anderson brought his work ethic with him to Cincinnati, and some players called his spring training "Stalag 17."[6] GM Howsam insisted on a clean-cut look for the team: no facial hair, no long hair, and suit jackets for traveling, which Anderson supported and enforced. He believed that mannerisms and dress carried over into a kind of self-discipline that helped his players work together as a team.

But probably more central to Sparky's success as a manager was the way he cared about his players. He allowed them to question him, and even encouraged it. He said, "I know there are managers who would never allow themselves to be put on this level with their own ballplayers, but as far as I'm concerned, it's a form of communication."[7]

The 1971 season was not a good one; the Reds finished below .500 and tied for fourth place. The off-season brought the "Big Deal." The Reds traded first baseman Lee May, second baseman Tommy Helms, and utility man Jimmy Stewart to the Houston Astros for second baseman Joe Morgan, infielder Denis Menke, pitcher Jack Billingham, and

outfielders César Gerónimo and Ed Armbrister. Cincinnati made the trade to gain speed at second base and third base, essential for playing on Astroturf.

Besides being known as Sparky, Anderson was called "Captain Hook" because he never hesitated to pull a struggling pitcher out of the game. The Big Red Machine was not blessed with superior starting pitching, and in an age when complete games were still common, Anderson's tendency to replace pitchers during a game drew notice. He said, however, that he could always sense when a pitcher was just about to lose his effectiveness. His players realized that while he cared for players as individuals, he would not cater to one man. Second baseman Joe Morgan said, "In his passion for winning, he will not ever put the feelings of any individual above the team."[8] Television cameras frequently followed Anderson's path from the dugout or the mound to show him avoiding stepping on the baseline.

The Reds returned as NL West Division winners in 1972 and faced the Pirates again in the NLCS. This time the series went five games with the Reds coming out on top. The finish was so exciting that before the World Series against the Oakland A's, Anderson made a statement he later regretted. He told the press that the two best teams in baseball had already played a dramatic series (Cincinnati and Pittsburgh) and that the World Series would be anticlimactic. Although he said what he really thought, the statement fired up the Oakland team. After the Reds lost the first two games in Cincinnati, Anderson realized how much he had underestimated his opponents. The Reds eventually lost the Series in seven games. But the Big Red Machine was building momentum.

In 1973 the Reds again won their division but lost to the New York Mets in the NLCS, three games to two. In 1974 the Reds finished second behind the Los Angeles Dodgers, despite winning ninety-eight games.

The Reds teams of 1975 and 1976 secured the label of dynasty and are considered among the best clubs of all time. In 1975 they took first place early in June and never relinquished it. Pitcher Don Gullett was on his way to a remarkable season when he fractured his thumb. Without their star pitcher, the rest of the staff had to pick up the slack. Because the Reds' bullpen was strong, the "Captain Hook" strategy was key. And with hitters like Morgan, Rose, George Foster, and Ken Griffey Sr. batting .300 or better and Bench and Pérez driving in more than one hundred runs, the Big Red Machine usually outscored their opponents anyway. The Reds finished the season 20 games ahead of the second-place Dodgers, with 108 wins, and swept Pittsburgh in 3 games during the NLCS.

The 1975 World Series has gone down as one of the greatest ever. As the Series opened, Sparky began feeling the pressure. He was more cautious this time about feeling overconfident. The Boston Red Sox were the American League champs after sweeping the Oakland A's in the ALCS. The opening game in Fenway Park was an eye-opener for the Big Red Machine when they faced the pitching mastery of Luis Tiant and lost 6–0. After winning Game Two by scoring twice in the ninth inning, the Reds won Game Three at Riverfront Stadium in extra innings. Tiant pitched the Red Sox to another victory in Game Four, but the Reds came back to win Game Five. When the Series returned to Boston, rain delayed play for seventy-two hours. The extra days off allowed Boston to bring back Tiant for another start. Game Six, however, proved to be worth waiting for—the game that many, including Sparky himself, say was the single best game in World Series history.

Anderson removed pitcher Gary Nolan for a pinch hitter in the top of the third inning, trailing 3–0. The Reds got to Tiant this time and evened the score in the fifth. By the eighth inning, leading 6–3, the Reds were thinking the championship was in the bag. After Pedro Borbon allowed a single and a walk, he got the hook and was replaced by Rawly Eastwick, who retired the next two bat-

ters. Then Bernie Carbo, a former Red, came in to pinch-hit. Carbo had already had a pinch homer in Game Three, and Sparky figured he didn't have another in him. But on a 2-and-2 count, Carbo drove the ball over the center-field wall to tie the game. After the Reds were retired in order in the ninth, the Red Sox loaded the bases with nobody out—but were unable to score. In the eleventh inning, Red Sox outfielder Dwight Evans made a spectacular catch on a line drive by Morgan, robbing him of a possible home run and then doubling up Griffey off first base. The Reds threatened in the twelfth but didn't score. In the bottom of the twelfth Pat Darcy, the Reds' eighth pitcher of the game, faced catcher Carlton Fisk, who hit a high fly ball down the left-field line. As Fisk ran to first base, he—and everyone else in the park—wondered if the ball would stay fair. Fisk jumped up and down waving his arms toward fair territory in what has become an iconic image. It was a homer, barely, hitting the foul pole. The Red Sox won, sending the Series to a deciding Game Seven. Sparky later said, "How can a manager of a losing team call it the greatest game ever played? Well, winning or losing, a man can't lie to himself."[9]

Game Seven was a come-from-behind affair with the Reds finally coming out on top, 4–3, and winning their first world championship under Anderson. Sparky was unprepared for the media blitz that continued to follow him into the next season and the expectation of winning another championship, but he soon learned to make the media his friend and to encourage his players to do so also. Pete Rose said, "He didn't make an enemy out of the press. He used it. And he taught us how to use it."[10] Later, Lance Parrish echoed this sentiment in Detroit: "Sparky let us know it wasn't fair to treat the media any differently than we would treat anyone else. They had a job to do."[11]

Pete Rose and Joe Morgan led the league in several offensive categories in 1976, and while the Reds had no big-winning pitchers, they did have seven pitchers who won at least eleven games. After their 102-win regular season, the Reds did not lose a postseason game, sweeping the Philadelphia Phillies in the NLCS and then the New York Yankees in the World Series.

During that World Series, a reporter asked Anderson to compare his catcher to Yankees backstop Thurman Munson. Sparky said, "Don't ever embarrass nobody by comparing him to Johnny Bench."[12] Sparky meant it as a general statement. When he returned home to California, he wrote Munson a letter of apology.

In 1977 the Reds finished second behind the Dodgers, and although 1978 was a better year, they finished second again. The Big Red Machine was being dismantled. Bob Howsam retired after the season. Winning was expected in Cincinnati, and Anderson was fired late that year. He was upset about how it happened. The Reds had just finished a tour in Japan, and management did not want to fire Sparky before that had been completed. But it was late, and most Major League clubs had already chosen their managers for the coming season. The firing was unpopular with the fans in Cincinnati and with the players. Joe Morgan said, "Sparky's firing was wrong and to this day, I don't understand it."[13] It was a blow that Sparky didn't see coming.

Anderson was about to sign a long-term contract to manage the Chicago Cubs in 1979 when Detroit Tigers general manager Jim Campbell got wind of the deal. He contacted Sparky, who realized that the team was filled with young players. Anderson had enjoyed mentoring young players in his Minor League days. At the press conference announcing his hiring, Anderson made another of his infamous predictions, saying the team would win a world championship in five years.

With talent like Ron LeFlore, Steve Kemp, Alan Trammell, Lou Whitaker, Kirk Gibson, Lance Parrish, Jack Morris, and Dan Petry, Sparky was confident. He also realized that discipline and professional conduct would have to be taught. Gibson later

said, "He wanted me to learn the game of baseball and learn how to treat people right. It took four to five years to get through to me."[14]

As he did in Cincinnati, Anderson kept an open-door policy. Players were encouraged to speak their minds, but Sparky had the final say. He called the team "rougher than a three-day beard." He started with fundamentals, drilling the players until their skills became routine. He insisted on coats and ties for traveling, saying, "If you carry yourself proudly, you look like a pro."[15]

In 1981 the Tigers surprised the American League by making an East Division pennant run during the second half of the strike-split season. In 1983 the team began to show its potential by winning ninety-two games. The next season was magical.

The 1984 Tigers led their division wire to wire, starting off by winning nine straight games, as part of an unbelievable 35-5 start to leave their opponents in the dust in what became a 104-win season. What Sparky had in Detroit, which he had never had in Cincinnati, was two superior starting pitchers to lead his rotation: Jack Morris, who pitched a no-hitter in early April, and Dan Petry. Reliever Guillermo "Willie" Hernandez, acquired in a trade in late March, was an All-Star while winning the American League Cy Young and Most Valuable Player Awards. Trammell led the team in batting with a .314 average. Parrish was an All-Star again that year, won the second of three straight Gold Gloves, and hit thirty-three home runs.

When the team clinched the AL East on September 18, Anderson felt vindicated. He remembered thinking, "No one will ever question me again."[16] No matter what happened in the postseason, the best team, he said, was the one that had won 104 games in the regular season and wore a big Old English "D" on its home uniform.

The Tigers swept the Kansas City Royals in the AL Championship Series. Sparky took a team to the World Series for the fifth time in his career, this time against a National League club, the San Diego Padres. The first game was close, with Detroit winning, 3–2. After the game Lou Whitaker complimented his manager: "When Sparky came to us from Cincinnati, he brought us back to fundamentals. We had a lot to learn and it's paying off."[17] The Tigers lost Game Two, but that was the only game they would lose, and they became world champions before the hometown crowd.

After the Series, Sparky's wife wanted him to quit. He thought about it. It had been a tough year. He was proud of the team and happy for the city of Detroit, but for five years he had struggled to try to prove Cincinnati wrong for firing him, and with the success of Detroit that year, the pressure he put on himself became almost unbearable. He had to get back to the business of baseball and to enjoying the game again. He couldn't do that if he quit.

There would be no back-to-back championships for Anderson in Detroit. In 1985 and again in 1986 the team finished third. The 1987 Tigers were not expected to do much better and early in May were in next-to-last place. Anderson chose that time to make another prediction, saying his team would be in the race by the end of the season. The Tigers started putting together some winning streaks. Before a season-ending series in Detroit against the Toronto Blue Jays, the Tigers were one game behind Toronto. Detroit finished with a flourish, winning three straight one-run games to clinch the AL East title, although the Tigers lost to Minnesota in five games in a best-of-seven ALCS.

The team that year had no outstanding talent save for Trammell, who finished second in the voting for Most Valuable Player. Anderson said, "We had no business running with the big boys. It was pure determination."[18] Pitcher Jack Morris said, "In 1984, we probably had the best club I ever played on in Detroit. In '87 we were less talented but typical overachievers. We didn't realize we weren't that good."[19]

Sparky's efforts with the team that year won him his second American League Manager of the Year Award. He said, "When I look back on that year, I still feel a high. The guys on that team can be proud of themselves for the rest of their lives."[20]

In 1988 the team finished second behind the Red Sox, but 1989 saw the Tigers lose 103 games. For a man who wanted to win more than anything else, it was a horrible year. Anderson was also experiencing personal problems, as his daughter was undergoing a painful divorce in California and he felt guilty about his own absence from the family.

Anderson, who believed that because baseball had blessed him he had a responsibility to give back to the community, was always participating in charity events. In May of that year he attended an event at Children's Hospital and afterward grew so fatigued that Tigers president Jim Campbell sent him home to California to rest. When Sparky left Detroit, he believed he wouldn't manage again. He blamed himself for Detroit's terrible year, but with the team he had and the injuries they suffered, even Sparky Anderson could not coax a winner. He was finally able to give up his obsession for winning after spending seventeen days away from the team. He said, "My greatest gift today is knowing I have a tomorrow."[21]

Anderson continued to manage mediocre teams in Detroit through 1995. That season, during spring training, he drew a lot of attention for refusing to manage replacement players during a player strike. But he said later that that was not the whole story. He knew that management would never open the season with replacement players; it was a ruse. "I [had] managed 25 years at that time in the major leagues, and I was no joke. I wasn't going to be part of a joke. That was the biggest travesty I have ever seen in my career."[22]

Sparky was granted a leave of absence and returned to manage that year when, as he predicted, the strike was settled and the replacement players were dismissed. He retired after the season. While rumor said he was forced out of the game, Anderson had been considering retiring for some time. He left as one of baseball's winningest managers, sixth all-time as of 2012. He was the first manager to win the World Series in both leagues. In 1984 and 1987 he won the American League Manager of the Year Award. He was inducted into the National Baseball Hall of Fame in 2000 and is also in the Cincinnati Reds Hall of Fame. In his retirement he considered himself a Red rather than a Tiger because of the man who had hired him. "People [in Detroit] said, 'Why wear a Reds cap? Why not a Tigers cap? You were in Detroit for 17 years.' I said, 'Because of Bob Howsam. Without Bob Howsam, I don't ever get to Detroit,'" Anderson said.[23]

His number 10 was retired by the Reds in 2005 and his number 11 was retired by the Tigers in 2011. In 2006 the California Lutheran University baseball field in Thousand Oaks, California, was named after Anderson.

Anderson's return visits to Detroit were not all that frequent in retirement. He stayed away from the final game at Tiger Stadium in 1999. But he turned up in uniform at the Tigers' spring training home in Lakeland, Florida, in 2003 to give support to new Detroit manager Alan Trammell, one of his protégés. Sparky also showed up at the twenty-fifth-anniversary gathering of the 1984 Tigers championship team in Comerica Park in Detroit. Tigers teammates noted Anderson looked frail. His last public appearance was in July 2010 at his Hall of Fame induction ceremony, when he had to be helped off the stage.

After the 2010 World Series ended, Anderson's family said that Sparky was in hospice care as he was suffering from the effects of dementia. On November 4, two days after the family's announcement, Anderson died at the age of seventy-six.

Chapter 4. **George Scherger**

Mark Armour

"He knows more about baseball than I'll ever know," Hall of Fame manager Sparky Anderson once said of George Scherger.[1] Pete Rose, answering skeptics about his own ascension to player-manager in August 1984, told the press not to worry. "I have George Scherger [as bench coach], who just happens to be the smartest baseball man in the world. He'll keep me from making mistakes, I am sure."[2] Scherger never played or managed in the Major Leagues but left his mark over a five-decade career in the game.

George Richard Scherger was born on November 10, 1920, in Dickinson, North Dakota, to John and Veronica Scherger. George had three younger brothers, Joseph, Leo, and Donald. The Schergers still lived in Dickinson in 1930, but sometime soon after they moved to Buffalo, New York. George starred in football, basketball, and baseball at St. Joseph Collegiate Institute, an all-boys Catholic high school in Buffalo, graduating in 1940. By high school he had acquired his lifelong nickname of Sugar, though later in life he was often called Sugar Bear.

Scherger signed with the Brooklyn Dodgers out of high school and played fourteen years in their farm system. He was a second baseman, about 5 feet 9 and 170 pounds, batting and throwing right-handed. He was a good defensive player who stole a lot of bases for the era but had very little power—just thirteen Minor League home runs in fourteen seasons. The Dodgers had a very large Minor League system, and Scherger spent most of his time in its lowest levels. He began in Superior, Wisconsin, in the Northern League in 1940, and by the end of the 1942 season had played for four Class D teams.

Scherger then joined the U.S. Army and eventually

The first move Sparky Anderson made when he became a big league manager was to hire George Scherger, fulfilling a promise.

the Army Air Corps. He spent most of his three years at Fort Bragg, North Carolina, running the base's gymnasium. The base library was located above the gym, and he soon began dating the librarian. Mozelle Spainour, a native of Winston-Salem, had degrees from Appalachian State University and the University of North Carolina at Chapel Hill.[3] The two hit it off. Scherger was discharged as a technical sergeant in early 1946, and on February 23 he and Mozelle were married in Buffalo.

The twenty-five-year-old Scherger reported back

to the Dodgers, who sent him to their Danville, Illinois, club in the Three-I League. He hit .243 in his ascension to Class B, and it was becoming clear that he was not going to be a Major League player. The Dodgers saw something else in him, however, and asked him to manage their Kingston, New York, club in the North Atlantic League. He was back at Class D but on a new career track. "I wasn't a very good player," recalled Scherger of his Minor League career. "I was a guy who was enthusiastic and liked to play. They made me a manager at age 26 so you can see how bad I was."[4] He spent ten more years in the Dodgers system as a player-manager.

His first team, in Kingston, won the league pennant, though in midseason Scherger was transferred to another Class D team, in Thomasville, North Carolina. He had his best year as a player with the 1948 Olean, New York, club, hitting .324 in full-time duty. After he spent two years in Trois-Rivieres, Quebec, his 1951 Ponca City, Oklahoma, club ran away with the league pennant. In these years Scherger occasionally got his name in the *Sporting News* because of a fracas with an umpire, drawing suspensions at least twice, in 1947 and 1951.[5]

He spent two seasons in Santa Barbara, California, where in 1953 fate had him cross paths with a young shortstop from nearby Los Angeles named George "Sparky" Anderson. Anderson was nineteen and in his first season of professional ball, while his new manager was thirty-two, but both men loved the game and were driven to succeed. "Winning was everything to George," recalled Anderson. "In fact, George believed you should win every night. You know you can't, but why admit it?"[6] Anderson deeply respected his manager and watched closely. "George could be tough, but he was always fair and considerate," Anderson remembered. "He knew kids like me could make a lot of errors and he tolerated that, but bonehead plays, mental mistakes, and indifferent attitudes were something else."[7]

Years later Anderson and Scherger often reminisced about their days in the Minor Leagues and the long bus rides through small towns. "George was one of those guys who believed that once you got on the bus you drove until you got there," recalled Anderson. "Sometimes it took hours and hours and he wouldn't allow comfort stops. We'd agitate him and his neck would get redder, but he'd just sit there, staying awake, staring straight ahead."[8]

After three more seasons, winning the league playoff in 1954 for Newport News, Virginia, and then taking the regular-season pennant the next season for the same club, the thirty-six-year-old Scherger seemingly walked away from baseball after a last-place finish with Cedar Rapids, Iowa, during the 1956 season. Having seen much of the country in the previous ten years, the Schergers had settled in Charlotte, North Carolina. In 1957 Mozelle was hired as the first full-time librarian at Charlotte College, later known as the University of North Carolina–Charlotte. George began working at the local A&P supermarket, helping to raise the couple's four children—sons George Jr., Joseph, and Daniel and daughter Teresa.

After four years out of the game, in 1961 Scherger decided to give baseball another go, returning to the Dodgers system to manage. In his first year back, with the Panama City, Florida, team he skippered a twenty-year-old second baseman named Bobby Cox. He spent two years in Salisbury, North Carolina, winning the Manager of the Year Award in both seasons and capturing the league title in 1964. After another year with St. Petersburg in 1965, he again left baseball. This time he lasted only a single season away from the game.

Scherger joined the Reds system in 1967, managing Tampa in the Florida State League. Bob Howsam had taken over the Reds and, along with farm director Sheldon "Chief" Bender, had begun to remake the organization. In the Minors, the Reds wanted their players to be in great shape and fundamentally sound, and Howsam hired new managers whom he believed could provide this kind of discipline: Scherger; Don Zimmer, who began his managerial career in the Reds system in 1967; and Sparky Anderson, whom Howsam hired for the Cardinals in 1965 and then for the Reds in 1968. By 1969 Scherger ran the Reds' Minor League spring training camp, and then he took over the Reds' Gulf Coast League club when the season started in June.

Anderson and Scherger had stayed in touch since their season together in Santa Barbara back in 1953. After one year in the Reds system, Anderson was the third base coach for the expansion San Diego Padres in 1969. In October 1969 Howsam shocked everyone by hiring the relatively unknown, thirty-five-year-old Anderson to manage the Major League club. The day he got the job, Anderson called Scherger in Charlotte and asked him to join his coaching staff. After thirty years, Scherger had reached the big leagues.

Scherger initially served as Anderson's bench coach and also was in charge of coaching defense, both the infielders and the outfielders. When Richie Scheinblum joined the club in 1973, Anderson pointed out Scherger on the field. "Who's he, the hitting coach?" asked the outfielder. "No, he's the fielding coach, and a guy I'd like you to know well."[9] In the coming years Scherger would spent a lot of time working with George Foster and Dan Driessen, two young players who struggled with defense when they started out. "He's not too old to wield a mean fungo stick," said Foster. "He can run you all over the outfield until your tongue hangs out."[10] When Pete Rose famously switched to third base in the middle of the 1975 season, it was Scherger who came to the park early every day to hit ground balls to him.

Scherger remained with the Reds for Sparky Anderson's entire nine-season run with the club, working later at first base and subsequently at third, participating in four World Series, and winning two titles. But through all of the success, he continued to work winters at the A & P supermarket back home in Charlotte. "We had four kids to put through college," he explained. "The kids went to Catholic schools all the way and that cost us too. We've

been catching up with the World Series money."[11] There were additional perks to the job. After the 1978 season the Reds team went to Japan to play a series of games. Upon their return, Rose gave each of the team's coaches a new four-wheel-drive Jeep.[12]

Despite all of the success, soon after their return from Japan Reds general manager Dick Wagner fired Anderson and his staff. Scherger accepted a job managing the Reds' Nashville club, returning to the Minor Leagues at the age of fifty-eight. In midsummer Anderson became the manager of the Detroit Tigers, and there were rumors that Scherger would head to Detroit with him. Scherger decided to finish the season with Nashville and soon signed a two-year deal to stay in the Reds organization. He would not be with Nashville, who broke their working agreement with the Reds because they would not allow their affiliates to use a designated hitter, putting their clubs at a decided disadvantage. Despite the handicap, Scherger shepherded the Sounds to the 1979 Southern League championship.

Scherger managed the next three years in Tampa; Waterbury, Connecticut; and Indianapolis. The 1982 Indianapolis Indians were the first Triple-A club he managed in twenty-three seasons of Minor League managing. The Indians won their division and then won the American Association playoff as well, earning Scherger the 1982 *Sporting News* Minor League Manager of the Year Award. "I'm tickled pink," he said about the award. "It's a real surprise. This has to rate as one of the best things ever to happen to me in baseball."[13] Once again, his success came despite the Indians' being the only club in the league that did not use a designated hitter. (The Indians did use one in the 1982 pennant race because of a depleted pitching staff.)

At the conclusion of the 1982 Minor League season, Scherger joined the Reds' Major League coaching staff on September 7. The Reds were going through a terrible season and had replaced Manager John McNamara in late July with third base coach Russ Nixon on an interim basis. There was speculation that Scherger might be in line for the job for 1983. Instead, the Reds rehired Nixon, who kept Scherger as his bench coach. "I would enjoy the opportunity to manage on the Major League level," said the sixty-two-year-old Scherger, "but not at the expense of my good friend Russ Nixon."[14]

Scherger remained a Reds coach for four more seasons, working for Nixon and then Vern Rapp. In August 1984 the Reds reacquired Pete Rose from Montreal and made him player-manager. Rose leaned heavily on Scherger. "He's been a baseball man for 45 years and he has the players' respect," said Rose. "The days I'm in the lineup he'll be running the show."[15] This arrangement lasted through the 1986 season, leading to some debate as to how the team was being managed. Outfielder Gary Redus, who had publicly suggested that Rose was playing himself at the expense of better players (like Redus), also doubted how much managing Rose was doing. "I thought of George Scherger as the manager," said Redus.[16]

After the 1986 season Scherger retired from baseball after forty-seven years (with time off for the Army and two brief retirements). In June 1987 he agreed to return to manage Nashville but lasted for only a single game before realizing his mistake. Other than helping Anderson out in spring training a few times, he retired for good.

He lived out the rest of his days in Charlotte. Mozelle had worked as the librarian at UNC–Charlotte for many years before retiring herself in the late 1970s. She died in May 1993, after forty-seven years of marriage. "She liked helping people and got a great kick out of working with the kids," George said. "And she kept a whole mess of books around."[17]

Scherger died on October 13, 2011, at his Charlotte home. He was survived by his three sons, his daughter, two brothers, ten grandchildren, and eight great-grandchildren. He did not make it to the Major Leagues as a player, but he played a large role in the careers of many who did and on one of history's greatest teams.

Chapter 5. **Alex Grammas**

Maxwell Kates

There was never an Alex Grammas question on *Family Feud.* However, if Richard Dawson, the late and longtime host of the popular game show, had asked a hundred of his contemporaries how they remembered Grammas, the survey would invariably have pointed to three answers: his flawless fielding, his excellence as a third base coach, and his Hellenic heritage. As a National League utility infielder for ten years, Grammas drew favorable comparisons to a young Phil Rizzuto. After retiring he was a third base coach for a quarter century, mainly for teams managed by Sparky Anderson. Forever proud of his ancestry, Grammas in 1976 became the first Greek American ever to manage a Major League team for a full season.

Peter Grammatikakis was a Greek immigrant who left his home in Agios Dimitrios for Birmingham, Alabama, early in the twentieth century. Attracted by the reputation of the southern metropolis as a "Magic City," he truncated his name to Grammas and established himself in the wholesale candy trade. Peter married Angeline, the American-born daughter of Greek immigrants from Geraki. Their second son, Alexander Peter, was born in Birmingham on April 3, 1926. Both Alex and his older brother, Cameron, loved baseball and seized any opportunity to pursue the national pastime between grammar school and Greek school. Both brothers served in World War II before playing college baseball at Mississippi State University.

Alex maintained that Cameron was the better player: "He has played A-ball at Colorado Springs and hit about .335. . . . They were going to send him back out to Colorado Springs the following year. [He] just didn't want to do it, so he quit. I wish he

After a ten-year career as a Major League infielder, Alex Grammas spent another twenty-eight years coaching and managing in the big leagues.

hadn't because he would have made it—no question about it," Grammas recalled in a 1998 book on Greeks in the game.

After he graduated with a bachelor's degree in business in 1949, Alex was signed to his first professional contract by Doug Minor of the Chicago White Sox. He batted .327 for Muskegon in the Class A Central League and was promoted in 1950 to Memphis, where he led Southern Association shortstops in fielding. Before that season, on January 29, 1950, Alex married the former Tula Triantos. Traded to the Cincinnati Reds organization in 1951, he continued to impress with his quick fielding and timely hitting. On loan to Kansas City of the American Association for one year, he led the league's shortstops in put-outs and assists. The Pittsburgh Pirates valued Grammas and his defensive abilities enough to look into acquiring him in a proposed six-player trade in 1952 with Ralph Kiner as the headliner in the swap. Although the Pittsburgh deal fell through, the Reds offered Grammas in another trade the following winter. On December 2, 1953, he was dealt to the St. Louis Cardinals for pitcher Jack Crimian and $100,000.

Measuring 6 feet tall and weighing 175 pounds, Grammas could not have been more excited about making his Major League debut as a Cardinal: "I was hoping [they] would get me. I can't think of anything better than playing next to Red Schoendienst. He's the best there is in the majors," Grammas said. Finishing tied for third in the National League with a record of 83-71 in 1953, the Cardinals under new owner August A. Busch viewed Grammas as "the missing piece" to transform the team into bona-fide contenders.

Unfortunately, Grammas's enthusiasm proved costly during his first spring training with St. Louis. On February 21, 1954, he injured his right arm during a sliding drill. Although x-rays proved negative and Grammas made the varsity squad, he spent his rookie year trying to regain confidence after suffering the painful injury. A year after batting .307 in the Minor Leagues, he hit only .264 with fifty-seven runs and twenty-nine RBIs playing for the Cardinals. Grammas scored three runs (once after reaching on an error and twice after walking) before collecting his first big league hit, a single off Cincinnati's Harry Perkowski on April 19, 1954, in a 6–3 Cards win at home. And he did not hit his first home run until September 3, when he parked a Paul Minner pitch in a losing effort to the Chicago Cubs. (Grammas had gone 0-for-4 against Minner in his big league debut, a 13–4 Opening Day loss

to the Cubs at Busch Stadium in St. Louis on April 13.) As for the Cardinals, they finished the season in sixth place out of eight teams with a record of 72-82, twenty-five games behind the New York Giants.

Although Grammas led the senior circuit in fielding average in 1955, he batted only .240. Early in the 1956 season, on May 16, he was traded back to Cincinnati along with outfielder Joe Frazier for infielder-outfielder Chuck Harmon. After years of obscurity, the Reds found themselves in a pennant race with the Brooklyn Dodgers and the Milwaukee Braves. Manager Birdie Tebbetts credited Grammas with making "a big difference in our ballclub . . . since we've been using him." The Reds finished third, two games behind Brooklyn and one behind Milwaukee.

Grammas's confidence improved in 1957, particularly on the heels of a triple play executed against the New York Yankees in a spring training contest. Gil McDougald was in scoring position at second base with Mickey Mantle on first when Yogi Berra hit a line drive to the Cincinnati shortstop. Grammas put McDougald out at second, then caught Mantle in a rundown. During the 1957 season, Grammas, playing behind All-Stars Johnny Temple, Roy McMillan, and Don Hoak, had only ninety-nine at bats. He hit .303, second on the Reds only to Frank Robinson's .322. The following campaign marked Grammas's worst pro season to date.

The 1958 Redlegs finished below .500 and in mid-August Tebbetts was replaced by Jimmy Dykes when Cincinnati dropped toward last place. Despite the team rebounding and eventually finishing fourth, Grammas lost the shortstop position in mid-July and primarily played third base, along with several starts at second. His season batting average ended at .218, over eighty points lower than the previous year.

The Reds traded Grammas back to the Cardinals in a six-player deal on October 3, 1958. During his second tour of duty in St. Louis, he earned the reputation of carrying "a sharper bat, a better arm, surer hands, and [handling] three positions well." Batting .269 in 1959, Grammas, then thirty-three years old, spent time teaching younger players the value of maintaining a proper attitude as a team player. Tim McCarver remembered, "I was 17 years old when I first came up with the Cardinals, just up from high school. My first night on the bench [a September 1959 game], Henry Aaron was up with a couple of guys [on]. I liked Henry Aaron a lot growing up. I let out with one of those 'Come on, Henry!' or something to that effect. Everyone naturally looked at me and Alex Grammas came over and said, 'You know, up here in the big leagues, we tend to cheer for our players, not the opposition.'"

Traded again on June 5, 1962, this time to the Cubs, Grammas completed his playing career in Chicago a year later. His lifetime statistics in ten National League seasons included 236 runs, 90 doubles, 10 triples, 12 home runs, 163 RBIs, and a .247 batting average. By then, the Grammas family had expanded to include daughters Lynn and Mary Ann, along with twin sons Peter and Alexis. The patriarch needed to plan for his family's future.

During the off-seasons, Grammas worked in the produce business with his uncles. The experience was valuable preparation for a supermarket venture he entered into with his friend Harry Walker. The business partnership proved to be an important strategic alliance when Walker was hired to manage the Pittsburgh Pirates in 1965. After managing the Cubs' Texas League affiliate at Fort Worth in 1964, Grammas was hired by Walker and began the first of twenty-five seasons as a Major League third base coach. He remained a Pittsburgh coach for five years before resigning at the end of the 1969 season, having managed the last five contests the Bucs played on an interim basis after Larry Shepard was fired. Pittsburgh general manager Joe L. Brown offered a glowing recommendation of Grammas, both as a coach and as a man. When the obscure thirty-five-year-old George Lee "Sparky" Anderson was hired to manage the Cincinnati Reds in 1970, Grammas was his choice as first lieutenant.

"I coached third base myself for Preston Gomez the year before. On my one season on that job, I watched all the other third base coaches in the league. I thought Grammas was the best and Eddie Yost of the Mets, next best," Anderson told Si Burick of the *Dayton (OH) Daily News*. "I told [General Manager Bob] Howsam I needed a real professional at third base, and I'd like to offer the job to Grammas. I called Alex and told him I was hoping for a relationship like [Al Lopez had] with the White Sox coaches." For nineteen of the next twenty-two years, Grammas remained a valuable member of Sparky Anderson's coaching staffs.

As the Reds prepared to open the new Riverfront Stadium, a dynasty was rising in Cincinnati. Nobody dared to ask "Sparky Who?" after the Reds opened the 1970 season with a torrid .700 winning percentage in their first one hundred games before tapering off, as it were, to 102-60 and a National League West Division title. The Reds swept the Pirates in three games during the NLCS before losing in the World Series to Baltimore. After the Reds disappointed in 1971, tumbling to a fourth-place tie with Houston, they pulled off a blockbuster deal with the Houston Astros, bringing, among others, All-Star and eventual Hall of Fame second baseman Joe Morgan to the Queen City. Grammas helped Morgan improve his defensive abilities and later successfully converted outfielder Pete Rose to a third baseman. However, if you ask Grammas today, he will reserve his highest praise for his prize pupil, a young shortstop from Venezuela named Dave Concepción.

"You're talking about a guy I love. He's probably the finest infielder I ever had the pleasure to work with. If not the most talented, he's near the top. He even named his son after me, David Alejandro," Grammas said in a 2009 interview. As Sparky Anderson later told sports reporter Dan Ewald, "Concepción had the tools but he needed a lot of polish. Alex Grammas spent hour after hour teaching him the tricks. Grammas and David sweat and bled from all the work they put in together. Grammas hit David more ground balls than Donald Trump has dollar bills . . . and Grammas taught him to concentrate on situations. It wasn't good enough to field the ball. He had to learn what to do after he got it."

The Reds won the NL West easily in 1972 before facing a challenging Pittsburgh Pirates team in the NLCS. The Reds and Pirates split the first four contests, forcing a deciding Game Five before a packed house in Cincinnati. Pittsburgh was leading, 3–2, as the game entered the bottom of the ninth inning. As Pirates reliever Dave Giusti waited to deliver the first pitch to Johnny Bench, a commotion ensued at home plate. Grammas remembered "standing at third base and I didn't know what was going on." He was later told that Bench's mother wandered down to the railing to offer words of encouragement, advising, "Johnny, this is it. Let's go. Do something." Bench, the National League's Most Valuable Player in 1972, listened to his mother and tied the game with a lead-off home run to right field. A pair of singles by Tony Pérez and Denis Menke brought Bob Moose in from the Pittsburgh bullpen. George Foster, at second base as a pinch runner for Pérez, made it to third on César Gerónimo's fly ball. With two outs after a Darrel Chaney pop-up, the entire stadium seemed to be on their feet as Moose uncorked a wild pitch to pinch hitter Hal McRae, sending Foster racing safely home for the 4–3 victory. For the second time in three years, Cincinnati was going to the World Series (which they lost to Oakland in seven games). For Grammas, it was "the most spine-tingling game I was ever connected with."

The Big Red Machine won their division again in 1973, although they lost to the New York Mets in the NLCS, before going all the way in 1975, defeating the Boston Red Sox in a sterling seven-game World Series. Game Seven was Grammas's last in a Cincinnati uniform before he was hired to manage the Milwaukee Brewers. Even as a player, he was deemed the most likely of his teammates to succeed as a manager. Now he would be challenged to manage a struggling franchise that had never in its brief history won more than seventy-six games per season. Not even the presence of Hank Aaron could prevent a late-season meltdown in 1975, as the Brewers lost fifty-nine of their last eighty-four games to finish at 68-94. Despite the financial security of a three-year contract, Grammas had his work cut out for him.

"When you take a ballclub that ended up the way the Brewers did last year, you've really got to be happy if you can wind up playing .500 ball. That means winning 13 games more. That's more realistic than to think we can win the pennant," he said. Leading the Brewers both on the field and by example was, once again, Hank Aaron. Grammas admitted years later to Larry Stone of the *Seattle Times* that he "was proud to have Hank on [his] team," describing the home run king as "the kind of guy everybody liked." Aaron was the first to admit that by 1976 his skills were deteriorating. Facing California's Dick Drago at County Stadium on July 20, Aaron hit his 755th career home run without any accompanying media fanfare. Nobody would have known it would be his last in a Major League uniform—and the highlight of an otherwise disappointing season for the Brewers.

An omen of the 1976 campaign presented itself early in the schedule, on April 10. The Brewers trailed the visiting New York Yankees 9–6 in the bottom of the ninth inning when third baseman Don Money hit a walk-off grand slam. Or did he? Before delivering the pitch to Money, Yankees reliever Dave Pagan did not notice first base umpire and fellow Canadian Jim McKean call time out as requested by the Yankees' Chris Chambliss. Never one to shy away from a protest, Yankees manager Billy Martin insisted that the home run should be nullified. McKean upheld Martin's protest, and Money subsequently flied out. The Brew Crew's rally was stymied as New York topped Milwaukee, 9–7.

Despite the promise of success with a Sparky Anderson protégé at the helm, the Brewers ended the 1976 season in the American League East cellar; posting a record of 66-95, they finished thirty-two games behind the Yankees. Grammas took the disappointment in stride, offering that "it's a little difficult to adjust to . . . but you have to be realistic. If not, you drive yourself crazy and I have no intention of driving myself crazy."

Clearly a roster overhaul was in order for the Brewers in 1977. Power-hitting George Scott was traded back to the Boston Red Sox for slugging first baseman Cecil Cooper after calling the Brewers "the laughingstock of baseball." After a weak season at the plate, catcher Darrell Porter was packaged with pitcher Jim Colborn to the Kansas City Royals for a trio of young players, outfielder Jim Wohlford, pitcher Bob McClure, and utility man Jamie Quirk. Acquired via the free-agent route was third baseman Sal Bando. With Don Money moving to second base and Robin Yount emerging as one of the brightest young shortstops in baseball, the Brewers opened the 1977 season with a formidable infield. If only infielders could pitch. Jerry Augustine led the squad with eighteen losses (and twelve wins) for a team that went 67-95. Only the haplessness of the expansion Toronto Blue Jays prevented a second consecutive last-place finish for the Brewers.

Despite his popularity among the fans in Milwaukee, Grammas lacked the support of all his players. The alienation began when he imported from Cincinnati the dress code that prohibited players from having facial hair. A significant minority of the Milwaukee roster in 1975 sported Fu Manchu mustaches. Along with Colborn, Porter, Scott, and Yount, Brewers players Gorman Thomas, Kurt Bevacqua, and Pete Broberg were all depicted on their 1976 Topps cards wearing their Fu Manchus. Under the stewardship of Grammas, the free-spirited players were required to shave their whiskers against their will by Opening Day 1976. Discontent with the manager continued in 1977 to the point that utili-

ty player Mike Hegan told reporter Lou Fitzgerald that "Alex Grammas is a nice guy, but as a manager he makes a good third-base coach."

Hegan's immediate release proved to be a pyrrhic victory for Grammas. The manager was not given the opportunity to complete his three-year contract, as he became one of the casualties in the November 20, 1977, front-office upheaval known as the Saturday Night Massacre. Again sardonic in his outlook, Grammas allowed, "I'm sure the Brewers are going to be a much better team." He was right; they went 93-69 for George Bamberger in 1978.

When one door closed in Milwaukee, another, in Cincinnati, reopened, and Grammas returned to the Reds in 1978. Sparky Anderson was ecstatic that "Grammas is back with us. . . . He will coach again at third base. I have said 'Greek' is the best at that job, so there is where he will be stationed." It was a brief homecoming for Grammas, as the Reds finished in second place. Under new general manager Dick Wagner, second place was no longer good enough, and Anderson was fired. While Anderson began the 1979 season in exile, Grammas had accepted the Atlanta Braves' offer to coach third base. However, when Anderson was hired to manage the Detroit Tigers on June 12, Grammas seemed to be a natural fit for the coaching staff.

"With Grammas, I had such a good rapport from the bench to the third-base coach's box that, after a while, we didn't even have a regular sign," Anderson recalled. "In the early days, I found myself giving him the wrong sign at times, but he realized it and would change it to the right thing. Once in a while, he'd even change the right sign, like a quarterback checking off the coach's play at the line of scrimmage because the defensive alignment wasn't right for the strategy. Alex would hear a whistle on the other side and realize they anticipated what we intended to do, so he did something else."

Grammas followed Anderson to Detroit in 1980 and had the opportunity to coach two more bright infield pupils, shortstop Alan Trammell and second baseman Lou Whitaker. Although experts scoffed at the manager's prediction of a world championship within five years, the Tigers produced precisely that. After winning thirty-five of their first forty games in 1984, the Tigers spent the entire season in first place before dispatching the Kansas City Royals in three games during the ALCS, then defeating the San Diego Padres, four games to one, in the World Series.

With Detroit struggling in its quest to defend its title in 1985, a left-handed starter was on General Manager Bill Lajoie's shopping list. Meanwhile, the Texas Rangers had a southpaw they were eager to trade. Remembering him as "the best pitcher—not only in the American League," Grammas recommended the pitcher in a trade. On June 20, 1985, the Tigers welcomed native Detroiter Frank Tanana back home. The crafty southpaw lent stability to the Tigers' rotation for eight years and was the winning pitcher in the decisive final game of the 1987 season, pitching a 1–0 shutout over the Blue Jays to win the AL East over second-place Toronto.

Although the Tigers contended yet again in 1988, success would be short-lived, as Detroit posted the worst record in baseball, 59-103, in 1989. Veterans who had contributed to the 1984 success were ineffective, retired, or playing elsewhere. They had been replaced by a new batch of players, younger and cheaper and uncomfortable with an older coaching staff; these players were not afraid to voice their concerns to the front office. Consequently, despite winning eighty-four games in 1991, the Tigers released three of their coaches that year, among them Alex Grammas. At age sixty-five, he decided it was time to retire.

His baseball career behind him, Grammas returned to Birmingham to pursue his favorite hobbies, fishing and golf. In 1992 he reaped the dividends of the eight years he spent at Greek school as a child when he traveled to Greece for the first time.

"All my life, my father was telling me good things about Greece," Grammas recalled. "When he was

talking, I was laughing, but when I saw with my own eyes, I realized he hadn't said enough about Greece. I love Greece very much. . . . When I walked up to the Acropolis and saw the Parthenon, the hairs on my head were standing straight up. I couldn't believe it." He returned to Greece several times, and a later trip was the most special for him.

"I decided to take the entire family to Greece—all 21 of them. I thought it was important for my grandchildren to learn about their heritage and see where their ancestors came from," Grammas said in 2009. "We visited Athens, took a cruise of the [Greek] islands, and stayed overnight at the house where my father was born. I'll tell you—the day we arrived, they announced Athens was getting the Olympics. The entire city went mad. You've never seen anything like it."

Alex Grammas devoted more than a half century of his life to baseball as a player, coach, and manager. He played ten years in the Major Leagues, coached an additional twenty-five, and earned two World Series rings. He gained the respect and admiration of students and peers and delighted in watching his pupils become stars. Dave Concepción became one of the most successful shortstops in Cincinnati before teaching the trade to another budding superstar, Barry Larkin. Grammas continued to live in Birmingham in retirement and in 2012, at age eighty-six, said he enjoyed good health. His philosophy on life advised that "nothing can be stopped except time, so please enjoy every minute."

The *Family Feud* survey says that Alex Grammas listened to his own advice.

Chapter 6. **Larry Shepard**

Andy Sturgill

Serving as the pitching coach for the Big Red Machine is a bit like being the drummer in Billy Joel's band. Even if you're an integral part of an exceptional team, only the most devoted and hard-core observers will ever know your name as opposed to that of the headline-grabbing main attraction. While the Reds' offense and its stars made headlines as the force that drove the Machine, Shepard and his pitchers more than held up their end of the bargain as Cincinnati became the National League's dominant team in the 1970s.

Lawrence William Shepard was born on April 3, 1919, in Lakewood, Ohio, just to the west of Cleveland. He was the third of four sons born to Frank and Viola Shepard, joining older brothers Frank and Richard, and, later, younger brother Robert. Shepard's father worked as a general agent at a steamship office, while his mother stayed home with the boys. Four years older than Larry's father, Viola was raised by German-born parents and was a widow when she married Frank in 1913. In 1933 the family moved to Montreal, Quebec. Larry attended the city's McGill University.

Shepard made his professional baseball debut in 1941 as a right-handed pitcher with the Trois-Rivieres Renards of the Class C Canadian-American League. The twenty-two-year-old won fifteen games and lost eleven to finish tied for tops on the team in wins and second in innings pitched and ERA. The Trois-Rivieres club sold Shepard's contract to the New York Giants, but in November, with the United States on the verge of entering World War II, Shepard enlisted in the army, and the deal was nullified. Shepard missed the next four seasons while in the army.

Sparky Anderson delegated the entire pitching staff to the well-respected Larry Shepard.

After he returned to baseball in 1946, Shepard spent six seasons pitching in the Brooklyn Dodgers' Minor League system. After two good but not special seasons at Nashua, New Hampshire, and Pueblo, Colorado, in 1948 Shepard became the player-manager of the Class D Medford, Oregon, Nuggets in the Far West League. It proved to be a banner year for Larry, as the team finished in second place and he posted a 22-3 record (leading the league in victories) and married Joyce Hamilton.

For the next three seasons Shepard was the pitcher-manager for Billings in the Pioneer League.

The stay in Montana marked the high point of his playing career; as he logged three straight twenty-win seasons and led the team to the league championship in 1950.

After the 1951 season Shepard, by then in his thirties, was drafted out of Billings and the Brooklyn organization by the Hollywood Stars of the Pacific Coast League, an affiliate of the Pittsburgh Pirates. At Hollywood Shepard was exclusively a pitcher; the team was managed by Fred Haney, who would go on to win a World Series managing the Milwaukee Braves in 1957. For the Stars, Shepard, pitching mostly in relief, was 6-4 with an ERA just over 3.00 in 107 innings as Hollywood won the Pacific Coast League championship.

Shepard again became a playing manager in 1953, in South Carolina with Charleston of the South Atlantic League, then spent two seasons in Williamsport, Pennsylvania, with the Eastern League before going to the Lincoln Chiefs of the Western League in 1956. So taken were the Shepards with Lincoln, Nebraska, that they made the city their permanent home.

Shepard pitched in eighteen games while managing Lincoln in 1956 but, at age thirty-seven, left the playing field in 1957. Lincoln won the league championship in both of his seasons there.[1] The team was run by Dick Wagner, who two decades later was instrumental in bringing Shepard to the Reds.

Promoted to manager of the Pirates' Triple-A team in Salt Lake City in 1958, Shepard had a brief swan song as a player, pitching in seven games as a thirty-nine-year-old. In 1959 he led Salt Lake City to the Pacific Coast League championship. In 1961 the Pirates moved Shepard to the Columbus, Ohio, Jets of the International League, who immediately won the league championship, a notable achievement because the team had so many injuries that Shepard was forced to use twenty-three different infield combinations.[2] The Jets won the title under Shepard's guidance again in 1965. Having won five Minor League championships and having prepared players such as

Donn Clendenon, Steve Blass, Dock Ellis, Manny Sanguillen, Manny Mota, Wilbur Wood, and Willie Stargell for the Major Leagues, Shepard moved on after the 1966 season. He had hoped to take over the Major League club when it needed a new manager before the 1965 season but was passed over for Harry Walker. Shepard instead became the pitching coach with the Philadelphia Phillies for the 1967 season, his first Major League job after twenty-five years in professional baseball.[3]

The 1967 Phillies finished fifth with a record of 82-80. The pitching staff posted an ERA of 3.10, fourth in the National League. After the season Shepard worked with the Phillies team in the Florida Winter Instructional League. While he was in Florida he got the chance he had waited for his entire career: he was named manager of the Pirates, at least partly due to his familiarity with the many Pirates he had managed in the Minor Leagues.[4] The Pirates had had Shepard in mind since early September, when the Phillies played in Pittsburgh and Shepard talked about the job with Pirates general manager Joe L. Brown. (Manager Walker had been fired on July 18.) After he was hired Shepard said, "I had been walking on air ever since I first met with Brown and waited daily for this phone call. I phoned my wife right away because she was slowly developing an ulcer. This is our dream come true." In addition to taking over a dream job as a Major League manager, Shepard got a salary that was about twice as much as the most he had ever made in one Minor League season.[5]

The 1967 Pirates had finished in sixth place, and Danny Murtaugh had managed the last seventy-eight games. Shepard set his sights high. "I'm shooting for the pennant," he said. "I'll be disappointed if the Pirates don't win it because I think we have what it takes."[6] The Pirates began the Shepard era with an opening night one-game series at Houston. Joyce Shepard and the couple's twelve-year-old son, Larry, traveled to Houston for the game, and the Pirates led 4–2 heading into the bottom of the ninth. The Astros scored three runs after two were out to win the game and spoil Shepard's debut as skipper.

Shepard took the loss hard. He dressed in silence and uttered not a word on the team's midnight flight from Houston to San Francisco, where the Pirates were to begin a series the next day. Later he said, "I take defeats hard. And I try to take them myself. I don't want to talk and don't like people talking to me."[7] As the season progressed and the team struggled, Shepard had difficulty sleeping and maintaining an appetite; he lost nearly thirty pounds. He described a ten-game losing streak in July as "the worst experience of my life."[8]

Sleepless nights, ten-game losing streaks, and all, Shepard guided the Pirates to an 80-82 record and a sixth-place finish (out of ten teams) in 1968, earning another one-year contract to prove his mettle as a manager. The 1969 team won its first four games and held second place into early June before spending the rest of the season in either third or fourth in the new National League East. Showing his penchant for internalizing the wins and losses, Shepard missed about a week in July after suffering chest pains. He had not had a heart attack but was kept in the hospital for several days as a precaution.[9] Despite a respectable record of 84-73, Shepard was fired the morning after the Pirates' doubleheader sweep over the Phillies before fewer than three thousand home fans on September 25. At age fifty, released from the job of his dreams, Shepard stood at a professional crossroads. He could not have known how nicely things would fall into place for him.

After being fired, Shepard returned home to Nebraska to evaluate the next step in his professional life. "I was a very discouraged and broken-hearted man at that point," he said. "I could see my baseball career behind me."[10] But a brighter future beckoned. In October 1969 Cincinnati's Bob Howsam hired Sparky Anderson as manager. Anderson knew Shepard from the time they had spent as rival managers in the International League, and Wagner, Howsam's assistant, respected Shepard from their time together at Lincoln. Anderson asked Shepard to be the Reds' pitching coach, and Shepard accepted. Also added to the Reds staff was Alex Grammas, who had been Shepard's third base coach with the Pirates.

Often the success of a manager or head coach in professional sports is dependent on the leader surrounding himself with good, capable people and allowing them to do their job. With the Reds, Anderson understood that he did not know a whole lot about pitching and that Shepard did, and Anderson more or less turned things over to him. As Daryl Smith wrote in *Making the Big Red Machine*, "[Sparky] had two basic philosophies when it came to pitchers. First, he wasn't going to listen to them; he was only going to listen to the expert, and the expert wasn't the pitcher, it was pitching coach Larry Shepard. What his pitchers tried to tell him didn't hold any weight. In fact, he didn't care what they thought. What he did want to hear was what 'Shep' had to say. He trusted Shepard completely."[11]

With that trust Shepard went about improving the performance of the pitching staff. The 1970 squad posted an ERA nearly half a run better than in the preceding season and decreased its home runs allowed from 149 to 118. Shepard stressed improving the pitchers' level of conditioning (and throwing more change-ups). Not content to just talk about improved conditioning, he often led the staff in wind sprints.[12] As the season wore on and the Reds ran ahead of the pack in the National League West, more attention was given to the turnaround among the team's pitchers. Anderson credited Shepard. "I have not met with my pitchers since the spring," he said. "I've turned them all over to Larry. Larry's got the pitchers thinking like they're a separate team. The pitchers want very badly to hold their end up. Then it's up to the hitters to get the runs."[13]

Amid all the acclaim for the Reds' offense, Shepard was quick to stand up for his pitchers. "Granted that we are a hitting team with the likes of Pete Rose, Joe Morgan, Johnny Bench, and the rest, but our pitchers have to be doing their share for us to have enjoyed the success we have. But somehow, they're the last to get recognition," Shepard said.[14]

Shepard demanded a lot from his pitchers and had high expectations of them. He poked the staff by saying things like, "It's tough to win with the Reds because the offense doesn't *always* score six runs."[15] Reds beat writer Bob Hertzel wrote that Shepard "complimented and chastised, punished and rewarded, psyched and created this staff."[16] Shepard rode the staff hard and called them "dumb ass" when they messed up.[17] Jack Billingham, who pitched under Shepard for six seasons, recalled Shepard as "always thinking, always teaching. Larry was a perfectionist."[18] Shepard sat next to the impatient Anderson during games, always available to answer any query from the notorious Captain Hook. Shepard, of course, was also available to call down to the bullpen at any moment to instruct a pitcher to begin warming up.

While he could be blustery and difficult, there was another side to Shepard. Steve Blass, who pitched for Shepard in the Minor Leagues and with the Pirates, fondly recalled him as a great instructor for young pitchers and referred to him as "[my] pitching dad."[19] He was a devout Catholic, loyal friend, and sometimes provider of comic relief. In 1976 amid the hoopla of Mark Fidrych and his practice of talking to the baseball, Shepard said that as a pitcher he had done the same thing and had even gone so far as to smack the ball when it was getting hit too much. As a pitching coach with the Reds he would "kill" a baseball that wasn't providing the desired results. Shepard would walk to the mound, take the ball from the pitcher, and hit it a few times. "When a team makes a couple of errors or gets a couple of long hits, it's time to kill the baseball," he said. The intent was to break the tension and relax the pitcher.[20] The comedy Shepard provided was not always intentional, however. Severely limited by hip and leg

issues, he had a hip replacement and lost mobility in the process. Once Shepard stood near the plate like a hitter before a start, and as Billingham warmed up he accidentally buzzed Shepard, who went sprawling and had to be helped up. Another time the pitchers were in a meeting in which Anderson was dressing them down, and as he turned to Shepard to ask if he had anything to add, Shepard tilted too far back in his chair and fell over as the staff struggled not to burst out in collective laughter.[21]

Together with the quick-triggered Anderson, Shepard mapped out a plan of "defense from the bullpen" in which the duo would allow the team's offense to determine when a pitching change had to be made. The reliance upon the bullpen was made possible by the effectiveness of veteran relievers Pedro Borbon and Clay Carroll and later by the duo of Rawly Eastwick and Will McEnaney.

Despite the success of the team and the pitching staff, only five of the Reds' thirty-four All-Star Game selections from 1970 to 1976 went to pitchers.[22] But while the pitchers missed out on individual accolades, under the direction of Anderson and Shepard they piled up the only stat that really matters: wins. From 1970 through 1976 the team was 683-443 (.607) and won five division titles, four pennants, and two World Series.

The team began to disintegrate in the new free-agency era, and Anderson was fired after the 1978 season following consecutive second-place finishes. Shepard and the rest of the staff were also let go, with all but Grammas offered other positions in the organization. Ever loyal to Anderson, Shepard declined and served as the pitching coach of the San Francisco Giants in 1979, where he took considerable blame for the decline in the pitchers' performance since the previous season. After the 1979 season Shepard retired at the age of sixty, after thirty-nine years in professional baseball.

In retirement Shepard returned to life in Lincoln full-time alongside his wife, Joyce. Living in the city that housed the University of Nebraska, Shepard routinely offered advice to Cornhusker pitchers. He stayed in Lincoln for the rest of his life; he was ninety-two when he died on April 5, 2011. Joyce and two of his brothers had died earlier. Shepard was buried at Calvary Cemetery in Lincoln.

Chapter 7. **Ted Kluszewski**

Paul Ladewski

The area known as Argo is located eight miles west of Chicago's old Comiskey Park in Summit, Illinois, a low-down, five-figure village in Cook County known for a corn milling and processing plant that is among the largest of its kind—and has the odor to prove it. It was also home to Ted "Klu" Kluszewski, the 6-foot-2, 225-pound mountain of a man with the famous fifteen-inch biceps whose legend in baseball history will live even longer and go farther than the home runs he hit decades ago.

Kluszewski has often been referred to as one of the most underappreciated players of the post–World War II era, one whose accomplishments as a player and a coach have remained under the radar far too long. In the mid-1950s Klu was the original Big Red Machine, a long-ball hitter and run producer without peer. In the four seasons from 1953 to 1956, he averaged 179 hits, 43 homers, and 116 RBIS, numbers every bit as impressive as those of Eddie Mathews (152-41-109) of the Milwaukee Braves and Duke Snider (180-42-123) of the Brooklyn Dodgers in the same period. It's not a stretch to believe that if Kluszewski had stayed healthy and productive for four or five more seasons, he would have joined Mathews and Snider in the Hall of Fame. Despite an abbreviated career, his 251 homers while he was with Cincinnati rank fifth on the Reds' all-time list.

Born on September 10, 1924, Theodore Bernard Kluszewski attended Argo High School in Summit, where he excelled in football. His father worked in a local factory. As a youth, Klu's baseball experience consisted mostly of sandlot games. Indiana University recruited him primarily as a football player, but he also played baseball there, and his 1945 season

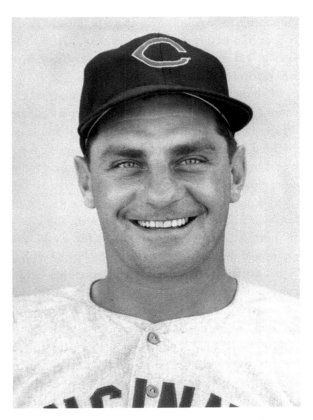

A longtime hero in Cincinnati as a power hitter, Ted Kluszewski was the hitting coach for one of history's greatest offenses.

ranks as one of the best for a two-sport athlete in the school's history. As a center fielder, Kluszewski hit .443, a school record that stood for fifty years; then the star end and kicker helped lead the Hoosiers to their only outright Big Ten football championship. The squad, which also included future NFL players Pete Pihos and George Taliaferro, finished with a 9-0-1 mark, the only unbeaten Hoosiers football team.

If not for World War II, Kluszewski most likely would have embarked on a professional football career. During the war the Reds held spring training at the Indiana campus in Bloomington because Major League teams were forbidden to train in the South. One day they invited the kid to take some hacks at batting practice. As legend has it, Big Klu promptly launched a few rockets over an embankment nearly four hundred feet away. After they picked their jaws up off the ground, team officials offered him a $15,000 contract, which he accepted.

With the bonus in hand, Kluszewski married Eleanor Guckel in February 1946. Eleanor was a fine athlete herself, excelling at softball, and Klu later credited her with helping his Major League career by taking films of him at bat and in the field from seats close to the field.

Making his professional debut for the Reds' Columbia (South Carolina) farm team in the Class A South Atlantic League in 1946, Kluszewski was an immediate sensation, leading the league with a .352 batting average and driving in eighty-seven runs in ninety games. He made his Cincinnati debut in April 1947 but logged only ten at bats with the Reds, spending most of the season with Memphis of the Double-A Southern Association. Again he tore up the league, winning the batting crown with a .377 average.

In 1948 Kluszewski returned to Cincinnati to stay for ten full seasons. It wasn't long before his large biceps prompted Klu to cut off the sleeves of his jersey, one of the boldest fashion statements in baseball history. At first he did it because the sleeves were restricting his swing, but after a while it became part of his persona. "I remember the first time that I saw Ted in those cutoff sleeves," former White Sox teammate Billy Pierce said of Klu's trademark style nearly a half century later. "They were good-sized. He was a big man. A big man."[1]

Despite those massive arms, Kluszewski did not immediately become a home run hitter at the Major League level. He hit only twelve as a rookie in 1948 and just eight in 1949, though he showed overall improvement as a hitter by lifting his batting average thirty-five points, from .274 to .309. He showed his power potential for the first time in 1950, hitting twenty-five home runs and driving in 111 runs to go along with a .307 batting average. After a dip in 1951 (.259-13-77), Klu had sixteen home runs in 1952 while raising his average to .320. His big breakthrough came a year later.

In 1953 Kluszewski finally blossomed as big-time slugger, as his .316 batting average, forty home runs, and 108 RBIs translated into a seventh-place finish in the Most Valuable Player vote. A career year followed in 1954, when he led the NL with forty-nine home runs. He hit .326 (fifth overall), slugged .642 (third), drove home 141 runs (first), and finished a close second to New York Giants outfielder Willie Mays in the MVP vote. In the All-Star Game at Cleveland, he delivered an RBI single and a two-run homer in consecutive innings, the latter of which broke a 5–5 tie in an eventual 11–9 loss. Klu was at his best when the stars came out, as he hit .500 in four midsummer classics.

Kluszewski did the brunt of his damage in the cozy confines of Crosley Field, which produced one of the highest home run rates of the decade, but he wasn't known for front-row jobs. What separated Kluszewski from the rest of the musclemen was his off-the-charts discipline at the plate. He totaled thirty-one fewer strikeouts (140) than home runs (171) in his four peak seasons. Of the ten times in Major League history that a player hit at least forty homers with fewer strikeouts, three were by Kluszewski. The others on the list: Lou Gehrig (twice), Johnny Mize (twice), Mel Ott, Joe DiMaggio, and Barry Bonds.

"Everybody moves at his own pace," Billy Pierce said many years later. "I mean, we had a Nellie Fox who jumped around all the time. Sherm Lollar couldn't move very fast no matter what happened. But both gave you everything they had on the field and Ted was the same way. He worked at his own pace, and he had a pretty good career that way."[2]

Kluszewski didn't make many mistakes in the field, either, although his detractors argued that the low error totals were the result of an inability or reluctance to move more than one step either way. If you believe in range factors, though, Big Klu was well above average in this regard before his achy back came into play. He led the league in fielding percentage in a record five consecutive seasons, largely the result of excellent hands and nimble footwork.

"Everybody knows Ted could hit a baseball," said the late Bill "Moose" Skowron, the former New York Yankees first baseman who crossed paths with Big Klu many times in their careers. "What some people don't know is that he was a hell of a first baseman and a hell of a nice guy, too. And he always played in those short-sleeve shirts. He was built like a rock, you know."[3]

Kluszewski might have had a long run as one of baseball's top sluggers if not for a back injury that resulted from a clubhouse scuffle during the 1956 season. The disc problem proved to be Delilah to Klu's Samson, as he would never be the same power hitter again. After the 1957 season, one in which Klu was limited to a half-dozen homers and twenty-one RBIS in sixty-nine games, he was dealt by the Reds to Pittsburgh in return for Dee Fondy, another veteran first baseman.

In 1958, his only full season with the Pirates, Kluszewski produced a mere four home runs and thirty-seven RBIS in one hundred games, but he had a positive influence on a young, talented team that was on the move. Before he left, Klu made history at Forbes Field on May 9, when he went deep against Philadelphia Phillies pitcher Robin Roberts leading off the twelfth inning, the nineteenth walk-off homer to decide a 1–0 game since the turn of the century.

Big Klu began the 1959 season with the Pirates but was reduced to part-time status behind Dick Stuart and Rocky Nelson. He had started only twenty games and had logged just 122 at bats by late August when the White Sox, looking to add power for the stretch and (hopefully) the World Series,

traded outfielder Harry "Suitcase" Simpson and Minor League pitcher Bob Sagers for Kluszewski on August 25.

While the thirty-four-year-old Kluszewski was deep into the back nine of his career at the time, news of his return to Chicago was well received by South Siders. "Certainly, the attitude of the fans was positive about the trade," said John Kuenster, who covered the 1959 pennant winners as a *Chicago Daily News* beat writer. "Ted was a nice guy, a popular guy. He was well known in the area and his return was very well received there."[4] At the very least, the consensus went, Klu could do no worse at the position than thirty-five-year-old warhorse Earl Torgeson, a .226 hitter at the time, or twenty-four-year-young prospect Norm Cash, a .231 hitter who was new to the pressure of a pennant race.

Besides, the righty-dominated lineup had been rather "Kluless" for months. The veteran lefty provided a much-needed option for a "Go-Go" Sox team that was overly dependent on speed and defense at the time. "We didn't have a regular first baseman," Pierce recalled. "When we got Ted, we all thought it was a very, very good thing for us, because he gave us a strong left-handed hitter with a good reputation. We never thought he was past his prime but that he would help us. We were very glad to have him on our ballclub."[5]

What Kluszewski lacked in glitzy numbers, he made up for in stature. His mere physical presence gave the Second City a sliver of security, a reason to flex its own muscles for a change. "Ted was a quiet fellow, but he had been with a winner in Cincinnati and had many accomplishments in his career," Pierce said. "A fellow like that is a kind of automatic leader on the team. He gave us stability, which was very good for us."[6]

As it turned out, Kluszewski didn't quite turn back the clock in the final weeks of the regular season, but he had his moments. The most significant took place in Chicago on September 7, when the White Sox defeated the Kansas City Athletics in a

Labor Day doubleheader. In the opener Kluszewski contributed a key run-scoring hit in a 2–1 victory; in the nightcap he slugged a pair of homers and drove home five runs in a 13–7 rout. As a result of the sweep, the White Sox maintained a 4½-game lead over the second-place Cleveland Indians, who scored an emotional sweep of the Detroit Tigers by 15–14 and 6–5 the same day.

While Kluszewski had rather modest statistics in the final thirty-two games of the regular season—.297 batting average, two homers, ten RBIs—the hidden numbers suggest the White Sox were deeper and better because of him. "Ted was a great asset for us," Pierce said. "He was an important cog in the middle of the lineup."[7] With Klu as protection in the cleanup spot, outfielder Jim Landis immediately picked up the pace in the third hole. The offense produced more runs (4.5 vs. 4.3 per game) and the team won at a higher rate (.625 vs. .607) with Big Klu than without him.

But it was his performance in the 1959 World Series against the Dodgers that made South Side fans forever remember the Kluszewski trade as one of the greatest Brinks jobs in White Sox history; a local boy who made very, very good one unforgettable season. In the six World Series games, Kluszewski hit .391, slugged three home runs, and drove in ten runs. His 1.266 OPS (on-base plus slugging) was just plain silly.

Kluszewski smashed two home runs in an 11–0 rout of the Los Angeles Dodgers in the Series opener. "Oh, man, the two home runs that Ted hit . . . ," Pierce smiled at the thought of them. "That was exciting. I mean, there we were in the World Series. . . . The fans were excited, we were excited, everybody was excited."[8] Witnesses said Comiskey Park never rocked the way it did in the moments after Kluszewski took reliever Chuck Churn for a ride to the upper deck in the fourth inning. The two-run blow not only sealed the victory, but it did much to "chuck" Churn, as it turned out. The pitch was his last in the big leagues.

Until outfielder Scott Podsednik went deep to decide Game One of the 2005 World Series, Kluszewski's monster blast stood as the most memorable home run in team history. "There was a similar feeling with the two home runs," said John Kuenster. "They gave White Sox fans a reason to think, 'Maybe we will win this thing after all,' although in the case of the 1959 team, it didn't turn out that way."[9] Alas, the Dodgers won four of the next five games to become world champions.

Kluszewski left the team for the Los Angeles Angels in the expansion draft after the 1960 season—he had hit .293 with five homers in eighty-one games—but not before he was involved in the most controversial play of the 1960 campaign. In a game at Baltimore on August 28, Kluszewski hit a dramatic pinch-hit, three-run homer against Orioles starter Milt Pappas in the eighth inning to give his team a 4–3 lead. Or so it seemed. The umpire crew agreed that time had been called before the pitch was thrown and the home run was wiped out. After teammate Nellie Fox was ejected from the game, Kluszewski flied out to end the threat. The White Sox went on to drop a 3–1 decision and fell three games out of first place.

Before Kluszewski retired one year later, he exacted a sliver of payback at the same site. In the first game in Los Angeles Angels history, Big Klu took Pappas deep with a man on base in the first inning, the first home run in franchise history. One inning later he greeted rookie John Papa with a three-run homer to set the wheels in motion for a 7–2 victory. Kluszewski finished his final big league season with a .243 batting average, fifteen home runs, and thirty-nine RBIs in 107 games.

Kluszewski returned to the Reds after retiring as a player, and his impact on the team was no small one. He was the Reds' hitting coach for nine seasons in the 1970s, a decade that the Big Red Machine dominated as few other offenses in NL history had done. In 1986, after he had become a hitting instructor in the Reds' Minor League system, Kluszewski suffered a heart attack and underwent emergency bypass surgery. On March 29, 1988, a massive heart attack took his life. He was sixty-three years old.

That the funeral service in suburban Cincinnati was a virtual Who's Who of baseball said as much about Kluszewski the person as Big Klu the athlete. Pete Rose, Johnny Bench, and Tony Pérez were among those who paid their respects. Stan Musial and Joe Nuxhall did, too. During the 1988 season the Reds wore black armbands in memory of their late teammate. There wasn't an arm large enough to do justice to Big Klu, a big man in more ways than one.

Chapter 8. **Preseason Outlook**

Mark Armour

As the Cincinnati Reds prepared for the 1975 season, they had reason for cautious optimism. The club had plenty of talented players, including some of the biggest stars in the game, and they had been a strong team for several years. There were at least two reasons for the caution: the Reds, despite their great regular-season success, had been unable to finish the deal in the postseason—they had not won the World Series in thirty-five years; and the Los Angeles Dodgers, one of baseball's stronger teams, were in their division (the NL West) and were the defending league champions.

The Reds had taken their big step forward in 1970, winning 102 games and reaching the World Series. That club developed some holes the very next year before being transformed after the 1971 season via a big trade with the Astros—bringing second baseman Joe Morgan, outfielder César Gerónimo, and pitcher Jack Billingham, among others, on board and getting the team back on top. The 1972 club was led by five offensive stars: Morgan, MVP catcher Johnny Bench, first baseman Tony Pérez, left fielder Pete Rose, and center fielder Bobby Tolan. The club had solid starting pitchers (Billingham, Ross Grimsley, Gary Nolan) and a great, flexible bullpen (led by Clay Carroll, Tom Hall, and Pedro Borbon). The club finished 95-59 in a strike-shortened season, winning the division by 10½ games before defeating the defending champion Pittsburgh Pirates in the NLCS. In the World Series they were heavy favorites against the upstart Oakland A's, who had won ninety-three regular-season games and then lost their best player, Reggie Jackson, to a severe left hamstring injury in the deciding game of the ALCS. Instead, the A's prevailed in a pitching-dominated World Series, scoring just sixteen runs in seven games but winning four times—with each of their victories being by one run.

The 1973 club was largely unchanged and rolled to a 99-63 record, the best in baseball. The Reds actually trailed the Dodgers by four games on August 30, but Los Angeles proceeded to lose nine consecutive games while the Reds began a 13-2 stretch. On September 16 the Reds were 6½ ahead, a stunning advance of 10½ games in seventeen days. The Reds' offense was marred by a terrible year from Tolan, who hit .206 and lost his starting outfield job, but was aided by the breakthrough of shortstop Dave Concepción. Billingham (nineteen wins) and twenty-two-year-old Don Gullett (eighteen) led a deep pitching staff. The Reds were firing on all cylinders going into the NLCS, in which they faced the New York Mets, who had won just eighty-two games to barely capture the NL East, the worst first-place team in big league history. Shockingly, the Reds were toppled three games to two, as for the second straight year they were shut down by a good pitching staff during a postseason series. The Reds hit .186 and scored just eight runs in the five-game series.

In 1974 the Reds won their typical 98 games, the second-highest total in baseball. This time, however, the Dodgers won 102 games and took the NL West, denying the Reds a postseason berth. The Reds were loaded with All-Stars having good seasons, but the Dodgers led wire to wire with their own collection of excellent players.

Heading into 1975, this latest Reds team appeared to be loaded again. Bench, still just twenty-seven, was the biggest star in the game, with two MVP Awards, seven Gold Glove Awards, and seven All-Star Games

Thanks to men like Joe Morgan, the Reds were the cofavorites to win the NL West in 1975.

to his credit already. Pérez at first base had averaged more than 103 RBIs per year over the previous eight seasons. Morgan had been electrifying in his three years with the club, hitting over .290 with surprising power, averaging more than 115 walks and sixty steals per year. At shortstop, Concepción had hit over .280 the past two years and had won his first Gold Glove in 1974. Left fielder Pete Rose, perhaps the most consistent star in baseball, had hit just .284 in 1974, his lowest average in a decade, but still had set career highs with 106 walks and forty-five doubles and led the league in runs scored.

At the other three positions, Manager Sparky Anderson had options. César Gerónimo was a tremendous defensive center fielder who would likely give way to George Foster against left-handed pitchers. The lightning-fast Ken Griffey was set to play right field, ably backed by Merv Rettenmund and Dan Driessen. Third base, a trouble spot the past couple of years, would be manned by the slick-fielding but weak-hitting John Vukovich, acquired in the offseason from the Milwaukee Brewers.

The Reds' pitchers were often criticized for not carrying their weight, but this view was largely unfair. It was the offense, after all, that had failed in the 1972 and 1973 postseasons, and looking ahead, Anderson seemed to have another deep and flexible staff. Billingham had won nineteen games each of the previous two seasons, while Gullett, still just twenty-four years old, had won eighteen and seventeen. Fred Norman, acquired in the middle of the 1973 season, and Clay Kirby, picked up before the 1974 season, were dependable third and fourth starters. For his remaining starter Anderson was hoping for a comeback from the twenty-seven-year old Gary Nolan, who had been 15-5 with a 1.99 ERA before getting hurt late in the 1972 season and had pitched in just two games in the past two seasons. The return of Nolan would give Anderson one of the best rotations in the game.

One of the reasons Anderson's starters remained under the radar was that he was quick to use his bullpen, a trait for which he earned the nickname Captain Hook. The Reds had finished third in the league in ERA in 1974 but Anderson used a five-man rotation and gave a lot of innings to his top relievers. Over the previous three years Pedro Borbon had averaged ten wins, 127 innings, and a 2.87 ERA. Clay Carroll finished 12-5 with a 2.16 ERA over one hundred innings in 1974, and he had been anchoring the Reds' bullpen for seven years. Anderson also had Tom Hall and rookies Pat Darcy and Will McEnaney to hand the ball to, which he would certainly be doing.

Unfortunately, the Dodgers, defending NL champs, looked equally strong. Los Angeles also had a great offense, led by Jim Wynn, MVP Steve Garvey, Ron Cey, Davey Lopes, and Bill Buckner. The team's excellent pitching staff included Don Sutton and Andy Messersmith, along with ace reliever Mike Marshall, who had won the Cy Young Award for his amazing season: 15-12 and a record-breaking 208⅓ innings in relief.

None of the other four teams in the NL West (Atlanta Braves, San Francisco Giants, San Diego Padres, and Houston Astros) were expected to keep up with the Dodgers and Reds. In *Street and Smith's Official Yearbook*, among the more respected baseball annuals of the day, Ross Newhan picked the Dodgers to repeat, citing the Reds' age and the previous year's failure, which was sure to weigh on the team.[1] Zander Hollander's *Complete Handbook of Baseball* agreed, as did the annual *Major League Baseball 1975*.[2] The Churchill Downs Sports Book in Las Vegas listed the Dodgers as 4–5 favorites to win the division.

But not everyone was ready to bury the Big Red Machine. "The Reds have devastating bats up and down their lineup," wrote the *Sporting News*, "and their pitching will be better than adequate, especially if Gary Nolan succeeds in his comeback from shoulder trouble."[3] The Dodgers had their own comebacking hurler, Tommy John (recovering from his famous surgery), who did not appear to be ready.

"Everybody is picking the Dodgers to repeat," opined Roy Blount Jr. in *Sports Illustrated*, "but everybody may be wrong. The Reds look better."[4] The Reds' season would begin on April 7, and seven of their first ten games would be against the Los Angeles Dodgers.

Chapter 9. **Pete Rose**

Andy Sturgill

AGE	G	AB	R	H	2B	3B	HR	TB	RBI	BB	SO	BAV	OBP	SLG	SB	GDP	HBP
34	162	662	112	210	47	4	7	286	74	89	50	.317	.406	.432	0	13	11

The 1970 All-Star Game, at Riverfront Stadium in Cincinnati, was tied at 4–4 with two out in the bottom of the twelfth inning. For the National League, Pete Rose was on second base and Billy Grabarkewitz on first. When Jim Hickman lined pitcher Clyde Wright's offering to center field, hometown hero Rose broke from second base. Rounding third as center fielder Amos Otis came up throwing, Rose barreled toward home plate, but between Rose and home plate stood catcher Ray Fosse, awaiting Otis's throw. Just as the ball arrived, Rose plowed into Fosse, sending the catcher sprawling with an injured shoulder. Rose touched the plate with the winning run, but not before putting himself and Fosse in harm's way in what was essentially an exhibition game.

Ten years later the Philadelphia Phillies were two outs from the first world championship in their ninety-seven-year history, but they were in big trouble. The Phillies were up three games to two and were ahead 4–1 in Game Six, but the Kansas City Royals had loaded the bases with one out on a walk and two hits. Pitcher Tug McGraw's first pitch to the Royals' Frank White was popped up foul near the first-base dugout, and catcher Bob Boone rushed over to secure the critical second out. Disaster almost struck. The ball bounced from Boone's mitt. Just as it was about to hit the ground, Phillies first baseman Pete Rose snatched it from certain calamity, recording the out. McGraw then struck out Willie Wilson to clinch the 1980 World Series title for the Phillies.

Pete Rose is among the most controversial figures in baseball history. His skill, reckless abandon, and desire to win endeared him to millions of baseball fans, but that same hard edge combined with personal missteps to give his detractors more than enough fodder to tear him down. Through baserunning and bravado, girlfriends and gambling, one thing is indisputable: Pete Rose was an outstanding baseball player.

Peter Edward Rose was born on April 14, 1941, at Deaconess Hospital in Cincinnati, Ohio, the third of four children born to Harry Francis Rose and LaVerne Bloebaum Rose. Most friends called his parents Pete and Rosie.[1] With his sisters, Caryl and Jacqueline, and his younger brother, David, he grew up in the Anderson Ferry section of Cincinnati. Harry worked for Fifth Third Bank for more than forty years, but his real claim to fame was as a semipro athlete. He boxed and played baseball, softball, and football well into his forties. Harry chased all of his athletic pursuits with the same reckless determination that became his son's hallmark. Harry was determined to make his son an athlete from an early age and always stressed to him that when you play, you play to win. Pete's father once told an amateur baseball coach that Pete would play for the team, but only on the condition that he be allowed to switch-hit. He was eight years old.[2]

Pete attended Western Hills High School, a local incubator of baseball talent (twelve alumni, including Rose and Don Zimmer, have played Major League baseball). He excelled in football and baseball. He did not, however, excel in the classroom and as a result was forced to repeat the ninth grade. He could have avoided this fate by attending summer school, but his father objected on the ground that it would take time away from summer baseball.[3] Because of this extra year Rose was ineligible

On a team of stars and leaders, no star burned brighter in Cincinnati baseball than Pete Rose, who starred for the Reds for sixteen seasons.

to play baseball for Western Hills during his senior season, so he played in a semipro league, where he attracted the attention of scouts. Rose's uncle Buddy Bloebaum, who had played in the Minors and was then a bird-dog scout for the Reds, had made it his goal to have the young Rose sign with the hometown team. On the day that Rose graduated from Western Hills in 1960, Uncle Buddy told the family that the Reds were willing to sign Rose for $7,000 plus another $5,000 if he made the Majors. Years later Rose recalled, "I don't remember ever wanting to be anything but a professional athlete and it's a good thing I became one because I never prepared for anything else."[4]

After signing, Rose reported to the Class D Geneva Redlegs of the New York–Penn League, where he displaced a young Cuban named Tony Pérez at second base. Rose hit .277 in his first professional season. Pérez moved to third base and eventually to first, where he joined Rose as one of the key cogs in the Reds machine of the 1970s. After hitting .331 for the Class D Tampa Tarpons in 1961

and .330 with the Single-A Macon Peaches in 1962, Rose was invited to spring training with the Reds in 1963. While there were no great expectations for the young Rose, he impressed with his hitting, and Manager Fred Hutchinson had it in mind to keep Rose on the active roster to start the season. Many Reds veterans did not want to see Rose make the squad—he would be replacing their buddy, Don Blasingame—but he hit so well that he gave the team no choice but to take him north.[5]

Just shy of his twenty-second birthday, Rose made his Major League debut by starting on Opening Day 1963 at home against the Pittsburgh Pirates. He started his Major League career 0-for-12 before lining a triple into the gap in left-center field off Pittsburgh's Bob Friend. Hitting .273 and scoring 101 runs, Rose was named the National League Rookie of the Year. In July he met Karolyn Engelhardt at the River Downs racetrack in Cincinnati, and the two were soon married. Rose left his own wedding reception in order to attend the Parade of Stars dinner put on by Cincinnati's baseball writers.[6]

ANDY STURGILL

The 1964 season was not as smooth for Rose (.269, sixty-four runs scored), but he bounced back strong in 1965 and established himself as one of the better hitters in the National League. He led the league with 209 hits, made his first All-Star team, and hit .312. It was the first of his fifteen .300-or-better seasons.

Throughout the 1960s Rose continued to establish his credentials as a premier player. He twice led the league in hits (1965 and 1968), led the league in runs scored in 1969, and won his first two batting titles in 1968 and 1969. In 1969 he also won the first of consecutive Gold Gloves as an outfielder, after having moved out of the infield in 1967, and recorded twenty outfield assists in 1968.

Rose's prominence brought his no-quarter-asked-none-given style of play into the spotlight. Perhaps no athlete in any sport has ever squeezed more production out of his ability than Rose, and nobody has ever wanted to win more. Joe Morgan, Rose's teammate with both the Reds and Phillies, wrote, "Pete played the game, always, for keeps. Every game was the seventh game of the World Series. He had this unbelievable capacity to literally roar through 162 games as if they were each that one single game."[7] Rose was aggressive but smart, possessed superior instincts, and always hustled.[8]

Perhaps no word is used in connection with Rose more than "hustle." He knew of its importance to his big league career, once saying, "I didn't get to the majors on God-given ability. I got there on hustle, and I have had to hustle to stay."[9] It became an enduring part of Rose's persona through the nickname that defined him, Charlie Hustle, bestowed upon him by Whitey Ford, who saw him sprint to first after a walk during a spring training game.[10] "That's the only way I know how to play the game" became Rose's standard response in explaining his approach on the field.[11] Los Angeles Dodgers broadcaster Vin Scully once quipped that Rose "just beat out another walk."

In many ways Rose was a walking baseball con-

tradition. He was aggressive and combative on the field but was accommodating and a great quote for the media. He was selfish—playing for stats, money, fame—but also unselfish—he always picked up the check, routinely invited teammates to live with him, and willingly changed positions several times during his career, all for the benefit of his team or teammates.[12] He loved being around smoke and alcohol but did not smoke or drink himself.[13]

As good as Rose had been in the 1960s, the 1970s were even better for him and the Reds. Led by new manager Sparky Anderson in 1970 and sparked by the arrival of second baseman Joe Morgan and center fielder César Gerónimo in a trade with Houston after the 1971 season, the Reds dominated the National League for most of the decade. Driven by its powerful offense, the Big Red Machine captured four pennants and two World Series titles between 1970 and 1976.

On the field Rose served as the Machine's lead-off hitter and catalyst, infusing the Reds with his desire to win and intimidating opponents in the process. He caused an uproar before Game Five of the 1972 World Series against Oakland when he intimated to the press that Catfish Hunter wasn't all that great, then backed up his bravado by homering off Hunter to lead off the game and then getting the game-winning hit in the ninth off ace reliever Rollie Fingers. A year later Rose started a bench-clearing melee in the National League Championship Series against the Mets with a hard takeout slide of Met shortstop Bud Harrelson and wrestled Harrelson to the ground in the ensuing ruckus. Rose's fire led the Reds on the field, and the group of Rose, Johnny Bench, Tony Pérez, and Joe Morgan controlled the clubhouse during the 1970s, in large part with a good-natured humor that left no one immune to serving as the butt of a joke.[14]

Rose's finest all-around season was probably 1973, when he won his third batting title (.338), had 230 hits, scored 115 runs, and was named the National League's Most Valuable Player. Despite his personal achievements, the Reds' season ended with a Game 5 NLCS loss to Harrelson and the Mets. In 1974 the thirty-three-year-old Rose saw his average dip below .300 for the only time between 1965 and 1979, and whispers began that he was on the downside of his career.

After missing the postseason in 1974, the Reds and Rose came back with ferocity in 1975. He led the league in runs scored and doubles for the second season in a row, and the Reds blew away the National League West with a 108-54 mark. After some early inconsistency at the hot corner, Anderson asked Rose, on May 2, to move to third base for the good of the club—starting the next day. Rose complied, and throughout the remainder of the season he wore out coaches George Scherger and Alex Grammas by having them hit ground balls to him at third.[15] Rose was never exceedingly fluid or swift at third, but he was serviceable. The move allowed Anderson to insert slugger George Foster into the Reds' lineup in left field, and many have pointed to this as the inflection point when the Big Red Machine became THE Big Red Machine. Rose first took the field at third base when the Reds hosted the Braves on May 3, and from that point through the end of the regular season the team posted a mark of 96-42 (.695) and finished twenty games ahead of the Dodgers.

In the NLCS the Reds swept the Pirates in three games to advance to the World Series against Boston. This Series has gone down as one of the greatest in baseball history, with the high point coming during the epic sixth game that ended with Carlton Fisk famously waving his game-winning home run down the left-field line to stay fair in the bottom of the twelfth inning. Throughout the seesaw affair, many participants later testified, Rose could not stop babbling, "Isn't this great? This is the best game I've ever played in. Isn't this great? People will remember this game forever. Isn't this great?," or other such remarks.[16] He repeated this comment to Sparky Anderson after the game, but he also prom-

ised his manager that the Reds would win Game Seven.[17] The next night the Reds defeated the Red Sox, 4–3, to capture the first World Series championship for the Big Red Machine after Series losses in 1970 and 1972. The title was Cincinnati's first since 1940, and hometown hero Rose was named Series MVP after hitting .370 with a .485 on-base percentage. Rose later said he never saw the ball better than he did in the 1975 World Series, that it "looked like a beach ball."[18] For Rose, the season was capped in December when *Sports Illustrated* named him its Sportsman of the Year.

The 1976 regular season played out in a remarkably similar fashion. Rose again led the league in runs scored, hits, and doubles and posted numbers similar to his 1975 totals across the board. The Reds again won more than one hundred games, swept through the NLCS (this time defeating the young Philadelphia Phillies), and swept the New York Yankees in the World Series.

While the Reds looked invincible on the field, the game off the field was changing like never before. Faced with the new economics of baseball in the aftermath of an arbitrator's decision that granted players the right to earn free agency, Reds general manager Bob Howsam and president Dick Wagner decided not to participate in the competition for players. Faced with the impending departure of free-agent starting pitcher Don Gullett, the Reds traded Tony Pérez and left-handed reliever Will McEnaney to Montreal for pitchers Woodie Fryman and Dale Murray. Without Pérez, Gullett, and McEnaney, the 1977 Reds slumped to second place. But it would be difficult to lay any of the blame at the feet of Rose. He had his standard season—he played every game, hit .311, and made the All-Star team—but the season was not without some drama. In the aftermath of the Pérez trade, Rose and his agent, Reuven Katz, played hardball with the Reds in salary negotiations. He had made $188,000 in 1976 and, after watching free-agent Reggie Jackson sign a huge deal with the Yankees, requested $400,000 for 1977. When the

ANDY STURGILL

team balked, Rose took his case public through the media, expertly explaining his position to the fans, opening up the possibility of playing out his option and hitting free agency if he was not treated fairly, and galvanizing public opinion behind him. Eventually, on the eve of the 1977 season, Rose signed for two years at $752,000, far more than the $425,000 the team had originally offered.[19]

Rose continued to pad his baseball résumé. In 1977 he passed Frankie Frisch's record for the most hits by a switch-hitter, and then on May 5, 1978, with a single against the Montreal Expos, became the thirteenth Major Leaguer to reach three thousand hits. Greeting him at first base after the milestone hit was his old pal Tony Pérez. Rose notched two hits at home against the Cubs on June 14 and proceeded to get a hit in each of the next forty-three games, offering what remains through the 2013 season as the most serious threat to Joe DiMaggio's record fifty-six-game streak. When the streak reached thirty games the national media began to descend on him and, ever the quote machine, Rose offered, "Fine with me. I like talking about my base hits."[20] Over the course of the streak Rose hit .385 with eighteen multihit games and struck out only five times in 182 at bats. He passed Tommy Holmes's thirty-seven-game mark from 1945 to set a new National League record and was not stopped until, after forty-four games, he went 0-for-4 on August 1 in Atlanta as Gene Garber struck him out to end the game. The Reds again finished second in the NL West. After the season Sparky Anderson was fired, and Rose, with his two-year contract expired, was allowed to enter free agency.

By most accounts Rose wanted to remain in Cincinnati for the rest of his career, and Katz, his agent, had even floated the idea of a lifetime contract. The Reds were not interested, so it was pretty well understood that Rose would leave Cincinnati. While it would be hard to argue that his play on the field had declined, Rose at this time was in the middle of a nasty divorce, and his hard lifestyle and even

alleged associations with gamblers made the decision for the Reds to move on a bit easier.[21]

On the open market Rose had no shortage of suitors, and the bidding war that developed for his services included various enticements. August Busch Jr., owner of the St. Louis Cardinals, offered Rose his own beer distributorship; Pirates owner and horse farmer John Galbraith offered race horses; and Ewing Kauffman of the Kansas City Royals offered stock in his pharmaceutical company.[22] However, one team had caught Rose's eye as early as 1976: the Philadelphia Phillies. When the Big Red Machine squared off with the Phillies in the 1976 NLCS, Rose opined to Joe Morgan, "That team's got talent. All they need is a leader."[23] After losing to the Reds in the playoffs in 1976, the Phillies won the NL East again in 1977 and 1978, only to lose the NLCS to the Dodgers both times. With the Phillies desperate to get over the hump and win their first World Series in franchise history, Rose seemed a natural fit, but it appeared that the Phillies could not afford him. Seeing an opportunity for a mutually beneficial relationship, Phillies executive Bill Giles asked the local television station that carried their games, WPHL, for an additional $200,000 in broadcasting rights fees if the team signed Rose, anticipating increased viewership. The station agreed, and on December 5, 1978, Rose signed with the Phillies for four years and $3.2 million. (The Phillies sold $3 million worth of tickets in the next thirty days.[24]) Still at issue was what position Rose would play; the Phillies' best player was third baseman Mike Schmidt, a brilliant hitter and fielder. A spring training deal sent first baseman Richie Hebner to the New York Mets, opening a spot for Rose, who to that point in his career had played three games at first.

The 1979 Phillies slumped to a fourth-place finish, but Rose more than held up his end of the bargain. He hit .331 with a league-leading .418 on-base percentage and a career-high twenty stolen bases. In the midst of a late-season slide, the Phillies fired

Manager Danny Ozark and replaced him with their high-strung scouting director, Dallas Green. Green had been a pitcher for the Phillies in the 1960s and had given up Rose's only grand slam, a fact that Rose often reminded the manager of.[25]

In 1980 the Phillies returned to the postseason and, after a subpar—for Rose—regular season (.282), the NLCS gave Rose the stage to show exactly why he had been brought to Philadelphia. With the Phillies trailing the Astros in the best-of-five series two games to one, Rose singled with one out in the top of the tenth inning. After an out, Greg Luzinski ripped a ball into the left-field corner and Rose broke from first determined to score the go-ahead run. He tore around third, casting nary a glance at third base coach Lee Elia, and rumbled toward home and Astros catcher Bruce Bochy. "I know Pete Rose," said Joe Morgan, back playing for the Astros, "Pete Rose was never going to stop." As the relay from shortstop Rafael Landestoy neared the plate, Rose unloaded a forearm to Bochy's jaw as the ball bounced away. Rose scored the go-ahead run and the Phillies closed out the game in the bottom of the inning.

The next night, in the winner-take-all Game Five, the Phillies were down 5–2 in the top of the eighth inning against Nolan Ryan. With the bases loaded and no outs, Rose stood in against Ryan and the two baseball legends engaged in an epic seven-pitch at bat with Rose ultimately earning a walk and an RBI to cut the lead to 5–3 and chase Ryan from the game. For once Rose did not sprint to first base but arrogantly threw his bat toward the dugout and stared out at Ryan as he swaggered down to first. Philadelphia ended up taking a 7–5 lead, gave it up in the bottom of the inning, and finally won it in the tenth to clinch their first pennant in thirty years. While second baseman Manny Trillo was named the NLCS MVP, Rose reached base thirteen times in twenty-five plate appearances, and his attitude energized his team. The Phillies dispatched the Royals in six games to win their first World Series in

the team's history, and Rose's purpose in signing with the Phillies was fulfilled.

Rose broke Stan Musial's National League hits record in the first game back after the end of the 1981 player strike and hit .325 for the season. After two subpar seasons for the club, the Phillies acquired forty-one-year-old Tony Pérez and thirty-nine-year-old Joe Morgan to join the forty-two-year-old Rose on the Phillies for the 1983 season. The team was dubbed the Wheeze Kids, a takeoff on the Phillies' youthful 1950 pennant winners, the Whiz Kids. After the Phillies sputtered to a record just above .500 halfway through the season, Manager Pat Corrales was replaced by Paul Owens. From that point, the Phillies raced ahead of the pack, winning the East by six games. Rose was hitting only .248 at the end of August, and his playing time was diminished significantly during the stretch drive in favor of rookie Len Matuszek. Rose hit only .220 in fifty September at bats. Due to roster rules at the time, Matuszek was ineligible for postseason play, and like an old warhorse on its last charge at the enemy, Rose hit .344 in nine postseason games as the Phillies beat the Dodgers in the NLCS before losing to Baltimore in the World Series. Three days after the World Series ended, Rose was released by the Phillies.

Perhaps needing a gate attraction more than a forty-three-year-old hitter, the Montreal Expos signed Rose in January 1984. He played in ninety-five games for the Expos, then was traded back to Cincinnati on August 16, where he became player-manager. Rose played at first base and as a pinch hitter, in pursuit of Ty Cobb's Major League hits record. He reached that milestone on September 11, 1985, at home against the Padres with a looping single to left off Eric Show for the 4,192nd hit of his career. As fans stood and cheered and teammates swarmed around him, Rose tearfully embraced his fifteen-year old son, Pete Jr., in the area around first base.

Rose played through the 1986 season but never officially filed for retirement. His accomplishments were staggering. As of 2011 he was the leader in hits, games played, at bats, plate appearances, singles, and times on base. He was second in doubles and sixth in runs scored and retired with a lifetime .303 batting average. He won an MVP, a World Series MVP, a Silver Slugger Award, and two Gold Gloves. His teams won six pennants and three World Series.

Rose stayed on as manager of the Reds through the beginning of the 1989 season, by which time his life had become very interesting. He had been suspended for thirty days in 1988 for shoving umpire Dave Pallone, but what sat before Rose a year later was far more serious. Allegations arose that he had bet on Major League games in violation of the sport's most sacred rule. Commissioner A. Bartlett Giamatti retained John Dowd to investigate the matter, and the Dowd Report was presented to Giamatti in May. The report's most stirring conclusion was that Rose had in fact bet on baseball during his tenure as Reds manager. In late August 1989 Rose and Giamatti agreed to a settlement in which Rose would be declared permanently ineligible from baseball, with the ability to ask for reinstatement after one year. Meanwhile, Rose steadfastly maintained that he had not bet on baseball.

Less than a year later, in April 1990, Rose pleaded guilty to charges related to income tax evasion and served five months in the federal penitentiary in Marion, Illinois. After the tax due, interest, and fees had been paid, he was released from prison in January 1991.

Being placed on the permanently ineligible list barred Rose from attending official ceremonies, with the exception of the All-Century Team presentation during the 1999 World Series. His number, 14, which certainly would have been retired by the Reds, has been issued by the team only once since his banishment, and then to his son Pete Rose Jr. during the younger Rose's brief tenure with the club in 1997.

After fifteen years of vehemently denying that he had bet on baseball, Rose, in his book *My Prison without Bars* (2004) admitted that he had. However, even this could not be done without controversy, as the book coincided with the announcement of that year's Hall of Fame class.

In his seventies and still a fixture at baseball card and autograph shows, Rose spent more than twenty hours a week greeting fans and signing autographs at Caesar's Palace in Las Vegas for much of the decade of the 2000s. So long as the individual paid the autograph fee, Rose would sign anything, including the Dowd Report and his mug shot from his tax-evasion charges.[26]

It's all part of the hustle.

Chapter 10. **Tom Hall**

Mark Armour

AGE	W	L	PCT.	ERA	G	GS	GF	CG	SHO	SV	IP	H	BB	SO	HBP	WP
27	0	0	.000	0.00	2	0	1	0	0	0	2	2	2	3	0	0

Tom Hall's physique, usually listed as 6 feet and 150 pounds but occasionally lighter, earned him the enduring nickname "The Blade." Teammate Ted Uhlaender once quipped, "He wouldn't sink two inches if he walked on quicksand."[1] But Hall was also an excellent pitcher for several years, rocketing through the Minor Leagues to become one of the game's most dependable relief pitchers. His peak was brief, due to injuries, but he helped four teams to the postseason.

Thomas Edward Hall was born in Thomasville, North Carolina, on November 23, 1947. When he was four years old his family moved to Riverside, California, a place he still called home over sixty years later. Hall took to baseball at a young age, playing Little League through Connie Mack League for several years. He was usually a first baseman, being tall, skinny, and left-handed. His coach noticed that every ball he threw to another base tailed at the end, requiring his teammates to lunge for his throws. Inspired, the man decided to try young Hall at pitcher, where his tailing fastball would not be a handicap. By the time he reached Ramona High School he had become an all-conference pitching star. "I really liked to play football," Hall remembered, "but I was just a little too thin."[2] Bobby Bonds played baseball at rival Riverside Poly High School at the same time, and he and Hall remained close friends for the rest of Bonds's life.

After high school Hall attended Riverside Community College, earning team M V P honors in 1966. His skinny frame likely kept him from getting drafted out of high school the previous year. "When I first saw him," recalled Twins executive Clark Griffith (son of team president Calvin), "he was 5-10 and

Tom Hall's best years were behind him by 1975, but he had already been an excellent pitcher on four postseason teams.

weighed about 130 pounds. But he could throw! He struck out everyone." When Calvin went to see Hall he was "warned not to make any evaluation until after I had seen him throw."[3] Hall was drafted by the Minnesota Twins in the third round of the January 1966 amateur draft and signed with scout Jesse Flores in late spring.

Hall's ascent through the Minor Leagues was rapid. He spent the summer of 1966 with the Gulf Coast Twins in Sarasota, Florida, and finished 6-4 with a 1.94 earned run average, leading the short-season league with one hundred strikeouts, seven complete games, and four shutouts, enough to earn him all-league honors after the season. He also got in three late-season games with Orlando (Class A) and managed a 1-0 record and a 2.12 ERA in seventeen innings. "When I first signed with the Twins, I threw basically a fastball and curveball, but as the hitters got better I developed a slider and began to move up the organization quite fast," Hall said in 2009.[4]

Hall spent the 1967 season with the Wisconsin Rapids in the Midwest League and had another outstanding year. Working as a starter, he finished 14-5 with a 2.16 ERA and 177 strikeouts in 167 innings and was again named to the league All-Star team. In August he was called up by his marine reserve unit and missed the league playoffs, which his team lost to Appleton. He stayed in the service for six months, missing the start of spring training in 1968. When he got back he trained with the Twins and pitched well, but he was behind in his training and was farmed out. "My time will come," Hall related. "Maybe next year."[5]

In April Hall joined Charlotte (North Carolina) of the Double-A Southern League and continued his great pitching, going 6-3 with a 1.36 ERA. Of his ten starts, seven were complete games and three were shutouts. On June 9 he was brought up by the Twins, who were temporarily short of pitchers. His first stint with the Twins lasted just one appearance—two shutout innings against the Senators—before he was sent down to Triple-A Denver. With the Bears, Hall was 4-1 with a 2.81 ERA in six starts, enough to get him back to Minnesota in early August. This time he stuck around a while.

Hall's first start, in New York's Yankee Stadium on August 9, was inauspicious. He faced six batters and retired none of them, departing down 3–1. "I remember I was very nervous," Hall recalled. "I couldn't throw a strike if I had to lay it on the table."[6] The Twins rallied to win the game, and Hall started and beat Washington four days later. For

the Major League season he pitched in eight games and 29⅔ innings, finishing 2-1 with a 2.43 ERA. Not a bad beginning for the twenty-year-old lefty.

Hall reported to the Twins' camp in 1969 to play for their rookie manager, Billy Martin, who had managed him in Denver the previous year. Hall was in the starting rotation at the beginning of the season and hurled a two-hit shutout in his second start, on April 18. Martin used him as both a starter (eighteen games) and a reliever (thirteen), and Hall ended up 8-7 with a 3.33 ERA in 140⅔ innings. He pitched to two batters (retiring both) in the Orioles' three-game sweep of the Twins in the playoffs.

The next year new Twins manager Bill Rigney also used Hall in a variety of roles, and he pitched outstanding baseball—11-6 with a 2.55 ERA in 155⅓ innings. In September he started seven times, put up a 5-0 record with a 1.84 ERA, and nearly copped the league ERA title. Hall was 6⅔ innings short of qualifying, while Oakland's Diego Segui won the crown with a 2.56 ERA in exactly 162 innings. "I'm a little more relaxed this season because I have some experience," Hall related. "And I am keeping the ball low; in 1969, I was high."[7] Hall also logged 184 strikeouts, an astonishing 10.7 strikeouts per nine innings, far higher than Cleveland's Sam McDowell's league-leading total (among qualifiers) of just under 9.0. "Maybe it's because he's so skinny," said Rigney. "He stands out there and batters figure he can't blister it. Then, when they find out he can, it's too late."[8] He started Game Two of the ALCS against the powerful Orioles but allowed four runs in 3⅓ innings as the Orioles won easily. Hall came back with two shutout innings the next day, but Baltimore completed another sweep.

Early in his career Hall spent at least two weeks every summer with the Marine Reserve, along with occasional weekend duty. This was not uncommon during the Vietnam era and placed an added burden on managers trying to establish regular roles for their team. Hall was available enough in 1971 to log 129⅔ innings, though he was a bit less effective

(4-7, 3.33). The Twins fell out of contention, and after the season decided that they needed to acquire a true relief ace. As a result, they dealt Hall on December 3 to the Cincinnati Reds for relief pitcher Wayne Granger. The Reds had a strong and deep bullpen but thought they needed a left-hander.

Hall took to his new league well. In 1972 he had a spectacular 10-1 record, with eight saves and a 2.61 ERA. Under the tutelage of pitching coach Larry Shepard, Hall added a change-up to his fastball, curve, and slider. The Reds' bullpen included Clay Carroll, Pedro Borbon, and Hall, and manager Sparky Anderson got them all a lot of work. Hall also started seven games, earning a 3-1 record in this role, including a three-hit shutout with twelve strikeouts against the Cardinals on May 14. As a reliever Hall pitched nearly two innings per appearance. "He has a deceptive fastball," said Anderson. "Before the batter realizes it, the ball is on top of him. And it's usually a strike."[9] Johnny Bench, his catcher, called him "a great guy to have on the club. All you've got to do is ask him to do something, and he'll best himself to do it."[10]

In the 1972 postseason Hall pitched six times, totaling 15⅔ innings, allowing just one run (0.57 ERA). He won Game Two of the NLCS, entering against Pittsburgh with two in the fifth inning, striking out Willie Stargell with two Pirates on base, and finishing the game, allowing just two hits and a run. "Hall has as much savvy as any pitcher on our staff," said Bench after Hall's victory. "He didn't pitch a masterful game, but he made the right pitches in the right spot."[11] In four World Series game appearances versus Oakland, Hall allowed zero runs in 8⅓ innings.

Still just twenty-five years old, Hall was used in a similar role in 1973, starting seven games and working as a multiple-inning reliever, and he finished 8-5 with eight saves and a 3.47 ERA in 103⅔ innings. Hall had a rough time during the five-game NLCS loss to the Mets. He appeared in three games for two-thirds of an inning, giving up three hits, three walks, and four earned runs to post a horren-

dous 54.00 ERA. In 1974 he pitched a career-low sixty-four innings, and his ERA rose again to 4.08 to go along with his 3-1 record. On May 3, when his ERA stood at 1.00, Hall cut the middle finger of his pitching hand on a tile soap dish in the shower at Pittsburgh's Three Rivers Stadium. He was disabled for two weeks and the injury hampered him for longer. A couple of years later he filed a lawsuit against Three Rivers Stadium and the Pirates for the incident, which caused a loss of blood and emotional trauma.[12] It is not clear how this lawsuit was resolved, but Hall never pitched as well as he had in the year prior to the mishap.

After two brief appearances in 1975, on April 15 the Reds traded the twenty-seven-year-old Hall to the New York Mets for fellow lefty hurler Mac Scarce. The move was mostly about the Reds' abundance of relievers, as Scarce went to the Minors and never appeared in a game with Cincinnati. The Mets needed pitchers. "I think it's a steal for us," said Hall's new teammate Tom Seaver. "Hall's got a great arm, and he's not that old."[13] Hall pitched in thirty-four games for New York, including four starts, and managed a 4-3 record despite an elevated 4.75 ERA, part of a trend that saw his ERA more than double in three years.

After pitching five games and with a 1-1 record for the Mets early in 1976, Hall was traded on May 7 to the Kansas City Royals, where he finished an undistinguished season (1-1, 4.45) for the AL West Division–winning club. In the ALCS versus the New York Yankees, Hall pitched to two batters during the pivotal sixth inning of Game Three, getting Chris Chambliss to ground into a force play, then allowing a run-scoring single to Graig Nettles. For his postseason career Hall pitched 22⅔ innings in thirteen games, finishing 1-1 with a 3.57 ERA.

Hall pitched in six games for the Royals in 1977 before drawing his release on June 14. He finished his professional career with eleven games for Tacoma, the Triple-A affiliate of the Twins. His last pitch came before he reached the age of thirty. "I had a rotator cuff strain," he recalled, an injury that was not as repairable then as it would be a generation later.[14]

Hall next worked with Rohr Aerospace for three years before being laid off in 1981. He then hooked on with the U.S. Post Office and was a mail carrier for twenty-one years. In November 2002 the fifty-five-year-old Hall retired from working life.

Hall married the former Grace Jean Mitchell in October 1969, and the couple raised two children: Kristi and Thomas. As of 2012 Hall still lived in Riverside, California, not far from where he grew up and learned to love the game. The Riverside Sports Hall of Fame, which inducted him in 2005, says on its website that Hall enjoys fishing, bowling with his son, and taking trips with his wife to Morro Bay. An excellent pitcher for several years, Hall remained rooted to his hometown and the family and life he created there.

Chapter 11. **Bill Plummer**

Michael Fallon

AGE	G	AB	R	H	2B	3B	HR	TB	RBI	BB	SO	BAV	OBP	SLG	SB	GDP	HBP
28	65	159	17	29	7	0	1	39	19	24	28	.182	.291	.245	1	0	2

Role players have long existed in baseball. At least since 1910, when roster numbers were set at twenty-five active players and forty reserved players, teams have kept bench players who filled certain key situational roles. And this tendency has only increased as the game has evolved over time and player specializations have proliferated. During the 1970s, no one typified the career role player more than Bill Plummer.

Born on March 21, 1947, in Oakland, California, William Francis Plummer moved with his family at the age of eight to horse country in Anderson, California, in the northern part of the state. His father, William Lawrence Plummer, was a former Minor League pitcher who, after a twenty-five-year career with the Oakland police, retired to ranch and teach his son the game. "He was a gruff man," said Plummer in later years, "but big-hearted. A good man." The elder Plummer kept Bill from becoming a Little League pitcher, worried that it would ruin his son's arm as it had his. "I used to throw a little relief, but he wouldn't let me throw a curveball. He taught me a forkball."[1] Plummer played basketball as well as baseball, and while at Shasta College in Redding, California, he was named to the all-conference hoops team before deciding to make a career of baseball.

Signed out of college in 1965 by the St. Louis Cardinals as an eighteen-year-old, 6-foot-1, 190-pound catcher, Plummer first played for the Cardinals' Rookie League team in Sarasota that summer. In forty-two games he played well enough—batting .265, providing solid defense behind the plate, and playing in the Florida Rookie League All-Star Game—to be moved up to the Cardinals'

Bill Plummer spent eight years backing up the greatest catcher of all time, which got him two World Series rings.

Class A team in Cedar Rapids, Iowa, right before the end of the season. In 1966 Plummer played in Low-A for the Eugene (Oregon) Emeralds (Northwest League), struggling at the plate (.144 batting average and just one home run in forty-six games) and, uncharacteristically, behind it (seven passed balls). In 1967 Plummer's season went slightly more smoothly. With Modesto (California), another Single-A team, he raised his batting average to .234 and played better defense—but even so, the Cardinals did not protect him from the Rule 5 draft by placing him on their forty-man roster. In late November 1967, Plummer was taken in the Rule 5 draft by the Chicago Cubs.

Plummer may have been simultaneously well served and paid a grave disservice by the rules of the draft. Being chosen by the Cubs gave him a higher profile than he might otherwise have earned over the next several seasons. At the same time, it might also have significantly hindered Plummer's development as a player. Because the Cubs had to keep him on the Major League roster for the entire season, lest they lose rights to him, Plummer stayed on the bench in 1968, appearing in just two games and recording no hits in two at bats. (Starting catcher Randy Hundley appeared in a record 160 games that year.) Plummer figured enough in the Cubs' future plans that he was sent after the season to the Arizona Instructional League, where he played well against many of the league's future star players.

Plummer was listed on the Cubs' forty-man roster, but on January 9, 1969, the team traded him to the Cincinnati Reds. The Reds assigned Plummer to Triple-A Indianapolis, and it was there that he began to blossom as a player. In 1969 he batted .248 with seven home runs in 104 games. More importantly, his defensive skills improved. Early in his Minor League career, Plummer had been rated as a "good receiver who can hit with power but with a lot to learn."[2] After three seasons at Indianapolis, he was upgraded somewhat: "Ready for majors now if somebody gives him chance. Solid receiver with good arm, shows increasing power at plate."[3] In 1971 Plummer completed his best year as a ballplayer—.266 batting average, seventeen home runs, and co–team MVP at Indianapolis—and he was increasingly viewed as Major League ready.

The Reds, faced with a play-him-or-trade-him situation, chose to trade their longtime backup to Johnny Bench, thirty-one-year-old Pat Corrales, in favor of the younger player. Plummer joined the Reds' twenty-five-man roster to stay in 1972. From the start his role in Cincinnati was clear, if unrewarding: He was there to back up Bench, who was one of the team's franchise players. While Plummer would play occasional games at first and third base, he otherwise filled his role uncomplainingly for seven seasons. Here's how *Sports Illustrated* described the typical work day for Plummer toward the end of his stint with the team, in July 1977: "Bill Plummer of the Cincinnati Reds is diligent and conscientious about his work. He gets to the park early, takes batting and infield practice, runs in the outfield, sings the Star-Spangled Banner, then sits down and spends the rest of the game trying to steal signs. Bill Plummer is the replacement for Johnny Bench, on the bench. . . . He knows this is all there is. 'I'm almost a player without a function,' he sighs."[4]

Everyone, including Plummer himself, knew his was a thankless job. In 1974 a reporter seemed surprised that Reds pitcher Fred Norman preferred having the backup catcher behind the plate when he was pitching. Plummer, who overheard the exchange, told the reporter simply, "He likes my ugly face to throw at."[5] Another time, on a cold night in Pittsburgh in 1976, Plummer reportedly helped some of the other bored bullpen occupants build a fire. "We broke up all the wood we could find," he recalled. "Ripped it off from under the stands, anywhere."[6] The fire nearly caused a major catastrophe when it smoked fans out of the stands near the bullpen— but at least it was an event to break up the endless monotony of the role player.

Aside from the Reds' two World Series titles in 1975 and 1976, and one other World Series in 1972 (during which he failed to make a single appearance), Plummer's career between 1972 and 1977 had few highlights. In those six seasons, Plummer came to the plate just 871 times; his batting average broke .200 only twice. Plummer holds the dubious distinction of recording the lowest batting average among all National Leaguers in the 1970s: a paltry .189.[7] However, until the Reds let their thirty-one-year old backup catcher become a free agent rather than re-sign him just before the 1978 season, Plummer's role on the Reds was rarely questioned.

"Around the National League," wrote Barry McDermott in *Sports Illustrated*, "Plummer is regarded with an unusual degree of respect."

It was often suggested that the cause of Plummer's ineffectiveness at bat was simply how rarely he got to play. Plummer's teammate Pete Rose wondered to McDermott what Plummer would be capable of if given the chance to play two months straight. "He's a physical fitness nut, and if hard work means anything, he would do all right."[8] Rose may have had a point. Meanwhile, despite Plummer's weak lifetime batting record, in one three-week stretch from mid-August to early September 1972 when Bench was playing elsewhere in the field due to a broken finger, Plummer stepped in and hit .254 (17-for-67). His highest seasonal batting average, .248, came in 1976, another season in which Bench struggled with injuries. While Bench was out of the lineup during the first two months of the season, Plummer hit .290. Plummer's single biggest game at the plate came in St. Louis on June 6 of that season, when he drove in seven runs with a single, triple, and homer.

Opponents viewed Plummer as tough and powerfully built, a threat if not in actuality then at least in idea. He was also comparable to the Gold Glove–winning Bench behind the plate. Among teammates, Plummer was a guy you'd want to have on your side. "When former teammate Clay Carroll got into a little disagreement in a San Diego bar," McDermott wrote, "Plummer rescued him with a right cross that floored one rambunctious soul as well as two or three others packed tight behind him." Sparky Anderson, who coached Plummer in the Minors before becoming his skipper in Cincinnati, vouched for his backup catcher's character: "He's a man. He doesn't like what he does. Nobody would like being a caddie. But he handles it."[9] Even many years later, his better-known, better-paid teammates had nothing but praise for the man they called Plum. "He played hard, with pride," Ken Griffey Sr. said in 1992. "His playing record was affected greatly by playing seven or eight years behind Johnny Bench.

He could have been a starter for anyone else. But he never complained."[10]

Plummer only shrugged at such sentiments, saying that while he used to "pray for 300–400 at bats" to show what he could do, "complaining doesn't change anything." Though he did regret that he was often embarrassed when he stood at the plate, "because you feel like your talent has rotted. It's like you haven't played tennis for two months and you try to play and stumble all around. This game's the same way, except you've got 50,000 people watching you and a guy gets you out although you feel like you're better than he is."[11]

After his release from the Reds, Plummer's playing career wound down quickly. At age thirty-one, he signed a one-year contract with the Seattle Mariners for their second season as an American League expansion team in 1978. "It was a milk-and-cookie crew compared to the world-champion mentality I was used to," Plummer said of that team. "Nothing against the kids they had here, but they didn't play like they were worried about losing their jobs, and that's what the Reds demanded. Remember, what you expect from people is what you're going to get."[12] That season Plummer bounced between the Minors and the big leagues, playing backup to Bob Stinson and batting .215 on a team that lost 104 games. In 1979 Plummer tested free agency and, after getting a nibble from Montreal, settled back with the Mariners with another one-year contract. After spring training he was sent to the Mariners' Triple-A team in Spokane, where he spent the whole season as a player-coach for Manager Rene Lachemann. On October 4, 1979, the Mariners released Plummer, and shortly after, Plummer announced his retirement as a player, adding that he, ever the role player, would welcome a chance to manage in the Minor Leagues. He didn't have to wait long.

By the time of his retirement, now three years removed from the swagger of the Big Red Machine, Plummer's character had somewhat changed from his heyday as a hard-living, hard-fighting teammate.

MICHAEL FALLON

Through the late 1970s Plummer had increasingly turned toward Christianity. "I realized I needed to change," he said some years later of his years with the Reds. "I don't think it was wildness. I think it was being young. You take things to extremes. I was a little too cocky, too macho. I got myself into situations where there were fights, yes, mostly in bars. I should have been scared, but I was busy being indestructible."[13] This change may also have been inspired by the example of his father, who had taught his son about life and about the game. Bill Sr. died in 1979, never having had a chance to see his son manage.

In 1980 Plummer was assigned to manage the Mariners' High-A team in San Jose (California League), and in 1981 he managed the Wausau (Wisconsin) Timbers to a title in the Midwest League. By then, partway through the 1981 season, Lachemann had been called up to manage the struggling big league club. In 1982 Plummer went to work for his old manager as the Mariners' bullpen coach. The role was a good opportunity for Plummer to learn but also to show what he could do—such as helping to lower the team's ERA from a league-worst 4.23 in 1981 to a fourth-best 3.88 in 1982. "I learned a lot from Lach and from Dave Duncan about handling pitchers," Plummer said later. "Of course, I developed my own ideas, too, from years as a catcher. I always took pitchers' success or failure personally. After all, I was the one who called the pitches."[14] The position was also a curse, as Seattle managers in those years rarely lasted longer than a season or two. Lachemann was fired less than halfway through 1983, and Plummer found himself managing in the Minors again. In 1984 and 1985 he was the skipper of the Mariners' Double-A team, the Chattanooga (Tennessee) Lookouts, and in 1986 and 1987 he took over the helm of the Triple-A Calgary Cannons.

If Plummer had been, for the bulk of his baseball career, stuck in the shadows as a role player, 1987 brought him his first opportunity to take several steps toward the floodlights. That year Plummer took Calgary, after its 1986 record of 66-77 and last-place finish in the Northern Division of the Pacific Coast League, to an 84-57 record and first place. (Calgary would lose in the league championship playoffs, three games to one, to the Albuquerque Dukes.) In 1988, buoyed by this success, Plummer returned to coach with the Mariners, splitting time for the next few years as the team's bullpen and third base coach. In 1991 Plummer was the third base coach under Manager Jim Lefebvre for the Mariners' first winning team (in its fifteenth year of existence). The franchise was on a high, but Lefebvre was not popular with the players, who complained that they were never sure where they stood with him. The Mariners' front office, feeling that the team could do still better, fired Lefebvre at season's end and after some deliberation chose Plummer in December 1991 as the tenth manager in the franchise's short history. The new manager immediately sought to distance himself from the previous manager and give the Mariners a fresh start. "We want to look ahead," Plummer said. "The Mariners have spent too much time looking back."[15]

At the time it appeared Plummer was poised for managerial success. As one of several Reds players managed by Sparky Anderson who went on to become Major League managers (along with Pete Rose, Tony Pérez, Pat Corrales, Ray Knight, Hal McRae, and John Vukovich), Plummer had a distinguished pedigree.[16] The Mariners also had a stable of young talent—such as third baseman/designated hitter Edgar Martinez, pitcher Randy Johnson, young centerfielder Ken Griffey Jr., and second baseman Bret Boone. And the plain-shooting, straightforward, forty-five-year-old Plummer seemed the perfect choice to keep the team on a winning track.

But success was elusive from the get-go for the new manager, as the Mariners suffered through a series of early losing streaks and fell into a 15-25 hole by May 20. One big drag on the team was its main off-season acquisition, left fielder Kevin Mitchell, for whom the Mariners had traded three relief pitchers to the San Francisco Giants and who was struggling with injuries while the team's bullpen was performing poorly. On May 26 Plummer got into a public feud with his star pitcher, Johnson, over the pitcher's decision to pull himself out of a game. By early August the atmosphere around the team seemed desperate. "I am doing everything I can to help the ballclub win," Plummer told a beat reporter on August 3. "I haven't had very good results, but on the other hand, a manager is only as good as his players. If players aren't doing as well as they should be, then [management] has to make decisions on who needs to go. If that happens to be me, I have to accept it."[17] A fourteen-game losing streak in September not only broke the team's back but likely sealed Plummer's fate. On October 13, 1992, after the team finished with the American League's worst record, 64-98 and thirty-two games out of first place in the AL West, Plummer was fired. It was just a few days more than a year since he had been hired. Plummer's only comment was typically brusque: "It goes with the territory."[18]

After two years off, Plummer returned to managing in the Minor Leagues in 1995. He continued to manage, in stints of one or two years, through 2008, when he wrapped up a season managing the Triple-A Tucson Sidewinders in the Arizona Diamondbacks system. While he had some success—winning one Double-A league championship and helping turn around the Diamondbacks' farm system—Plummer was never again considered for a Major League manager position.

A member of the Shasta County (California) Sports Hall of Fame, Plummer in 2012 was a resident, with his wife, Shelly, of Redding, a town of about ninety thousand that is twelve miles from where he grew up in Anderson. At the time, he worked as the Diamondbacks' Minor League catching coordinator. He has three grown children, Billy, Gina, and Trish, from a previous marriage.

Chapter 12. **Don Gullett**

Charles F. Faber

AGE	W	L	PCT.	ERA	G	GS	GF	CG	SHO	SV	IP	H	BB	SO	HBP	WP
24	15	4	.789	2.42	22	22	0	8	3	0	159.2	127	56	98	2	3

A three-sport star in high school, Don Gullett became a professional baseball player at the age of eighteen. After a short stint in the Minors, he became the mainstay of the Cincinnati Reds pitching staff. Before he was twenty-five years old he was being compared to Sandy Koufax and seemingly was headed for Cooperstown. But misfortune struck. In short order he suffered a broken thumb, a dislocated ankle tendon, injuries to his neck and shoulder, and as the last straw a double tear of his rotator cuff, from which he was unable to recover. He pitched his last Major League game at the age of twenty-seven, his dreams of the Hall of Fame over too soon.

Donald Edward Gullett was born on January 6, 1951, near Lynn, Kentucky, in Greenup County in the northeastern part of the state (across the Ohio River from Portsmouth, Ohio). The sixth of eight children of Lettie and Buford Gullett, he grew up playing baseball and basketball with his brothers. His younger brother, William, played one Minor League season with the Detroit Tigers organization. In addition to playing sports, Don enjoyed hunting and fishing with his father.

But it was not all play for the youngster. To supplement the family income, as a teenager he worked on neighboring farms in the summers, pitching bales of hay and doing other strenuous tasks.

Gullett attended McKell High School in South Shore, Kentucky, where he compiled an amazing athletic record. As a senior he was All-State in baseball, basketball, and football. His exploits on the gridiron made him a schoolboy legend. In one game against Wurtland High School he scored an unbelievable seventy-two points as he ran for eleven touchdowns

The best pitcher on the mid-1970s Reds, Don Gullett had a 109-50 record, one of history's best. Unfortunately, illness and injury curtailed what would have been an even better career.

and kicked six extra points. He once scored forty-seven points in a basketball game against Wurtland and was recruited by major colleges for both basketball and football. "But I always knew baseball was my first love," he said.[1] His record for McKell High School was about thirty wins and four losses. His best performance came when he pitched a perfect game, striking out twenty of the twenty-one batters he faced.

Drafted by the Cincinnati Reds in the first round of the 1969 amateur draft, the fourteenth pick overall, young Gullett was signed by scout Gene Bennett for a reported bonus of $25,000. He was assigned to Bradenton (Florida) of the rookie-level Gulf Coast League, but he never played there. Instead he was sent to Sioux Falls (South Dakota) of the Single-A Northern League. During the two-month season he won seven of nine decisions, compiled a 1.96 earned run average, and struck out eighty-seven batters in seventy-eight innings. Then he returned to Kentucky's Greenup County and married Cathy Holcomb, a cheerleader whom he had met when both were students at McKell High School.

Gullett's short stint with Sioux Falls comprised the whole of his Minor League experience. He went to spring training with the Reds in 1970 as a non-roster invitee. (Married for less than three months, Cathy wanted to accompany her husband to Florida, but she had to finish high school.) At 6 feet and 190 pounds, Gullett was powerfully built and could really fire the fastball. "I was exceptionally impressed with the poise shown by Don Gullett," Manager Sparky Anderson said. "Time will tell if he is ready now for the big leagues or if he still needs another year of minor-league ball."[2] Gullett himself had few doubts. "I figure management wouldn't have invited me in the first place if they hadn't felt I had a chance to make the club," he opined.[3] On April 5 Gullett was promoted to Cincinnati's Major League roster.

The left-hander made his big league debut on April 10, 1970. In San Francisco, Gullett relieved Ray Washburn in the fifth inning with the bases loaded and two outs. He retired Tito Fuentes on a fly ball to the shortstop. Gullett gave up a walk and a single with two out in the sixth, but he struck out Willie Mays to end the inning.

Two days later, the Reds were leading the San Francisco Giants 6–3 with two out in the bottom of the ninth inning, when Gullett was called in from the bullpen. The rookie induced Ken Henderson to pop up for what appeared to be the game-ending final out. However, first baseman Johnny Bench and second baseman Tommy Helms collided as both went for the ball, which dropped safely, allowing two runs to score. Anderson replaced his young moundsman with Wayne Granger, who got the final out to preserve the 6–5 victory.

Six days later, at Crosley Field, Gullett secured his first big league win by pitching five scoreless innings of three-hit relief in the Reds' 12–2 romp over the Los Angeles Dodgers. "In time, he'll be nothing but a star. We're seeing a star being born right before our eyes," said Anderson.[4] The rookie spent most of 1970 in the bullpen, starting only two games while relieving forty-two times. On August 23, against the New York Mets, he struck out six batters in a row, tying the National League record for consecutive strikeouts by a relief pitcher. Gullett struck out eight of the twelve batters he faced in this contest. By this time sportswriters were comparing the young lefty to Koufax. Anderson thought such comparisons were premature. "Of course, any comparison of Gullett with Koufax now would be ridiculous, but I have reason to believe this kid's going to be a great pitcher," the manager said.[5]

Cincinnati won the National League West in 1970 and swept Pittsburgh in the NLCS. Gullett picked up two saves. In Game Two he relieved in the sixth inning with the Reds leading 2–1, with two Pirate runners on and two outs and Willie Stargell at the plate. Gullett retired Stargell on a fly ball to right field, struck out the side in the seventh, and saved the game by pitching hitless ball over the final 3⅓ innings. In Game Three the drama was packed into the top of the ninth inning as the Reds led, 3–2. With two outs and Roberto Clemente on first base, Anderson again brought Gullett in to face Stargell, who singled, sending Clemente to third base as the potential tying run. Up came Al Oliver, who grounded out to second base to end the game and win the NL pennant for the Reds. In the World Series against the Baltimore Orioles, the Reds lost in five games. Gullett pitched well, appearing in three games and giving up only one run in 6⅔ innings, but he was unable to pick up a save.

In 1971 Gullett became a full-time starter, winning sixteen games while losing six, leading the league in winning percentage with .727, and posting an exemplary 2.64 earned run average. In the fourth start of his Major League career, Gullett pitched his first complete game, shutting out the Dodgers 2–0. Despite his stellar work, the Reds had a losing record of 79-83, so he had no postseason opportunity in 1971.

Bad luck struck Gullett in 1972. His strength was sapped, his fastball slowed, he tended to tire early in games. After undergoing tests, he was diagnosed with hepatitis. When he was well enough to return to the mound, Anderson assigned him to the bullpen. That year Gullett had the only losing season (9-10) in his entire career. Without much help from their young pitcher, the Reds still came out on top in the National League West. To the surprise of almost everybody Anderson selected Gullett to start the first game of the NLCS against Pittsburgh. The Pirates scored three runs on four hits in the first inning to take a lead they never relinquished. Gullett went six innings and allowed five runs to suffer the loss. The Reds took two of the next three games to tie the series at two wins apiece. Gullett started the deciding Game Five. He pitched into the fourth inning before Anderson replaced him with Pedro Borbon with the Reds on the short end of a 2–1 score. Borbon immediately gave up another hit to give the Pirates a 3–1 lead. However, the Reds rallied and won a dramatic game 4–3 by scoring two runs in the bottom of the ninth.

In the World Series the Reds lost two of the first three games to Oakland. Anderson nominated Gullett to start Game Four. The southpaw pitched well enough for seven innings, holding the A's to only one run on five hits, but the Reds were unable to

score, and Gullett departed for a pinch hitter trailing 1–0. The Reds rallied to take a 2–1 lead in the eighth inning, and Gullett stood to be the winning pitcher until the A's scored two runs in the ninth to win, 3–2. Oakland won the Series in seven games.

With his strength not yet fully restored after his bout with hepatitis, Gullett spent over a month of the 1973 season in the bullpen. Nevertheless, after closing the season with nine consecutive victories, he posted a career-high eighteen wins while losing eight. During a no-decision, on August 18, Gullett surrendered the 660th and final career home run hit by Willie Mays. The Reds won the National League West again in 1973 but lost the NLCS to the New York Mets three games to two. Gullett started Game Two and pitched very well, but Jon Matlock of the Mets was even better. Gullett was lifted for a pinch hitter in the fifth inning with his team trailing 1–0. In Game Four Gullett relieved Fred Norman in the sixth inning and pitched four innings of shutout baseball, keeping the score tied at 1–1. Clay Carroll got credit for the win when Pete Rose hit a twelfth-inning home run to give the Reds a 2–1 victory that evened the series at two games. However, Tom Seaver wrapped up the series for the Mets with a 7–2 win in the fifth game. Gullett relieved in the critical fifth inning of Game Five and walked the only Met batter he faced.

Gullett's early success was based on a blazing fastball, a change-up, and excellent control. By 1974 he had added a forkball to his pitching repertoire. When the ball neared the plate, it dropped, quickly and sharply. The new pitch enabled him to fool batters. "The forkball has made the difference," Gullett said, "even though 75 to 80 percent of my pitches are still hard stuff. It used to be, though, that when I got behind I was throwing what they were looking for—the fastball."[6]

In 1974 Anderson said, "It's the only Hall of Fame battery active in baseball today." The manager was speaking of Johnny Bench and Don Gullett. "Barring an injury, [Gullett] is almost sure of making the Hall of Fame. With Gullett's body and the way he stays in shape, I know he's going to pitch until he's at least 35. So, doing that you know he's going to win at least 250 games with the start he has. And anything over 250 has to rate a pitcher serious consideration for the Hall of Fame."[7] Anderson had the one caveat—barring injury. And injuries would eventually keep Gullett from attaining the career victory total Anderson predicted. Anderson had good reason to expect great things for the young left-hander. The three best southpaws of the previous generation—Warren Spahn, Whitey Ford, and Sandy Koufax—were in the Hall of Fame. When Gullett celebrated his twenty-fifth birthday in 1976 he had already won ninety games—many more than Spahn (eight), Ford (forty-three), and Koufax (fifty-three) had won by that age.

In 1975 Gullett got off to an excellent start. By June 11 he had already won eight games against three losses and had a 2.09 earned run average. He seemed on his way to the All-Star Game and a twenty-win season. But disaster struck on June 16 in the ninth inning of a game against Atlanta. When making the second out, Larvell Blanks hit a line shot that fractured the pitcher's left thumb. Gullett earned his ninth victory but was sidelined for two months. When Gullett returned from the disabled list on August 18 he hurled five scoreless innings in a 3–2 Reds victory over St. Louis. It was an extraordinary performance, considering that he was pitching after a two-month layoff. "I feel like a music teacher watching a great pianist at work," said pitching coach Larry Shepard. "He gives me goose bumps."[8] In the remainder of the season the lefty won five more games and lost one to finish the year at 15-4.

With their star pitcher healthy again, the Reds easily captured the NL West and took on the Pirates again in the NLCS. Gullett started the first game for the Reds and went the distance, winning 8–3. His biggest thrill came not from his pitching, but from his hitting. He batted in three runs

with a single and a home run. The homer was the first, and only, of his Major League career and the first ever by a pitcher in an NLCS game. "It was really exciting. I'm elated," the young man said. "It was my greatest day in my life in baseball."[9] But, he added, it was not his greatest day in sports, not equal to the eleven-touchdown game against Wurtland. The Reds ousted the Pirates in three straight games and qualified to face the Boston Red Sox in the 1975 World Series.

Gullett faced Luis Tiant in the Series opener, and the game was a pitchers' duel for six innings. Plagued by unaccustomed wildness, Gullett gave up seven hits and four walks during the first six innings and had to wriggle out of several jams, but he did not allow any runs until the seventh inning. Tiant led off that frame with a single to left. Dwight Evans bunted back to the pitcher. Instead of taking the easy out at first base, Gullett attempted to get Tiant going to second. Gullett slipped, threw wildly, and both runners were safe. Suddenly there were two runners on base and nobody out. Denny Doyle singled to left and the bases were loaded. Carl Yastrzemski drove Tiant in with a single to right for the first run of the game. Gullett was removed, but the uprising continued against relievers Clay Carroll and Will McEnaney. The Red Sox scored six runs in the inning en route to their 6–0 victory.

With the Series tied at two games apiece, Gullett faced Reggie Cleveland in Game Five. The lefty gave up one run in the first inning and didn't give up another hit until the eighth. The Reds took a 6–1 lead into the ninth, but Gullett weakened, giving up two singles and a double before Rawly Eastwick relieved to get the final out and preserve the victory. After the Series was delayed three days by rain, Boston won Game Six on Carlton Fisk's dramatic twelfth-inning home run. Gullett was well rested for Game Seven—perhaps too well rested. He hadn't pitched in six days. In the third inning he gave up two hits and walked four to fall behind 3–0, despite striking out the side. Gullett lasted four innings before Merv

Rettenmund batted for him in the fifth. "I wanted to go with Gullett," Anderson said later. "I stayed with him a long time. But after it was three nothing, I had to pinch-hit for him."[10] The Reds came back to win the game, 4–3, and the world championship. The 1975 World Series replaced that Wurtland game as Gullett's biggest thrill in sports.

After the Series was over Gullett went back to his Greenup County farm and his Black Angus cattle. He had purchased seventy-five acres of a farm where he had pitched hay as a teenager. The deeply religious Gullett told a national television audience, "I'd like to thank my Maker who gave me the ability to go out and pitch in a World Series."[11] He gave additional religious testimony on television, which led to invitations to speak to many church groups. Gullett practiced what his religion taught. Drinking, carousing, womanizing, and a wild nightlife were not part of his lifestyle. For recreation he preferred hunting, fishing, and listening to country music.

Anderson expected great things from his ace pitcher in 1976. The manager asserted that Gullett was the best left-hander in the National League. "Barring another injury," Anderson said, "I figure Don's a cinch to win 20 or more this season."[12] However, Gullett could not avoid injury. On May 20 he suffered a muscle spasm in his neck, which kept him out of action until June 5. In late July he came down with neck and shoulder miseries that sidelined him until the end of August. An inflammation between his left shoulder and his neck bothered him all season. Despite these difficulties, Gullett won eleven games and lost only three in 1976, for a winning percentage of .786. His earned run average was a very respectable 3.00. By October the southpaw was ready for the postseason. The Reds won their division again and swept Philadelphia in the NLCS, three games to none. Gullett pitched a gem in the opening game of the series, giving up only two hits and one run in eight innings. Eastwick allowed two runs on four in the bottom of the ninth but held on as the Reds won 6–3.

The New York Yankees won the American League pennant, and the Reds swept them in four games in the fall classic. Gullett was Cincinnati's pitcher in the opening game. He had a 5–1 lead through seven innings. In the top of the eighth Gullett retired Mickey Rivers, the first batter he faced, but hurt his ankle on his last pitch to the Yankee center fielder. When Roy White followed with a single to left, the Reds' pitcher grimaced in pain. Anderson came to the mound, and Gullett left to a standing ovation. Borbon relieved and preserved the victory. X-rays revealed a dislocated tendon in Gullett's right ankle, and the ankle was placed in a cast. The Reds won the next three games to become the first National League club to win two consecutive world championships since the New York Giants of 1921 and 1922.

In 1976 veteran players with expiring contracts could play out their options and become free agents for the first time in history, and Gullett chose this path. His agent, Jerry Kapstein, had asked for a longer contract than the Reds were willing to offer. A dozen clubs bid for his services, and the New York Yankees prevailed with a six-year, $2 million contract. They recognized that the pitcher had a history of injury problems but, noting that the young man had the best winning percentage among active pitchers, they were willing to gamble on his health.

During the off-season baseball's newest millionaire took a sportswriter on a tour of his Greenup County farm. The reporter wrote that Gullett was quiet, courteous, respectful, and deeply religious and knew the meaning of a good day's work. At that time the family consisted of Don, Cathy, and two children—Don Jr. and Tracey. A third child, Angela, was born in February 1980. Because he was on the road during the baseball season, Gullett had to have help with farm work. When he could, Gullett did a lot of the work himself. However, the scribe wrote, he always found time for hunting and fishing.

On April 10, 1977, Gullett made his debut as a Yankee. The Two-Million-Dollar Man, as the *New*

York Daily News dubbed him, pitched well but gave up a pair of home runs to Sixto Lezcano as the Bronx Bombers went down to a 2–1 defeat at the hands of the Milwaukee Brewers. The injury jinx reared its ugly head again just over two weeks later. Pitching in Baltimore, Gullett slipped and fell, spraining his left ankle and pulling a neck muscle. At the end of July he missed six weeks with a sore shoulder. Still, he managed to win fourteen games while losing only four and led the American League with a .778 winning percentage.

The Yankees won the AL East and faced Kansas City in the ALCS. Gullett started the first game for New York and lasted only two innings, giving up four runs in his short stay on the mound during a 7–2 loss. Yankee manager Billy Martin said that Gullett had a shoulder injury and probably wouldn't pitch again in the series. The Yankees came back to defeat the Royals, three games to two, and earned another trip to the World Series.

To the surprise of many, Gullett started the first game of the Series against the National League champion Dodgers. With the Yankees leading 3–2 in the ninth inning it appeared Gullett had a great chance to win the game. However, after he allowed a hit and a one-out walk, Gullett was taken out. Sparky Lyle relieved and allowed a single that gave the tying run. Lyle shut the Dodgers down the rest of the day, with the Yankees winning 4–3 in twelve innings.

The Yankees won three of the first four games of the Series. When Gullett faced the Dodgers in Game Five, his club needed only one more win to clinch the World Series. In the fourth inning Steve Yeager hit a three-run home run off a forkball that stayed high, to make the score 5–0. Gullett was removed with one out in the fifth and eventually charged with the loss. However, the Yankees got their fourth victory and the 1977 world championship by winning Game Six.

An aching left shoulder limited Gullett to only eight appearances in 1978. Before he could make his first start, he was placed on the disabled list. After coming off the disabled list on June 3, he won four of his first six starts and pitched two complete games. On July 9 he faced the Milwaukee Brewers and could not get out of the first inning. He allowed four runs on three hits and four bases on balls in two-thirds of an inning and was charged with the loss. It was the last time he ever pitched in the Majors, his playing career over at the age of twenty-seven. On September 29 he underwent surgery for a double tear of his rotator cuff. Although unable to play in the 1978 World Series, he was on the Yankees' roster. Gullett is one of the few men in the history of baseball to be on the roster of four consecutive World Series champions—Cincinnati in 1975 and 1976 and the Yankees in 1977 and 1978.

After the surgery Gullett was unable to pitch again. The Yankees released him on October 30, 1980. He closed out his career with 109 wins and 50 losses, for a winning percentage of .686, second only to Whitey Ford (.690) among all left-handed pitchers with a minimum of 100 wins.

After his release Gullett returned to full-time farming. One morning in February 1986, while working on his farm, he complained of chest pains. Still active at age thirty-five, strong, athletic, working on his farm, he did not seem like a candidate for a heart attack. But he was smoking up to three packs a day and consuming coffee by the gallon. He spent a month in the hospital undergoing tests. His physician, Dr. Grant Stevenson, said, "I'm puzzled by what happened to Don, other than the fact he's still a smoker."[13] The doctor decided that no surgery was necessary but ordered Gullett to exercise, stop smoking, cut down on coffee, go on a low-sodium diet, and take a prescription blood thinner.

Gullett stopped smoking and continued working on his farm, but he was still drinking lots of coffee by 1989. He also worked as an assistant baseball coach at Greenup County High School, which had absorbed the old rivals McKell and Wurtland through consolidation. In December 1989 Gullett became a pitching coach for Cincinnati's farm club

CHARLES F. FABER

in Chattanooga. During his first spring on the job he suffered a heart attack. In June 1990 he underwent triple-bypass heart surgery at the Cleveland Clinic.

After recuperating, in 1991 Gullett coached for Cincinnati's farm club in Nashville. On May 24, 1993, he was back in the big leagues as pitching coach for Cincinnati. The Reds did not do well the next several years, losing more games than they won most seasons. Manager Dave Miley and pitching coach Gullett were fired on June 20, 2005. Soon there were changes at the top levels of the organization, and Gullett was back in the club's good graces. He began working in various capacities for the Reds, most notably in their player-development program.

In 1993 Gullett was inducted into the Dawahares-Kentucky High School Athletic Association Sports Hall of Fame. Could another Hall of Fame—perhaps the one in Cooperstown—have beckoned him had he not been plagued by injuries? His bust is not in Cooperstown, but his portrait is painted in a mural on the floodwall protecting downtown Portsmouth, Ohio, from the ravages of Ohio River floods.

Chapter 13. **Tom Carroll**

Gregory H. Wolf

AGE	W	L	PCT.	ERA	G	GS	GF	CG	SHO	SV	IP	H	BB	SO	HBP	WP
22	4	1	.800	4.98	12	7	2	0	0	0	47	52	26	14	2	3

Recalled from the Minor Leagues near midseason by the Cincinnati Reds in both 1974 and 1975, Tom Carroll was a hard-throwing right-handed pitcher who began his career by winning his first four decisions as a starter in 1974. With the Big Red Machine cruising in 1975, Carroll's four wins helped stabilize the staff when their ace, Don Gullett, was injured in mid-June. Once hailed as the Reds' top Minor League pitching prospect, Carroll was beset by arm miseries that prematurely ended his Major League career after those two seasons.

A native of Oriskany, New York, Thomas Michael Carroll was born on November 5, 1952, the first of seven children (four boys and three girls) born to Daniel and Jeanette Carroll. In the town of twelve hundred residents in central New York, Tom grew up in a house with an old, fenced-in tennis court. "I recall my father taking me [on the tennis court] one day," he said of one of his first memories about baseball, "and tossing me a red rubber ball and how I liked to hit."[1] With his brothers, Tom modified the court, removed the net, and created a miniature baseball diamond with their own set of rules. "We used the tennis court to great advantage," he recalled. "Hitting the ball over the fence meant a lot of running, so we made a rule that if you hit the fence with a line drive it was a home run and if you hit it over the fence it was an out. We learned early on to hit line drives."[2] Learning to hit, field, and throw on the court, Tom and his brothers were well prepared when they began playing Little League baseball. When his father accepted a job as a personnel executive at Allegheny Ludlum that necessitated a move to Pittsburgh in 1965, Tom remained with his grandmother in Oriskany so he could fin-

Tom Carroll won four of five decisions for the 1975 Reds but never pitched in the Major Leagues again.

ish the season as a pitcher and shortstop on Oriskany's highly competitive Pony League team, which played in a statewide tournament.

Starring as a pitcher and fielder from 1968 to 1970 on the baseball team at North Allegheny High School in Pittsburgh (where he also played junior varsity basketball), Carroll had a unique opportunity to play baseball in the summer. "The Little Pirates, a team sponsored by the Pittsburgh Pirates, recruited in the metropolitan area [and] is where I really got my basic training as a pitcher," Carroll said. His team was managed by a former Minor

League player, George Schmidt. "I actually made the team as an outfielder. I was playing left field one day and someone hit a ball [to me] with a runner on third base. I was able to get a good jump on the ball and threw him out. From that point on I was told that I'd be a pitcher."[3] Playing about sixty games per summer and instructed by Pirates scouts, Carroll attracted attention as a tall, hard-throwing pitcher.

After graduating from high school at the age of seventeen, Carroll was drafted by the Reds in the sixth round of the 1970 amateur draft. "There was some question about whether I would sign or go to college," he recalled. "I had a scholarship offer from the University of Iowa and I had signed a letter of intent." Even after Elmer Gray, the Reds' scout for the area, visited him at home, Carroll was unsure what to do. "I didn't make the choice right away. The Reds flew me and my father to Cincinnati and put us up in a hotel. They invited us to Riverfront, which was under construction. Russ Nixon, who'd be my coach the next two years, gave us a tour." Impressed and excited by the immediacy of Major League baseball, Carroll signed for a "few-thousand-dollar bonus" and an allowance for eight semesters of college.[4]

Carroll reported to Bradenton, Florida, in June 1970 with other Reds draftees and young players to attend a two-week training camp, after which the Reds assigned players to either the GCL Reds in the Rookie Gulf Coast League or the more competitive Class A Sioux Falls (South Dakota) Packers in the short-season Northern League. "It was clear that Sioux Falls was the team players competed for," Carroll said. The instructional camp introduced the players to the Reds' core philosophy of mental awareness and fundamentally sound baseball. "Each morning, [Minor League instructor] Ron Plaza would walk into the players' area and start a whiteboard talk with, 'Gentlemen, today we're going to go over the . . .'" Carroll recalled. "Ron's depth of knowledge on fundamentals was great and the Reds were noted for having players

that were a cut above in that regard and it all came back to those whiteboard sessions and related demonstrations on the field."[5]

Along with future Reds Ken Griffey, Will McEnaney, Joel Youngblood, and Pat Zachry, the seventeen-year-old Carroll was assigned to Sioux Falls. Carroll found himself away from home for the first time. "I had a great roommate, Jim Mavroleon," he said. "He looked out for me and it made the transition easier."[6] (Mavroleon left organized baseball after two seasons in the Reds' farm system.) Carroll tied for the lead on the short-season team with four wins in nine decisions and had an impressive 2.83 earned run average in eighty-six innings.

The owner of a fastball and curveball, Carroll began to experiment with a change-up at Sioux Falls under Manager Russ Nixon. Assigned to the Florida Instructional League after the season, Carroll honed the pitch. "Scott Breeden, who was our Minor League pitching instructor, taught me how to throw [the] change-up. I refined it that season in winter league ball and used it to some effect in Tampa. It became a great pitch for me. I could put it where I wanted, it sank, and [I had my motion] down."[7]

With great confidence, Carroll began the 1971 season with the Tampa Tarpons in the Class A Florida State League and achieved immediate success, which he credited to his close work with Nixon, who had been moved to Tampa as manager. "Russ had been around . . . and had caught a lot of pitchers. In my career, the catchers were most influential."[8] While tying for the league lead with eighteen victories (and only five losses) and a sparkling 2.39 ERA in 192 innings, Carroll was tabbed by Reds general manager Bob Howsam as the team's top young pitching prospect.[9]

After studying at Duquesne University in Pittsburgh in the off-season, Carroll moved to Florida, where he found a job to support himself. "I worked for a company and we moved wire bales. It probably was not the wisest thing to do in the off-season. And it affected me."[10] Assigned to the talented Trois-

Rivieres (Quebec) Aigles in the Double-A Eastern League in 1972, Carroll complained of tight muscles all season and was limited to eighteen starts and only one complete game in 104 innings pitched. Struggling with velocity and control, he limped to a 6-10 record and saw his ERA jump almost a full run per game, to 3.38.

Determined not to repeat his year with Trois-Rivieres, Carroll pitched in the Florida Instructional League after the season and was committed to improving his physical fitness and endurance, but he stayed away from any heavy lifting. "I really worked hard in the off-season to get my legs in the best shape they had ever been in. And then over the years I found that it really helped."[11] The Reds were impressed with Carroll's progress despite his 1972 record and promoted him to Triple-A, the Indianapolis Indians, for the 1973 season.

Beginning his fourth year of Minor League ball, Carroll played for Vern Rapp, a longtime former Minor League catcher who had developed a reputation for producing Major League players since taking the reins of the Reds' top farm team in 1969. "Vern took a genuine personal interest in the players . . . developing not only a player, but also a person," Carroll said. "You sensed that as a young person. That made instruction in pitching more digestible. And he had a catcher's knowledge of pitching."[12]

Described by the *Sporting News* as "lean," the 6-foot-3, 190-pound Carroll was in the best shape of his life, and his pitching responded.[13] "After spring training workouts," he said, "I'd play handball to keep my legs in shape and my agility, but also to stretch my arm out."[14] While completing four games in a six-game stretch of starts in late May and June, Carroll tossed a two-hit shutout against the division-leading Iowa Oaks on June 6 and then a one-hit gem over the Wichita Aeros on July 23, prompting Manager Rapp to boast, "Early in the year, Tom was a seven-strikeout, seven-walk pitcher. But he has really come around well. I think the teams he's faced will argue that he's not just a thrower any-

more. I guess hard work, desire, and determination are the reasons why he's improved."[15] Deflecting attention, Carroll maintained that his success was due to Rapp's help with his mechanics and delivery. "He worked with me on my motion and it paid off," Carroll said of his improved control. "I learned a lot from him. His instruction was instrumental in me becoming a Major Leaguer."[16]

Though still inconsistent (a ten-walk outing against the Evansville Triplets on August 18 was followed by a masterful complete-game victory with thirteen strikeouts over Iowa on August 24), Carroll was considered the top pitcher in the American Association with Omaha's Mark Littell, a Kansas City Royals farmhand.[17] With fifteen wins and a 3.88 ERA in 174 innings pitched, Carroll was added to the Reds' forty-man roster after the season.[18]

The twenty-one-year-old Carroll went to his first spring training with the Reds in 1974 and was among the last players cut. He moved to the Minor League camp and was assigned to Indianapolis, which was stacked with pitching prospects and veterans. Thirteen of the sixteen pitchers on the Indians' roster that season had or would have Major League experience. Carroll was unable to establish the kind of dominance he had the season before, and his ERA hovered around 5.00 in mid-May. "In 1974 I was in a rhythm where I'd have three good starts, a so-so one, and then a bad one," said Carroll. "I thought that was pretty good for a young guy in Triple-A. Vern said, 'No, no, if you want to get to the Major Leagues, you need to string together seven or eight good starts. And on the days when you don't have your great stuff, you still gotta have a good start.' That was sobering, but it gave me a target."[19]

On May 24 Carroll pitched the best game of his life, a no-hitter over the Omaha Royals. "I remember how easy it was. I didn't have the smoothest motion or the best control [in my career]," Carroll said with a chuckle about his 104-pitch masterpiece. "It was just one of those days when things just happen naturally."[20] He got stronger as the game progressed and said that he drove toward the plate more forcefully with his left arm in order to keep his fastball down.[21]

Sporting an 8-4 record in sixteen starts, but also with a 4.92 ERA in ninety-seven innings, Carroll was called up by the Reds in July to replace Roger Nelson as the fifth starter on a strong staff that included Don Gullett, Clay Kirby, Jack Billingham, and Fred Norman. "Vern Rapp said he wanted to see me," Carroll said of his recall. "We were in the Hotel Fort Des Moines in Des Moines, Iowa. I really wasn't thinking I'd be going to the big leagues. Rapp said, 'Son, you're going to the big leagues.' That had to be one of the greatest days of my life."[22]

With temperatures approaching one hundred degrees on the Astroturf at Riverfront Stadium, Carroll made his Major League debut on July 7, 1974, in Cincinnati and earned the victory by pitching two-hit, one-run ball for seven innings against the NL East–leading St. Louis Cardinals. After setting down the side in the first inning, Carroll gave up a home run to Ted Simmons in the second. Striking out six and walking six, Carroll threw 101 pitches and was relieved by his former Indianapolis teammate and Reds roommate Will McEnaney, who had been called up with him.

In his next start, on July 12, Carroll pitched in front of friends and family in Pittsburgh and led the streaking Reds to their eighth win in nine games as he won game two of a doubleheader, 4–3. Pitching into the ninth inning, Carroll was in command the entire game except for the third inning, when the Pirates scored three unearned runs after two were out. "This kid is just like Don Gullett. He's quiet, never complains, but he's got [courage]," said Reds manager Sparky Anderson.[23] After a no-decision against St. Louis where he singled off his boyhood idol Bob Gibson, Carroll won again by pitching eight innings of four-hit ball against the San Diego Padres, surrendering their only run on an RBI double to Cito Gaston in the fourth inning. "Carroll has a mind like a sponge," said Reds pitching

coach Larry Shepard, who was impressed with his ability to throw strikes. "He soaks everything up you tell him."[24]

The Reds' bats had been abnormally quiet in the first quarter of the season, causing the reigning division winners to fall ten games out of first place by the time Carroll was called up. With the offense of the Big Red Machine hitting full stride in July and August, Carroll pitched six innings on August 11 against the Mets in New York to win his fourth consecutive decision, leaving the Reds 5½ games behind the division-leading Dodgers. "We're making a man out of Tom in a hurry, throwing him right into the middle of this pennant race," said Anderson.[25] With a fastball made more effective with his change-up, Carroll's success made for good copy. "Back in Indianapolis, I just reared back and tried to strike out the hitters. Up here, I try to keep the ball down low," Carroll said.[26]

But after Carroll made a few ineffective starts and the pennant race tightened, Anderson juggled his rotation during the last month of the season, preferring to pitch his four established starters. After his 4-0 start, Carroll lost three decisions, started just three games, and relieved in three in September and early October. "I got off to a nice start," he said. "My view was that as long I was in the rotation, I'd find my way. Unfortunately, after a bad game or two, I'd be pulled. For someone who pitched every fourth or fifth day for years, it was harder to get into a rhythm when you had lapses between starts."[27] While the Reds finished in second place behind the Dodgers in the NL West, Carroll finished 4-3 with a 3.68 ERA in 78⅓ innings pitched.

Though the short-hair and no-facial-hair policy of the Reds during those years may be well known, other matters of attention to detail may not be. "The Reds were strict," Carroll recalled. "Once we were in uniform, we had multiple sets. The general manager [Bob Howsam] noticed that my colors were slightly off—that my pants and shirts were not matching—and he called down and I had to change." The Reds players got along well with one another and a genuine sense of camaraderie ruled. Carroll said that rookies were treated well. "Pete Rose was especially good to the young players, inviting them to his house, taking them out for dinner on the road," he said. "Pete doesn't get a lot of good press. Morgan and Bench also looked out for the younger players. Terry Crowley, Clay Carroll, Merv Rettenmund, Jack Billingham, Fred Norman also come to mind in that way."[28]

With Gary Nolan returning to Cincinnati in 1975 after missing almost two years with shoulder problems, the Reds staff reckoned to be one of the deepest in the Major Leagues in 1975. Despite his success the previous season, Carroll found himself the sixth starter in a five-man rotation and was assigned to Indianapolis so that he could pitch every day. Initially refusing to report to the Indians and drawing a short suspension, Carroll returned to Vern Rapp's team. With a record of six wins and six losses in sixteen starts, Carroll earned another call-up to the Reds in mid-June when staff ace Don Gullett fractured his thumb on a line drive by the Braves' Larvell Blanks. Though his ERA was significantly lower than in 1974 (3.09 from 4.92), so too was his strikeout ratio, causing Carroll deep concern. "In 1974 I'd been pitching better in Indianapolis than in 1975," he said. "I could feel, despite the fact that I was called up, that my arm was not the same. I was struggling more with velocity."[29]

With the Reds in first place, Carroll reeled off 7–3 and 2–0 victories over the Astros and Braves after his promotion. He lasted just 1⅔ innings during his third start, in Cincinnati versus Houston on June 30, but started again two days later and, after surviving a very shaky first inning, pitched more effectively, but not enough to keep his spot in the rotation. Through mid-July he saw intermittent duty as a long reliever and spot starter but lacked consistency. On August 2 he pitched shutout ball for 6⅓ innings against the Dodgers for his fourth and what proved to be his last Major League win. "I was

concerned because my arm was not the same. . . . I was living on my wits in 1975. I could feel my arm going. It wasn't so easy to throw hard anymore."[30] When Gullett returned in August, Carroll was sent back to Indianapolis.

Reflective and articulate, Carroll told this author, "I had a realistic assessment why [I was sent down]. I can't be angry. I can be frustrated, but not angry with the decision. The nice thing about pitching is your performance is captioned clearly." He was called up again in September, too late to be added to the postseason roster, relieved twice, giving him twelve appearances for the season (seven starts), and finished with four wins in forty-seven innings and a 4.98 ERA. Though he couldn't play, he was in uniform for the NLCS against Pittsburgh and for the Reds' dramatic World Series victory over the Boston Red Sox. For a twenty-two-year-old whose passion was baseball, it was frustrating to watch but not participate, especially having contributed during the regular season. The team voted him a three-quarters World Series share even though he was on the roster for just half a season. One of his few sources of disappointment: "I didn't hear anything about a World Series ring over the winter. The rings were passed out during spring training. I guess somewhere along the line it was determined I didn't deserve a ring."[31]

Spring training in 1976 was cut to three weeks after the owners locked out the players in 1976. With the trade of Clay Kirby and Clay Carroll in the off-season and lingering concern over Gullett's injury the season before, Carroll was considered one of the front-runners for a spot in the rotation. Facing stiff competition from Pat Darcy, a surprise eleven-game winner in 1975, and top prospects Santo Alcala and Pat Zachry, the twenty-three-year-old Carroll still suffered from a lack of velocity and was again among the last pitchers cut. He was assigned once again to Indianapolis.

Playing for Manager Jim Snyder, Carroll occasionally displayed his once-promising potential—

throwing a one-hit shutout over the Tulsa Oilers on June 26—but struggled with the Indians, going 9-12 with a bloated 5.38 ERA. With their deep farm system and young starters, the Reds found Carroll expendable and traded him in the off-season to the Pittsburgh Pirates for pitcher Jim Sadowski (who never appeared in a game for the Reds), thus initiating Carroll's strangest season in baseball.

Carroll remained a Pirate for only a month before he was chosen by the Montreal Expos in the annual Rule 5 draft after the Pirates did not add him to their forty-man roster. Expos general manager Charlie Fox was excited about offering Carroll a change of scenery, saying, "We honestly believe he's a young man with big-league potential."[32] Working with Expos pitching coach Jim Brewer and roving instructor Eddie Lopat in spring training, Carroll had a good shot to make the team, which had lost 107 games in 1976.[33] "I had the best spring training I ever had, statistics-wise," he said, "but I wasn't throwing hard and I think it was pretty obvious. For someone who had been primarily a fastball pitcher, it was not good. I was cut on the last day."[34]

Assigned to the Denver Bears in the American Association to start the 1977 season, Carroll struggled to throw his fastball and surrendered nineteen earned runs in nine innings. "My arm was getting so bad that I asked if I could go to West Palm Beach," he said. "I had had a good year in the hot weather in Florida [in 1971] and I thought I could loosen things up."[35] Playing for first-year manager Felipe Alou in the Class A Florida State League, Carroll continued to struggle and was released after pitching just eighteen innings.

Carroll attempted two unsuccessful comebacks in the next three years. Vern Rapp, the most influential coach in his career, was in his second year as skipper of the St. Louis Cardinals and arranged an invitation to the team's Minor League spring training camp in 1978. "I just called and told him that I'd like to give it one more chance," Carroll said, but he was not offered a contract. Out of baseball

entirely in 1979, a healthy and physically fit Carroll thought a year's rest might rejuvenate his sore arm and signed a contract in 1980 with the Alexandria (Virginia) Dukes of the Single-A Carolina League, a team without a Major League affiliation. "I was twenty-seven and wasn't sure what I wanted to do. Baseball is a great magnet, especially when you've grown up with it and it's been your life. It's hard to break away," he said. After seventeen innings, he realized that it was time to move on and retired from baseball.[36]

In parts of two seasons with the Cincinnati Reds, Carroll won eight games and lost four while posting a 4.16 ERA in 125⅓ innings. In the Minors he was 66-56 with a 3.96 ERA.

Carroll has since had a successful career with MITRE, a not-for-profit, federally funded research and development center where he has served as an analyst and department chief engineer. In 2012 he was managing the Financial Integrity Division, leading MITRE work programs for the Treasury Department, the Federal Reserve Board, and financial regulators. But the transition to life away from baseball was not easy for him. "It took a while to find my way as far as a post-baseball career, but I did," he said. "I am fortunate to be in work that is as exciting as baseball."[37] With an MA in international affairs from Georgetown University, since 2008 Carroll has also been an adjunct professor in the Georgetown University School of Foreign Service, where he teaches courses on international security.[38]

Carroll and his wife, Elizabeth, resided with their two sons in Hamilton, Virginia, in 2012. Carroll enjoyed occasionally coaching in youth leagues and speaking to teams. He credited his success in his post-playing career to baseball, which taught him to work in teams, deal with pressure, and come to terms with the everyday grind.

Chapter 14. **April 1975 Timeline**

Mark Miller and Mark Armour

All headlines below are from the next day's edition of the *Springfield (OH) News*.

April 7—ANDERSON PLACES GREAT SIGNIFICANCE ON REDS' WIN—The Reds begin their quest for a world championship in their traditional home opener, defeating the Dodgers 2–1 in fourteen innings. A crowd of 52,526 saw George Foster hit an infield single to score César Gerónimo with the winning run. Ace Don Gullett allowed just five singles in 9⅔ innings.

April 9—CONCEPCIÓN WARMS UP FOR PINCH-HIT ROLE—Entering the bottom of the ninth inning trailing 3–2, Dave Concepción's pinch-hit game-ending single to center off Dodgers All-Star reliever Mike Marshall scored Darrel Chaney with the winning run in the 4–3 Reds victory. Concepción had been on the bench nursing a sore groin and Chaney, his replacement, had singled in the tying run before Concepción's hit.

April 10—REDS SWEEP DODGERS SERIES—The Reds beat the Dodgers 7–6, completing an opening series sweep with three come-from-behind victories over their main NL West rival. At one point in this game the Reds trailed 5–0 before Tony Pérez drove in the winning run on an eighth-inning double. George Foster, playing center field in his first start of the year, hit two home runs to key the comeback.

April 11—SPILLNER BAFFLES REDS, NORMAN TAKES LOSS—The Reds suffered their first loss of the season in San Diego as Padres pitcher Dan Spillner allowed ten hits and three walks but only two runs as the Padres defeated the Reds 5–2. The Padres scored three runs in the first inning off Fred Norman, which proved to be enough.

April 12—PADRES BEAT REDS AGAIN, NOLAN SUFFERS LOSS—The Reds suffered their second straight defeat in San Diego, 3–2, as Gary Nolan allowed single runs in each of the first three innings. Pete Rose had half of the Reds' six hits.

April 13—GULLETT NASTY TO PADRES—Left-handed ace Don Gullett threw a 10–0 two-hitter to defeat the Padres and avoid the sweep. Dave Winfield and Randy Hundley provided the only Padres offense with singles. The Reds, on the other hand, finally broke through with a big hitting day, clubbing fourteen hits, including three from Morgan and two from Gullett.

April 14—MARSHALL "AT BEST" AS DODGERS FINALLY BEAT REDS—The Reds made the short drive from San Diego to Los Angeles to start a four-game series against the defending league champion Dodgers, starting off with a 5–2 defeat. Mike Marshall, the reigning Cy Young Award winner, pitched 2⅔ innings of relief, snuffing out an eighth-inning rally by striking out Johnny Bench and getting Tony Pérez to hit into a force play.

April 15—DODGERS TAKE SECOND IN A ROW OVER THE REDLEGS—LA's Don Sutton pitched a brilliant one-hitter, giving up only a seventh-inning home run to Johnny Bench, on a day when the Reds traded reliever Tom Hall to the Mets for pitcher Mac Scarce. The 3–1 loss evened the Reds' record at four wins, four losses, the same record as the Dodgers.

April 16—WYNN'S GRAND SLAM HOMER SPARKS L.A. PAST REDS—The Dodgers were trailing the Reds 6–2 with the bases loaded and two outs in the bottom of the seventh. Dodger center fielder Jim Wynn swung, just trying to meet the pitch thrown by reliever Pat Darcy. The ball carried into the left-field stands and tied the game. Steve Garvey's ninth-inning single off Clay Carroll knocked in the winning run in the 7–6 Dodger victory.

April 17—DODGERS SWEEP REDS' SERIES, DRIESSEN ERROR FATAL—A home run by César Gerónimo and an RBI single by Pete Rose gave the Reds a 4–3 lead heading into the bottom of the ninth. But a Steve Garvey single tied the game in the ninth and the Dodgers won in the eleventh when first baseman Dan Driessen misplayed a ball hit by Willie Crawford, allowing Jim Wynn to score the winning run. The Reds dropped to 4-6, two games behind Los Angeles.

April 18—PÉREZ FINDS CURE FOR SLUMP— Back home after their dreadful West Coast road trip (one victory in seven games), the Reds defeated the Houston Astros 5–2 behind a complete-game five-hitter from Don Gullett and the hitting of Tony Pérez, who singled and homered. Pérez, who had come into the game hitting .095, had a .450 spring training average but struggled once the bell rang to begin the season.

April 19—LATE RALLY CRUISES REDS PAST HOUSTON—The Reds, trailing 7–1 after four innings, came back to score a 9–8 victory. The three-run ninth-inning rally was fueled by a Tony Pérez home run and ended on a two-out run-scoring single by Dave Concepción. Pete Rose, Concepción, and Johnny Bench combined for nine hits, including three doubles.

April 20—RICHARD CAST SHADOW OVER REDLEGS—Cincinnati finished up its four-game series with the Astros by splitting a doublehead-er. Pete Rose's ninth-inning two-run home run, his fourth hit of the game, ended the 5–3 victory in the opener. Clay Carroll picked up his second win in two games. In the nightcap, 6-foot-8 Astros right-hander J. R. Richard pitched 8⅔ innings and won 7–6. Joe Morgan's three-run home run in the ninth off Fred Scherman brought the Reds to within one run, but former Reds reliever Wayne Granger came on to strike out Johnny Bench to nail down the victory.

April 21—THIRD BASE STILL PROBLEM, ERRORS BEAT REDS 4–3—The Reds fell one game back under .500 as they lost to the San Francisco Giants, 4–3 in ten innings. The Giants scored in the top of the tenth when rookie Doug Flynn, a late-inning replacement at third base for John Vukovich, could not field a ground ball by Chris Speier. It was originally ruled an error, though it was later changed to a single. Sparky Anderson was becoming more exasperated by the play of Vukovich at third base, while he alternated George Foster, Ken Griffey, and César Gerónimo between center and right fields.

April 22—REDS USE ERROR TO TRIUMPH, NIP GIANTS 5–4—The power and speed of Joe Morgan helped defeat the Giants. The score was 4–4 when Morgan doubled with one out in the bottom of ninth inning. With two outs, Morgan headed to third on a Charlie Williams wild pitch and scored the winning run when catcher Marc Hill threw the ball down the left-field line, attempting to throw Joe out.

April 23—REED, BLANKS SPARK BRAVES, REDS LOSE IN 11TH, 5–4—Once again the Reds were forced into overtime, their fourth extra-inning game of the season, losing in Atlanta, 5–4, in eleven innings. Both Don Gullett and Ron Reed pitched complete games, and the Braves came out on top when a Larvell Blanks double scored Mike Lum. In his first defeat of the season Gullett pitched 10⅔ innings, allowing ten hits. Johnny Bench's three-run homer tied the game in the fifth, but neither team scored for the next six innings.

April 24—BENCH GLAD PÉREZ STAYED WITH REDS—Tony Pérez, who had been the subject of trade rumors during the off-season, had three hits and three RBIS, scoring on a sixth-inning double by Ken Griffey off Phil Niekro. It broke a 1–1 tie on the way to an 11–3 victory over the Braves as the Reds banged out eighteen hits. Johnny Bench and Dave Concepción also had three hits and Jack Billingham earned a complete-game victory, as the Reds got back to a .500 winning percentage at 9-9.

April 25—FORSCH QUIETS REDS' STICKS, SPARKY PROTESTS—The Reds had fifteen hits, but the home-team Astros won the game, 6–4. Sparky Anderson filed a protest over a seventh-inning interference call against Merv Rettenmund, who was breaking up a double play at second base. Larry Dierker got the win as Houston used five pitchers during the game.

April 26—REDS THROTTLE ASTROS, 9–3—Ken Griffey's bases-loaded double highlighted a five-run fourth inning that helped the Reds beat the Astros 9–3. Left-hander Fred Norman secured his first victory of the season with a complete-game eight-hitter. An RBI single by Joe Morgan and Johnny Bench's first-inning home run got the Reds going, as they eventually led 9–0 after four innings.

April 27—REDS TAKE ADVANTAGE OF HOUSTON—The Reds scored four runs in the top of the tenth inning to defeat the Astros, 6–2. Gary Nolan (eight innings) and Pedro Borbon (two) combined to hold back Houston. A key play during the Reds' tenth inning occurred when umpire Ed Vargo ruled that Astros catcher Milt May missed touching home plate on an attempted force play. Houston used four pitchers in the inning and Johnny Bench's two-run single capped the scoring.

April 29—GIANTS NIP REDS IN NINTH—On the Reds' second trip to the West Coast, in April, the Giants tied the game in the bottom of the eighth when Clay Carroll hit Horace Speed with the bases loaded, then won the game on a Chris Speier double in the bottom of the ninth, 4–3. The Reds had gone ahead in the seventh on a triple by George Foster, now hitting .320 but still without a regular position to play.

April 30—MORGAN IS PRAISED, REDS WHIP GIANTS 4–1—Though César Gerónimo had three singles, Tony Pérez homered, and Ken Griffey tripled, it was Joe Morgan who earned the praise from both teams' managers. Joe had three hits and two stolen bases, along with his great fielding. Jack Billingham and Will McEnaney combined to allow the Giants only one run as the Reds crawled back over .500 to end the month. Morgan was hitting .405 with a .551 on-base percentage and fifteen stolen bases.

NL West Standings, April 30, 1975

TEAM	W	L	GB
Los Angeles	15	8	—
San Diego	11	10	3.0
Cincinnati	12	11	3.0
Atlanta	12	12	3.5
San Francisco	10	11	4.0
Houston	8	16	7.5

Chapter 15. **Ken Griffey**

Charles F. Faber

AGE	G	AB	R	H	2B	3B	HR	TB	RBI	BB	SO	BAV	OBP	SLG	SB	GDP	HBP
25	132	463	95	141	15	9	4	186	46	67	67	.305	.391	.402	16	10	1

Baseball lore is rich with stories of fathers and sons playing catch in the backyard, of fathers and sons bonding at a baseball park. Ken Griffey's father never played catch with him, never bonded with him at a baseball park, or anywhere else for that matter. Nevertheless, the youngster grew up to be a key member of Cincinnati's Big Red Machine and the father of a future member of the National Baseball Hall of Fame.

George Kenneth Griffey was born on April 10, 1950, in Donora, Pennsylvania, one of five children of Ruth and Joseph "Buddy" Griffey. In his youth Buddy was an outstanding athlete, a left-handed third baseman who played on an All-Star team with Stan Musial. A halfback, he won a football scholarship to Kentucky State University, met Ruth, then returned to Donora. Located on the Monongahela River in Washington County, about twenty miles south of Pittsburgh, Donora is the birthplace of three famous athletes—Musial, Griffey, and Ken Griffey Jr. Environmentalists recognize it as the site of one of the worst air-pollution disasters in American history. In late October 1948 a temperature inversion combined with toxic emissions from U.S. Steel's smelting plants to create a death-dealing smog. Twenty residents died; thousands were sickened by the calamity. Buddy Griffey was an employee of American Steel and Wire, a subsidiary of U.S. Steel, but his family escaped the ravages of the smog. However, the company closed the plant in 1952 and transferred Buddy to Cleveland. When Ruth refused to join him in Ohio, the couple divorced. Ruth and the children lived on welfare for fifteen years.

In high school Griffey became a star in four sports—baseball, basketball, football, and track.

On a team filled with speedy players, no man on the Reds was as fast as Ken Griffey.

In baseball he was a hard-hitting, base-stealing, fine-fielding center fielder. In basketball he was outstanding, once scoring forty points and collecting twenty-seven rebounds in a game against Charleroi Area High School. It was in football, though, that he received his greatest acclaim. He played alternately at end and halfback and specialized in long runs after catching passes thrown by the quarterback, his younger brother Fred. The two set many passing records for the Donora High School Dragons, who had two consecutive undefeated seasons. Although the baseball and track seasons overlapped, Griffey was able to compete in both sports. He participated in the 220-yard dash, the low hurdles, and the high jump. In May 1969 he set a Washington County record in the high jump at 6 feet, ¾ inch. He was named the Donora community's Athlete of the Year in 1969.

After graduating from Donora High School that spring, Griffey briefly joined an American Legion team in nearby Charleroi. In the June 1969 amateur baseball draft, Griffey was selected by the Cincinnati Reds in the twenty-ninth round. Of the prospects drafted by the Reds that year, two—Don Gullett and Rawly Eastwick—would eventually join Griffey on the Reds. According to the writer Joe Posnanski, Griffey was drafted solely because of his speed. Scout Elmer Gray had taken a stopwatch to one of the Donora High School games and was amazed at how quickly Griffey could get down the first-base line. On Gray's recommendation, the Reds drafted Griffey. They would need speed when they moved into the new Riverfront Stadium with its artificial turf. Posnanski wrote that the Reds gave Griffey a red jacket and five pairs of socks in lieu of a signing bonus.[1] Although he had offers of college scholarships to play football, Griffey signed with the Reds. He needed the $500 a month they offered him.

Griffey was sent to Bradenton, Florida, to play for the Reds of the Gulf Coast Rookie League. The nineteen-year-old outfielder appeared in forty-nine games in his first professional season and hit a respectable .281. In 1970 he was promoted to the low Single-A Northern League's Sioux Falls (South Dakota) Packers and the next year to the Tampa Tarpons in the Florida State League. He caught fire with the Tarpons, hitting .342 and stealing twenty-five bases in eighty-eight games. This productivity earned him a late-season promotion and a full year at Trois-Rivières (Quebec) of the Double-A Eastern League, where in 1972 he hit .318 with fourteen home runs and stole thirty-one bases. Clearly he was on his way.

In 1973, for Indianapolis of the Triple-A American Association, Griffey hit .327 and earned a pro-

motion to the Reds when outfielder Bobby Tolan went on the disabled list. The twenty-three-year-old Griffey made his big league debut in Cincinnati on August 25 against the St. Louis Cardinals. His first Major League hit came in the third inning when he doubled to left off Tom Murphy. He hit well the rest of the regular season, posting a .384 average in twenty-five games, though he was just 1-for-7 in the NLCS loss to the New York Mets.

Griffey split the 1974 season between Indianapolis and Cincinnati, hitting .251 in the big leagues. He spent 1975 with the Reds as the full-time right fielder. According to Joe Morgan, the addition of Griffey as a full-time member of the Reds played a major role in the club's improvement during the 1975 season. "He was the best fastball hitter I had seen," Morgan wrote. "It did not matter where you pitched him, in, out, up, or down, he was always able to handle heat. He had speed, he could throw, he was smart in the outfield and never missed a cutoff man."[2] The installation of Griffey enabled the Reds to move César Gerónimo to center field full-time, George Foster to left field, and Pete Rose to third base. These switches strengthened the Reds tremendously. Griffey hit .305 with an on-base percentage of .391 and scored ninety-five runs. However, despite his speed, he stole only sixteen bases that season. There was a reason: at the start of the season Griffey had batted sixth, seventh, or even eighth. When Manager Sparky Anderson moved him up to hitting mainly second in the lineup, he told Griffey, "Kenny, I'm moving you up to the number two spot in the lineup. That's because I think you're a great hitter. But there's one thing you need to know. From now on I don't want you stealing any bases. You got Joe Morgan hitting after you, and he's the best damn player in the game of baseball, and he doesn't like when people steal bases when he's batting. It distracts him. So you don't steal."[3]

Although he resented having his greatest asset—his speed—taken away from him, Griffey did not complain. On the 1975 Reds Anderson and the four stars (Morgan, Tony Pérez, Rose, and Johnny Bench) ran the team. The other players were expected to do as they were told. Much later Griffey said, "I could have been a whole hell of a lot different player. I could have been a very selfish player. I could have been like Joe Morgan. . . . Joe knew he couldn't run with me. I could have stolen just as many bases as he did. I could have stolen more bases. Back in 1973, I was the best there was at stealing bases. . . . Sparky told me I couldn't steal bases because it bothered Joe's hitting. . . . I sacrificed for the team. I always sacrificed for the team."[4]

The Reds won 108 games in 1975, finishing 20 games ahead of Los Angeles in the NL West. When the Reds faced Pittsburgh in the NLCS, Anderson shuffled his lineup. Morgan wanted to bat second, and Anderson obliged by dropping Griffey to seventh. Although he did not think he deserved the demotion, Griffey kept his feelings to himself. He hit a two-run double as the Reds won the first game, 8–3. Batting lower in the order, Griffey was not restrained from stealing bases. He led off the sixth inning of Game Two with a single. He stole second base. He stole third base. He danced off third base. Ken Brett, the left-handed Pittsburgh pitcher flinched. The umpire called a balk, sending Griffey home. The Reds won, 6–1.

Griffey's speed was instrumental in winning Game Three. The score was tied in the tenth inning. Leading off the frame, Griffey startled the Pittsburgh defense by dropping a two-strike bunt in front of the plate and beating the throw to first base. He advanced to second on a balk by Ramon Hernandez, moved to third on a groundout by Gerónimo, and then scored the lead run on a sacrifice fly by pinch hitter Ed Armbrister. The Reds added an insurance run and held the Pirates scoreless in the bottom of the tenth to win, 5–3, completing the sweep of the series. In the three games Griffey had four hits, scored three runs, batted in four, and stole three bases.

After the Reds lost the first game of the World Series to Boston, they trailed 2–1 heading into the

ninth inning of Game Two. The Reds rallied for two runs, capped by a tie-breaking double by Griffey that proved to be the winning hit. In Game Seven he scored the tying run in the seventh after walking, stealing second, and scoring on a single by Rose. With the game still tied in the ninth, Griffey again walked, reached second on a sacrifice bunt, and scored what proved to be the winning run on a single by Morgan. In the seven games Griffey finished 7-for-26 (.269) with three doubles and a triple.

In 1976 Griffey had perhaps his best year at the plate, hitting .336 with an on-base percentage of .401 and tallying 111 runs, seventy-four RBIs, and thirty-four steals. Going into the last days of the season Griffey was locked in a duel for the batting title with Bill Madlock of the Chicago Cubs. Griffey was playing nearly every day, while Madlock was allegedly picking his spots and sitting against tougher opponents. With the division already clinched, several of Griffey's teammates urged him to protect his thin lead by taking a few days off. Anderson left the decision up to the player, though telling him that playing was the manlier thing to do. Griffey played. On the last day of the season he was hitting .338 to Madlock's .333. If Griffey did not play, Madlock would have to go 4-for-4 to catch him. Anderson now suggested that Griffey should sit, which he did. During the Reds game against the Braves, the Reds received reports that Madlock had gone 4-for-4 and was now leading the race for the batting championship by one-thousandth of a percentage point. Griffey needed to get into the game. Anderson sent him in as a pinch hitter and kept him in the game for a second at bat, but Griffey struck out each time. Madlock won the title, .339 to .336.

The Reds repeated as National League and World Series champions in 1976, sweeping the Philadelphia Phillies in the NLCS and the New York Yankees in the World Series. Griffey hit .385 in the playoffs, though just 1-for-17 in his return to the Series. After the season, the *Sporting News* named him to their NL All-Star team.

After the championship years, Griffey played five more seasons in Cincinnati and remained a consistently excellent performer. In 1977 he scored a career-high 117 runs, second in the National League, and hit .318. In these four years with the Reds he averaged .300 in five hundred games. He made his third All-Star team in 1980 and won the game's MVP Award for his 2-for-3 performance, which included a home run off Tommy John. After the 1981 season Cincinnati traded Griffey to the Yankees for two prospects, a poor trade for the Reds.

Although Griffey's years as a star were behind him, he still had many years as a contributing player ahead of him. He played semiregularly for four and a half years for the Yankees, batting .285 with extra-base power and good defense in the outfield. In June 1986 he was traded to the Atlanta Braves for outfielder Claudell Washington and infielder Paul Zuvella and continued to hit well as a platoon outfielder. In August 1988 the thirty-eight-year-old returned to Cincinnati, where he was the fifth outfielder, occasional first baseman, and a pinch hitter into the 1990 season.

In late August 1990 Griffey was released by the Reds and was quickly signed by the Seattle Mariners. In Seattle Griffey made history as he played on the same team with his son, Ken Griffey Jr. On August 31, against the Royals, the duo played together for the first time and hit back-to-back singles in the bottom of the first. On September 14 at Anaheim they did even better, hitting back-to-back home runs off Kirk McCaskill. Griffey Sr. hit .377 over the final month of the 1990 season, good enough to get invited back the next year as a forty-one-year-old. In the final eighty-five at bats of his career, often playing beside his son, he hit .282.

Perhaps in reaction to the neglect of his own father, Griffey has taken a great interest in the fortunes of his sons, Junior and Craig. When Junior and Senior were together on the Mariners, the father said, "A lot of times I'd look over to center field, and this is no lie, I still see the hat too big for his head, a baggy uniform, and he's got number 30 across his chest and back. That's a father-son game I was remembering when he was just a little kid and I was with the Reds. . . . Relationships between fathers and sons are unique and different in certain ways."[5]

Ken and Alberta "Birdie" Griffey were married young. Junior was born soon after his nineteen-year-old father had been drafted by the Cincinnati Reds. Junior and Birdie accompanied Griffey to his various Minor League locales, but Junior's memory goes back only to Cincinnati. Contrary to stories that Junior had the run of the clubhouse, his mother said he was allowed in only after victories.[6] A second son, Craig, was born in 1971, and the two sons are equal in their father's affection. Craig played in the Minor Leagues for seven seasons, reaching the Triple-A level briefly before retiring in 1997. Junior had a long and distinguished career in the Major Leagues and is almost certainly headed for the Hall of Fame.

The athletic genes that were passed down from Buddy Griffey to the two Kens and Craig have not lost their potency. In 2012 Junior's son, Trey, accepted a scholarship to play football at the University of Arizona. As with other members of the family, Trey's greatest asset may be his speed. At his high school in Florida he played both wide receiver and safety. (Craig's speed had helped him earn a football scholarship as a defensive back at Ohio State University before he left the Buckeyes to play professional baseball.)

As of 2012 Ken and Alberta lived in Winter Garden, Florida. He was inducted into the Cincinnati Reds Hall of Fame in 2004. In 2010 Griffey was the batting coach for the Dayton Dragons, the Reds' affiliate in the Low-A Midwest League. In 2011 he was named manager of the Bakersfield Blaze, the Reds' farm team in the High-A California League, and he was rehired for the 2012 season.

Chapter 16. **Fred Norman**

Doug Wilson

AGE	W	L	PCT.	ERA	G	GS	GF	CG	SHO	SV	IP	H	BB	SO	HBP	WP
32	12	4	.750	3.73	34	26	1	2	0	0	188	163	84	119	0	9

Describing his philosophy of building pitching staffs, Sparky Anderson once remarked, "To get the real top-flight pitchers, you have to strip yourself of so much talent that if you make such a deal, you find you don't have enough left to win. So you try to obtain a pitcher who has pitched well against your club."[1] This philosophy found its perfect match in Fred Norman, who had been a Reds-beater for the San Diego Padres. The 5-foot-8, 170-pound left-hander was picked up for very little in return in 1973 and became a dependable starter for the duration of the Cincinnati dynasty.

Fredie Hubert Norman was born on August 20, 1942, in San Antonio, Texas, into a large family with six siblings. The family soon moved to Miami, where Fred established himself as one of the best young baseball players in the area, becoming a regular member of Little League All-Star teams. In 1958 he pitched the Miami Pony Graduates All-Star team to the U.S. Championship game in Springfield, Illinois.

Despite his short stature, Norman was a phenomenal athlete for Miami Jackson High School. In addition to being a diving champion, he was on the basketball team and was featured in a pictorial in *Life* magazine in 1961 demonstrating his trampoline prowess. But the baseball diamond was where he made his mark. He was simply overpowering as a high school pitcher. More than twenty years later when old-timers discussed the hardest-throwing high school pitchers in South Florida history, Norman's name was mentioned alongside that of Steve Carlton of North Miami High. Former Reds shortstop Woody Woodward, who played against Norman for Coral Gables High School, said, "He was

One of Bob Howsam's best deals landed Fred Norman from San Diego in 1973.

really fast. Every time I faced him, I lost a thousand dollars in bonus money."[2] Despite some scouts' belief that Norman lacked the height to ever be a consistent member of a starting rotation, the Kansas City Athletics signed him for a bonus estimated at $40,000 to $65,000 after he graduated from high school in 1961.

Norman got off to a rough start in the Minors, going 1-7 with a 5.70 earned run average and sixty-four walks in 53⅔ innings at Double-A Shreveport (Louisiana). This was the start of an odyssey that would take him through ten different Minor League

79

and five Major League cities over the ensuing ten years. In 1962 he improved his control somewhat and began building a reputation as a strikeout pitcher, fanning 228 batters in 165 innings while going 10-10 for Class B Lewiston (Maine) and Class A Binghamton (New York). He struck out eighteen batters in a nine-inning game and twenty in a ten-inning game. In 1963 he set an Eastern League record with 258 strikeouts in 198 innings for Binghamton. But Norman also built a reputation for wildness, with a large number of walks and a habit of being pounded when his pitches were up in the strike zone. He pitched in two games for Kansas City in both 1962 and 1963 but the A's were unimpressed and traded him to the Chicago Cubs for outfielder Nelson Mathews after the latter season.

While in the Cubs organization, Norman developed problems with his mechanics and struggled for several years. Particularly frustrating was the 1964 season at Salt Lake City and Fort Worth, in which he was a combined 3-14 with an ERA over 7.00. He made a few brief, dismal appearances with the Cubs before they gave up on him and traded him to the Los Angeles Dodgers on April 26, 1967.

A turning point in Norman's career came after a serious shoulder injury sidelined him for a large part of the 1967 season. The next season at the Dodgers' Double-A team at Albuquerque, under the tutelage of future Major League pitching guru Roger Craig, he became a pitcher and not just a thrower. His record improved to 13-6 with a 2.62 ERA at Triple-A Spokane in 1969. Losing his great fastball would turn out to be Norman's ticket to the Majors. "At the time, I didn't ever imagine that the arm injury would eventually help me out," he said in 1975. "But now as I look back, I guess it was a blessing."[3]

Norman experienced his first extended time in the Majors in 1970 with the Dodgers. The twenty-eight-year-old pitched with little success over several months as a middle reliever and mop-up man, however, and was released late in the year and claimed by the St. Louis Cardinals. Back in the Minors at Tulsa in 1971, he underwent another turning point as Manager Warren Spahn helped him become a more polished pitcher. "He taught me the mechanics and psychology of pitching, after all those years," Norman said.[4] Spahn also helped him perfect the screwball that he had been fooling around with since 1963. Norman responded with a 6-1 record, including a no-hitter. He was then traded to the Padres in June 1971 with outfielder Leron Lee for pitcher Al Santorini and finally got the opportunity to pitch regularly in a Major League rotation.

Norman soon learned that pitching for the three-year-old Padres was a challenge in self-preservation. The team that backed him up included the likes of shortstop Enzo Hernandez, who had the curious statistics of thirty-three errors and twelve RBIS in 143 games in 1971. Norman's record of 3-12 for the Padres that season was not deserved, as his ERA was a respectable 3.33. Only once in his eighteen starts that year did the Padres score as many as three runs. Developing a slider to complement his fastball, screwball, curveball and change-up, he improved to 9-11 the next year but again had numerous fine outings wiped out by lack of support. To get those nine wins, Norman had to pitch six shutouts. He impressed managers around the league, particularly Sparky Anderson of the Reds. He struck out fifteen Reds while pitching a shutout in September 1972 and was 4-1 with two shutouts against the National League–champion Reds that year.

Norman started the 1973 season with a 1-7 record. The struggling Padres were desperate for cash to help keep the team in San Diego and were willing to deal some of their players to get it. Just before the June 15 trading deadline, Norman was sent to the Reds for outfielder Gene Locklear, Minor League pitcher Mike Johnson, and a reported $150,000. The Reds had been floundering in fourth place with serious pitching problems caused by injuries and an overworked bullpen. Norman arrived in Cincinnati, shaved off his mustache and got a haircut to please

Sparky Anderson, then stepped into the starting rotation. He made an immediate impact with complete-game shutouts in his first two games. He narrowly missed a third in his next start, giving up a two-out ninth-inning home run in a 4–1 win. Norman won seven of his first nine starts for the Reds and keyed a turnaround that swept the Reds to the division title. He started Game Four of the NLCS against the New York Mets, pitching well with only one hit and one run over five innings. The Reds eventually won the game in twelve innings but lost the deciding Game Five the next day.

Norman picked up where he left off in 1974 and quickly showed that he especially liked his new home, as by June of that season he had a career record of 15-3 at Cincinnati's Riverfront Stadium. He went on an early season tear, winning eight of ten decisions, and was pitching the best baseball of his career before he suffered a torn muscle in his left rib cage while batting and missed two weeks in early June. Upon returning, he developed some bad habits that he related to favoring his injured side, and he struggled to find consistency thereafter, finishing the season at 13-12 with a 3.15 ERA.

Norman started slow in 1975, was in and out of the rotation early, then won ten of eleven decisions after June and ended up 12-4 with a team-leading 119 strikeouts. In that season, as the Reds went a record forty-five straight games without a complete game (the club won thirty-two of those games), personal records for starting pitchers took a backseat to the team as a whole. The Reds won 108 games and took the division by 20 games. Norman was tabbed as the starter for Game Two of the NLCS and responded by beating the Pittsburgh Pirates 6–1. He went six strong innings, gave up four hits and one run, and helped himself with a sacrifice fly in the fourth inning.

In the World Series against the Boston Red Sox, Sparky Anderson, wary because lefties had been battered in Fenway Park all year, shuffled the rotation and skipped Norman, pitching Jack Billingham

in Game Two in Boston. Norman was not happy, feeling that he had earned a Series start. "I'm upset," he told reporters. "I believe I should be pitching. I believe I'm one of the guys who got us here."[5] He got his start in Game Four, back in Cincinnati, but was knocked out in the fourth inning after giving up seven hits and four runs and took the loss as the Red Sox won 5–4. Norman made one other appearance in the Series, pitching in relief in the third inning of the famous Game Six as the Reds captured the title in the seventh game.

One of Norman's more memorable games came against the San Francisco Giants at Riverfront on April 17, 1976. The nationally televised game was interrupted for thirty-five minutes when an estimated five thousand to ten thousand honeybees descended on the field while Norman was on the mound. Undeterred, he pitched a four-hit shutout. In a way the game symbolized the plight of the starting pitchers of the Big Red Machine—they pitched well, the team won, but all too often something else grabbed the headlines and created the buzz around the team.

In 1976 Norman was removed from the starting rotation after being battered by the Phillies on April 26 and then walking five Mets in two innings in early May. After returning as a starter, he won eight of nine decisions from June 13 to August 5 with three shutouts and an ERA of 1.18, prompting Anderson to admit he had made a mistake. "The guy who didn't start him all that time was awful dumb," said Anderson. "I won't mention any names but he's got a 10 on the back of his uniform."[6] With Don Gullett injured and others struggling, Norman was the most effective pitcher on the staff in midseason. In August Anderson told reporters, "Right now Fred is the best pitcher in the league."[7] Norman finished the 1976 season 12-7 with a 3.10 ERA.

Norman was the starter in Game Two of the 1976 World Series against the New York Yankees at Riverfront Stadium. The game was the first Sunday night World Series game in history; Commissioner Bowie Kuhn was reluctant to buck the NFL's Sunday afternoon television ratings. In a cold evening matchup against Catfish Hunter, Norman kept the Reds close, giving up one run in the fourth inning, then two in the seventh that tied the contest before being relieved by Billingham. Tony Pérez won the game with a two-out single in the ninth inning. The performance of Norman and Billingham prompted *Los Angeles Times* columnist Jim Murray to write, "Million dollar baby [Hunter] got trimmed by two five-and-ten-cent-store arms."[8]

While not having a huge contract like the free agent Hunter, Norman was anything but a cheap arm. He possessed five quality pitches—a fastball, curve, slider, change-up, and screwball—which he could throw on any count. He was described as a crafty, tough competitor, a bulldog. He was also frequently referred to as "Little Freddie Norman" by writers. He provided the Reds with a reliable starter for seven years. The daily trials of dealing with Captain Hook could wear on any pitcher's confidence, but Norman took it in stride. Anderson sometimes felt that Norman tended to nibble too much when he was in a slump, going to too many full counts instead of challenging hitters. Anderson also occasionally complained to reporters about what he called Norman's "mad scientist act," in which he constantly tinkered with his grip and experimented with different ways to get hitters out. But Anderson valued Norman for the fact that he was rarely injured and was a consistent winner. Because of his serious manner and the fact that he was closer to Anderson's age than other players (only eight and a half years separated them), he was one of the few players Anderson would allow to question his methods (albeit privately). Norman was a valuable member of the underrated starting rotation of the Big Red Machine. While they did not possess an overwhelming ace other than the oft-injured Gullett, the staff worked very well in providing Anderson with six to seven solid innings before turning the game over to the bullpen and the big hitters. The underappreciated value of this was only too

evident in 1977 when several slots in the rotation were no longer able to fill this role and the Reds fell to second place.

Throughout his years in Cincinnati, Norman was frequently noted in yearbooks and on the back of baseball cards to be an "eligible bachelor." That ended in February 1977 when he married. He and his wife, Cindy, were joined by son Joey in 1978.

Norman won a career-high fourteen games in 1977 but, like the entire team that season, he was inconsistent; he had a streak of six wins, followed by seven straight losses, then five straight wins. His final record was 14-13. He followed up with a 11-9 record in 1978 and 11-13 in 1979—his only losing season with the Reds. On September 5, 1979, he beat the Giants for his one hundredth career victory. His final appearance for the Reds came against the Pirates in Game Three of the NLCS that year, when he pitched two innings and gave up four runs on four hits (two home runs) as Pittsburgh swept the Reds in three games.

After the 1979 season Reds general manager Dick Wagner showed little interest in the thirty-six-year-old pitcher and Norman played out his option, signing with the Montreal Expos for $450,000 for two years in December 1979. Along with earning big money for the first time, Norman found the 1980 season brought frustrations as he divided his time between the bullpen and Manager Dick Williams's crowded doghouse. He did not get a start until July 28, when he defeated the Reds and finished with a 4-4 record and 4.13 ERA in forty-eight games. After struggling in spring training in 1981, Norman was released by the Expos on April 2.

Norman had a record of 85-64 in seven seasons with the Reds. His reliability is attested by the fact that since 1945 only three men have won ten or more games for the Reds in seven consecutive seasons: Jim Maloney, Tom Browning, and Norman. He retired with a career Major League record of 104-102 with an ERA of 3.62. As of 2012 he resided in Julian, North Carolina, near Greensboro.

Chapter 17. **Rose to Third**

Rory Costello

Pete Rose roamed around the diamond during his twenty-four big league seasons. Depending on when one saw him, the picture of Charlie Hustle with a glove on his hand varied. He was primarily a second baseman from 1963 through 1966. He shifted to the outfield in 1967 and played eight full seasons there through 1974—even winning a pair of Gold Gloves in 1969 and 1970. During the final phase of his career, from 1979 through 1986, he was a first baseman.

Yet Rose also played third base in about 18 percent of his games—chiefly from 1975 through 1978. His move from left field to third base in early May 1975 often receives credit as a pivotal moment in the success of the 1975 Reds—and with good reason. The batting order became much more potent because Rose continued to set the table and George Foster soon took over left field. Also, keeping Rose's bat in the lineup over light-hitting utility types John Vukovich, Doug Flynn, and Darrel Chaney did not come at a cost in defense. As Rose emphasized to sportswriter Joe Posnanski for a July 2009 article in *Cincinnati* magazine, "I wasn't a great third baseman. But I worked my ass off. I don't know if people realize how hard I worked."[1]

And quite simply, the team began to win consistently. When Rose made his first start at the hot corner on May 3, 1975, Cincinnati was playing only .500 ball (12-12). The rest of the way, the Reds went 96-42 (.696).

There was a good bit of history behind the move. Third base had been an unsettled spot for Cincinnati during the mid-1960s. In fact, Rose had gotten a brief trial there at the beginning of the 1966 season, and it didn't work out. From 1967 through

1971, Tony Pérez played at third, out of his natural position. That move as well was enabled by Rose's switch from second base to left field. Pérez shifted to first base in 1972 after the blockbuster November 1971 trade with Houston, in which the Reds obtained infielder Denis Menke and dealt away slugging first baseman Lee May (among several other players). Menke hit a combined .218 during his two seasons as the primary starter at third base, though, and so he was shipped back to the Astros for pitcher Pat Darcy.

In 1974 the team stuck Dan Driessen's bat at third base. A natural first baseman, he was rocky with the glove at third (.915 fielding percentage at that position in 122 starts). Catcher Johnny Bench also started thirty games there, and various other players accounted for the remaining ten.

General Manager Bob Howsam did not view Driessen as a viable ongoing option—in fact, he never appeared at third base again during his remaining thirteen seasons in the Majors. That December, the *Sporting News* ran an article titled "Howsam Sees Safety in Numbers at Hot Sack." The GM mentioned four players who could compete for the third base job in 1975:

Arturo DeFreites: This young Dominican eventually played thirty-two games for the Reds in 1978 and 1979. In that brief big league career, he was mainly a pinch hitter, playing a bit at first base and in the outfield—but not at third (his part-time position in the Minors).

Joel Youngblood: Cincinnati's second-round draft pick in 1970, Youngblood went on to a fourteen-year career in the Majors, mainly in the outfield. When the San Francisco Giants put him at third base regularly in 1984, his fielding percentage was an abysmal .887.

Ray Knight: Knight, a tenth-round pick in 1970, was a very good true third baseman who had gotten his first Major League trial in 1974. He remained in the Minors in 1975–76 but eventually took over at third base with Cincinnati in 1979 after Rose left the Reds via free agency. Knight later won a championship and was the World Series MVP with the New York Mets in 1986.

John Vukovich: The Reds obtained this utility man in an October 1974 trade. The article said, "While Vukovich has an outstanding glove, his bat is suspect."[2]

Before spring training in 1975, according to Reds beat writer Earl Lawson, "listening to Howsam, one gathers that DeFreites rates as the No. 1 candidate among the youngsters." Darrel Chaney, mainly a shortstop, was also in the mix.[3] Sparky Anderson told Vukovich, "The third base job is wide open."[4] Vukovich got the opportunity, based largely on his defensive ability, and though there was talk of a platoon, he started most of the games at third base in April.

As had been feared, though—despite expressions of confidence from the brass in the off-season—Vukovich didn't hit. In fact, as Joe Posnanski described at length in his 2009 book *The Machine*, Anderson hung the derisive nickname Balsa on him for his soft bat.[5] Chaney and Flynn got some starts, but the three players were hitting a collective .157 (14-for-89) on May 2 when the exasperated Anderson felt he had to make a move to secure more offensive production from his lineup.

Posnanski also provided much colorful inside detail on various other aspects of the situation. There was the way Anderson asserted his authority over the team, as seen in his handling of Vukovich. There was the flash of inspiration that spurred Anderson

to try Rose at third. But above all, there was the psychology involved. When Cincinnati's manager in 1966, Don Heffner, had moved Rose, it was an order. Anderson didn't tell, he asked.[6] Appealing to Rose's desire to help the team made it happen (though when the Hit King was chasing Ty Cobb's record as player-manager in 1985, another motive was visible). Previous insight came from John Erardi and Greg Rhodes, who wrote *Big Red Dynasty* (1997). They noted that Anderson also had to find playing time for his many well-qualified outfielders and Dan Driessen—and that preserving his own job was also a part of moving Rose. Howsam, who was away in Arizona, thought it was a mistake when he saw the box score of the May 3 game—and said, "Oh my God" when he found out it was for real. Reds broadcaster Marty Brennaman talked about Rose's initial adventures in the field. Erardi and Rhodes also recounted how Rose's teammates "were all over him" for his unpolished play.[7]

As a United Press International feature described it that July, "Pete Rose plays third base like a mad bull. He barricades the ball, stomps after it, or hurls himself in its vicinity, whatever he feels it takes to catch, stop or somehow slow down the ball. . . . 'Finesse!' he shouts. 'I don't play with finesse. Aggressive. That's what I am. That's the way I play third base.'"[8]

Further Rose quotes were entirely in character. "I love to play third. You know why? 'Cause I get to touch the ball after each out. . . . Third base is more fun than the outfield. I feel more a part of the game. Closer to it." He made the same point that he did to Posnanski more than thirty years later: "Hard work. I work hard, that's it. I think if you work hard enough you can do just about anything, or come close to it. I may not look too smooth out there, but I'm working, I'm getting the job done."[9]

Rose committed just thirteen errors in 349 chances at third in 1975, a respectable .963 fielding percentage. When asked that July if hitters were able to bunt on him, the reply was again as one would expect. "'Yeah, three or four have tried it,' says Rose with a hard, straight face. The subject is serious to him. 'But I threw 'em out. No problem.'"[10] Fielding in the postseason wasn't a problem either, as he cleanly handled all the relatively few chances that came his way.

In his 2004 biography, *Pete Rose: Baseball's All-Time Hit King*, author William Cook noted another important dimension of the move. "[Rose] remarked that the advantage it gave the Reds, other than getting the powerful bat of George Foster into the lineup, was that it gave the Reds a set lineup to play every day. Sparky Anderson agreed with that assessment, stating that after he moved Rose to third and inserted Foster in left he concerned himself mainly with the Reds' pitching and hardly paid any attention to the starting eight for the rest of the season."[11]

Rose started an average of 157 games a year at third with the Reds from 1976 through 1978. There was precious little game time for his backups, first Bob Bailey and later Ray Knight. After the 1978 season, Rose signed with the Philadelphia Phillies. He shifted to first base for the Phillies—reflecting the presence of Hall of Famer Mike Schmidt at third. Rose returned to the outfield with some frequency in 1983 and again in 1984, by which time he was with Montreal. However, he played only five more games at third (all in 1979).

Nonetheless, Pete Rose's years at the hot corner formed a vital chapter in his career. If this move hadn't taken place, perhaps the Los Angeles Dodgers might have won the NL West—and the pennant—for five straight years. In that case, nobody would have written books about the Reds dynasty.

Chapter 18. **Clay Carroll**

Derek Norin and Mark Armour

AGE	W	L	PCT.	ERA	G	GS	GF	CG	SHO	SV	IP	H	BB	SO	HBP	WP
34	7	5	.583	2.62	56	2	27	0	0	7	96.1	93	32	44	3	3

Clay Carroll was a popular relief star in the heyday of the fireman, a bullpen workhorse who could be used in a variety of difficult situations. From the end of June 1968 through the 1975 season, he saved a then Cincinnati Reds record 119 games and compiled a 1.39 earned run average in twenty-two postseason games. Carroll was named to the 1971 and 1972 National League All-Star teams and was named the *Sporting News* Fireman of the Year in 1972 after saving what was then a Major League record of thirty-seven games. He recorded victories in Game Four of the 1970 World Series and in Game Seven of the 1975 World Series, the game that brought the Reds their first world championship in thirty-five years.

Carroll got the nickname Hawk from teammates.[1] He was known as a fierce competitor who at the same time kept the Cincinnati bullpen entertained and loose. "Did you ever hit anybody on the head with a ripe tomato?" he once asked in the bullpen. "It sure makes a funny noise and there's a way it flattens out to really mess up a guy's hair."[2] He became the leader of the relief corps—with Carroll, Pedro Borbon, Tom Hall, and later Will McEnaney and Rawly Eastwick, it was the excellent but unsung facet of the great Big Red Machine teams.

Clay Palmer Carroll was born on May 2, 1941, in Clanton, Alabama, a textile-mill town about midway between Birmingham and Montgomery. He was one of nine children. "When I was a kid, most of the people worked in the cotton mill," he recalled of his struggling hometown. "My father worked there 40 years, and when I grew up I worked there a couple years too."[3] Carroll later recalled his father making forty-five dollars per week but putting aside enough

The Hawk, Clay Carroll, was one of the best relief pitchers in baseball for several years and the leader of a deep Cincinnati bullpen.

for each of his kids to get a weekly Popsicle.[4] It was the only world the boy knew, as Carroll never left the town until he was a teenager. "I was working for a cafe as a curb service boy in Clanton. The owners took me with them to Tallahassee, Florida, for a few days when I was 15. That was the first time I was ever away from home."[5]

"Lucky, I had this arm and I liked playing baseball," said Carroll. "Did it every chance I got when I wasn't working in that mill, or loading watermelons onto trucks, or whatever job came around. I went to school and I was good at sports."[6] He played well enough to draw the attention of at least one club. Former Major Leaguer Dixie Walker signed Carroll for the Milwaukee Braves as an amateur free agent in 1961 for $1,000.

Carroll said, "I was anxious to sign and get to playing ball. So when Mr. Walker offered me the $1,000, I took it. All I want to do now is get the experience I need and get to the major leagues. I know if I make good the money will come."[7]

Walker invited Carroll and Braves pitching coach Whitlow Wyatt to his home shortly after Carroll signed. "I knew only one thing about pitching then," Carroll remembered a few years later. "I just threw the ball as hard as I could although I knew how to throw a good curveball. Mr. Wyatt showed me how to throw a changeup and slider. And he taught me my motion and follow-through. Now I feel experience is my big need. I'm shy and quiet by nature, but I'm gaining confidence."[8]

Carroll began his professional career with Davenport (Iowa) of the Class D Midwest League, where he finished 7-10 with a 4.20 ERA. The next year he led the Class C Pioneer League in victories, sporting a 14-7 record for Boise, striking out 223 hitters in 181 innings while pitching sixteen complete games. He split both the 1963 and 1964 seasons with Austin of the Texas League and Denver of the Pacific Coast League, the top two affiliates in the Braves system. After winning eleven and ten games over the two years, Carroll was called up to Milwaukee in September 1964.

Carroll's first trip to the big show was a smash success. He pitched 20⅓ innings in eleven games and allowed just four runs (all in his lone start), good for a 1.77 ERA. He won his first game on September 26 in Philadelphia (this was the fifth straight loss by the first-place Phillies during their infamous ten-game losing streak), and the next day he bought several copies of the newspaper and pointed out his picture in it to people in the hotel lobby.[9] He had

come a long way from Clanton, Alabama. He won another game four days later.

Carroll started the 1965 season in the Majors but was sent down on June 1, returning in early August. For Milwaukee Carroll went 0-1 with a 4.41 ERA in nineteen games. He played for two months for the Atlanta Crackers, the Triple-A affiliate of the Braves, and pitched thirteen games, all starts, finishing 3-6 with a 2.42 ERA. After the season the Milwaukee Braves became the Atlanta Braves.

In 1966 Carroll again made the big league club. This time he stuck around the entire season and had an excellent year. He led the NL (and set a new Braves record) with seventy-three appearances while recording an 8-7 record with eleven saves and a 2.37 ERA. "Clay has done a fine job for us," said new manager Billy Hitchcock. "He'll go out there any time you need him and he'll give you a good job." Carroll also had not lost his boyish wonder at his station. "Even when he wins a game now, he walks about this high off the ground," said his catcher, Joe Torre, holding his hand out. "He's really on a cloud."[10]

The 6-foot right-hander usually played at about 200 pounds, but in the 1966 and 1967 seasons he got his weight up to about 215 pounds, which he later blamed for his poor 1967 season, during which he was used as both a starter and a reliever. His ERA shot up to 5.52 to go along with his 6-12 record. In July Carroll was demoted to Triple-A Richmond for a few weeks, but his 0.82 ERA got him back to Atlanta quickly. He initially balked at the demotion, saying he'd quit and "go into police work."[11] (Carroll had been a deputy sheriff in Clanton in the off-season, so it was not necessarily an idle threat.) In any event, he stuck with baseball and after the season took off the weight by riding his bike in the hills around his hometown.[12] He showed up in 1968 back at 200 pounds.

Carroll began the 1968 season with the Braves and was 0-1 with a 4.84 ERA on June 11 when he was involved in a big trade with the Cincinnati Reds.

He was sent to the Reds with pitcher Tony Cloninger and infielder Woody Woodward in exchange for pitchers Milt Pappas and Ted Davidson and infielder Bob Johnson. Although Pappas and Cloninger were the big names in the deal, the Reds acquired Carroll hoping that he might benefit from a change of scenery. "Just give me work. All I want do is help the team," Carroll said. "Honestly, I haven't been keeping track of times I've pitched. There have been times when my arm muscles have been a little bit tired but I've never had a sore arm. Anyway, it just proves what I've always contended. You can't be effective if you don't get enough work. Maybe you do lose a little zip off your fastball after you've worked a lot, but you've got three other things going for you—control, rhythm, confidence—they're things you don't have if you're just sitting around doing nothing."[13]

Carroll was outstanding for the Reds the remainder of the season, appearing in fifty-eight games and 121⅔ innings, finishing with a 2.29 ERA and seventeen saves, and teaming with Ted Abernathy to form an excellent late-inning tandem. The next year he again had a heavy workload, pitching 150⅔ innings in seventy-one games, with a 12-6 record and a 3.52 ERA. During the off-season the Reds had obtained reliever Wayne Granger, who ended up getting most of the save chances and had a great season.

One of Carroll's big thrills came on May 30, 1969, in St. Louis, when he hit a two-out tenth-inning home run off Bob Gibson to beat the Cardinals, 4–3. "You should see the smile on Carroll's face when he returned to the dugout. He looked like a cut watermelon," said Manager Dave Bristol. "Hey, Clay! Where would that homer have landed down in Clanton?" asked teammate Jimmy Stewart. "Deep in the corn patch!" Carroll retorted. "I don't want to brag but I knew it was a homer as soon as I hit it."[14]

Sparky Anderson took over as manager of the Reds in 1970, and he continued to give a big role to Carroll. In sixty-five games the pitcher was 9–4

with a 2.59 ERA. His manager was impressed. "Clay throws a fastball, slider, a slip pitch, and curves at different speeds," beamed Anderson. "And he gets them all over." Carroll added, "I've got so much confidence in my curve that I don't hesitate to throw it on a 3-and-2 count."[15] Carroll recorded the Reds' only victory in the 1970 World Series. He pitched 3⅔ innings in relief in Game Four, allowing only Brooks Robinson's eighth-inning single, after the Reds came back to take the lead and win 6–5. Carroll pitched in four of the five games, allowing no runs in nine innings.

Carroll continued to pitch outstanding baseball for the next five years in Cincinnati. In 1971 he finished 10-4 with a 2.50 ERA in ninety-three innings and was selected to his first All-Star Game. After the season the Reds traded Granger to the Minnesota Twins for pitcher Tom Hall, and Anderson began to use Carroll more at the end of games. He responded with a 6-4 record and thirty-seven saves, a new Major League record (broken many times with the advent of the "closer" role). "Remember, Sparky," Carroll told Anderson before every game, "I'm up there in the tree. If you need me, just give me a call." Carroll struggled early in the 1972 season, when Anderson told him to forget his secondary pitches and just throw hard, but recovered nicely.[16]

A rough start in 1973 got Carroll demoted to more of a set-up pitcher, but he still managed eight wins and fourteen saves, despite his elevated 3.69 ERA. Anderson employed a deep and talented bullpen for many years, and Carroll bounced back with a 12-5, 2.15 season in 1974, then 7-5, 2.62 in 1975. In the fabled 1975 World Series, Carroll pitched in five games and allowed two runs in 5⅔ innings. In Game Seven he pitched two hitless innings and earned the victory. For his postseason career, Carroll pitched twenty-two innings with a 1.39 ERA, earning a 4-2 record. In his final effort, he helped his team win the World Series.

After the 1975 season the Reds traded Carroll to the Chicago White Sox for pitcher Rich Hinton and Minor League utility man Jeff Sovern. The Reds were loaded with fine relievers, and shedding the veteran's salary was the economical choice. As a member of the Reds for 7½ seasons, Carroll finished 71-43 with a 2.73 ERA.

The thirty-five-year-old Carroll pitched in twenty-nine games for the White Sox in 1976, going 4-4 with six saves and a 2.56 ERA, numbers in line with his pitching over the previous several years. Nevertheless, the next spring the White Sox sent him to St. Louis for pitcher Lerrin LaGrow, and Carroll was again a workhorse, throwing ninety innings with a 2.50 ERA. On August 31, with the White Sox unexpectedly in a pennant race, the Cardinals dealt Carroll back to Chicago for three players, and he finished the season there. The White Sox released Carroll on March 30, 1978.

Now thirty-seven years old, Carroll signed with the Pirates as a free agent and pitched the 1978 season in their organization, spending most of the year at Triple-A Columbus (Ohio) before making two appearances for the Pirates late in the season. After being released by Pittsburgh in mid-October, he signed with the Milwaukee Brewers in mid-April 1979, making twelve appearances for Triple-A Vancouver before retiring.

The years since Carroll left baseball have been marred by one tragic day. He had married Judy Haynes in September 1964, and the couple had three children, Brett, Lori, and Connie. The couple settled in Bradenton, Florida, but divorced in 1981. In April 1981 Carroll married Frances Nowitzke, a widow who had two children of her own. He remained close to his three children and active in their lives.

His world was shattered on November 16, 1985, when twenty-six-year-old Frederick Nowitzke, Frances's son, murdered Frances and eleven-year old Brett (his stepbrother), while wounding Carroll in the face, in a horrific shooting rampage. Nowitzke had been acting bizarrely for some time, and there was a family history of mental illness. He pleaded innocent by reason of insanity but was found guilty of the two murders and one attempted murder. On appeal, the verdict was overturned on grounds of prosecutorial misconduct and a retrial was ordered. Nowitzke was again found guilty, and as of 2012 was still incarcerated.

Carroll later relocated to Chattanooga, Tennessee, and worked in construction. He was inducted into the Cincinnati Reds Hall of Fame in 1980 and has made appearances at team Hall of Fame events and at Reds fantasy camps. In 1992 Carroll was inducted into the Alabama Sports Hall of Fame. He is recognized as an important cog in the great Reds teams of the 1970s.

Chapter 19. Merv Rettenmund

Jacob Pomrenke

AGE	G	AB	R	H	2B	3B	HR	TB	RBI	BB	SO	BAV	OBP	SLG	SB	GDP	HBP
32	93	188	24	45	6	1	2	59	19	35	22	.239	.356	.314	5	6	0

By his own account, Merv Rettenmund was a "scuffler" more than a ballplayer. He never found his niche as a regular starter with the Baltimore Orioles, but he starred as a super-sub and was a key cog for the Orioles as they won three consecutive American League pennants, from 1969 to 1971. He twice led the team in batting average in those years while playing all three outfield positions. More than that, Rettenmund always seemed to find himself as part of a winner—as a player and coach, his teams reached the postseason in thirteen of his thirty-three seasons in Major League baseball (through 2008). He played in four World Series, winning championships in 1970 with the Orioles and in 1975 with the Cincinnati Reds. Later he became one of the game's top pinch hitters with the San Diego Padres and California Angels.

After he retired as a player, Rettenmund became one of the most respected hitting coaches in baseball, and he was on staff for three more World Series—with the Oakland Athletics in 1989 and 1990 and the San Diego Padres in 1998. He once called his job as a hitting coach "50 percent comedian, 25 percent psychologist, and 25 percent teacher," but his methods worked.[1] Led by Hall of Famer Tony Gwynn, who won half of his eight batting titles under the tutelage of Rettenmund, the Padres set franchise records in nearly every offensive category in the 1990s. In a rare move for a coach, Rettenmund remained with the team through three managerial changes in San Diego.

Mervin Weldon Rettenmund was born on June 6, 1943, in Flint, Michigan. His father, Weldon, worked for many years with General Motors, as did his uncle and his Swiss-born grandfather. His moth-

Merv Rettenmund started his career as if he would be a perennial All-Star but instead turned into a fourth outfielder for a decade. He later became one of the game's most respected batting coaches.

er, Dolores (nee Tucker), was from Carsonville, a small village in eastern Michigan. Dolores's grandfather had emigrated from England.[2]

Merv came from an athletic family. His mother and sister, Susan, both played softball. "There was always an opportunity to play," he recalled.[3] In his spare time, Weldon played baseball in semipro leagues around Flint and he was good enough to earn a tryout with the Detroit Tigers. He turned down their contract offer, however, and "always regretted it." When Merv had his own chance to sign with the Tigers after high school, Weldon urged his son not to pass it up. But Merv opted for college instead.[4]

Baseball was always Rettenmund's ambition. "I'd go to games at Tiger Stadium all the time, see those guys in their uniforms and watch them play," he recalled. "I thought, 'Gosh, I'd love to do that.'"[5] In addition to baseball, the speedy teenager also starred as a halfback in football at Southwestern High School in Flint.

After graduating from Southwestern High School in 1961, he spent the summer as a hard-hitting catcher on Michigan's top American Legion team, the Buick Colts. The Colts won city and state championships—Rettenmund hit .588 to earn the Kiki Cuyler Award as the state tournament MVP—and went on to play at a regional tournament in Princeton, Indiana. "That's the summer Merv really developed," said Legion teammate Wayne Schmitz, who later played in the Atlanta Braves organization. "Scouts wanted to sign him right then."[6]

During the Princeton tournament, Rettenmund was approached by Ray Louthen, the baseball and football coach at Ball State University in Muncie, Indiana. As Rettenmund recalled, "I had been considering Western Michigan or Michigan State—I was looking at them, but I don't know if they were looking at me, you know? . . . Ray Louthen came up to me [at Princeton] and said, 'If you'll come play for us, I'll give a scholarship to your cousin and to your friend.'" It was a football scholarship, Rettenmund said, "so they could bring more players in."[7] Rettenmund took it.

At Ball State, Rettenmund broke the school's single-season rushing record, held by Timmy Brown, who played for the Philadelphia Eagles and Baltimore Colts. Rettenmund was good enough to get drafted by the Dallas Cowboys—much to his surprise, because he had played just three games as a senior because of injuries. In baseball he was a two-time All-Indiana Collegiate Conference first-team selection, hitting .321 in his career. He later became

a charter member of the Ball State Athletics Hall of Fame.[8] In 1966, two years into his professional career, he earned his bachelor's degree in education.

Rettenmund also met his wife, the former Susan Clark, at Ball State. She was from Findlay, Ohio, a Spanish major who would later accompany him on trips to Latin America and South America for winter ball when he was in the Minor Leagues. Travel always plays a major role in the life of a ballplayer, and Merv and Susan loved it. In the off-seasons they began taking trips around the world—including a cruise to Antarctica. "The Red Sea, Jordan, Israel, Ireland . . . pretty much anywhere you can think of, we've been there," he said. The Rettenmunds married in 1964 and had their first child, Cyndi, in 1965. In 1970 they welcomed their second daughter, Christy.[9]

In November 1964, just a few weeks after Merv and Susan were married, Baltimore Orioles scout Jim Terrell signed Rettenmund as an amateur free agent, with a reported $15,000 bonus. He was sent to Single-A Stockton to finish out the year and returned to the California League for his first full professional season in 1966. He hit .307 with twenty-one home runs in 127 games to earn a spot on the California League All-Star team. In 1967 he continued his quick ascent up the Minor League ladder by hitting .286 before a shoulder separation sidelined him late in the summer. That winter he played in Venezuela and hit .313 for Manager Luis Aparicio. Because of the injury, he said, "I couldn't lift my arm. But the one thing it did was it cut my swing down. I think it was the turning point of my career. I really became a good hitter."[10]

As a result, Rettenmund made the 1968 Orioles roster out of spring training. His Major League debut came on April 14, when he struck out as a pinch hitter against the Angels' Clyde Wright to end the game. He made three more appearances that week, getting two hits and walking once, before being sent down to Triple-A Rochester (New York) when pitcher Pete Richert was activated from National Guard duty. In Rochester the sweet-swinging right-hander flourished, hitting .331 with twenty-two home runs to earn International League MVP and Rookie of the Year honors, as well as the *Sporting News*'s Minor League Player of the Year Award. When outfielder Curt Motton was injured in late August, Rettenmund was called up to Baltimore for good.

Three days after Rettenmund's call-up, he was sent in to pinch-hit for Ellie Hendricks in the bottom of the ninth inning. He homered on the first pitch he saw from Oakland reliever Warren Bogle to beat the A's, 5–3.[11] Rettenmund batted .265 in the final month as Manager Earl Weaver moved him up and down the lineup. He was a valuable utility man for the Orioles in their championship years, but he never settled into a regular position.

There was also no room for a rookie outfielder to break into Baltimore's lineup. Future Hall of Famer Frank Robinson, who had won the American League's Triple Crown (home runs, RBIs, and batting average) in 1966, held down the fort in right field, while Paul Blair was considered the game's best defensive center fielder and Don Buford was a solid starter in left field. In the 1969 World Series against the upstart New York Mets, Rettenmund made his only appearance as a pinch runner in a Game Two loss. The Orioles lost the Series in five games, in one of baseball's biggest postseason upsets.

By 1970, Rettenmund's ability was getting hard to ignore. Preseason work with batting coach Jim Frey turned him into a stronger hitter to the opposite field, and he got off to a hot start, hitting .333 in April. But he still couldn't break into the lineup as an everyday starter. So Rettenmund became the Orioles' "noble substitute," spelling the regular outfielders when they were tired or slumping. It took an injury to Paul Blair, who was hit in the face by a pitch on May 31, to finally give Rettenmund the chance to start. He did not take it lightly. "We expected to win every game," he recalled. "It was not a showcase [for prospects]. You were expected to produce."[12]

Rettenmund did. During the second half of the season, he batted a blazing .373, hitting safely in sixteen of seventeen games between July 26 and August 15. He had three four-hit games in a five-week span, finishing the year with a team-high .322 average and eighteen home runs. In the league playoff against the Twins he started Game Two and played well—he walked twice, stole a base, and had an RBI single in the ninth inning during a decisive seven-run ninth-inning uprising in an 11–3 victory. The Orioles went on to win the pennant the next day in Baltimore. In the World Series, against the Cincinnati Reds, he did not get a chance to start until the fifth game and did not learn of the opportunity until late in the Orioles' Game Four loss.

"I was sitting in the manager's office during that [eighth] inning," he recalled. "You can see the game better that way, you can get a better view on TV than you can from the dugout. I watched [Lee] May hit his home run and Earl comes running in. Boy, is he pissed. He starts yelling, 'Get your feet off that damn desk! Get your ass out of this office! . . . Oh, and by the way, you're starting tomorrow!' That's how I found out I was playing.'"[13]

Rettenmund made the most of his opportunity. In the third inning, after the Orioles had taken a 4–3 lead, he singled home Boog Powell and then scored on Dave Johnson's RBI single with one out. In the fifth he added to the Orioles' World Series–clinching victory with a long home run down the right-field line off Tony Cloninger. The Orioles cruised from there, winning 9–3, and celebrated the franchise's second championship deep into the night. "It's a moment you'd like to have kept the rest of your career," Rettenmund recalled. "You think it'll never end. . . . I was thinking, after winning all those pennants, that in spring training what we were doing was getting our pitchers ready for the playoffs, you know? We thought that's how it would always be."[14]

Rettenmund's confidence was sky-high. Teammate Mark Belanger liked to say then, "Merv always says two things in life are certain: There will

JACOB POMRENKE

be snow in the winter and I'll get my two hits." Second baseman Johnson recalled the quote a little differently: "Death, taxes and my three hits."[15]

Whatever the case, the twenty-eight-year-old Rettenmund continued to hit like a machine in 1971—leading the team again with a .318 average, good for third in the American League behind Tony Oliva and Bobby Murcer—no doubt helped by the fact that he finally was receiving steady playing time in the Orioles' lineup, even if he was never sure which position he would play until he got to the ballpark. Rettenmund started fifty-eight games in right field, thirty-four in left field, and thirty-seven in center field and logged more innings (1,170) than any other Orioles outfielder. At the plate, he set career highs with 75 RBIs, 81 runs, 15 stolen bases, and 491 at bats in 141 games. His performance earned him a few MVP votes at the end of the year as the Orioles swept the Oakland A's in the ALCS to clinch the pennant.

In the 1971 World Series Rettenmund earned a spot in the Orioles' lineup as Baltimore prepared to defend its title against the Pittsburgh Pirates. His three-run home run off Dock Ellis in the third inning of Game One proved to be just enough of a margin for Dave McNally, who shut down the Pirates on three hits, but the Orioles ultimately fell in seven games. Game Seven ended when Rettenmund, representing the tying run, grounded out sharply to shortstop.

Surprisingly, the Orioles relieved the crowded outfield by dealing Frank Robinson, their biggest star and leader, to the Los Angeles Dodgers in November. With Robinson gone, Rettenmund inherited the starting job in right field and got the chance to play regularly. But injuries plagued him from the beginning. During a four-hit day in Detroit, he dove for a ball and landed awkwardly on his right shoulder. The next day he couldn't lift his arm. In August he suffered a torn abdominal muscle and was placed on the disabled list.[16] In between, he suddenly, inexplicably lost the ability to hit.

His batting average fell below .300 on the season's second day and it never returned. By the end of the year, Rettenmund was hitting .233—an eighty-five-point drop from his team-leading average the previous season. He couldn't figure it out. One theory suggested that Weaver put extra pressure on Rettenmund to supply the Orioles' power with Boog Powell and Brooks Robinson getting older and Frank Robinson no longer around. So Rettenmund tried to change his stance to pull the ball and hit more home runs—then made other variations, such as keeping his bat still and holding his hands lower—and all the adjustments disrupted his swing. Years later, Rettenmund explained his slump this way: "I had a weird swing. And when it was broke, I knew what was wrong and everybody could tell me how to fix it, but I just couldn't fix it."[17]

He dismissed the idea that Weaver played a role in the slump, explaining that he was too easily satisfied as a young player: "You cause these things yourself. I had two goals when I started playing. One, to be a .300 hitter in the Major Leagues, and two, to make x number of dollars. . . . That's all I wanted to do. And after two years in the Majors, I had been doing everything I wanted to do. I didn't have any more goals and I didn't know how to set any more goals. I got myself in a mental rut."[18]

Rettenmund got off to a poor start in 1973, hitting .230 before the All-Star break, and after severely bruising his chest crashing into the outfield wall in Kansas City in late May, he lost his job in right field. After a one-year hiatus from the postseason, the Orioles were rolling along to another AL East Division title. The club benefited from a powerful farm system that continued to produce strong outfield prospects—before, it had been Blair, Dave May, Terry Crowley, and Rettenmund; now Don Baylor, Al Bumbry, and Rich Coggins were muscling in for more playing time. When Rettenmund's slump continued in the ALCS, in which he hit .091 in a losing effort against the Oakland A's, he too was deemed expendable.

Rettenmund was given a fresh start with the Cincinnati Reds, who traded for the thirty-year-old in a five-player deal that sent pitcher Ross Grimsley to Baltimore in December 1973. Rettenmund seemed pleased to go from one winning franchise to another, but moving to the National League did not help his hitting get back on track.

In two seasons with the Reds, he batted just .227 and drove himself deeper into despair at the plate. He later said the slump also carried over to his outfield play—"I got to dropping fly balls, which I never did"—and it even affected him driving to the ballpark. "I put so much pressure on myself in Cincinnati," Rettenmund said, adding that it got so bad that he took to swinging at the first pitch in nearly every at bat "so they wouldn't have time to put my average on the scoreboard!" After making three pinch-hit appearances in the 1975 World Series, he was swapped to San Diego in a trade for infielder Rudy Meoli during spring training the following year. He and Terry Crowley, his old friend and teammate who was sent to the Atlanta Braves the same week, celebrated by taking a joyride all around the Reds' practice field in Tampa, Florida.[19]

In the sunny climate of Southern California, and no longer fighting to start every day, Rettenmund began to relax and enjoy the game. And just as suddenly as it began, his debilitating slump seemed to be far behind him. "I could hit fine," he said. "I could hit the curveball. I was pinch-hitting and having success at it. . . . I started having fun again." In 1977 he became one of the league's top specialists—setting a Padres franchise record with twenty-one pinch-hits in sixty-five at bats and setting two National League records as a pinch hitter, by walking sixteen times and appearing in eighty-six games.[20]

Rettenmund signed as a free agent with the California Angels in 1978 and was an asset off the bench, hitting the first pinch-hit grand slam in team history on May 6. In 1979 he helped the Angels to their first postseason appearance by hitting .263 in seventy-six at bats. In the ALCS that year, he returned to Baltimore along with three other former Orioles—Don Baylor, Bobby Grich, and Larry Harlow—to face their old team, still piloted by Earl Weaver, whom Rettenmund has called the smartest manager he knew in baseball. "The only way to measure a manager is by how his guys produced for him, and guys *played* for Weav," he recalled.[21] Weaver's players outperformed Rettenmund's Angels teammates in the ALCS, winning Baltimore's fourth and final pennant for the Hall of Fame manager. Rettenmund was limited to just four plate appearances during two of the four games.

That off-season, Rettenmund began to consider life after playing baseball. His education degree made him well suited for teaching, and coaching was the next best thing. For years, he had helped his teammates—many of them among the best in the game—tinker with their swings, observing what worked and what didn't to develop his own philosophies on hitting.

More than most coaches, hitting coaches work in almost total obscurity. Rettenmund often said that his work ended when the game began, having spent most of his day under the stands in the batting cages or the video room, tutoring players.[22] But his reputation as a hitting coach over three decades did not escape notice.

After retiring as a player in 1980, Rettenmund joined the Angels' coaching staff under Manager Jim Fregosi. With California—and later the Texas Rangers and the Oakland A's in the 1980s—his primary responsibility was to work in the farm system, teaching young prospects in the Minor Leagues how to improve their focus and discipline at the plate. But when his former teammate Baylor started the 1981 season with three hits in sixty-five at bats, Rettenmund was asked to help. Said Manager Gene Mauch, "Merv came in . . . and both [Bobby] Grich and Baylor went crazy with the bat. If there's any connection to having him here and what we did . . . he's got to be the greatest hitting instructor there is."[23]

JACOB POMRENKE

In 1989, after serving three years as Oakland's roving hitting instructor, Rettenmund moved up to become Tony La Russa's hitting coach with the A's, who won pennants in both years Rettenmund was on the coaching staff. Rettenmund maintained that the 1989 A's were the best team he'd ever seen, better even than the two championship teams he played on, the 1970 Orioles and the 1975 Reds.

"That team had thunder, and tons of speed. Oh man, they were loaded," he said of the A's dynasty. "The Orioles had pitching and defense, but they didn't have the thunder. The Reds had thunder and they had the speed. . . . The difference is, the A's had four quality starters and [Dennis] Eckersley waiting in the bullpen. The Reds always worried about pitching."[24]

Rettenmund's third World Series ring, he said, was more satisfying than the two he had earned as a player. "That's when you finally realize how difficult it is," he said. "[As a player], the game was easy. But [winning], it's not always going to happen like that."[25]

In 1991 Rettenmund returned to San Diego—the city he and Susan had made their permanent home since he was traded there more than a decade earlier—as a hitting coach with the Padres. He began working with then-four-time batting champion Tony Gwynn, or as Rettenmund liked to call him, "the 'man with the little hands,' the greatest hitter I've ever seen."[26]

It was a match made in hitting heaven. Gwynn had battled injuries on the field and dissension off it to hit for one of the lowest averages of his career, .309, in 1990. Rettenmund, a gregarious personality who was easy to talk to and loved to discuss hitting as much as Gwynn did, helped the pudgy outfielder reach new heights for the rest of the decade. The future Hall of Famer never hit below .317 again and won four consecutive batting titles from 1994 through 1997 to tie Honus Wagner's National League record with eight in his career.

Rettenmund said the most amazing quality about Gwynn was his consistency: "We'd hit off the tee every day. I think there were years when he hit off the tee 365 times. . . . And he never ducked a pitcher. Some guys will take a day off against a Randy Johnson. Tony would be in there every time."[27] He added that he rarely discussed mechanics with Gwynn, knowing full well that the only time Gwynn stopped hitting was when his knee was hurting.

Other Padres benefited from having Rettenmund as their hitting coach, among them Steve Finley, Ken Caminiti, and Gary Sheffield, the latter of whom made a run at the Triple Crown in 1992 (he won his only batting title but finished third and fifth, respectively, in home runs and RBIs). Rettenmund said the nine years he spent with San Diego were the best times of his career.[28]

After leaving the Padres in 1999, he bounced around with three organizations (Atlanta, Detroit, and Toronto) before returning to the San Diego coaching staff in mid-2006. Instantly, the Padres—who ranked last in hitting, runs, and home runs at the time—began a surge to the NL West Division title. "That was one of the most gratifying years I've ever had," Rettenmund said. "And I know better than to think it was just because of my presence. But that was very gratifying."[29]

Rettenmund was fired partway through the 2007 season and, after more than four decades in baseball and in his mid-sixties, he said he didn't plan to get back into full-time coaching again. In between trips around the world with his wife and spending time with his grandchildren, he offered private hitting instruction to youths in the San Diego area. He occasionally attended Padres games at nearby Petco Park—"I like to watch. But I like it more when they score some runs!" he said of his offensively challenged former team.[30]

He said he has as much energy as ever. "I feel great, I'm exercising a lot. I might get back in one day, but not at the big league level. . . . I'd go help out at spring training, evaluate some guys in camp, something like that. I still love it."[31]

Chapter 20. **May 1975 Timeline**

Mark Miller and Mark Armour

All headlines below are from the next day's edition of the *Springfield (OH) News*.

May 2—BLANKS IS VILLAIN AGAIN AS BRAVES DEFEAT REDS—For the second time in a week, light-hitting Braves shortstop Larvell Blanks provided extra base-hit power, this time a home run, in the Braves' ninth inning to defeat the Reds, 6–5. The two-out long ball came off reliever Clay Kirby. The victory moved the Braves into second place in the NL West over the Reds and Giants, 3½ games behind the first-place Dodgers.

May 3—REDS' NOLAN STOPS ATLANTA, ROSE STARTS AT THIRD—In a surprise move, Pete Rose started the game at third base, on a day when Foolish Pleasure was victorious in the 101st Kentucky Derby. Rose played errorless baseball at third for six innings before moving back to the outfield for the final three. Gary Nolan, who made only two appearances in 1973 and 1974, achieved his first win since October 1972 with a 6–1 victory over the Braves. Dan Driessen started the game in left field in place of Rose.

May 4—BOB WATSON NIPS CONCEPCIÓN FOR THE MILLIONTH RUN; REDS WHIP ASTROS—"The Countdown Is One" read the Riverfront Stadium scoreboard as Major League Baseball planned to acknowledge the one millionth run scored in big league history. "I never ran faster," said Dave Concepción when he hit a fifth-inning home run off Phil Niekro. "I saw everyone jumping and cheering and thought: 'I got it, I got it.'" It wasn't to be, as Astro Bob Watson had scored a few seconds earlier in San Francisco. More important-

ly, Concepción's homer, and four hits from Johnny Bench, helped Don Gullett defeat the Braves, 3–2.

May 6—SPARKY'S EXPERIMENT WORKS, ROSE HITTING SPARKS REDS—The Reds won their third straight with Pete Rose at third base. Although "still not relaxed" at the hot corner, Rose collected four hits to raise his batting average to .330 and propelled the Reds and Jack Billingham to a 7–3 victory over the visiting Padres. Joe Morgan collected three hits, including a triple and home run.

May 7—BENCH FEELING BETTER, CAUSING NL PAIN—Fred Norman spotted the Padres two runs in the first three innings before the Reds stormed back with ten unanswered tallies to prevail, 10–2. Tony Pérez tied the score with a two-run home run in the fourth, but Johnny Bench put it out of reach with a grand slam in the fifth. Bench had been scuffling with an injured shoulder but was showing signs of coming to life. César Gerónimo added three singles to the cause, and the Reds took over sole possession of second place in the NL West with a 16-12 record.

May 8—PADRES, BEHIND LOCKLEAR'S 4-FOR-4, STOP REDS—Padres ace Randy Jones allowed just four singles in a masterful four-hit 3–0 shutout of the Reds, salvaging one win in the three-game series. Gary Nolan also pitched the full nine innings, but left fielder Gene Locklear reached him for four hits, including two doubles, and Dave Winfield homered in the fourth inning.

May 9—MORGAN'S PLAY SAVES REDS, GULLETT GETS VICTORY—Joe Morgan was the star in the Reds' first trip to New York in 1975, leading the Reds to a 4–3 win over the Mets. He capped the Reds' four-run fifth-inning rally with a two-run single and also made the game's key defensive play, in the third. With the bases filled with Mets, he ranged far to his right to spear Jesus Alou's hard shot up the middle, turning it into an inning-ending double play. Don Gullett scattered eight hits in six innings to gain his fourth victory and got relief help from Pedro Borbon, Will McEnaney, and Clay Carroll.

May 10—REDS HAND METS SIXTH STRAIGHT LOSS—The Reds made it two straight in New York behind the strong starting pitching of Clay Kirby and 3⅔ no-hit innings of relief from Will McEnaney. George Foster, now a full-time member of the Reds' lineup, hit his fifth home run, and Ken Griffey got three of the Reds' eight hits in the 7–1 win.

May 11—METS APPLAUD PHILLIPS, GUNS DOWN ROSE, REDS??—The Mets took the final game of the series, 3–2, with an eighth-inning run that allowed Tom Seaver to best Jack Billingham. The Reds nearly broke the 2–2 tie in the top of the eighth, but Pete Rose, trying to score from first on Ken Griffey's double to center field, was gunned down by the relay throw from shortstop Mike Phillips. In the bottom half, Phillips led off with a single and later scored on a single by Rusty Staub.

May 13—ROOKIE SOUTHPAW STOPS REDS, 4–0—In the Reds' first trip to Philadelphia, Phillies rookie Tom Underwood tossed a six-hit shutout to stifle the powerful Reds, 4–0. Merv Rettenmund, in a rare start, managed two singles, while Gary Nolan and Pedro Borbon allowed single runs in four different innings. It was still early, but the Reds had dropped to 4½ games behind the Dodgers.

May 14—PHILS BLANK REDS AGAIN—Dick Allen, who had abruptly retired from the White Sox

the previous August, returned to baseball (and his former team, the Phillies) and received three standing ovations over the course of the game. He managed a single in three at bats, but the Phillies' 4–0 victory was largely due to Steve Carlton's seven-hit shutout. Frustrated manager Sparky Anderson was ejected by umpire Terry Tata in the first inning. The Reds' scoreless streak had reached twenty-six innings.

May 15—REDS DROP TWO, FALL 5½ BEHIND—The Reds finally got on the scoreboard but still dropped a doubleheader to the Phillies, 6–3 and 5–3, running their losing streak to five. In the first game the Reds committed three errors, including one by César Gerónimo that led to four unearned runs in the ninth inning to give the Phillies the game. Two more errors in the second game did not help either. The Reds were back to .500, at 18-18.

May 16—REDS DROP SIXTH IN ROW TO EXPOS—The Reds lost their sixth straight, 4–2, their longest losing streak since 1971. Jack Billingham pitched well in defeat, but the Reds had scored just ten runs in their six losses. Pete Rose managed two hits and was batting .303, seemingly unaffected by the move to third base.

May 17—REDS SNAP STREAK, MCENANEY GETS WIN—Following a pregame meeting and a tirade by Sparky Anderson, Ken Griffey and Johnny Bench homered in the tenth inning to defeat the Expos, 5–3, and break their six-game losing streak. Will McEnaney gained his first victory of the season in relief of Fred Norman and Pedro Borbon. Would this be the spark the club needed?

May 18—REDS "BACK ON TRACK," NOLAN IMPRESSIVE—Gary Nolan pitched a four-hit complete game, beating the Expos 6–1. Pete Rose and George Foster spurred the offense with solo home runs. An impressed Sparky Anderson commented that Nolan had pitched so well that his record should be 5-2 rather than 2-3.

May 20—TORRE FINDS REMEDY FOR SLUMP: GULLETT AND REDS—Joe Torre, hitting just .197 during his first season with the New York Mets, had four hits, two off Reds starter Don Gullett, as the Reds dropped the first game of their eight-game home stand, 6–2. Johnny Bench homered for the seventh time in the eighth inning.

May 21—PÉREZ SPARKS BIG RUN OUTBURST AS REDS DRUB METS—With Tom Seaver on the mound for the Mets, the Reds fell behind, 3–0, early and things looked bleak. But the bats came alive, the Reds knocked Seaver out in the fifth, and they rapped out thirteen hits in an 11–4 victory. Tony Pérez connected for his sixth home run of the season and drove in four runs, Dave Concepción homered, and little-used rookie Doug Flynn finished the scoring with his first Major League homer, a three-run shot off Tom Hall, who was a Red just a few weeks before.

May 23—PÉREZ RETURNING TO FORM—Tony Pérez's two-run home run in the first inning put the Reds on top to stay as they coasted to a 5–2 victory over the Phillies. Gary Nolan pitched into the seventh inning, and Clay Carroll backed him with 2⅔ innings of scoreless relief. Pérez's homer was his seventh, tying Bench for the team lead.

May 24—REDS SCORE UNEARNED RUN IN 11TH, BEAT PHILS, 3–2—Joe Morgan singled home César Gerónimo with an unearned run in the eleventh inning to give the Reds a 3–2 win. Starter Pat Darcy could not get through the fifth, but relievers Pedro Borbon, Rawly Eastwick, and Clay Carroll worked 6⅓ of scoreless relief, Carroll picking up the victory. The Reds' two runs in regulation had come from Johnny Bench's two solo home runs.

May 25—REDS DOING THEIR THING, NIP PHILADELPHIA—"No one can stop us when we are doing our thing," crowed Joe Morgan after his two hits helped the Reds to a 4–3 victory and a sweep of the three-game series with the Phillies. Clay Kirby outpitched Jim Lonborg for the victory. The big blow was a two-out, three-run double by César Gerónimo in the third inning.

May 26—BENCH'S SLAM GETS GRAND RECEPTION FROM FANS—The Reds swept a double-header from the visiting Montreal Expos, 4–3 and 5–4, extending their winning streak to six games. In the first game the Reds scored what turned out to be the winning run on a seventh-inning balk by Woody Fryman. In the nightcap the Expos built up a 4–0 lead, but the 25,034 fans at Riverfront Stadium "went berserk" when Johnny Bench hit a grand slam to cap a five-run fifth inning. Once again, the bullpen was brilliant in preserving Don Gullett's fifth victory. Bench's homer was his tenth of the season and gave him the league lead.

May 28—REDS WIN SEVENTH IN ROW, PULL WITHIN 1½ OF THE DODGERS—Gary Nolan tossed a two-hit shutout in a 6–0 Riverfront Stadium victory. Pepe Mangual and Rich Coggins doubled for Montreal's only hits. Joe Morgan homered in the game to give Sparky Anderson his five hundredth career victory. The Reds' seven-game winning streak was their longest in two years.

May 30—CARDS SNAP REDS' STREAK, WIN IN NINTH 5–4—Lou Brock's second hit of the night came in the bottom of the ninth and gave the Cardinals a 5–4 victory. The Reds had tied the game in the top of the inning on Pete Rose's two-run double. The Reds' attack was led by Johnny Bench's eleventh home run. Rawly Eastwick took the loss for the Reds in relief.

May 31—GULLETT HURLS REDS PAST CARDS, SMACK THREE HOME RUNS—Joe Morgan, George Foster, and Ken Griffey homered for the Reds as Don Gullett hurled a four-hit shutout against the Cardinals. Morgan's homer came off Bob Gibson, whose record fell to 1-5. Gibson became the second former Cy Young Award winner to be defeated by the Reds in a week and the fourth in May (Phil Niekro, Tom Seaver, Jim Lonborg, Gibson). The Reds finished 16-10 for the month of May.

NL West Standings, May 31, 1975

TEAM	W	L	GB
Los Angeles	30	20	—
Cincinnati	28	21	1.5
San Francisco	23	22	4.5
San Diego	24	24	5.0
Atlanta	22	27	7.5
Houston	20	31	10.5

Chapter 21. **Johnny Bench**

Mark Armour

AGE	G	AB	R	H	2B	3B	HR	TB	RBI	BB	SO	BAV	OBP	SLG	SB	GDP	HBP
27	142	530	83	150	39	1	28	275	110	65	108	.283	.359	.519	11	12	2

A generation after Johnny Bench's last game, he remains the gold standard for baseball catchers of any era. By the age of twenty he had redefined how to play the position, and by twenty-two he was the biggest star, at any position, in all of baseball. Catching eventually took its toll, moving him to the infield by his early thirties and to retirement by age thirty-five, but his first decade with the Cincinnati Reds was enough to make him most experts' choice as the greatest catcher who ever played the game. Ten Gold Gloves, two Most Valuable Player Awards, and his central role in two world championships made him an easy choice for the Baseball Hall of Fame at the early age of forty-one.

Johnny Lee Bench was born on December 7, 1947, in Oklahoma City, the son of Ted, a truck driver, and Katy Bench. The family moved a few times in the area but eventually settled in Binger, about sixty miles west of Oklahoma City, when Johnny was about five. He had two older brothers, Teddy and William, and a younger sister, Marilyn. It was in Binger that Johnny remembered first playing ball, using, as many kids from his generation recall, balls and bats kept together with electrical tape. Ted had been a ballplayer, playing in high school and in the U.S. Army, but by the time World War II ended he was too old. Instead, he poured his dreams into his three boys, all of whom played organized ball in the area. Ted started a boys' team when Johnny was six, buying the uniforms and driving the team to games in his truck. Johnny played catcher right away. "My father said catching was the quickest way to the big leagues, because that's what they wanted," Bench recalled.[1]

Bench remembered being inspired watching fel-

Johnny Bench might have been the most famous star in the game in 1975, in the middle of his great career.

low Oklahoman Mickey Mantle on television as a kid. Mantle was from Commerce, nearly three hundred miles away, but his rise to stardom helped plant a seed of possibility in the youngster's head. By the second grade Bench was telling his teacher that he was going to be a Major League ballplayer, and within a few years he was practicing his autograph to prepare for his future. He played catcher and pitcher throughout his youth in organized leagues, from Little League through American Legion. While starring in both basketball and baseball at Binger High School (he was All-State in each sport) and excelling academically (valedictorian in his class of twenty-one), he did a lot of hunting and worked hard—picking cotton, working in the peanut fields, and mowing lawns. His high school years were also marred by a tragic accident—a bus carrying his baseball team lost its brakes and rolled down a fifty-foot ravine, killing two of Bench's friends and teammates. Bench was knocked unconscious but otherwise escaped physical harm. The details of the event remained with him for many years, however.[2]

In June 1965, in baseball's first free-agent draft for amateurs, the Cincinnati Reds selected Bench in the second round, the thirty-sixth overall pick. Bench briefly considered attending college on a baseball/basketball scholarship but instead signed with Cincinnati scout Tony Robello for $6,000 plus college tuition. Bench was assigned to Tampa of the Florida State League, where he played with Bernie Carbo and Hal McRae. He hit .248 with two home runs but drew good reviews for his defense. The next spring he trained with the Reds, also in Tampa, and the eighteen-year-old was confident. "To tell the truth," he recalled, "I wasn't overwhelmed."[3] While some youngsters take years to feel comfortable with their Major League teammates, Bench immediately felt, and acted, like a leader.

Reds manager Don Heffner considered keeping the eighteen-year-old Bench in 1966 but instead sent him to Hampton, Virginia, to play for the Peninsula Grays in the Single-A Carolina League. All he did there was win the league Player of the Year Award, hitting .294 with twenty-two home runs before being called up to Triple-A Buffalo (New York). Before he left, the Peninsula club retired his uniform number 8. Bench's stay in Buffalo was not so kind—in his very first inning for the club he took a foul tip on his right thumb and broke it, ending his season. What's more, on his long drive back to Binger, driving a 1965 Ford Fairlane he had bought with his bonus money, he collided with a drunk driver and wound up in the hospital.

Again, as in the bus crash in high school, Bench felt lucky to escape, only having to endure twenty-seven stitches in his scalp.

Still just nineteen, Bench returned to Buffalo in 1967 and starred, hitting .259 with twenty-three home runs and playing great defense. Buffalo was a veteran team, filled with former Major Leaguers in their thirties. Bench later credited the veterans in the club for being supportive and not resentful of his future and promise. Steve Boros, who roomed with Bench, was particularly helpful, teaching the youngster how to focus on the game with all the distractions available to a young man away from home.[4] After the season Bench was named the Minor League Player of the Year by the *Sporting News*.

The Reds promoted Bench in late August and he started twenty-six games down the stretch for a team out of contention. He got his first hit off the Phillies' Chris Short on August 30 and his first home run off the Braves' Jim Britton in Atlanta on September 20. Bench did not hit well that month (.163 and the one homer) but the Reds saw enough to make a commitment, trading two-time Gold Glove and three-time All-Star catcher Johnny Edwards (just twenty-nine years old) to St. Louis to clear the way for the twenty-year-old Bench. In March 1968 he was one of five young players featured on the cover of *Sports Illustrated*, beneath the headline "The Best Rookies of 1968."[5]

Bench's rise to stardom was rapid. After playing briefly in two early season contests, he got his first start on April 17 and stayed in the lineup for eighty-one straight games. In all, he caught 154 games, a record for a rookie catcher, and hit .272 with fifteen home runs and eighty-two RBIs. These were excellent numbers in 1968, when the league average was .243. Bench's power numbers led all league catchers, and his forty doubles were third in the league for all players. Though he started slowly, by September he was batting fourth for the team that scored the most runs in the league. Bench was selected to his first All-Star Game, catching the ninth inning of the National League's 1–0 victory in Houston's Astrodome, and was named the NL Rookie of the Year after the season.

It was for his defense that Bench garnered the most praise. Of his throwing arm, which would keep would-be base stealers honest for the next decade, Roy Blount Jr. wrote, "It is about the size of a good healthy leg, and it works like a recoilless rifle."[6] Bench had grown to 6 feet 1 and 200 pounds, but he seemed both larger and more agile. He had huge hands—he could palm a basketball in high school and could hold seven baseballs in his throwing hand (a feat he was often called on to perform for the cameras). He caught one-handed, one of the first catchers to do so, with his right hand resting behind his back to protect it from foul tips—Bench had broken his thumb in Buffalo in 1966, after all. He used a hinged catcher's mitt, rather than the prevalent circular "pillow" style, allowing him to better make plays on bunts or on plays at the plate. After Bench took a high throw and tagged out a Chicago runner in his rookie year, Cubs manager Leo Durocher exclaimed, "I still don't believe it. I have never seen that play executed so precisely."[7] Herman Franks, the Giants' manager (and former Major League receiver), saw Bench make a similar play against his club and said afterward that Bench was the "best catcher I've seen in 20 years."[8] It was no surprise when he became the first rookie catcher to win a Gold Glove for his defense.

Along with his great catching, Bench stood out for his confident leadership at a young age. The Reds' pitchers marveled at how great a game he could call, how well he knew the league's hitters so quickly. In 1967, during his late-season call-up, the nineteen-year-old went out into the infield and told veteran shortstop Leo Cardenas to reposition himself for the upcoming batter. Cardenas screamed at his catcher and did not move, but this did not change Bench's belief that he had acted properly. In his rookie year he would often go out the mound and tell the pitcher to bear down, or throw harder, or not be afraid

to throw the curve to the next hitter. The twenty-year-old once deigned to instruct Jim Maloney, the team's star pitcher, who stared at him in disbelief. Manager Dave Bristol waved Bench back to the plate, then smiled and told the pitcher, "You know, he's right." Maloney soon came around. "So help me, this kid coaches me. And I like it. . . . When you're in a big sweat and nervous, he can calm you down more ways than I have ever seen."[9]

One of the best players in the game as a rookie, Bench got better still. His world-class defense remained stellar, as he won Gold Gloves in his first ten seasons and became arguably the greatest defensive catcher in history. In 1969 he hit twenty-six home runs, drove in ninety runs, and batted .293, establishing himself as the best-hitting catcher in the game. He started his first All-Star Game, hitting a long home run and a single, before getting robbed of a second home run by Carl Yastrzemski's leaping grab over the left-field fence at Washington's RFK Stadium. The Reds rode their great hitting into the NL West race before ending in third place, four games behind the Atlanta Braves.

After the 1969 season the Reds hired Sparky Anderson as manager, promoted a few key rookies, and became a juggernaut. The 1970 club had a ten-game lead in mid-June and never looked back, finishing with 102 wins and an easy division title. Bench led the way with an astonishing season, topping the league with forty-five home runs and 148 RBIs and easily capturing the league MVP Award. Although the season ended in disappointment in a five-game World Series loss to the Baltimore Orioles, Johnny Bench had become as big as baseball star as there was—a twenty-two-year-old seemingly without weakness on the field, and a handsome and articulate person off the field. Not surprisingly, he was besieged with endorsement opportunities and banquet invitations. He went to Vietnam with Bob Hope and the USO, golfed with Arnold Palmer, talked and sang on talk shows, appeared in the television program *Mission Impossible*, and began hosting his own weekly television show in Cincinnati. As Bench later put it, "My push for visibility during the offseason, even at age twenty-two, was intentional."[10]

After giving Bench a heavy workload in his first two seasons, Anderson began "resting" him by playing him at other positions for entire games or for partial games—in 1970 he started games at first base and all three outfield positions, for a total of twenty-two games. His biggest offensive performance of 1970 came in a July 26 game at the new Riverfront Stadium in which he played left field: 4-for-5, including three home runs, all off Cardinals pitcher Steve Carlton. Throughout the remainder of his prime catching years, Bench generally started twenty or thirty games at other positions, keeping his bat in the lineup while giving his legs a bit of a rest.

The 1971 season was a bump in the road for the Reds (who fell to fourth place) and for Bench (who hit just .238 with twenty-seven homers). The team played without an injured Bobby Tolan all year and also had off years from Tony Pérez and several other players, and Bench's drop of 87 RBIs (from 148 to 61) is telling both for Bench's performance and for the fewer base runners ahead of him. He still won his usual Gold Glove and hit a long home run off Vida Blue in the All-Star Game at Detroit's Tiger Stadium. But for Bench, it was a humbling season.

Fortified by the acquisition of second baseman Joe Morgan and others in the off-season, Bench and the Reds stormed back in 1972, winning the division by 10½ games and returning to the postseason. In the bottom of the ninth inning of the decisive Game Five of the NLCS, Bench's dramatic lead-off home run to right field against Pittsburgh's Dave Guisti tied the contest before the Reds plated another run to win the NL pennant. Bench led the way with a league-leading forty home runs and 125 RBIs while also drawing one hundred walks, for a club that lost a seven-game World Series to the Oakland Athletics. The most memorable image of Bench from that Fall Classic is one he would like to forget. In the top

of the eighth inning of Game Three in Oakland, Bench was facing Rollie Fingers with runners on second and third and one out. The Reds were leading 1–0 in the game but trailing in the series, 2–0. When the count reached 3-2, Oakland manager Dick Williams came out to the mound and pointed to Bench and first base, a clear signal that he wanted to walk the slugger. The A's catcher, Gene Tenace, after returning from the conference on the mound stood to receive an intentional ball, then slyly resumed his position as Fingers threw a slider on the outside corner that Bench took with his bat on his shoulder. A memorable moment, but Bench could take solace that the Reds held on to win the game.

Late in the 1972 season a routine physical examination turned up a growth on Bench's lung that the doctors could not identify. Telling only close friends and the Reds management, Bench played the end of the season and the postseason with understandable worry hanging over his head. He finally had an operation on December 9. The surgeon had to make a twelve-inch incision under his right arm and break a rib, finally extracting a benign lesion that Bench likely got from breathing an airborne fungus. After several weeks of pain from the operation, Bench went to spring training fully healed.

The next two seasons were excellent ones for Bench and the Reds, though the club began to get a reputation as a great team that could not finish it off in October. The 1973 club won ninety-nine games, the most in baseball, yet lost the playoff series to a New York Mets team with eighty-two wins. The next year they won ninety-eight games but lost the NL West to the Dodgers. Bench contributed twenty-five home runs and 104 RBIs to the 1973 club, then thirty-three and 129 in 1974, his third time leading the league in RBIs.

The Reds finally broke through with their long-expected championship in 1975, winning 108 games (the most in the NL in sixty-six years) and defeating the Pittsburgh Pirates in the playoffs and the Boston Red Sox in a dramatic seven-game World Series. Bench hit a big double to start a decisive rally in the ninth inning of Game Two and homered off Rick Wise to begin the Cincinnati scoring in Game Three, but all that took a backseat when he embraced Will McEnaney, a famous image captured on the cover of *Sports Illustrated*, after the final out in the final game. Personally, it was a difficult year despite his success. He hurt his shoulder in a collision at home plate in April and hit well through a lot of pain (twenty-eight home runs, 110 RBIS, .283 average) before battling the flu through most of the postseason.

Bench's off-field life also became very public during the year. He had always had a very active social life, a very eligible bachelor regularly photographed with models and actresses. This ended before the 1975 season when he married Vicki Lynne Chesser, who had been Miss South Carolina and a runner-up in the 1970 Miss USA pageant. Bench saw her in a toothpaste commercial and called her up for a date. The two had known each other for four days when Bench proposed and for seven weeks when they married. By the end of the 1975 season they were separated and divorced quickly. The two had a large, public wedding, and details of their rocky relationship inevitably found their way into the tabloids as well. Bench soon returned to his bachelor ways. "There used to be a lot of beautiful women down at the ballpark," said a friend. "Now, they're going to be back."[11] Bench remained single for the rest of his playing career.

The next season was another great one for the Reds, and Bench's life off the field was less stressful, but he battled cramps in his back that affected his swing and his throwing. His 135 games were then a career low, and he slumped to hit .234 with just seventy-four RBIS for a great offensive team. After what might have been his worst regular season, Bench tacked on his greatest postseason, hitting .444 with three home runs as the Reds swept the Philadelphia Phillies and New York Yankees in seven total games. "When Johnny Bench was born,"

Sparky Anderson told the press in the raucous clubhouse after the World Series, "I believe God came down and touched his mother on the forehead and said, 'I'm going to give you a son who will be one of the greatest baseball players ever seen.'" For Bench, after his down season, the feeling was even better than 1975; he called it a "personal triumph."[12]

Bench had his last big season in 1977, bouncing back to hit thirty-one home runs, drive home 109 runs, and bat .275 while capturing his tenth consecutive Gold Glove. The Reds fell to eighty-eight wins and second place in the NL West, and the Big Red Machine began to fade away. Tony Pérez was traded after the 1976 season, and within a few years Sparky Anderson, Pete Rose, and Joe Morgan were wearing different uniforms. Only Bench stayed on, signing a five-year contract at $400,000 per year after the 1977 season. It was big money for the time, but he could have gotten more had he signed elsewhere.

At the end of the 1977 season the twenty-nine-year-old Bench had played for ten years and many historians had concluded that he was the greatest catcher ever. He had had a couple of off years, slumps he attributed to catching every day. During his career he broke six bones in each foot from foul tips, twice broke his thumb, and also battled problems with his back and shoulder from collisions. After his playing career he had left and right hip replacements, injuries he dated back to his bus and car accidents as a teenager. Bench knew the price he paid but took pride in his reputation for playing with pain. "Are there times I wish I hadn't caught? Sure. But then I wouldn't have been Johnny Bench."[13]

Bench remained a star for a few more years, though minor injuries kept him out of the lineup or at other positions more and more. He played in just 120 games (with 96 starts at catcher) in 1978, though he continued to hit well (twenty-three home runs). He played a bit more in 1979 (130 games) for new manager John McNamara and drove in eighty runs. The revamped Reds' surprising division title brought Bench to the postseason for the sixth and final time, and he finished 3-for-12 with a home run in the three-game NLCS sweep by the Pirates. Bench played in ten postseason series and hit at least one home run in nine of them.

After one final season as a fine-hitting catcher (twenty-four home runs in 114 games), Bench played the infield for the rest of his career. He played first base and battled injuries during the strike-shortened 1981 season, then finished up with two forgettable years as a mediocre third baseman. As he might have said, he was no longer Johnny Bench. He announced his retirement from the game during the 1983 season and spent the rest of the summer playing to cheers at all the different National League parks. In his final at bat, on September 29, 1983, he stroked a pinch-hit two-run single off the Giants' Mark Calvert before the home crowd at Riverfront Stadium. Gary Redus pinch-ran, and Bench's magnificent career was over.

In the ensuing years, Bench remained a public figure around baseball. He broadcast games on radio and television and in the 1980s hosted *The Baseball Bunch*, a syndicated TV show in which a group of boys and girls learned the finer points of the game from Bench and other current or former players. He became a regular public speaker and was often called upon by the Reds or Major League Baseball to speak at a ceremony to honor an old teammate or a new ballpark. An avid and excellent golfer, he participated in many celebrity events during his career and in senior tour events once he turned fifty years old.

As of 2012 Bench was married to his fourth wife, the former Lauren Biachaai. Bench's son Bobby was born in 1989 and graduated from Boston University, and Johnny and Lauren had two sons, Justin and Joshua.

Bench was elected to the Baseball Hall of Fame in 1989, receiving 96 percent of the vote in his first year of eligibility. He had made the Reds Hall of Fame in 1986, when the club permanently retired his uniform number 5. He was named to Major League Baseball's

All-Century team as the top-ranking catcher, and many organizations have named him baseball's best-ever catcher. Since 2000 the Johnny Bench Award has been presented after the conclusion of the College World Series to honor the top Division I baseball catcher. In 2008 the Reds honored him again, with a bronze statue outside the new Great American Ballpark. Fittingly, the statue shows Bench in full gear throwing out a runner with his powerful right arm.

No one has ever done it better.

Chapter 22. **Pat Darcy**

Gregory H. Wolf

AGE	W	L	PCT.	ERA	G	GS	GF	CG	SHO	SV	IP	H	BB	SO	HBP	WP
25	11	5	.688	3.58	27	22	3	1	0	1	130.2	134	59	46	0	2

With his twenty-ninth pitch of the game on October 21, 1975, Cincinnati Reds relief pitcher Pat Darcy retired his sixth consecutive Boston Red Sox batter, Carl Yastrzemski, on a weak grounder to shortstop Dave Concepción to end the eleventh inning and keep the score tied in the most pressure-packed game of his life: Game Six of the 1975 World Series. Darcy, a twenty-five-year-old rookie and, surprisingly, the winner of eleven games during the regular season for Reds, had imagined such moments as a child. "For some reason," he remembered thirty-six years later, "as I was coming into Game Six, I flashed back to when I was a kid and remembered thinking, 'What would it be like to be on the mound at a critical juncture in a World Series game and have to make a good play? Could I do it?'"[1]

With consecutive one-out singles by Tony Pérez and George Foster, the Reds threatened in the top of the twelfth inning. A victory in Boston would give Cincinnati its first World Series championship since 1940. With mounting tension, Red Sox pitcher Rick Wise set down Concepción and César Gerónimo to end the inning. Calm and collected, Darcy went to the mound and threw his warmup tosses to Bench. Facing Carlton Fisk, he threw his thirtieth pitch and home plate umpire Satch Davidson signaled ball one. At 12:34 a.m. (ET), in the second-longest World Series game at the time (consuming four hours and one minute), Darcy then threw what he intended to be a hard, sinking fastball inside, but it sailed high. It was his only mistake of the game. Fisk unloaded a long high drive down the left-field line. He waved, pushed, and willed the ball to stay fair, and the result was one of baseball's most iconic

Most famous for throwing one of history's most famous home runs, Pat Darcy finished 11-5 on the 1975 Reds.

moments, Fisk's game-winning walk-off home run. Darcy and the Reds were the losers. But unlike the New York Yankees after Ralph Terry surrendered a Series-ending home run to Bill Mazeroski in 1960, Darcy and the Big Red Machine would get another chance, in Game Seven, which, because Fisk's winning blow came after midnight, would begin the same day. This time victory was theirs.

For Pat Darcy, the pitcher victimized by the Red Sox catcher, the pitch was the last one of his only full season in the Major Leagues. After an undistinguished five-year career in the Houston Astros' farm system, Darcy had been acquired by the Reds in 1974 and flourished under the tutelage of Manager Vern Rapp with the Triple-A Indianapolis Indians, earning a late season call-up to the Major Leagues. In 1975 Darcy emerged from relative obscurity to win his last nine decisions as the Cincinnati Reds' fifth starter on his way to a surprising 11-5 record. With the Reds' surfeit of starting pitchers he was limited to two relief appearances in the World Series. Then he was beset by shoulder problems in 1976, was sent back to Indianapolis in midseason, and never made it back to the Major Leagues

Patrick Leonard Darcy was born on May 12, 1950, in Troy, Ohio (twenty miles north of Dayton), the son of an FBI agent. When he was three years old, his father, Lyman, moved the family to Tucson, Arizona, after a brief period in New Mexico. "Like a lot of people, we moved out here because of illness in the family. My sister had asthma," Darcy said of the move to the dry, desert climate.[2] Young Darcy was involved with sports his entire childhood. At Rincon High School he starred on the baseball team from 1966 to 1968 as an outfielder and pitcher. In his senior season, the team, coached by Gilbert Carrillo and assisted by former Red Sox Minor League infielder Bill Mehle, finished second in the Class 5A state baseball tournament. After high school Darcy entered Mesa Community College, where he played baseball in 1969 as his team won the Arizona Community College Athletic Conference championship. A tall, lanky, hard-throwing, right-handed starting pitcher, Darcy attracted the attention of scouts but went undrafted that year and signed a free-agent contract with the Houston Astros in the summer.

Darcy was assigned to the Covington (Virginia) Astros of the Rookie-level Appalachian League, where one of his teammates was fellow nineteen-year-old pitcher J. R. Richard. Darcy was 2-2 in twenty-eight innings with a 5.46 earned run average.[3] He split the 1970 season with Williamsport in the short-season New York–Pennsylvania League and Raleigh-Durham in the Class A Carolina League.

With an impressive cumulative ERA of 2.93 in thirteen starts, Darcy was primed for stiffer competition in 1971, and he was one of the few bright spots for the 1971 Columbus (Georgia) Astros in the Double-A Dixie Association. With a deceptive 5-10 record, he was the victim of poor run support from a team that won just fifty-one games and lost ninety-one. Darcy's 2.56 ERA ranked fifth in the southern section of the league among starters with more than one hundred innings pitched and was his career low. The 6-foot-3 right-hander pitched a no-hitter on August 29 against the league champion Charlotte (North Carolina) Hornets, striking out ten.

Because of his flights of wildness (seventy walks and thirteen wild pitches in 123 innings in 1971), Darcy began the 1972 season back at Columbus and showed better control (fifty walks in 129 innings). He spent part of this season on the roster with his former high school teammate Jim Crawford, who later went on to pitch for Houston and Detroit. In August Darcy was promoted to Triple-A Oklahoma City, where he did not allow an earned run in sixteen innings pitched and shut out Denver on three hits.

Darcy went to spring training with the Astros in 1973 but spent the entire season with the Astros' new affiliate in the American Association, the Denver Bears. Despite suffering from a sore ankle all season, Darcy posted a 3.57 ERA, almost two runs better than the last-place team's ERA. Darcy was hit by a flying bat during a pregame drill on August 15 and required eighteen stitches in his right cheek.[4]

Darcy was considered one of the Astros' top pitching prospects. But in February 1974, hoping to improve its defense and make a push for the National League West title, the team traded him to the Reds for former All-Star infielder Denis Menke and cash. "The trade was a shock," Darcy said. "I grew up in the Houston organization and knew a lot of their players. . . . I was on their 40-man roster. Then

[General Manager] Spec Richardson called and said I was traded to Cincinnati. I said, 'Cincinnati?' I couldn't believe it."[5]

Darcy arrived at the Reds' camp and experienced a different culture. "Bob Howsam, the Reds' general manager, called and told me about the rules, especially about the haircuts. I knew about that because at Denver, I had pitched against Indianapolis [the Reds' Triple-A affiliate] a lot. So when I reported to the Reds, I went up to Sparky and said I knew the rules and got a haircut. He said, 'Fine kid, but get another haircut.' It wasn't short enough for Sparky."[6] But Darcy was impressed by the Reds' winning attitude and confidence. "I didn't know anybody on the roster but the culture at Cincinnati was so much different than Houston. Larry Shepard was the Reds' pitching coach and he came up to me and said, 'We don't lose 2–1 and 3–2 games here. We just don't do it.'"[7]

Assigned to the Reds' Triple-A affiliate, Indianapolis, Darcy excelled under Manager Vern Rapp and played for a first-place team for the first time in professional baseball. (The Indians won a division championship but lost to Tulsa in the league championship playoff.) On a pitching staff that included Joaquin Andujar, Tom Carroll, Rawly Eastwick, Gary Nolan, Pat Zachry, and other former and future Major Leaguers, Darcy won twelve games and his 3.41 ERA was the lowest among the starters. He was named to the American Association All-Star team. Darcy was rewarded with a September call-up to the Reds.

Thrust into a heated pennant race, Darcy made his Major League debut in a start at Riverfront Stadium against the Atlanta Braves on September 12. Darcy stifled the Braves' bats through seven innings, giving up just four hits and one run. He was lifted with two outs in the eighth after surrendering a home run to Darrell Evans and a single to Dusty Baker but was the winning pitcher in the 6–2 victory. Darcy singled with two outs in the fourth inning and later scored when Johnny Bench hit a grand slam. Darcy pitched in five more games, including another start (a no-decision) for the second-place Reds. He finished with a 3.71 ERA in seventeen innings pitched.

Darcy made the squad in 1975 and got the victory on Opening Day, pitching two scoreless innings against the Los Angeles Dodgers. "I got to know Pat pretty well in spring training," said Joe Morgan, impressed with Darcy's poise and control with runners on the corners and his one out in the fourteenth inning of the Dodgers game. "I could tell he had a lot of guts and wasn't going to panic."[8] On April 20 he made the first of his twenty-two starts that season, pitching seven innings of one-run ball against his former team, the Astros. Bothered by blisters on his pitching hand, Darcy missed several starts in late May and early June. On July 30 he pitched his only Major League complete game, a victory over the San Francisco Giants. The complete game was the first for a Reds starter in forty-five games, a record at the time. "[Darcy's] got the liveliest arm on the team," said Sparky Anderson, known as "Captain Hook" for his habit of pulling starting pitchers at their first sign of trouble.[9]

Winning his last nine decisions of the season, Darcy came out of relative obscurity to earn eleven victories. He posted a 3.58 ERA. "If Sparky would have started me more, I would have won 20," said the self-assured Darcy.[10] Described as a "nice-looking, surfer-type blond," Darcy, who volunteered at a mental health clinic in Tucson in the off-season, got along well with his teammates and had a reputation for being somewhat quirky.[11] "Darcy is completely uninhibited and has confidence in himself," said Reds pitching coach Shepard. "He's a right-hander, but with all of the eccentricities of a left-hander. . . . Who else would go out there in the outfield during batting practice and take yoga exercise?"[12]

Having pitched just twice in relief during the last two weeks of the season, Darcy saw no action in the NLCS against Pittsburgh, whom the Reds, winners of 108 games, swept in three games. In the World

GREGORY H. WOLF

Series he relieved Gary Nolan in Game Three and gave up one run in two innings during an exciting ten-inning victory.

"We arrived in Boston up three games to two, and got hit by three days of rain," Darcy recalled in 2011. "During those three days of rain, there wasn't a strength coach, nutritionist, or sports psychologist to be found. When it was time to play baseball, we just went out and played."[13] When he entered the game in the tenth inning of Game Six, Darcy was the Reds' eighth pitcher, tying a World Series record. He retired the Red Sox in order in the tenth and eleventh innings, but he noticed something. "I threw 28 pitches in those two innings and hadn't worked for quite a while," he said. (Between September 27 and the World Series, Darcy had pitched only two-thirds of an inning.) "I could tell I was losing some zip on my fastball."[14] After his fateful second pitch to Fisk, Darcy watched over his right shoulder as the arcing shot hit the foul pole and left-field umpire Dick Stello signaled a home run. "I thought it was going to be foul," Darcy said. "I have no excuses. I tried to get the ball low—and it sailed."[15]

"After Game Six, Sparky told me I'd done well to get the game into the 12th inning," Darcy said. "Nobody was despondent. Everybody just sat around saying what a great game it was, and that we'd get 'em tomorrow."[16] In another nail-biter, the Reds came back from a 3–0 deficit and won Game Seven 4–3 in Boston and thus the World Series when Joe Morgan singled home Ken Griffey in the top of the ninth inning. With the Reds' victory, as dramatic as Fisk's home run was, Darcy's name has not been assigned to baseball lore and memory like that of the Brooklyn Dodgers' Ralph Branca, whom Bobby Thomson victimized in 1951, or the Yankees' Floyd (Bill) Bevens, who was just one out from the first no-hitter in World Series history before surrendering a walk-off two-run double to the Dodgers' Cookie Lavagetto in 1947.

After one of the most exciting World Series ever, baseball started on a sour note in 1976 when the owners locked out the players from March 1 to March 17 over disputes on free agency and the free-agent draft. The reduction of spring training to three weeks caused havoc for pitchers. The Reds had made substantial changes in their staff in the off-season, trading starter Clay Kirby to the Montreal Expos and reliever Clay Carroll to the Chicago White Sox. Despite Darcy's surprising eleven-win campaign the previous year, he was not guaranteed a place in the rotation going into spring training. But he pitched well in the curtailed period and Don Gullett was injured, so Darcy won a spot. In his first start, on April 11 against the Astros, Darcy retired the first fifteen batters he faced before giving up three runs in the sixth inning but earned a win as the Reds scored nine runs. In his next start, five days later, he lost his spot in the rotation when he allowed twelve base runners in six innings against the Giants. After nine more appearances (two starts), Darcy was optioned to Indianapolis on June 16. "Darcy can't relieve and we just didn't have room for him in the starting rotation," Anderson said.[17] Darcy never made it back to the Major Leagues. His record for the Reds in 1976 was 2-3, with a 6.23 ERA in thirty-nine innings pitched.

At Indianapolis the rest of the season, Darcy suffered from shoulder problems and made only sixteen starts, going 5-7 as he suffered through his most frustrating season as a professional. With a 4.28 ERA in 103 innings at Indianapolis and limited opportunity for promotion, Darcy decided not to re-sign with Reds and played out his option. In March 1977 he was traded to the St. Louis Cardinals for pitcher Mike Caldwell. Assigned to the Cardinals' Triple-A affiliate in the American Association, the New Orleans Pelicans, Darcy continued to suffer from chronic arm and shoulder pains. Sporting a 12.60 ERA after just three appearances, the twenty-seven-year old was demoted to St. Petersburg in the Florida State League. Going from a World Series championship and the high life in October 1975 to cramped bus rides and fast food two years later in Class A baseball, Darcy quipped, "It is somewhat of a culture shock."[18]

After earning a respectable 7-6 record and 3.09 ERA for the Arkansas Travelers (Double-A Texas League) in 1978 despite arm troubles that limited him to sixteen starts, Darcy was out of baseball entirely in 1979. Released by the Cardinals, he signed with the Iowa Oaks, the Chicago White Sox's Triple-A team, for 1980. After walking fourteen batters in twelve innings, he was released.

A winner of ten consecutive decisions over the course of two seasons, Darcy finished his three-year Major League career with a 14-8 record and a 4.15 ERA in 186⅔ innings pitched. In his ten-year Minor League career, he posted a 55-59 record with a 3.47 ERA.

After baseball, Darcy enrolled at the University of Arizona and earned a bachelor's degree but noted, "It was hard to go back because I was almost 30 years old."[19] He began a new career in real estate and business in Tucson. With his wife, Judy, a longtime teacher in the Tucson Unified School District, Darcy had three children, Kimberly, Ryan, and Kathleen. Active in politics, Darcy ran twice for mayor of Tucson. He became a supporter of public parks and athletic opportunities for people of all ages in Tucson and Pima County. Darcy remained close to baseball, coaching Little League, semipro, and softball teams, and for decades, he has hosted a local radio sports talk program. Owing to his close relationship with former Reds general manager Bob Howsam, who was instrumental in bringing expansion baseball to Denver, Darcy played a pivotal role in making Tucson the Rockies' spring training headquarters in 1993.

"You can't dwell on it. . . . You have to move on from that moment no matter how big it is," Darcy said about serving up one of the most famous home runs in baseball.[20] With fond memories of his time on one of the best teams in baseball history, Darcy never lost his love for baseball.

GREGORY H. WOLF

Chapter 23. **Dan Driessen**

Gregory H. Wolf

AGE	G	AB	R	H	2B	3B	HR	TB	RBI	BB	SO	BAV	OBP	SLG	SB	GDP	HBP
23	88	210	38	59	8	1	7	90	38	35	30	.281	.386	.429	10	8	2

An integral role player on the Big Red Machine's World Series–winning teams in 1975 and 1976, Dan Driessen developed into a dependable, consistent, clutch-hitting first baseman over his fifteen-year Major League career. One of the best fielding first-sackers of his era, Driessen was the first designated hitter in the history of the National League when he starred for the Reds in the 1976 World Series against the New York Yankees.

Born on July 29, 1951, in Hilton Head Island, South Carolina, long before it established its reputation as a destination for wealthy tourists, Daniel Driessen was one of eight children raised by his mother in a poor, rural, and segregated area. "We had to struggle," Driessen told a sportswriter in 1978. "My father died when I was 5 years old."[1] Working odd jobs to help support his mother and siblings from a young age and with little money or opportunity for entertainment, Driessen developed a passion for baseball, which could be played almost year-round in the warm and humid climate. "I really learned from playing the game with my brothers," Driessen said.[2] Though many of the segregated and impoverished schools of the area could not afford to field sports teams, the region had a long and strong tradition of semipro teams for African Americans. By the age of fourteen Driessen had begun to play for the Hilton Head Island Blue Jays, with whom he faced seasoned competition for the next four years on the weekends while attending Michael C. High School.

Having distinguishing himself as a hard-nosed catcher for the Blue Jays, Driessen attracted the attention of Harold J. Young, the manager of the Boll Weevils, a black semipro team in Hardeeville, South

A backup at both first base and the outfield in 1975, Dan Driessen ended up with a solid fifteen-year career in the National League.

Carolina. Young persuaded the seventeen-year-old Driessen to join his team in 1969 and personally drove him back and forth from Hardeeville to Hilton Head Island, a two-hour round trip on country roads. Because the games attracted no professional baseball scouts, Young decided to take matters in his own hands. He was so impressed with Dan and his older brother, Bill, who was a star pitcher, that he wrote a letter to every Major League team about the two prospects.

In the summer of 1969 the Atlanta Braves invited the left-handed-hitting Driessen to a tryout camp in Greenwood, South Carolina, conducted by Bill Lucas, the Braves' general manager. "There must have been 300 people there," recalled Driessen. "[Lucas] kept getting me back to take swings."[3] The Braves signed three players and Driessen was the last one cut. Dejected, he returned home only to find a letter from the Cincinnati Reds telling him to report to Savannah, Georgia, to work out with the team's Double-A affiliate, the Asheville Tourists. Asheville manager Alex Cosmidis was impressed and sent for a Reds representative and scout. "Bill Jamison came and signed me," Driessen said, "and since this was late July or early August, they told me not to worry about that year and come to spring training [in 1970]."[4] Completely overlooked by scouts, the undrafted Driessen signed with the Reds as an amateur free agent on August 29, 1969. "All they gave me was a Reds yearbook and a plane ticket [to spring training]," Driessen said about the day he signed.[5]

After participating in the Reds' spring training in 1970, Driessen was assigned to the Class A Tampa Tarpons, where the eighteen-year old struggled. Provided formal coaching for the first time, Driessen was worn down by playing baseball almost every day in the Florida State League. Platooning at first base, he batted just .223 with no home runs and just three extra-base hits in 242 at bats.[6] The Reds brass was not concerned by Driessen's slow start. "The one thing you don't want to do is give up too quickly on a prospect," said team president/general manager Bob Howsam. "We don't release anyone until we're absolutely certain. We give him at least two years."[7]

Driessen honed his hitting skills with the Florida Instructional League in 1970. "[He's] the finest young hitter I've ever seen come into a major-league camp," said Minor League manager Russ Nixon, whom Ken Griffey credited for helping him develop as a confident and discriminating hitter.[8]

Returning to Tampa in 1971, Driessen teamed with the twenty-one-year-old Griffey to form the most potent one-two punch in the Florida State League. Starting at first base, Driessen finished with a .327 batting average, second in the league among qualifiers, while teammate Griffey batted .342 in eighty-eight games. The duo battered pitchers again in 1972 while playing for Trois-Rivieres (Quebec) of the Double-A Eastern League. Leading the team to a division crown, Driessen was named all-league first baseman and flirted with the batting title the entire season, ultimately finishing third with a .322 mark (and Griffey fourth at .318). "He reminds me of Tony Oliva," said his manager, Jim Snyder.[9] The Reds began touting Driessen as their number-one prospect and Manager Sparky Anderson was convinced that he would be a great Major Leaguer. "I like the kid's swing," Anderson said."[10]

After spring training with the Reds in 1973, Driessen was assigned to the Indianapolis Indians in the Triple-A American Association. On a team overflowing with Major League talent, including Griffey, George Foster, Ray Knight, and Joel Youngblood, Driessen distinguished himself by his sheer athleticism. Convinced that he could play almost anywhere, the Reds had experimented with Driessen (who threw right-handed) at third base in 1972 and decided to move him permanently to third base at Indianapolis in 1973. With the consistently productive Tony Pérez occupying first base on the parent club, the Reds eyed Driessen as the eventual replacement for thirty-two-year-old Denis Menke at third base. Against Triple-A pitching in 1973, Driessen had a torrid start, batting .409 in 181 at bats, but commented, "I can't get adjusted [at third base]."[11]

With the reigning National League pennant winners mired in third place in the NL West in early June and suffering from abnormally quiet bats, the Reds called up Driessen. "I thought I would have a few days to get my feet on the ground, but [Sparky Anderson] told me I would be in the lineup the next day," he said.[12] On June 9, 1973, Driessen made his Major League debut, playing third base against Fergie Jenkins and the Cubs in Chicago. At bat with the bases full and two outs in the first inning, Driessen struck out.[13] "I had idolized [Jenkins] and now I batted against him," Driessen said about his childhood hero. "He threw me pitches I could hit, but I was so nervous, I didn't do a thing."[14] To make matters worse, Driessen made an error on the first ball hit to him when he flubbed a ground ball hit by Randy Hundley. After grounding out and lining into a double play in his next two at bats, Driessen walked, scored a run, and later smashed a double during the Reds' seven-run ninth. "I like his stance," said Cubs manager Whitey Lockman. "He looks mechanically sound as a hitter."[15]

Nicknamed the Cobra for his quick, uncoiling batting style, the rookie helped wake up the Reds' dormant bats and spark the Big Red Machine to another NL West crown with a 99-63 record. Batting almost .400 after his first ten games, he was moved to third in the batting order. Anderson conceded that third base was not Driessen's best position, but he wanted his hot bat in the game. "I didn't play Driessen at all at third base during spring training because I never thought he could handle it," Anderson said. "I'm convinced now that he can be an accomplished third baseman."[16] Nonetheless, he often replaced Driessen in late innings of games and moved him to first base to spell Tony Pérez. "We had heard for three years that Dan Driessen could hit," said Johnny Bench; consequently, it was not a surprise when the Cobra quickly adjusted to Major League pitching, finished with a .301 batting average (his career high) and tied for third in the National League Rookie of the Year voting despite playing only two-thirds of a season.[17]

Aiming for a third appearance in the World Series in four years, the streaking Reds were a heavy favorite in the NLCS over the New York Mets, winners of seventeen fewer games. After splitting the first four games, the teams were tied, 2–2, in the bottom of the fifth inning of the deciding Game Five at Shea Stadium when Driessen committed a mental mistake that, in the eyes of many Reds fans accustomed to fundamentally sound play, made him a scapegoat for the unexpected loss. With the Mets' Wayne Garrett on second base with a lead-off double, Felix Millan, in an attempt to sacrifice, bunted hard back to the pitcher, Jack Billingham, who had an easy throw to third. However, Driessen, apparently thinking that Garrett could be forced out, stepped on the base instead of tagging him. Garrett slid in safely and the misplay started a series-winning four-run rally.

After working on his fielding technique in the Florida Instructional League with coach Ron Plaza, Driessen began the 1974 season with high expectations. "He's going to be one of the best hitters around if he keeps his feet on the ground," Anderson said.[18] On a second-place team, the twenty-two-year-old Driessen hit consistently all season, finishing with a .281 average and increasing his slugging percentage from his rookie year. Disconcerting to Reds brass, however, was his erratic play at third base, forcing Anderson to replace him in late innings with light-hitting Darrel Chaney or Ray Knight. In 122 games at third base (just 36 full games), Driessen committed twenty-four errors, and his .915 fielding percentage was the lowest for all Major League third basemen.

Meanwhile, there were few problems with Driessen's hitting. A prototypical line drive and spray hitter, he hit to all fields, which made him difficult to defend against. "We don't know where he's going to hit the ball," said Reds coach Alex Grammas in 1973. Grammas expected Driessen to develop a more pronounced home run stroke after he hit just four round-trippers in his rookie year. It took a while, but by 1977 Driessen had developed somewhat of a home run punch and was in double figures for seven of the next eight seasons, the only exception being 1981, when a players' strike wiped fifty-four regular-season games off the schedule. Driessen said he developed his quick, smooth, rhythmic swing from years of chopping wood for his family's wood-burning stove.

Though his career is most readily associated with the Big Red Machine's championship seasons of 1975 and 1976, Driessen lost his starting position at third base and was used primarily as a spot starter at first base and the outfield or as a pinch hitter in those seasons. He broke his wrist in the Florida Instructional League before the 1975 season when he collided with Gary Carter at first base. He missed the first week of the season.[19] When he came back, Anderson had opted to start the light-hitting John Vukovich at third base, but when that experiment failed, he moved Pete Rose from left field to third base and inserted Driessen in Rose's spot. However, Driessen, with sparse experience in the outfield, had problems tracking fly balls and was replaced by slugger George Foster in mid-May.[20]

Despite his reduction in playing time (he had fewer at bats in 1975 and 1976 combined than in 1974), Driessen never complained or served as a distraction. "I really appreciate it," Anderson commented about his attitude, "because it's hard for a guy to do, especially [one] who can hit."[21] Though teammates called him Sleepy for his laid-back demeanor, Driessen wanted to play more regularly and voiced his displeasure with pinch-hitting. ("I'm no pinch hitter. It's boring."[22])

Batting .281 in 210 at bats in 1975 as an important and versatile role player on one of the best teams in National League history, Driessen had his moments, including a walk-off three-run home run in the eleventh inning against the Padres on June 27; however, the season was frustrating for him. He saw no action in the NLCS against the Pirates and had only two unsuccessful pinch-hit appearances against the Red Sox in the World Series.

In light of Driessen's league-leading .331 batting average with Bayamon in the Puerto Rican Winter League in the off-season, Anderson was determined to play him more in 1976; however, his slow start (he was batting just .211 in mid-June) coupled with Rose's and Pérez's stellar play at third and first limited his playing time. Without consistent opportunities to start and establish his hitting rhythm, Driessen's batting average dipped to .247, but he knocked in forty-four runs with just fifty-four hits for the pennant winners.

Driessen's moment to showcase his talents on the national stage came when he became the first designated hitter in the National League, in the 1976 World Series against the New York Yankees. After going 0-for-4 in Game One, Driessen got two hits and scored a run in Game Two. Game Three may be his career highlight: he cranked two doubles and a home run, knocked in one run, and scored twice in the Reds' 6–2 trouncing of the Yankees. Were it not for Johnny Bench's record-setting performance (8-for-15), Driessen might have been named the MVP of the Series by hitting .357 (5-for-14) and scoring four times.

(Though the DH was instituted to start the 1973 season in the American League, it was still a relatively novel concept, at least for the National League and its fans. When asked how he spent his time on the bench during a cold game night in New York, Driessen said he watched the game in the clubhouse, drank coffee, or sat dressed in uniform in the sauna in order to stay warm.[23])

In December 1976 the Reds shipped the thirty-four-year old Pérez to the Montreal Expos, opening first base for Driessen. "Danny's performance in the World Series should have bolstered his confidence. . . . Batting .375 in winter league ball [in the off-season] should make him even more confident," said Reds hitting coach Ted Kluszewski.[24] Replacing a fan favorite, hobbled by a leg injury, and off to a slow start in 1977, Driessen expected some boos in the transition. After going 9-for-16 in late April (earning him NL Player of the Week honors), Driessen enjoyed the best year of his career, hitting an even .300 with seventeen home runs, a

GREGORY H. WOLF

career-high ninety-one RBIs, and thirty-one stolen bases, the most for a Major League first baseman in sixty years.[25]

Defensively, Driessen quashed any concerns that he would be a liability in the field. "He got a bad rap while playing third base," said Kluszewski, commenting on Driessen's transition to first base. "He psyched himself out. His success will depend on how quickly he becomes comfortable in the field."[26] Driessen developed into one of the league's best (and most underrated) defensive first basemen and led the league in fielding percentage three times (1978, 1982, and 1983).

Primed for their third consecutive NL West crown in 1977, the Reds were undone by poor pitching and finished second behind the Dodgers. A small-market team with limited resources, the Big Red Machine of the 1970s was being gradually dismantled by the advent of high-spending free agency, trades, and aging players; nonetheless, they competed for the division crown and sported winning records in every year from 1977 to 1981. As for Driessen, his 1977 breakout season proved to be an exception and he batted over .250 just once in the next four seasons.

Driessen became disgruntled with the Reds in 1981 when he felt he was being slighted in favor of aging icon Johnny Bench, who could no longer catch regularly. Batting just .197, Driessen was hit on the wrist by Bob Shirley of the Cardinals on May 2 and did not bat for over two weeks, while Bench played first. Upon his return, Driessen went 0-for-11 and was again replaced by Bench. Feeling insulted, Driessen lashed out at Manager John McNamara (Sparky Anderson had been fired after the 1978 season) and General Manager Dick Wagner. "I'm not a hothead, but it came to the point where I said the hell with all this," Driessen said. "I don't want to be a part of it. I didn't say anything wrong. I wanted to be traded."[27] Then Bench broke his ankle just a few days after Driessen's outburst. Driessen resumed his duties at first base but struggled at the plate, hitting just .236. "He looks lost up there," said an anonymous Reds player, "like he's lost his confidence."[28]

With trade rumors clouding Driessen's future in Cincinnati, 1982 was a shock for the Reds, who had the Major Leagues' best record in the strike-shortened season in 1981 but were not eligible for the postseason because of the split-season playoff format. "The whole [1982] season has been like a bad dream," Driessen said after the weak-hitting Reds lost a franchise-record 101 games. "I thought we'd at least play .500 ball."[29] Driessen led the team with seventeen home runs and fifty-seven runs batted in.

Bothered by a sore left knee in 1983 that required off-season surgery, Driessen batted .277, his best since 1977, but the Reds finished in last place for the second year in a row. A meaningless game for the Reds versus the Braves, but certainly meaningful for Driessen, occurred on September 13 when he fielded a grounder and stepped on first base to end the seventh inning. The ball had been hit by his nephew, Atlanta's rookie Gerald Perry, who would have a thirteen-year Major League career—mainly as a first baseman.

With constant rumors about his imminent trade, Driessen realized his days were numbered with the only franchise he knew. In his last four years in baseball (1984–87), Driessen undertook an odyssey in which he played for four Major League and two Minor League teams. Playing for new Reds manager Vern Rapp, Driessen began the 1984 season by hitting over .300 through early June despite the off-season surgery. Struggling in fifth place, the Reds traded Driessen to the Montreal Expos on July 26 for pitchers Andy McGaffigan and Jim Jefferson. "We didn't get [Driessen] to sit on the bench," said Expos manager Bill Virdon. "We hope he'll do something to our offense."[30] Though his batting average dropped from .280 to .269 for the season, Driessen was a more effective hitter for the Expos and belted nine home runs in 169 at bats and knocked in thirty-two on just forty-three hits, while playing first base with his typical grace.

Unable to duplicate his hitting successes for the Expos in 1985, Driessen had hit just six home runs and had driven in twenty-five runs by the end of July, and the Expos shipped him to the San Francisco Giants for pitcher Bill Laskey and utility man Scot Thompson at the trading deadline. While the weak-hitting Giants were on the way to a franchise-record one hundred losses, the thirty-three-year-old Driessen took over first base duties; however, his .232 batting average was one point lower than the team's NL-worst .233. Giants general manager and president Al Rosen, the architect of the team's turn-around over the next few seasons, began shopping Driessen in the off-season, but his $700,000-plus contract was an albatross. In spring training of 1986 Driessen fell victim to a top prospect when twenty-two-year-old rookie Will Clark earned the starting nod at first base. Finding no takers for Driessen and his contract, the Giants released him on May 1.

Driessen's final year and a half reflected his passion for the game and willingness to suppress his ego for team success. After his release from the Giants he agreed to a Minor League contract with the Houston Astros' Pacific Coast League affiliate, the Tucson Toros, with no guarantee that he would be called to the parent club. As the Toros' oldest player, Driessen batted .295 in seventh games, but with little power (five home runs and thirty-five RBIs); however, he proved to be a valuable acquisition. When the Astros' top slugger, Glenn Davis, was injured on August 31 in the middle of a pennant race, the team called up Driessen. Playing first base and pinch-hitting, Driessen helped the team clinch the National League West crown by going 7-for-24 in seventeen games. He was ineligible for the playoffs because he was not on the team's active roster by August 31.

The Astros released Driessen after the season but invited him to 1987 spring training as a nonroster player. When they did not tender him a contract, Driessen thought his career might be over. He went home to Cincinnati and worked out while his agent contacted teams. In June he signed a Minor League contract with Louisville (Kentucky), the Cardinals' Triple-A affiliate. He stayed at home as much as possible and drove to and from Louisville. "It's about 100 miles," Driessen said. "I'd make it in close to an hour and a half."[31] An accomplished Major Leaguer with more than seventeen hundred games under his belt, Driessen still thought he could play. "I'd made a commitment to play," he said. "I would at least finish out the season."[32]

The Cardinals called Driessen up at the end of August to provide some veteran leadership in the midst of a tight divisional race. In a scene of déjà vu, Driessen got his chance when Jack Clark, now the Cardinals' first baseman and top slugger, injured his ankle and missed the last three weeks of the season. After Driessen hit a big first inning two-run home run off Rick Sutcliffe at Wrigley Field on September 26, Lee Thomas, the Cardinals' director of player development, remarked, "He can still hit."[33] In storybook fashion, Driessen's two-run double on October 1 against the Expos helped clinch the NL East championship for the Cardinals. "I thought I could still play," said Driessen, who knocked in eleven runs with his fourteen hits during his month with the team. "I thought I'd be cheating myself if I didn't."[34]

In his first postseason since 1979, Driessen started against the Giants' right-hand pitchers in the NLCS. "It's nice to redeem yourself," he said after he cranked two doubles and scored the tie-breaking run in Game One.[35] Capping off his Major League career in a dramatic seven-game World Series against the Minnesota Twins, Driessen played against right-handers and manned first base for the first time in his World Series career. He went 3-for-13 with two doubles, an RBI, and three runs scored.

Driessen was out of baseball entirely in 1988 after being released by the Cardinals. In 1989 his urge to continue playing led him to the Mexican League, where he played for the Yucatán Leones, and then to the Fort Myers (Florida) Sun Sox in the short-lived Senior Professional Baseball Association for the 1989–90 and 1990–91 seasons.

Driessen played first base in 1,379 of his 1,732 Major League games. He finished his fifteen-year career with a .267 batting average and one of the top career fielding percentages (.995) for first basemen. Often overlooked, Driessen may not have fulfilled predictions that he'd be a superstar, but he was a consistent and dependable hitter throughout his career. "I wasn't real bigheaded about making the front page of the news," he said when he was elected to the Reds Hall of Fame in 2011. "I was just trying to win a game."[36]

After retiring from baseball Driessen moved with his wife, Bonnie, (they were married in 1976) and their three daughters to his hometown of Hilton Head Island, where he still resided in 2012. He started an excavating and trucking company. Driessen helped coach a local high school team, where he no doubt served as tangible proof that a youngster can emerge from obscurity and follow his dreams. "Playing baseball is something that I . . . always wanted to do," he said of his never-ending passion for the game. "People would ask me when I was small what I wanted to do when I grow up, and I'd tell them 'a major-league ballplayer.'"[37]

Chapter 24. César Gerónimo

Jorge Iber

AGE	G	AB	R	H	2B	3B	HR	TB	RBI	BB	SO	BAV	OBP	SLG	SB	GDP	HBP
27	148	501	69	129	25	5	6	182	53	48	97	.257	.327	.363	13	7	4

Playing on a squad that featured such top-rank stars as Johnny Bench, Pete Rose, Joe Morgan, and Tony Pérez made it challenging for other players to gain notice in their own right. During the 1970s it was easy to overlook the contributions of "other" Reds who made up the roster of Cincinnati's Big Red Machine. While César Gerónimo is sometimes slighted by the media and public, his exceptional arm, glove, and range in center field, and his timely hitting, helped him play an essential role in bringing two World Series titles to the Queen City. Indeed, his career was marked by historic events: Gerónimo scored one of the most significant and controversial runs in World Series history in 1975 and holds one distinction (as a strikeout victim) unlikely ever to be repeated by a Major Leaguer. Once he retired after the 1983 season, Gerónimo began contributing to the sport in another way: by improving the lot of Dominican youngsters who were pursuing their dreams (athletic, academic, and personal) against what were often overwhelming odds.

César Francisco (Zorilla) Gerónimo was born on March 11, 1948, in the municipality of Santa Cruz del Seibo, El Seibo Province, Dominican Republic. While it was quite common for Dominican children of this era to not receive much formal schooling, Gerónimo's parents worked diligently so that their son would not only be properly educated but would serve the Catholic Church as a priest. With this aim, Gerónimo was enrolled in the Santo Tomas de Aquino seminary at the age of twelve and remained there for five years. Eventually he withdrew and attended (and graduated from) high school. His father was quite happy, for he had wanted his

César Gerónimo used his long stride to win four Gold Gloves in center field for the Reds.

son to pursue an athletic career. Throughout his time in these settings, there was one constant in Gerónimo's life: a love of baseball, and particularly the New York Yankees. "I liked it at seminary, but I really wanted to be a ballplayer and I knew if I went on to become a priest that would never happen," he once said.[1]

Neither the seminary nor his high school fielded a baseball team, so César instead played basketball, soccer, and slow-pitch softball (on a club with his father). Gerónimo's success on this squad, predominantly because of his strong throwing arm, led to tryouts with the New York Mets and the Yankees, and the Yankees signed the nineteen-year-old prospect in 1967 as a pitcher-outfielder. (While blessed with phenomenal arm strength, he was awful at bat.) His first two teams were in rookie leagues: Oneonta in the New York–Pennsylvania League and Johnson City (Tennessee) of the Appalachian League. His lack of hitting was evident at both locales. Gerónimo played four games for Oneonta and hit a meager .100, followed by an even more anemic .071 in nineteen games for Johnson City. The next season the Yankees moved him to Fort Lauderdale in the Florida State League hoping he would find something resembling a reasonable stroke. While there was some improvement, it was marginal (a .194 average in 109 games and 324 at bats) and the notion of moving Gerónimo permanently to the mound gained acceptance.[2]

At about this time Gerónimo came to the attention of Grady Hatton, a scout for the Houston Astros, who recommended the outfielder to his boss, Assistant General Manager John Mullen. Then, at the 1968 winter meetings, Howie Haak, a scout for the Pirates, raved to Mullen about Gerónimo's arm and bemoaned the fact that Pittsburgh did not have room on its roster for the young Dominican. The conversation clinched Mullen's interest, and the Astros invested $8,000 on the unproven prospect, selecting Gerónimo in the third round of the Rule 5 draft.[3]

The Astros, as required by the draft rules, kept Gerónimo on the Major League roster for the entire 1969 season, using him mainly as a late-inning defensive replacement and pinch runner. Gerónimo got into only twenty-eight games and had eight at bats (two hits). For 1970, no longer required to keep him in the Majors or risk losing him, the Astros assigned Gerónimo to their Columbus (Georgia) affiliate in the Double-A Southern League, where he hit a more respectable .269 in seventy-four games, and called him up for forty-seven games (thirty-seven at bats) late in the season. Gerónimo played winter

ball and continued to work on both his hitting and fielding. Heading into the 1971 season, the Astros felt he could be useful as a pinch runner and pinch hitter. And there were those who believed that "if he were a regular, he would be the best fielder on the team."[4] He justified the Astros' faith in his defensive prowess by launching a strike from the left-field corner of the Astrodome to nail Duke Sims of the Dodgers at third base on Opening Day. But at the plate, while he had a few good stretches, he hit only .220 in ninety-four games (eighty-two at bats). Once again, he headed off to play winter ball in hopes of continuing to improve all facets of his game.[5]

Gerónimo's statistics in Houston were certainly not dazzling, and he was now playing behind All-Star center fielder César Cedeño, but once again fate intervened to boost his career prospects. In late November 1971 the Cincinnati Reds negotiated a swap that sent first baseman Lee May, second baseman Tommy Helms, and utility man Jimmy Stewart to the Astros in exchange for second baseman Joe Morgan, infielder Denis Menke, pitcher Jack Billingham, outfielder Ed Armbrister, and Gerónimo. For some, the young Gerónimo seemed little more than a throw-in. Reds general manager Bob Howsam, however, argued that because the Reds had moved to the spacious Riverfront Stadium, it was necessary to have outfielders with speed who could cover more ground. Reds manager Sparky Anderson said of Gerónimo, "Maybe he isn't the best I've seen getting a jump on the ball instinctively, but he reacts very well."[6]

Finally given an opportunity to play semiregularly, and helped by extensive work with batting instructor Ted Kluszewski, Gerónimo improved to .275 in 120 games (255 at bats) in 1972, many as a late-inning replacement. With the fleet veteran Bobby Tolan returning from an injury and manning center field, Gerónimo mainly played right field that season. Once again, he played winter ball, and he began the 1973 season as the Reds' center fielder, with the now-struggling Tolan shifting to right.

Gerónimo injured his shoulder while making a catch and then slumped badly to .210. There was some reason for hope, as he had raised his average from .149 in July and hit over .300 in September. Anderson argued that Gerónimo was still an asset to the Reds. "If a guy can save you a couple of runs with his fielding and throwing, it is just as important as driving home a couple of runs."[7]

After that dismal campaign, Gerónimo again headed home to the Dominican Republic to play baseball, where he got some well-timed assistance from his manager, Tommy Lasorda. The work paid off, as Gerónimo hit .281 in 150 games for the Reds in 1974 and earned the first of what would be four consecutive Gold Glove Awards. On July 17 he became the three thousandth strikeout victim of Bob Gibson, a feat he oddly duplicated on July 4, 1980, when he was the three thousandth victim for Nolan Ryan. Given his seminary training, Gerónimo was very philosophical about this "feat": "I was just at the right place at the right time," he said.[8]

In 1975, in his second full season holding a regular position, Gerónimo hit .257 and led the NL in outfield put-outs with 408. In the World Series against the Boston Red Sox, Gerónimo scored the winning run in Game Three, leading off the bottom of the tenth inning with a single, moving to third after a controversial collision between Boston catcher Carlton Fisk and pinch hitter Ed Armbrister, and scoring on a single by Joe Morgan.[9] For the Series, Gerónimo hit .280 (7-for-25) with two home runs, as the Reds won the classic in seven games.

Gerónimo had his best individual season in 1976 as he hit .307 with eleven triples, second in the league. The Reds again waltzed to the World Series and swept the Yankees. Gerónimo batted .308 while playing every inning for the second straight October.

Gerónimo hit .266 with a career-high ten home runs in 1977 and copped his fourth Gold Glove Award, but the Reds were overtaken by the Dodgers in the NL West, and many of the team's regular players began to depart. Pérez had been traded after the 1976 season, and Rose and Morgan soon left for free agency. Gerónimo stayed with the Reds through the 1980 season, but his hitting fell to .226, .239, and .255, and he was a part-time player most of that time.

In January 1981 the Reds dealt Gerónimo to the Kansas City Royals for infielder German Barranca. Gerónimo played the final three years of his career mainly as a defensive replacement, compiling only 324 at bats and hitting .240. He played his final game in the Majors on August 28, 1983, against the Texas Rangers. The Royals released him after the season. In 1,522 Major League games he batted .258 with fifty-one home runs and 392 RBIs.[10]

Gerónimo was always known as a quiet and reserved individual who brought much stability and class to the Reds' locker room. He and his wife, Elizabeth, were married in 1971 and had two children, César Jr. (born December 19, 1972) and Giselle (born December 17, 1975).[11] Given his religious training, it is not surprising that César got involved in causes linked to social justice after his departure from the Majors. First he was involved with the Federación Nacional de Peloteros Profesionales, which represented the interests of Dominican ballplayers in their dealings with the teams on the island. Later he worked at the training camp set up on the island by the Hiroshima Toyo Carp of the Japanese baseball league, a facility that Mark Kurlansky, in *The Eastern Stars*, called "one of the better appointed academies" on the island.

Gerónimo also was a founder and a board member of the Dominican Republic Sports and Education Academy, aimed at providing proper training, nutrition, and on-field instruction to young Dominican athletes and working to make sure they are educated, have a working knowledge of English, and are given basic instruction in financial matters.[12]

In other words, César Gerónimo continued to do the same caliber of work that he performed with the Reds during the Machine's glory days. He was not about bringing great attention to himself. He merely did the best he could to make it possible for his team (and then his countrymen) to succeed in the often-difficult world of baseball. While he never became a Catholic priest, in many ways in recent years he was involved in a type of ministry that his Jesuit instructors at the Santo Tomas de Aquino seminary would certainly approve. The Cincinnati Reds inducted him into their Hall of Fame in 2008.[13]

Chapter 25. John Vukovich

Andy Sturgill

AGE	G	AB	R	H	2B	3B	HR	TB	RBI	BB	SO	BAV	OBP	SLG	SB	GDP	HBP
27	31	38	4	8	3	0	0	11	2	4	5	.211	.286	.289	0	0	0

Hitting mammoth home runs and striking out ten hitters a game look great in highlights or on the back of a baseball card, but those who excel at these feats are few and far between. The soul of the game is the baseball lifer. Lifers count their number of spring trainings in decades, not just years. Lifers have played and coached in a dozen Major League parks that have long since been demolished. Lifers are men you would not recognize if they weren't wearing turf shoes or carrying around a fungo bat. Lifers are men like John Vukovich.

John Christopher Vukovich was born on July 31, 1947, in Sacramento, California, to John and Lena Vukovich and grew up in Sutter Creek, about forty-five miles from Sacramento. His father worked hard—very hard—to provide for his family. He ran a small beer distributorship, taught high school, and coached three sports, often working sixteen hours a day. Despite limited sight in one eye, he possessed enough baseball talent to have had the opportunity to play professional baseball, but his father (John's grandfather) had immigrated to America and taught his son that you work for a living, you don't play a game.[1]

Vukovich inherited his father's work ethic and carried it with him even from a young age. In addition to starring as an infielder for the baseball team at Amador County High School in Sutter Creek, Vukovich began driving a truck for his father's distributorship at the age of sixteen. After graduating from high school in 1965 he enrolled at American River College, a junior college in nearby Sacramento for which Dusty Baker and Dallas Braden also played. Vukovich was a first-round selection of the Philadelphia Phillies in the January 1966 phase of the am-

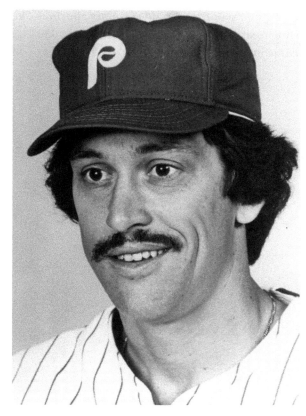

John Vukovich parlayed a .161 lifetime average into a long professional playing career and another two decades as a beloved coach.

ateur draft. He signed with the Phillies in May and used his $10,000 signing bonus to buy his father a new truck and himself a new Dodge Coronet 500, for which he paid $3,400 in cash.[2] Thus began a relationship with the Phillies organization that endured for most of his life. (Larry Bowa of Sacramento, a year and a half older than Vukovich, had been drafted by the Phillies the year before—both were scouted by Eddie Bockman. During their off-seasons as Minor Leaguers Vukovich and Bowa would find empty fields in Sacramento and pitch to each other for hours.)

The 6-foot-1, 187-pound Vukovich broke in with the Huron (South Dakota) Phillies of the Class A Northern League. He moved up through the Philadelphia system, playing excellent defense at third base and showing flashes of hitting ability, climaxed by a .275 season at Eugene (Oregon) of the Pacific Coast League in 1970 with twenty-two home runs.

The also-ran Phillies brought Vukovich up in September 1970 and he made his Major League debut on September 11 at Jarry Park in Montreal. He started at third base that evening and at shortstop in the following two games against the Expos, his only appearances with the Phillies that season. He got his first Major League hit, a single, off Expos starter Mike Wegener in the final game of the series.

Vukovich split his time between Eugene and Philadelphia in 1971. He began the season at Eugene and hit .308 in fifty-eight games before being called up in mid-June after veteran infielder Tony Taylor was traded to Detroit. With the Phillies, Vukovich hit .166 in seventy-four games, including sixty-two starts at third base. One highlight of the season came on June 23, when he grabbed a soft liner hit by Pete Rose for the final out of Rick Wise's no-hitter against the Reds, a game in which Wise also hit two home runs. That season Vukovich began dating Bonnie Loughran, an usher at Philadelphia's Veterans Stadium. They were married after the 1972 season, which Vukovich spent at Eugene.

While the couple were on their honeymoon, Vukovich was traded on October 31 to the Milwaukee Brewers with infielder Don Money and pitcher Bill Champion for pitchers Jim Lonborg, Ken Brett, Ken Sanders, and Earl Stephenson. "I didn't like it at first," Vukovich said of the trade. "I had followed Don throughout the Phillie organization, and I didn't want to do it again someplace else. But

the Brewer front office told me they had plans of using me as a utilityman. I felt better."[3]

Vukovich spent all of 1973 with the Brewers and got into fifty-five games, at first base, third base, and shortstop. He made his Brewers debut by starting at third base in an April series against Baltimore and impressed Orioles manager Earl Weaver, who said, "I can't believe some of the plays Vukovich made," and compared him favorably with Baltimore's future Hall of Famer Brooks Robinson.[4] But his struggles at bat prevented him from winning a permanent home in the lineup. His .188 batting average in 1974 was his highest yet in the Major Leagues.

In the fall of 1974 John and Bonnie had their first child, a daughter named Nicole. On October 22 Vukovich was traded to the Cincinnati Reds for pitcher Pat Osburn. The Reds had no established third baseman, and Vukovich was given a chance to compete for the starting role. "This will be the first time I've gone to camp with a chance to make a team," he said. "Sparky [Anderson, the Reds' manager] has made me no promises, but he has told me the third base job is wide open."[5]

Vukovich won the job, though Anderson was concerned about the level of offensive production that the squad would get from him and constantly griped about Vukovich.[6] During spring training, Anderson quipped that the bats Vukovich used must be made of balsa wood and pleaded with his hitting coach Ted Kluszewski to try to do something about it. In their season opener the Reds defeated the Los Angeles Dodgers, 2–1, in eleven innings. Vukovich robbed the Dodgers' Joe Ferguson and Davey Lopes of hits, and he hit a double. The performance was as much as anyone with the Reds could have wanted from third base, but it did not last. In a game against the Dodgers in Los Angeles on April 16, Anderson's distaste for Vukovich and his frustration with the team's slow start on offense boiled over. Anderson sent up Dan Driessen (who was hitting .000) to pinch hit for Vukovich (who was hitting .294) with the bases loaded and one out—in the second inning. Vukovich, feeling he had been showed up by his manager, smashed every lightbulb between the Reds' dugout and the clubhouse. Anderson dressed him down for his reaction the next day.[7] In later years Vukovich's resentment softened; years later, after Vukovich had died, Phillies director of baseball communications Greg Casterioto said that Vukovich had loved to tell the story.[8] But the incident ended his tenure as the Reds' starting third baseman. He started only five more games and played most often as a late-inning defensive replacement. He was sent down to Triple-A Indianapolis in late May to make room on the roster for reliever Rawly Eastwick and was traded back to Philadelphia for Minor League outfielder Dave Schneck in August.

Back in the Philadelphia organization, Vukovich spent most of his time in the Minors, appearing in only sixteen Major League games between 1976 and 1979, and he often considered quitting. Before the 1977 season Vukovich was offered a good job with a liquor company but turned it down because he loved baseball and needed only one hundred more days of Major League time to qualify for the players' pension plan.[9] He was invited to spring training with the Phillies in 1979 because of his loyalty to the organization but spent most of the season at Triple-A Oklahoma City, where he finally found his batting stroke, hitting .291 with twelve home runs and sixty-six RBIs. He was called up to the Phillies in September and never returned to the Minor Leagues.

Late in the 1979 season, with the Phillies underachieving after three consecutive playoff appearances, Manager Danny Ozark was fired and replaced by the team's fiery Minor League director, Dallas Green. During spring training in 1980, Green unloaded some veterans he thought were too complacent but kept Vukovich, who had appeared in only ten Major League games the previous season. Green, a self-described yeller and cusser, found a kindred spirit in Vukovich, a man for whom play-ing the game the right way was of utmost importance. "Vuke was a spearhead to that team," recalled Green. "He didn't play much, but he wasn't afraid to get up and scream and yell. He would tell the Bull [Greg Luzinski], Schmitty [Mike Schmidt], Bowa or any of the other guys when they needed to get off their butts."[10] "I have a very understanding wife," Vukovich said when asked why he continued to play even if only as a backup. "If not for her support and my love for baseball, I probably would have given it up several years ago. But I love it and she supports me."[11] In the spring of 1980 John and Bonnie's second child, a son named Vince, was born.

A hard-nosed competitor unafraid to take on the Phillies' stars, Vukovich also contributed on the field in 1980. With only two catchers on the roster, Vukovich volunteered to be the Phillies' emergency catcher, often catching in the bullpen before games to improve. He filled in admirably at third base in the middle of the season when Schmidt was sidelined with a hamstring injury. But overall he played in only forty-nine games, mostly as a defensive replacement. Vukovich was on the active roster but did not get into any games as the Phillies defeated the Houston Astros in the NLCS and the Kansas City Royals in the World Series. He remained with the Phillies through the strike-shortened 1981 season, his last as an active player.

After the 1981 season Green left the Phillies to be the general manager of the Chicago Cubs. Green imported a number of people from the Phillies at all levels of the Cubs baseball operation, including Vukovich, who joined new manager Lee Elia's staff as a coach. He was with the Cubs from 1982 through 1987 and managed the Cubs for one day during a mid-June doubleheader in 1986 between the tenures of Jim Frey and Gene Michael. Michael was fired in early September and Green tapped Vukovich to succeed him for the 1988 season. Before the appointment could be officially announced, Green met with executives from the Tribune Company, which owned the Cubs. A disagreement erupted and Green resigned. Vukovich refused to stay on as Cubs manager after Green's departure, and instead of preparing for his introductory press conference with the Chicago media, he flew home to Philadelphia.[12] Vukovich ended up as a coach with the Phillies under his old boss Lee Elia.

Vukovich remained with the Phillies for the rest of his life. He managed the team in its last nine games of the 1988 season after Elia was fired and then was a coach through the 2004 season on the staffs of Nick Leyva, Jim Fregosi, Terry Francona, and his longtime friend Larry Bowa.

Vukovich filled every role imaginable on the Phillies staff, serving as a bench coach as well as coaching at first base and third base. He worked with the infielders, went over scouting reports with pitchers, and ran every aspect of spring training.

While he harbored a desire to manage, Vukovich was unflinchingly loyal to the managers he worked under and always tried to make them look good. Just as in his playing days, he had no fear of telling players the truth in a straightforward manner, with big contracts and big egos not impressing him much.

Vukovich was a man's man, tough with a rawhide exterior. But those who broke through the shell spoke glowingly of a caring man with a huge heart. When John Kruk returned to the Phillies for their home opener in 1994 after cancer treatments, he was welcomed with a rousing ovation—and a glimpse of Vukovich in tears. "It meant so much to me that he cared so much," Kruk said of the memory.[13] In early 2000 outfielder Doug Glanville had made a key mental mistake in a game after his father had suffered a stroke on the other side of the country, and after the game ran into Vukovich in the clubhouse. Recalling that day years later, Glanville wrote, "[Vukovich] saw the anguish in my face, and he whisked me off into some back office and gave the hug that only a father can give a son. One that says to you, 'I will hold you up for as long as it takes until you can hold yourself up again.' And he did."[14] Before spring training in 2002 third baseman Scott Ro-

len made comments critical of the Phillies organization. During spring training Vukovich let Rolen know that he did not appreciate the comments, and the two spent a good while standing toe to toe and yelling at each other. A few days later Vukovich left the team to visit his father, who was ill at his home in California. Rolen paid for his first-class plane ticket for the trip.[15]

Vukovich was a baseball lifer, but baseball was not the only thing in his life. He was an avid outdoorsman who enjoyed hunting and fishing, sometimes with former Phillies owner Ruly Carpenter. He adored his wife, Bonnie, and his two children, Nicole and Vince. He would often take Vince on the team's road trips and spent endless time hitting him ground balls and throwing him batting practice. Vince went on to play baseball at the University of Delaware, was drafted by the Phillies in 2001, and played four seasons in the team's Minor League system.

In early 2001 Vukovich began experiencing headaches and he was persuaded to visit a doctor. Tests revealed a mass on the occipital lobe of his brain and surgery was performed to remove the mass. It proved to be benign, and just over a month later he returned to the third base coach's box for the Phillies. His sight in one eye was slightly diminished, but he got by on his experience and guile.

In 2004 Vukovich began his seventeenth season as a Phillies coach, eclipsing the previous team record of sixteen set by Mike Ryan. It was his twenty-fourth season in a Phillies uniform, surpassed only by his boss, Manager Larry Bowa, who was in his twenty-fifth season in uniform in '04. Just before the end of the season, in which the second-place Phillies finished ten games behind Atlanta in the NL East, Bowa was fired and replaced by Charlie Manuel. Vukovich had offers to coach elsewhere but accepted a role as a special assistant to Phillies GM Ed Wade, who felt he would "cast too large a shadow over the new manager." "I'm still not sure whether I was promoted or demoted," Vukovich quipped.[16]

In late 2006 Vukovich was diagnosed with another brain tumor and privately battled the disease for months before it ultimately claimed his life on March 8, 2007. He was fifty-nine. He was survived by his wife, Bonnie; brothers Rich and Bill Vukovich; son Vince; daughter Nikki (Vukovich) Stolarik; and three granddaughters, triplets Anna, Lena, and Stella, born to Nikki and her husband in 2006.

As news of Vukovich's death spread, the outpouring from the baseball world multiplied. Countless baseball men referred to Vukovich in familial terms—father, brother, best friend. Many celebrated his tough exterior and soft heart. Some remembered his passion and competitiveness. Others simply recalled his friendship.

A few days later the baseball world gathered with the Vukovich family to pay their respects. Vukovich's service at St. Andrew the Apostle Catholic Church in Gibbsboro, New Jersey, was a who's who of fifty years of Phillies history. Team executives, including Ruly Carpenter, Bill Giles, David Montgomery, Pat Gillick, and Ed Wade, were among the seven hundred people who showed up. Managers Dallas Green, Lee Elia, Jim Fregosi, Terry Francona, Larry Bowa, and Charlie Manuel attended. Phillies teammates, including Mike Schmidt, Garry Maddox, Greg Luzinski, and Tim McCarver, were there. Former players he coached, among them Curt Schilling, Lenny Dykstra, Darren Daulton, John Kruk, Mitch Williams, and Bobby Abreu, made the trip. Later stars like Jimmy Rollins, Chase Utley, Ryan Howard, and Pat Burrell were there too. The *Philadelphia Daily News* described the scene by noting that "across the church, tough and hard-bitten baseball men wept openly."[17] All came to say goodbye to one of the best of baseball's lifers.

In 2007 the Phillies honored Vukovich by wearing a black patch with "VUK" in white letters on the right sleeves of their jerseys. In August he was inducted onto the team's Wall of Fame with his wife, children, grandchildren, and brothers in attendance.

Jimmy Rollins chuckled at the thought of what Vukovich would think of a pregame to-do in his honor.

On the last day of the 2007 season the Phillies defeated the Washington Nationals at home while the Florida Marlins knocked off the New York Mets, to clinch the team's first division title and postseason appearance since 1993. The win was made sweeter by the fact that the Phillies had trailed the Mets by seven games with only seventeen games to play and had come all the way back to win the NL East outright. In the subsequent celebration among players and fans Pat Burrell, the team's longest-tenured player, pointed to the patch on his right sleeve and solemnly nodded his head up and down in recognition of the role Vukovich played in the success of that team and the young players who made it.

In an article in the *Philadelphia Daily News* shortly after Vukovich died, Paul Hagen summed him up as well as anyone possibly could. He wrote, "[In 2004], Vukovich was asked to describe himself. 'Family man, first,' he said. After that? 'Phillie,' he added with a grin. John Vukovich: Family Man. Phillie. Not a bad epitaph."[18]

Chapter 26. June 1975 Timeline

Mark Miller and Mark Armour

All headlines below are from the next day's edition of the *Springfield (OH) News.*

June 1—"BIG HITS" LIFT REDLEGS, ONE-HALF GAME OUT—The Reds got all their runs on a third-inning three-run home run by Joe Morgan and a fifth-inning two-run double by Johnny Bench, beating the Cardinals 5–1. Jack Billingham ran his record to 5-3 with a complete-game five-hitter.

June 3—REDS NAB 10TH WIN IN 11 GAMES, PIRATES EXPERIENCE BAD NIGHT—"It's always good to be in first," said Reds manager Sparky Anderson, whose club regained the NL West lead for the first time since April 14. The Reds defeated the Pirates, who committed three errors, 8–4. Joe Morgan led the offense with three hits, including a bases-loaded triple.

June 4—REDS GIVE UP WEST LEAD TO DODGERS, REUSS LOSES NO-HIT BID—The Reds fell to the Pirates 2–1 despite a good outing by Fred Norman. Pirates starter Jerry Reuss took a no-hitter into the seventh before a hard line drive by Dave Concepción struck him below the left kneecap, earning Concepción a single and forcing Reuss to leave the game. The Reds scored their only run in the frame, as Ken Griffey was thrown out at the plate to end the inning after he tried to score the tying run and turn his triple into an inside-the-park home run.

June 6—FOSTER NOT TRIVIAL IN REDS VICTORY, CLUBS NINTH HOMER—Pete Rose garnered three hits (including the twenty-four hundredth of his career) and George Foster hit a two-run homer, one month after Rose moved to third base to allow Foster to get a starting job in the outfield, helping the Reds to a 5–1 win over the Cubs. The hard-hitting Foster was still batting eighth in the Reds' powerful lineup. Don Gullett won his seventh game with a complete-game five-hitter.

June 7—REDS TRIUMPH, TAKE LEAD, HOMERS POWER 8–1 ROMP—Johnny Bench, Joe Morgan, and Dan Driessen slugged home runs and Jack Billingham threw a five-hitter as the Reds downed the Cubs, 8–1. The Reds moved into first place again, on their fourteenth victory in their last seventeen games. Bench's four RBIs gave him a league-leading forty-three for the season.

June 8—REDS WIN 16TH OF 19 IN TORRID STREAK, WHIP CUBS TWICE—Johnny Bench was the hitting star in the doubleheader sweep as he belted a seventh-inning two-run homer in the first-game 2–1 victory and his fifth-inning opposite-field single knocked in the go-ahead run in the second game, an 8–5 triumph, as Tony Pérez joined in with three hits and three runs batted in. Gary Nolan was the winner of the first game with his fifth complete game of the season and Pedro Borbon won the nightcap in relief of starter Clay Kirby.

June 9—REDS, BOMBED BY PIRATES, 9–2, SEE LEAD SLASHED—Reds starter Fred Norman lasted only one-third of an inning, giving up four hits and five runs, and the Pirates never looked back in their 9–2 romp. The Pirates' attack was led by four hits from Rennie Stennett and three each from Cincinnati native Dave Parker and Richie Zisk, with homers by Parker, Willie Stargell, and Zisk.

June 10—REDS, ANDERSON HAPPY TO SEE "FE-ROCIOUS" BUCS GO—For the second night in a row the Reds starter failed to last one inning against the NL East–leading Pittsburgh Pirates, as Pat Darcy recorded just two outs, allowing five hits and three runs. He was replaced by the previous night's starter, Fred Norman, who lasted 4⅓ innings and gave up four tallies. The hitting star for the Pirates during their 9–5 victory was Willie Stargell, who went 4-for-5, with three doubles and five runs batted in.

June 11—GULLETT FAR AHEAD OF PACE, NEW PITCH MAKES HIM 8–3—The Reds sorely needed a strong effort from their starting pitcher, and Don Gullett delivered, going the full nine innings in a 3–1 win over the Cardinals. St. Louis's catcher Ted Simmons broke up Gullett's bid for a shutout with a ninth-inning solo home run. Ken Griffey led the offensive attack for the Reds with three hits while Gullett added a double.

June 12—NOLAN'S GOALS MODEST, BUT PITCH-ING DRAWS RAVES—Gary Nolan won his seventh game in ten decisions by pitching six innings of shutout baseball before being relieved by Will McEnaney and Rawly Eastwick in a 10–1 Reds victory over St. Louis. Pete Rose led the way offensively with three of the club's fourteen hits.

June 13—REDS TAKE BATTING PRACTICE ON CUB'S PITCHING—Trailing 8–6 after seven innings, the Reds took the lead with five runs in the eighth and put it away with seven more in the ninth, holding on for an 18–11 victory. Among the Reds' twenty-four hits were five by César Gerónimo and four by Tony Pérez, while Johnny Bench, George Foster, and Pete Rose all homered.

June 14—CUBS ASSAULTED BY BENCH, PÉREZ, REDS LEAD SUSPENDED GAME—The relentless firepower of the Big Red Machine continued, as the Reds rolled out to an 11–3 lead before the game was suspended in the top of the ninth inning due to darkness. (The Cubs' Wrigley Field did not yet have lights.) Johnny Bench led the attack with two doubles and two singles, and César Gerónimo added three hits of his own (following his five-hit game yesterday).

June 15—ANDERSON, BENCH ANGRY, REDS LOSE THRILLER—The Reds started the day by completing their 11–3 victory from the day before, with Johnny Bench adding a fifth hit to his total in the ninth inning. In the regularly scheduled Sunday game, the Cubs snapped the Reds' four-game winning streak with a 4–3 victory. The Reds trailed 4–0 before Joe Morgan homered in the top of the eighth inning. Both Sparky Anderson, in the bottom of the eighth, and Johnny Bench, in the top of the ninth, were ejected by first base umpire Art Williams. Bench was arguing that he was safe on a play at first in the ninth that ultimately cost the Reds the game (a television replay showed Bench was correct). The Reds scored two in the ninth but left the bases loaded when George Foster flied out to center field.

June 16—VICTORY COULD BE COSTLY TO THE REDS—For the third time in 1975, Larvell Blanks of the Braves hurt the Reds with his bat, this time literally. His two-out ninth-inning line drive up the middle struck and broke the thumb of the Reds' ace, Don Gullett, whose stellar effort upped his record to 9-3. (The injury sidelined Gullett for two months.) Joe Morgan led the attack with three hits, including a double, a home run, and four runs batted in.

June 17—MORTON BEATS REDS BY GETTING MAD AT THEM—The Reds managed just three hits, two by Joe Morgan and one by Johnny Bench, off Atlanta's Carl Morton in a 5–1 loss at Riverfront Stadium. The Braves got a grand slam from Dave May and a solo shot by Darrell Evans to account for their runs.

June 18—BENCH EYEING RBI CROWN, WEIRD HIT SCORES TWO—In a 6–1 Cincinnati victory, Johnny Bench knocked in two runs, giving him a league-leading fifty-seven, on a double that bounced off the right knee of third base umpire Lee Weyer. Bench later autographed the ball he hit and gave it to Weyer. Jack Billingham pitched six innings, earning his seventh victory, and Will McEnaney picked up a three-inning save.

June 20—YES, GERÓNIMO CAN HIT, THREE-RUN HOMER—In Houston, Tom Carroll, taking the rotation spot of the injured Don Gullett, gave up three runs in six-plus innings to gain his first victory of the season, 7–3 over the Astros. The offense was paced by a three-run homer by César Gerónimo, his fourth of the season, off former Reds reliever Wayne Granger.

June 21—REDS TRIUMPH IN 14—Ace reliever Clay Carroll made a rare start, but he had long left the game when the Reds finally won in extra innings. The score was tied 4–4 after nine, and the Reds thought they had it won when a Tony Pérez homer and a George Foster double plated two runs in the top of the tenth. But after the Astros knotted the game again the bottom of the inning, the clubs put up three more scoreless frames before a two-out Ken Griffey single in the fourteenth inning gave the Reds a 7–6 lead that held up. The Reds outhit the Astros 21–9, getting four safeties from Foster and three each from Pete Rose, César Gerónimo, and Griffey.

June 22—DIERKER STYMIES REDS, NOLAN BOUNCED, 8–4—Larry Dierker did not exactly fool the Reds, allowing eleven hits and four runs in his complete-game victory, but the Astros chased Gary Nolan early and rolled to a fairly easy 8–4 victory. Ken Griffey got three more hits, and Tony Pérez homered in the eighth inning. The Reds' 42-27 record is among the best in the Major Leagues, but they have not shaken the Dodgers, who are just two games back in the NL West.

June 23—BENCH EYEING RBI TITLE, VARIETY MAY BE KEY—The Reds scored four runs in the third inning and slowly pulled away, winning 8–4 in Atlanta. Jack Billingham (8-3) was in control until he allowed three runs in the eighth to tighten things a little, and Will McEnaney finished it off. Dave Concepción had three hits and backup catcher Bill Plummer homered and singled to drive in three runs. Johnny Bench, playing right field, homered (number fifteen) and drove in four runs, giving him a league-leading sixty-one RBIs, eleven more than the Phillies' Greg Luzinski. Bench also led the league with twenty-eight doubles.

June 24—SPARKY RATES MORGAN HIGH, REDS WIN 10TH OF 13—Joe Morgan's three-run homer in the third inning accounted for all the scoring the Reds were able to muster against Atlanta's Phil Niekro, but it was all they needed. Pat Darcy, with relief help from Fred Norman and Pedro Borbon, shut out the Braves, 3–0. This marked the third time this season that the Reds had defeated Niekro, Atlanta's knuckle-balling ace.

June 25—REDS BLANK BRAVES, INCREASE LEAD TO FOUR GAMES—The Reds completed a three-game sweep in Atlanta's Fulton County Stadium with their second straight shutout, 2–0, this one tossed by Tom Carroll and Will McEnaney. The Reds managed only six hits against Carl Morton and scored both their runs on sacrifice flies. The Reds' infield turned five double plays during the game, after having turned four the night before.

June 27—DRIESSEN'S BLAST WIDENS REDLEGS LEAD—The Reds return home to take on the Padres, and the Machine keeps rolling along. The two clubs were locked in a 2–2 pitchers' duel with two outs in the eleventh inning before Dan Driessen ended the festivities with a three-run home run off Danny Frisella for a 5–2 win.

June 28—FOSTER'S HOMER GIVES REDS WIN AND LEAD OF 6½ GAMES—It was Farmers Night at Riverfront Stadium, and for the second day in a row it took an extra-inning home run to defeat the Padres. This time it was George Foster who ended things with a two-out, two-run blast in the tenth to give the Reds a 6–4 victory. Will McEnaney pitched two innings for his third win in relief.

June 29—REDS SET FIELDING RECORD, INCREASE LEAD AGAIN—In a split of a doubleheader with the Padres, the Reds set a Major League record by playing their fourteenth consecutive errorless game. Jack Billingham picked up his ninth victory in the opener, winning 4–1 with the aid of home runs from George Foster, Joe Morgan, and Merv Rettenmund. In the nightcap, the Padres' Brent Strom earned the complete-game 4–3 victory, surviving an eighth-inning two-run home run from George Foster. The Dodgers dropped their fifth straight, pushing the Reds' lead in the NL West to seven games.

June 30—OVERTIME WORK REWARDING FOR REDS, BEAT ASTROS IN 12TH—For the third time in four days an extra-inning walk-off homer thrilled the Riverfront Stadium crowd. Johnny Bench was the hero this time, blasting a two-out, three-run home run off Joe Niekro, Phil's brother, to win 9–6 and send their fans home happy. The game marked a Major League record fifteenth straight game the Reds played without an error. The Reds finished the month of June with a 21-7 record that put them firmly in control of the NL West race.

NL West Standings, June 30, 1975

TEAM	W	L	GB
Cincinnati	49	28	—
Los Angeles	43	36	7.0
San Francisco	37	39	11.5
San Diego	36	41	13.0
Atlanta	32	43	16.0
Houston	28	52	22.5

Chapter 27. **George Foster**

Cindy Thomson

AGE	G	AB	R	H	2B	3B	HR	TB	RBI	BB	SO	BAV	OBP	SLG	SB	GDP	HBP
26	134	463	71	139	24	4	23	240	78	40	73	.300	.356	.518	2	14	3

A right-handed, power-hitting outfielder, George Foster was a feared presence at bat and in the outfield for most of his eleven-year run with the Cincinnati Reds. Once he mastered the mental aspect of his game, Foster became a key ingredient in Manager Sparky Anderson's Big Red Machine of the 1970s. But as powerful as he was on the field, Foster led a very quiet life off it. A columnist once summed up Foster's discipline in his mind and on the field by writing, "It is against George Foster's convictions to smoke, drink, chew, curse or leave men on base."[1]

Born in Tuscaloosa, Alabama, on December 1, 1948, to George and Regina (Beale) Foster, George Arthur Foster spent his early life picking cotton and hoping, despite his small size, to be chosen for neighborhood ball game. When he was eight his parents separated, and he moved to Hawthorne, California, near Los Angeles, with his mother, his older brother, John, and his older sister, Mamie.

In Hawthorne Foster played in the same Little League as future Major Leaguer Dave Kingman. He played several sports at Leuzinger High School in Lawndale, California, but broke his leg playing basketball in his senior year and did not play baseball that spring. Instead, he established a workout routine, gained weight, and got stronger. After high school, while playing in a fall league, he was spotted by San Francisco Giants scout Jack French, and in late 1968, after playing baseball at El Camino Junior College in Torrance, California, Foster was drafted in the third round of the amateur draft by the Giants, the team of his boyhood hero, Willie Mays.

The Giants sent the nineteen-year-old Foster to their low-level Class A team in Medford, Oregon. The next season he advanced to Single-A Fresno, made the 1969 California League All-Star team, and led his team with fourteen home runs and eighty-five runs batted in. The 6-foot-1, 185-pound powerhouse was drawing attention, and the Giants called him up after the California League season.

Foster's first Major League hit was an infield single to third base off the Dodgers' Claude Osteen on September 27. The Giants and Foster repeated the process in 1970: He spent the season at Triple-A Phoenix, where he hit .308 but with less power and fewer RBIs than the season before. Again he got a late-season call-up, and on September 25 he hit his first Major League home run as a pinch hitter off San Diego's Pat Dobson. In 1971 Foster made the Giants' roster as a reserve outfielder, backing up Bobby Bonds, Willie Mays, and Ken Henderson. The reclusive Foster roomed with Bonds, who became his mentor and helped him adjust. Foster avoided the media and rarely engaged in small talk with his teammates, afraid of bothering anyone. His time on the bench, after playing every day in the Minors, sent him into a batting slump, and he lost fifty-four points off his batting average during May.

On May 29 the Giants traded Foster to the Reds for shortstop Frank Duffy and pitcher Vern Geishert. The trade turned out to be vastly one-sided in favor of Cincinnati. Duffy was traded to the Cleveland Indians after the season and Geishert never pitched again in the Majors. But Foster was sorely disappointed. The day he was dealt the Giants were in first place in the National League West Division and the Reds were near the bottom. He was discouraged, but the trade proved to be a bless-

It was the shift of Pete Rose to third base that finally made a regular player out of George Foster, and he took the opportunity and became a star.

ing for Foster, and for the Reds. Foster became the Reds' regular center fielder (in part because Bobby Tolan sat out the entire season with an Achilles tendon injury). Foster hit .241 with thirteen home runs for the season, including .234 with ten homers for the Reds. On September 16 in San Francisco he avenged himself against his old team by hitting a grand slam off Don McMahon in the eighth inning that assured the Reds victory. Still, despite flashes of excellence, Foster earned only a backup role in the Reds' outfield in 1972 after Tolan returned to the lineup. Foster played in fifty-nine games and hit just .200 with two home runs. His most memorable moment of the season undoubtedly was the deciding Game Five of the NLCS against the Pittsburgh Pirates, when, as a pinch runner, he scored the winning run from third base on a wild pitch by Bob Moose in the bottom of the ninth inning.

The dramatic finish to the 1972 NLCS brought Foster attention from the press but he made just two brief appearances as the Reds lost the World Series to the Oakland Athletics in seven games. And the next season he was sent back down to Triple-A Indianapolis. Sparky Anderson said, "What George needs to learn is to make contact. When he does, the ball really jumps off his bat."[2]

At Indianapolis in 1973, Foster roomed with Ken Griffey, who became a friend and later a teammate on the Reds. Griffey said of Foster, "At first we had a hard time communicating because he was so upset about being sent down, but after a while we'd just have such a good time on the field just laughing that he forgot his situation and started to play ball."[3] That season was a turning point for Foster. He soon accepted the reasoning that more playing time would only help. Anderson and his staff had hoped the stint in the Minors would help Foster to mature. He had the skills but needed to develop and improve his mental attitude. Foster's friendship with Griffey and others helped him to relax, and his hitting improved. This was also a time of spiritual renewal for Foster, who came to profess a strong

CINDY THOMSON

Christian faith. He worked to stay in shape, began to eat healthy foods, and shunned alcohol and tobacco. In September the Reds brought him up to the Majors, and he played in seventeen games, hitting .282 with four home runs. Anderson confirmed his previous assessment of Foster's ability, saying, "When George gets into a pitch, no one hits a ball harder than he does—not Willie Stargell, Willie McCovey, or Lee May."[4]

As his hitting improved, Foster began to admire another player's stained hickory bat and ordered one for himself. Foster's big, black, thirty-five-ounce, thirty-five-inch bat was well known. Foster joked about having integrated the bat rack.

The Reds won the NL West again in 1973 but Foster had been called up too late to be eligible to play in the postseason. Even so, he had impressed the Reds enough that he stuck with the team the next season. Anderson declared, "He'll never be a loud-mouth, but his new attitude will make him a better ballplayer."[5]

In 1974 the Reds had outfielders Griffey, César Gerónimo, and Pete Rose, and Foster was still a part-time player, but this time he was mentally prepared for the role. The hitting coach, former Reds power hitter Ted Kluszewski, worked with Foster on his batting stance, focusing on the inside pitches that Foster had been avoiding. Foster hit .264 with seven homers that season and broke through in 1975, when he became the regular left fielder after Anderson moved Rose to third base. Foster's batting average rose to .300 and he hit twenty-three home runs, helping propel the Reds to a World Series victory over the Boston Red Sox, their first Series championship since 1940. In the bottom of the ninth inning during the dramatic Game Six, Foster threw out the potential winning run at the plate to keep the game going. In the twelfth Foster actually caught and kept the Fisk home run ball after it ricocheted off the foul pole. The ball was sold at auction in 1999 for over $100,000. Foster hit .364 in the NLCS and .276 in the World Series. Anderson said, "Having George in left field made the difference in our ballclub winning the World Series."[6]

The 1976 season was even better for Foster. He hit twenty-nine home runs, had a league-leading 121 RBIS, and was voted to the National League's starting lineup for the All-Star Game in Philadelphia. He hit a two-run home run off Catfish Hunter, drove in three runs, and was named the game's Most Valuable Player. He was named the National League's Player of the Month in May and July and the Player of the Year by the *Sporting News.* He had been in contention for the Triple Crown (home runs, RBIS, and batting average) and finished second to teammate Joe Morgan in the voting for Most Valuable Player. After Morgan was announced as the MVP, Foster declared that he should have won the award, something he immediately regretted saying.[7] The Reds swept the Philadelphia Phillies in the NLCS and the Yankees in the World Series. Foster hit .429 in the Series (6-for-14) with four RBIS.

During the season Foster smashed the seventh home run ever to be hit into Riverfront Stadium's upper deck since the ballpark opened in 1970. In the ballpark's thirty-three-season existence only thirty-five home runs were hit there and Foster hit the most, six.

Deprived (in his mind) of the MVP in 1976, Foster responded with a better season the next year and copped the award on the strength of a .320 batting average and being the league leader in home runs (52), RBIS (149), and runs scored (124). Once again Foster was voted to the All-Star team (he was 1-for-3 with one RBI as the National League won). On July 14, just before the All-Star break, Foster hit three home runs in a game against Atlanta, and he wound up with twelve that month. Of his home run total that season, Foster said, "I saw the ball so well. It seemed almost any pitch would do."[8] Foster's home run total in 1977 was the most since Willie Mays hit fifty-two in 1965. The fifty home run milestone was not reached again until Detroit's Cecil Fielder hit fifty-one in 1990.

After the 1977 season Foster combined an exhibition tour to Japan (he was voted the MVP for the tour) with a honeymoon. He married Sheila Roberts on November 3. They later had two daughters, Starrine and Shawna.

In 1978 his batting average slipped to .281, but he again led the National League in home runs (40) and RBIs (120). But over the next two seasons his production fell as he battled injuries and missed playing time. He rallied in 1981 and drove in ninety runs in 108 games in the strike-shortened season. Before the next season, on February 10, 1982, Foster was traded to the New York Mets for catcher Alex Trevino and pitchers Jim Kern and Greg Harris. His nearly eleven-year run with the Big Red Machine was over.

Foster, thirty-three years old by this time, signed a five-year, $10 million contract with the Mets—the largest in the National League at the time—but struggled from the start. After seven straight seasons of hitting at least twenty home runs, he managed only thirteen in New York, and his batting average plummeted to .247. Mets fans took to booing him.

Foster improved his home run numbers in the next three years as the Mets vaulted into contention in 1984 after years of ineptitude. But by 1986, as the Mets were having one of their greatest seasons, the thirty-seven-year-old Foster was struggling in part-time play. A comment Foster made in August to a sportswriter appeared to accuse Mets manager Davey Johnson of favoring white players. "I'm not saying it's a racial thing. But that seems to be the case in sports these days," Foster was quoted as saying. "When a ballclub can, they replace a George Foster or a Mookie Wilson with a more popular white player. I think the Mets would rather promote a Gary Carter or a Keith Hernandez to the fans so parents who want to can point to them as role models for their children, rather than a Darryl Strawberry or a Dwight Gooden or a George Foster."[9] Foster told Johnson and his teammates that his comments had been taken out of context,

and some of the teammates supported him, but he was released the day the article appeared.[10] With a huge contract and lackluster performance, Foster was destined to be released anyway. The Chicago White Sox picked him up and he hit a home run (the 348th and last of his career) in his first game with the team, but he was released after three weeks.

Foster was a Minor League hitting instructor for the Reds in the late 1990s and later a special instructor with the team. He has also coached in high school and college. He has spent time as a corporate speaker and with a baseball training organization called the George Foster Baseball Clinic. In 2003 Foster was inducted into the Cincinnati Reds Hall of Fame.

During Foster's playing days he spent time with young baseball players, giving them equipment and instructing them on batting. Dayton, Ohio, sportswriter Hal McCoy, who covered Foster when he was with the Reds, called him "the greatest person in baseball," adding, "I mean as a person, not just as a player. He never raises his voice, no matter how harassed he may be by fans. I asked him once if he'd let me use his name for Building Bridges, an organization for underprivileged kids. He said, 'No, you'll have more than my name. I'll be there too.'"[11] Foster seeks to teach future ballplayers to work hard and believe in their abilities.

CINDY THOMSON

Chapter 28. **Terry Crowley**

Malcolm Allen

AGE	G	AB	R	H	2B	3B	HR	TB	RBI	BB	SO	BAV	OBP	SLG	SB	GDP	HBP
28	66	71	8	19	6	0	1	28	11	7	6	.268	.333	.394	0	6	0

They say I'm a good pinch-hitter, but maybe if I ever came to the plate 500 times, they might learn I'm a good hitter, period.

—Jim Henneman, *Sporting News*

One of Terry Crowley's favorite players when he was a teenager was the New York Yankees' pinch hitter par excellence Johnny Blanchard. "When he wasn't catching, he was a good pinch-hitter, so for some reason I liked him a lot," Crowley recalled.[1] So it's perhaps not too surprising that Crowley grew up to be an excellent Major League pinch hitter himself.

Terrence Michael Crowley was born on February 16, 1947, in Staten Island, New York, and grew up rooting for the Yankees. Despite his admiration for Blanchard, Crowley was a left-handed pitcher in high school and drew the attention of professional scouts. Starring at Curtis High in Staten Island, the school that sent Bobby Thomson of "Shot Heard 'Round the World" fame to the Major Leagues, Crowley got to pitch for the city championship as a junior. But he hurt his arm and couldn't even throw—much less pitch—when he returned for his senior year. Not surprisingly, the demand for Crowley's services in professional baseball dipped accordingly. "Some teams had made offers and said they would wait until my arm got better," he said. "But I couldn't realistically go away to play pro ball when I couldn't move my left shoulder."[2]

Instead, Crowley enrolled at the Brooklyn campus of Long Island University, the institution that Hall of Famer Larry Doby once attended on a basketball scholarship. Crowley never went back to the mound, but he got his baseball career back on

Terry Crowley grew frustrated with his role as one of the game's best pinch hitters, though his managers loved having him around.

track with a first-team All-American performance as a sophomore. By then married to the former Janet Boyle with a baby daughter, Carlene, he was drafted by the Baltimore Orioles in the eleventh round of the June 1966 amateur draft but was in no particular hurry to sign unless the price was right.

The Orioles inked one draftee after another, but Crowley kept refusing to sign. Scout Walter Shannon came to watch him play and, after following Crowley around "for a good two months," finally offered a bonus of $27,500 with only a few weeks remaining in the Minor League season.[3] Crowley signed, reported to Miami, and batted .255 in nineteen Florida State League games with only one extra-base hit in his first taste of professional baseball.

He returned to Miami in 1967 and batted .262 with a league-leading twenty-four doubles in 135 games. Surprisingly, Crowley, a 6-foot 180-pounder never known for his speed, added ten triples and twenty-one steals. However, he managed only three home runs and forty-nine RBIS. "The wind blew in from right field so hard, it was impossible for a lefty to hit a home run," Crowley remembered. "The whole league was like that."[4]

After the season the Orioles put Crowley on their forty-man roster. He played in the Florida Instructional League and was assigned to the Double-A Elmira Pioneers in 1968. "Crow" hit .271 without a home run in fifty-five Eastern League games playing for Cal Ripken Sr., but he earned a promotion to Triple-A Rochester (New York) after a red-hot June. There he began to hit with power for the first time as a professional, launching eight home runs to go with a .268 average in seventy-five games. The Orioles sent him back to the Florida Instructional League after the season, and Minor League director Jim McLaughlin speculated that "Crowley may just come up in September for a look after a season in Triple-A."[5]

That's exactly what happened, but not before Crowley overcame a slow start at Rochester to become a unanimous in-season All-Star selection by International League managers. He batted .282 with twenty-eight home runs and eighty-three runs batted in, walked sixty-nine times, and led the league with 246 total bases. On September 4, 1969, he fouled out to the catcher as a pinch hitter in his Major League debut at Tiger Stadium but notched three hits in his first start (against the Indians) when the Orioles returned home. He got into seven games that September, hitting .333 (6-for-18), and, at just twenty-two years of age, his future appeared very bright.

Nevertheless, Crowley was a long shot to make the Orioles in 1970. The team's 109 victories had given it the American League pennant in 1969, and no starting jobs were open in the outfield or at first base. Even two reserve outfielders had spots secured, but Crowley forced his way into the mix by hitting .380 in spring training during Grapefruit League play. Utility infielder Bobby Floyd became the odd man out, and Crowley was wearing a Baltimore uniform on Opening Day in Cleveland. He didn't get into the game but wound up in the hospital overnight when a foul liner one-hopped its way into the Orioles' dugout and struck him above the ear. He was fine, though, and started the series finale in right field.

Though Crowley began the season as the Orioles' twenty-fifth man, his contribution to the team's 108-54 record and second consecutive American League East title was substantial. His first Major League home run was a three-run blast off the Minnesota Twins' Dave Boswell at Memorial Stadium on May 1 that gave Baltimore a lead it wouldn't lose. Crowley added game-winning home runs in Detroit and Cleveland before the season was through. He batted .257 in eighty-three games (thirty-four starts). His totals of five homers and twenty RBIS in 157 at bats were pretty good, and his .394 on-base percentage was exceptional. Perhaps most telling was Crowley's .290 average as a pinch hitter, a difficult role for any player but particularly for a twenty-three-year-old rookie. "It's a job usually handled by a veteran," remarked Crowley. "It's a big adjustment to go from playing every day to pinch-hitting."[6]

He made only one plate appearance in the postseason but earned a World Series ring as the Orioles romped through the Twins in the ALCS and the Cincinnati Reds in the Series by winning seven times in eight games. "It was like, hey, this is the way it's supposed to be," said Crowley. "We pretty much had an All-Star at every position. We had a fantastic pitching staff. It was a great time."[7]

The Orioles hoped Crowley would head to Puerto Rico to sharpen his skills in the winter league,

MALCOLM ALLEN

but with daughter Carlene about to turn seven and sons Terry Jr. and Jimmy still in diapers, Crowley elected to stay home and be Daddy. When spring training rolled around for 1971, he pulled a hamstring in a running drill, didn't hit when he was able to play, and wound up getting sent back to Rochester. "It was an emotional adjustment, no doubt, going from the world champions back to the Minors," he said. "I had to fight not only the opposing pitchers, but my situation as well."[8]

Crowley was recalled to Baltimore a few times that season and managed only a .174 average in twenty-three at bats over eighteen games. At Rochester, he hit cleanup, played first base, and helped the team to a Junior World Series title by smashing five homers in the playoffs. Still, the season was a disappointing setback, and he did go to the Puerto Rican league that winter, trying to turn things around.

Fellow Orioles Don Baylor, Rich Coggins, Dave Leonhard, and Fred Beene were also on the Santurce (Puerto Rico) squad, but Crowley gained his most valuable experience of the winter away from the baseball field. Though physically fine, he'd been placed on the disabled list after a disagreement with Manager Ruben Gomez and found himself sitting around the pool one day when heavyweight boxing contender Joe "King" Roman happened by and the two became friends.

"I had boxed informally as a kid," Crowley recalled. "We always had the gloves, and my dad and uncles always taught me how to fight because they were into the fight game a little bit. When I actually started to fool around with Joe Roman, it was fun and I could handle myself a little bit. I could move around, and I found that doing it every day for the first time, I got to improve."[9]

In addition to sparring, Crowley spent about three weeks following the training regimen of Roman, who in 1973 became the first Puerto Rican to fight for the heavyweight championship. (George Foreman knocked him out in the first round.) "Boxers are fantastically dedicated guys," marveled Crow-

ley the following spring. "They get up at 4 o'clock in the morning and go out and run for an hour or so. Every morning. They never miss. I've never seen anyone work so hard in athletics and, boy, does it pay off. I feel in great shape."[10]

Crowley wasn't sure where he fit in the Orioles' plans heading into 1972, but one major obstacle had been removed when Baltimore traded Frank Robinson to the Los Angeles Dodgers. Crowley wound up more or less platooning in right field with his good friend and roommate Merv Rettenmund. "Merv Rettenmund was one of funniest, wittiest, sarcastic type guys that you could ever be around," said Crowley. "He was a great teammate. Guys loved him, and he was a really funny guy."[11]

Crowley got into a career-high ninety-seven games in 1972 and hammered eleven home runs in 247 at bats. In June he shared the cover of the *Sporting News* with teammates Don Baylor and Bobby Grich and received praise from Baltimore coach Billy Hunter in the accompanying story. "I am more surprised at what Crowley has accomplished than the other two," Hunter said. "We always knew that Terry was a natural hitter, but he has impressed me even more by working very hard at other phases of the game."[12] But a .193 second-half batting average dropped Crowley's season mark to .231, and the Orioles missed the playoffs for the first time in four years after a September swoon.

Crowley lifted weights with Rettenmund nearly every day that off-season at a Baltimore YMCA, seemingly in preparation for a great opportunity. The American League adopted the designated hitter rule for the 1973 season and Crowley made his first-ever Opening Day start and had two hits as the first DH in Orioles history. Veteran Tommy Davis, a two-time batting champion, seized the job in May, though, and Crowley wound up hitting just .206 with three home runs in fifty-four games. Fed up, he let it be known that he'd welcome a trade. The Orioles sold him to the Texas Rangers in early December for a reported $100,000.

After another winter in Puerto Rico to get some at bats, Crowley expressed optimism about joining a new team. "If I could get about 350 or 400 at-bats, I think I could hit between 15 and 20 home runs and help this club a great deal," he said. "I'll DH, play first or the outfield, platoon, anything. All I'd like is the opportunity to play in some predictable fashion."[13]

Crowley didn't even make it through spring training with the Rangers, however. Texas placed him on waivers and he ended up with the Cincinnati Reds. There he was reunited with Rettenmund, whom the Orioles had also traded away because he wasn't satisfied playing part-time. The pair of ex-Orioles earned one more World Series ring when the Reds went all the way in 1975 but mostly endured two miserable years of dwindling playing time and disappointing production with Cincinnati. Crowley hit .240 with one homer in 1974, then .268, again with a single homer, the following year, and saw his at bats drop from 125 in 1974 to 71 in 1975.

Just before the 1976 season opener, Cincinnati sent Crowley and Rettenmund packing in separate deals. The two friends were so glad to be leaving the Reds that, the *Sporting News* wrote, they went joyriding back and forth over one of the Reds' spring training fields in Tampa. More than three decades later, Crowley still wasn't talking. "No comment," he replied with a laugh. "Let [Rettenmund] tell you that story."[14]

Traded to the Atlanta Braves for pitcher Mike Thompson, Crowley was soon reminded that the grass is not always greener. After he went hitless in seven pinch-hit appearances, the Braves tried to option him to Triple-A. He refused, became a free agent, and wound up back at Rochester a few weeks later after re-signing with the Orioles. Baltimore brought him back to the big leagues in late June, and he hit .246, primarily as a pinch hitter the rest of the way.

Just before the 1977 season got under way, the Orioles, in a surprise move, decided to keep rookie first baseman Eddie Murray, and Crowley was sent back to Rochester again. "Very mad" is how he described his reaction.[15] With four children (daughter Karen arrived in August 1976) between seven months and thirteen years of age, being back at Rochester nine years after his first tour there was not a welcome career move. "I think I'm the best hitter in this league, but I have to prove it," Crowley said.[16]

"He doesn't belong in this league," observed Tidewater Tides skipper Frank Verdi.[17] "He was right," replied Crowley when the quote was relayed to him years later.[18]

Playing every day for the first time since 1969, Crowley set out to bat .300 with thirty home runs, and he accomplished his goal by the first week of August. The Orioles brought him back to the Majors a week later, and he remained a big leaguer for the next six years. "Terry has what you call a classic swing," observed Hall of Famer Frank Robinson. "It's one you don't tamper with."[19]

From 1977 through 1981, Crowley delivered a .310 average as a pinch hitter for the Orioles. "People say you can't carry Crowley for what he does," said Baltimore manager Earl Weaver midway through Baltimore's pennant-winning 1979 season. "But he's already got us three games."[20]

"I've been doing it for so long that people just naturally think I'm older," Crowley said in 1978. "I've been around for a while, and I've been in a couple of World Series. A year ago, people thought I was washed up, though I was only thirty years old."[21]

American League managers voted Crowley the circuit's best pinch hitter in 1979, and he made them look good in Game Three of that season's ALCS with a hit that would have driven in the pennant-clinching run had the Orioles been able to hold the lead in the bottom of the ninth inning. Baltimore did advance to the fall classic the next day, however, setting the stage for one of the most memorable hits of Crowley's career.

The Orioles were trailing the Pittsburgh Pirates 6–3 in Game Four of the World Series at Three Riv-

MALCOLM ALLEN

ers Stadium entering the eighth inning but pulled within a run when John Lowenstein smacked a two-run double to the right-field corner. After Pirates ace reliever Kent Tekulve issued an intentional walk to set up the double play, Crowley stroked a pinch-hit double to the same location as Lowenstein's hit to knock in the tying and go-ahead runs. Baltimore took control, three games to one, and Crowley's hit would be remembered even more fondly if the Orioles hadn't dropped the final three games of the Series.

"Once you get to the World Series, everything is gravy," Crowley said. "I had some pressure-filled pinch hits that got us to different pennant-winning teams. Not only that year, but other years that were pressure filled. If you get a hit, we win the game. If you don't, we drop into second place. But the one thing about the hit off Tekulve, people started to notice, 'Hey, this guy's done that before.' That was the one that probably got me the most notoriety."[22]

The Orioles won 100 games in 1980 and, though they missed the playoffs (the Yankees won 103), it was an especially gratifying year for Crowley. He got 233 at bats, the second-highest total of his career, blasted twelve home runs, and drove in fifty runs while batting .288. He was rewarded with a two-year contract extension to keep him employed through 1983.

Crowley was frustrated, however, when he found himself back in his familiar pinch-hitting role, struggling for at bats again in 1981. "I'm coming off one of the most productive years on the club," he said. "What's wrong with letting me prove I can do it again?"[23]

"Terry's got an awful lot of value as a pinch-hitter," Manager Earl Weaver said. "You can't be too good at your job, and that's his job. I think the object of everyone to help the club is to do what he does best, and one of the things Crowley does as well as anyone is pinch-hit. It isn't that I'm disappointed with what he can do as a DH, but he's excellent as a pinch-hitter."[24]

Though Crowley came off the bench to hit two home runs in 1982, including a walk-off grand slam against the Royals, his average as a pinch hitter dipped to .194 that season. Nevertheless, when the Orioles had to choose between Crowley and his friend Jim Dwyer for the final roster spot coming out of spring training in 1983, a story in a Baltimore newspaper was headlined "Dwyer Set to Go." Crowley hit .357 that spring, so it was a surprise when the Orioles decided to release him instead. Baltimore general manager Hank Peters called it "one of the toughest things I've ever had to do in this job."[25]

Crowley was about to accept an offer to become the Orioles' Minor League hitting instructor when the Montreal Expos called in late May. But he got only forty-four at bats all year, batted .182, and decided to call it a career as a player. "I had some phone calls to go play, but my back was hurting pretty good at that time, and I thought it best and wisest to get into my coaching career, to try to become a hitting coach."[26]

Crowley spent 1984 as the Orioles' Minor League hitting instructor, then served on Baltimore's Major League staff as the hitting coach from 1985 through 1988. In 1986 the Orioles drafted his son Terry Jr., a shortstop, in the eighth round. (Crowley's younger son, Jimmy, was the Red Sox's eleventh-round pick in 1991.) When the Orioles lost 107 games in 1988, all the coaches lost their jobs except the popular Elrod Hendricks. Crowley spent 1989 and 1990 working with Boston Red Sox Minor Leaguers.

He returned to the Majors in 1991, becoming the hitting coach for a Minnesota Twins club that surprised nearly everybody by going from "worst to first" to win the World Series. He remained there through 1998 and explained part of his approach to instructing hitters this way:

If they're good enough to get here to this level, then they must be doing something right. Unless there's something I see that absolutely prevents them from having success at this level, I'll basically leave them alone and try to help them improve their own style, to improve on their own.

You know, it's like a signature. If you can read it, it's not too bad, but when it gets to the point that I can't read it, I've got to straighten their swing out a little bit.[27]

In an earlier interview he noted, "If there's a hitter who's capable of hitting home runs, hitting with power and driving in runs, that's what I'll strive for. I'd hate to see a player just being a singles hitter if he could hit with some power."[28]

The way Crowley fought to get at bats during his playing career helped him communicate to his pupils the importance of making the most of every plate appearance. "Sometimes I go into detail with them to try to make them understand you can develop good habits just as well as you can fall into bad habits. Once you get in the groove and start hitting the ball good, you have to work as hard as you can to stay there, because in the blink of an eye you can fall into a slump or start to struggle."[29]

Crowley left Minnesota after eight seasons and returned to Baltimore in 1999 for a second stint as the Orioles' hitting coach that lasted a dozen years. He outlasted six managers and was invited back for a twenty-fifth season on a Major League staff in 2011 but opted for the reduced travel of a newly created hitting evaluator position instead. Crowley was to evaluate Oriole Major and Minor Leaguers, possible trade and free agent targets, and potential draftees.

"I think I was lucky. I had a pretty good swing, and I had some ability and I made the best of it. I would like to have played more. That's the only regret I have. I wish I could've played more, but I turned out to be a pretty good pinch-hitter, so I guess everything worked out."[30]

Chapter 29. **Pedro Borbon**

Jorge Iber

AGE	W	L	PCT.	ERA	G	GS	GF	CG	SHO	SV	IP	H	BB	SO	HBP	WP
28	9	5	.643	2.95	67	0	25	0	0	5	125	145	21	29	3	6

Given the offensive firepower of the Big Red Machine, it is quite easy to overlook the contributions of the pitching staff to the franchise's success and its two World Series banners. Clearly a run-scoring powerhouse that featured talents like Johnny Bench, Pete Rose, Joe Morgan, and Tony Pérez often simply pummeled divisional, National League, and World Series opponents into submission. Still, it is also necessary to highlight the contributions of players like Don Gullett, Gary Nolan, Jack Billingham, Clay Carroll, Tom Hall, and others who served at the pleasure or behest of Manager George "Sparky" Anderson (also known as Captain Hook), a man who never shied away from bringing in a reliever or juggling a starting rotation. One of the key members of this staff during the glory years of the 1970s, indeed one of the best relievers in all of baseball during this era, was a proud, intense, and very often temperamental Dominican named Pedro Borbon.

Pedro Borbon Rodriguez was born on December 2, 1946, in the town of Mao in what is now known as Valverde Province, Dominican Republic (it was part of Santiago Province until 1958). Sources on Borbon's life provide little information about his schooling, though some indicate that he never attended high school. Given the economic and social circumstances of Dominican society during this era, it is possible that Borbon received scant formal education. What he always possessed, however, was a fiery and competitive disposition, and this was manifested in part by his love for cockfighting from a young age. Borbon has also indicated that he did not play baseball until he was about sixteen. Given the ubiquity of the sport in the Dominican Re-

Year in and year out, Pedro Borbon was one of the most valuable relief pitchers in baseball and a favorite of Sparky Anderson.

public, this tale seems a bit far-fetched (though very much in keeping with his character).

Borbon claimed that he initially played catcher, until he was struck in the head by a bat as he reached for a pitch. This settled matters in his mind, and Borbon quickly made the switch to the mound, where he felt he would be safer (and could take greater advantage of his strong and resilient arm). In mid-October 1964, at the age of seventeen, he signed with the St. Louis Cardinals and was shipped off to his first farm system assignment, in Cedar Rapids, Iowa (Midwest League), for the 1966 campaign.

Borbon spent three years in the Cardinals system and pitched quite well: 6-1, 1.96 for Cedar Rapids; 5-4, 2.29 for St. Petersburg (Florida State League), and 8-5, 2.34 for Modesto (California League). Used almost solely as a relief pitcher (just three starts in the three seasons), he had still not advanced beyond Single-A ball after his third season, 1968. When he was not placed on the Cardinals' forty-man roster after that season, he became eligible for the Rule 5 draft and was selected by the California Angels. In order to protect him, the Angels had to keep Borbon in the Major Leagues for the entire 1969 season.

Borbon made his Major League debut on April 9, 1969, against the Seattle Pilots, pitching three shutout innings in relief of starter Andy Messersmith and earning an impressive victory. But his promising start was an aberration, as he pitched in just twenty-two games for the Angels and finished 2-3 with a 6.15 ERA. While the Angels believed a "sore arm" was to blame, he was included in a big trade they made in November with the Reds; Borbon moved to Cincinnati with pitchers Jim McGlothlin and Vern Geishert in exchange for outfielder Alex Johnson and infielder Chico Ruiz. The Reds needed starting pitching and coveted the twenty-six-year-old McGlothlin. Borbon was a minor part of the deal.[1]

Borbon did not make a positive first impression with his new ball club, as he was involved in what Commissioner Bowie Kuhn considered an "inexcusable and intolerable" act during a game in the Dominican Winter League in December. Borbon was fined severely by Major League Baseball as a result of two confrontations with umpires. Initially, he was fined fifty dollars and suspended for three winter league games, but Kuhn felt this was not sufficient. In February 1970 the commissioner raised the fine to $500 and suspended Borbon (and Rico Carty as well) for the following winter season. This was the first of several incidents in which Borbon's fiery temper tarnished his reputation with his MLB colleagues and officials.[2]

During the 1970 summer season, the young Do-minican fireballer spent most of his time with Indianapolis of the Triple-A American Association, where he finished 5-2 with a 3.30 ERA. He made it to Cincinnati for several weeks in midsummer but had a 0-2 record and a 6.75 ERA. The Reds breezed to the division title and the National League pennant, but Borbon played no part in the postseason festivities. He was later granted permission to return to play in the Dominican Winter League, toiling on the mound for the Tigres del Licey.[3]

The 1972 campaign saw Borbon's breakthrough for the Reds, and he produced excellent and flexible relief work the entire season. In one two-week stretch starting in late June, during which the Reds won thirteen of fourteen games, Borbon made five relief appearances, for a total of 14⅓ innings, yielding only one run and six hits while earning four saves and one win. "He can throw, and throw and throw," Anderson crowed. "Even when I don't plan to use him, he wants to throw in the bullpen." Coach Ted Kluszewski considered Borbon to possess a "million-dollar arm." For the season, the young Dominican finished 8-3 with a 3.17 ERA in sixty-two games and 122 innings, while the Reds went all the way to the seventh game of the World Series before falling to the Oakland Athletics. Borbon pitched nine times in the postseason; his only poor performance was in Game Seven of the Series, as he gave up the deciding runs to the A's and took the loss.[4]

While 1973 was in many ways the best year of Borbon's career on the mound (11-4, 2.16 ERA in eighty games and 121 innings), it was also the year in which he became involved in a fracas that helped cement his reputation as a hot-tempered player, all too willing to be involved in fisticuffs. On October 8, with the Reds playing the Mets during Game Three of the NLCS, Pete Rose and New York shortstop Bud Harrelson became embroiled in a fight after Rose's hard slide into second base. As a result of the ensuing wrestling match, both benches cleared. At the end of the fracas Borbon retrieved what he believed was his cap from the Shea Stadium turf. When he realized it was actually a Mets hat, he took a bite out of the offending article. Similar incidents occurred later on in Borbon's career (a fistfight with teammate César Gerónimo in the Reds' clubhouse, an altercation with Pirates pitcher Daryl Patterson in which Borbon bit his antagonist, and some run-ins at Cincinnati nightspots).[5] Through it all, Borbon continued to pitch consistently excellent and durable baseball. In the 1973 NLCS Borbon won Game One and saved Game Four, but the Reds fell to the Mets in five games.

The next four years were remarkably similar for Borbon. In fact, for the six-year period beginning in 1972, Borbon put up a 52-27 record, with a 3.06 ERA and seventy saves, averaging seventy-one appearances and 126 innings per season. Of course, the Reds were one of history's greatest teams in this period, winning four division titles and two World Series. In the victorious 1975 and 1976 postseasons, Borbon pitched in seven games. In his career he hurled in twenty postseason games, finishing with a win, three saves, and a 2.42 ERA.

Eventually the Reds dynasty faded away. The thirty-one-year-old Borbon had an 8-2 record in 1978 but his 4.98 ERA was a better indicator of his struggles. After he started 2-2, 3.43 in 1979, on June 28 the Reds dealt their veteran reliever to the Giants in exchange for utility man Hector Cruz. His first two appearances for San Francisco came against his old club—he earned a victory against the Reds on June 29 and picked up a save on July 1. Overall, however, the Reds were likely correct in their assessment that Borbon was no longer the pitcher he had been. He finished 4-3 for the Giants, but his ERA was 4.89. After he was released just before the 1980 season, Borbon signed with the Cardinals at the end of April but was let go after only nineteen innings pitched with an ERA of 3.79, giving up a home run in each of his last three appearances. His final game in the Major Leagues was on May 25, 1980. The following spring he was toiling for Monterrey in the Mexican League.[6]

Borbon was married to Griselda Ventura and they had three children, Pedro Jr., Harold, and Miguel. Pedro Jr. (born November 15, 1967, in Mao) followed in his father's footsteps and pitched in the Major Leagues between 1992 and 2003; the high point of his career came in 1995 when his Atlanta Braves won the World Series. When the young Pedro was a teen, his parents divorced and his relationship with his father became strained. "After the divorce, my dad was . . . mentally messed up. He felt like a failure. So he kind of disappeared from my life," he told a reporter in 1995. Pedro Jr. eventually moved to New York City to live with relatives, and he became a standout pitcher at DeWitt Clinton High School and later at Ranger Junior College in Ranger, Texas. Father and son did not see each other on a regular basis for many years, and the younger Borbon noted in a 1999 interview that the relationship was still a work in progress: "We talk every four or five months. There's a lot of fuel there. We don't want to put a match to it because it'll explode. So we talk like we just talked yesterday."[7]

Although Borbon's career was often marred by incidents of violence and poor judgment, his time in the Cincinnati bullpen was marked by much success, as he became the "go-to" reliever for one of the best teams in baseball history. After retiring from the Major Leagues Borbon continued to pitch in various minor and semipro leagues in Latin America and the United States. In 2011 he resided in Pharr, Texas, just across the border from Reynosa, Mexico, along with his second wife. The Reds inducted him into their Hall of Fame in 2010 in recognition of his contributions to the Big Red Machine.

Pedro Borbon died, at age sixty-five, on June 4, 2012, at his home in Pharr. He had been battling cancer. Among the many tributes from former teammates, Tony Pérez recalled, "I always enjoyed his company on and off the field. He was a great guy."[8]

Chapter 30. **Dave Concepción**

Joseph Wancho

AGE	G	AB	R	H	2B	3B	HR	TB	RBI	BB	SO	BAV	OBP	SLG	SB	GDP	HBP
27	140	507	62	139	23	1	5	179	49	39	51	.274	.326	.353	33	17	2

It's called the fall classic, and the 1975 World Series was indeed a "classic." The Series waged between the Cincinnati Reds and the Boston Red Sox was one of the more memorable championship battles, as a single run decided five of the seven games. Cincinnati shortstop Dave Concepción entered the Series hoping that the old saying "third time is a charm" would prove true. He had been to two other World Series, losing out both times: first to Baltimore in 1970 and then to Oakland in 1972.

In 1975 Boston won Game One at Fenway Park, shutting out the Reds by a 6–0 score, and the Reds were looking to balance the ledger before the Series headed to the Queen City. It was a rainy day in Boston on October 12 for Game Two. But the inclement weather did not hinder Boston starter Bill Lee. He held the Reds to one run and was clinging to a 2–1 lead entering the ninth inning. But after Johnny Bench's lead-off double chased Lee from the game, Dick Drago and his blazing fastball moved to the hill.

After Drago retired Tony Pérez on a groundout to shortstop with Bench taking third and George Foster flied to short left field, Concepción came to bat with two outs and the tying run ninety feet away. Concepción hit a 1-1 fastball into the dirt and the ball bounced high toward second base. Boston's Denny Doyle raced to his right and backhanded the ball, but it was too late for the second baseman to make a play. Bench scored the tying run, and Concepción was on first. Red Sox fans in the Fenway Park crowd fell silent. Concepción stole second base, sliding past the bag but getting back safely. Ken Griffey then doubled him home, and the Reds won 3–2 to even the Series. "I was just looking to make contact," Concepción said later. "That's all

Dave Concepción joined the Reds as a skinny kid known only for his defense, but he became one of the best shortstops in the game.

you can do in a situation like that against a fastball pitcher like Drago. I knew it was a hit once I got it past the pitcher."[1]

David Ismael Concepción Benitez was born on June 17, 1948, in Ocumare de la Costa, Aragua, Venezuela. His father, a truck driver, was against young Dave's pursuit of a career in baseball, instead hoping that he would make a living as a lawyer, banker, or doctor. After attending Agustin Codazzi High School, Concepción worked as a bank teller and played for a local amateur baseball team.

His coach, Wilfredo Calvino, was a scout for the Reds, and despite his father's wishes, young Concepción signed a contract with Calvino in September 1967 and joined Tampa in the Class A Florida State League in 1968.

Concepción's time in the Reds' Minor League chain was brief; by the end of the 1969 season he was playing for Triple-A Indianapolis. The twenty-one-year-old hit .341 for the Indians in 167 at bats and showed a high aptitude on the base paths. "Concepcion has the best baserunning instincts I've ever seen in a youngster," said Indians manager Vern Rapp. "He stole 11 bases in 12 attempts and he was only with us about a month."[2]

Concepción was promoted to the Reds for the 1970 season, but he faced veteran competition at shortstop in Woody Woodward and Darrel Chaney. When Concepción showed up at camp, standing 6 feet 2 and weighing just 155 pounds, Pete Rose joked that he wouldn't be in danger of pulling a muscle in his legs, that instead it would have to be a pulled bone. But Rose also acknowledged, "They tell me that the kid can play shortstop with a pair of pliers."[3]

Reds rookie manager Sparky Anderson took a liking to the youngster, as did hitting instructor Ted Kluszewski. Anderson made Concepción the starter, mostly for his defensive ability. Anderson didn't expect much offense from his young shortstop. But when Concepción's batting average rose to .270 in May, Kluszewski commented, "I've been saying all along that the kid's gonna be a pretty good hitter."[4]

Concepción's unexpectedly good hitting could not keep him in the starting lineup. He made fourteen errors through mid-June, and Anderson replaced him with the dependable Woodward. Woodward was a valuable commodity for the Reds, able to play every infield position and play them well. He solidified the position for a while, but by the time the second half of the season began, Concepción was back in the lineup. He made only eight more errors and batted a respectable .260 for the season. The Reds steamrolled through the National League West Division and had little trouble sweeping Pittsburgh in the NLCS, holding the Pirates to three runs in the three games. They were not as fortunate in the World Series, losing in five games to the Baltimore Orioles.

Concepción missed most of the 1971 exhibition season with a badly sprained right thumb, and when he returned to the team in late April, he was used as a utility man, playing second base, third base, and the outfield. He got his shortstop job back in early May but struggled at the plate that season and in 1972 with .205 and .209 batting averages. His career got an indirect boost after the 1971 season when a big trade brought second baseman Joe Morgan from the Astros. Concepción and Morgan established themselves as one of the better keystone combinations in Major League history. As teammates with the Reds, they appeared in four All-Star Games, starting three, and won two World Series.

Concepción was his own worst critic, and at times his being hard on himself caused subpar play to spiral further downward. Sparky Anderson decided that he needed a big-brother influence and asked veteran Tony Pérez to room with the youngster and mentor him. "He cannot stand 0-4 day. It kill him. I tell him very simple thing. 'Don't get your head down.' . . . 'If you don't hit now, you will next time.' . . . Things like this. Always I try to pick him up," Pérez explained.[5] Pérez also felt that marriage helped Concepción settle down. (Dave and his bride, Delia, were married in 1972. They had three children, David Alejandro, David Eduardo, and Daneska.)

Whatever the reason, Concepción emerged as a top-flight player in 1973. He was named to the All-Star team for the first time. He batted .287 and provided some punch at the bottom of the Reds' lineup. He posted the first five-hit performance of his career against San Francisco on July 5—with hit number five, in the bottom of the ninth inning, driving in the winning run.

Unfortunately for Concepción and the Reds, his season was curtailed by an injury. On July 22 the

Reds were breezing to a 6–0 victory over Montreal at home. Concepción was having a fine afternoon with three hits and two runs scored. On first base in the seventh inning, he took off as Denis Menke hit a smash to Expos shortstop Larry Lintz. As Lintz threw Menke out at first base, Concepción never stopped and raced to third base. As he slid in to the base his left leg folded underneath him. The fibula, a long bone between the knee and ankle, was broken and his ankle was dislocated. His season was over. "It probably cost us the league championship," said Rose.[6] The Reds won the NL West but lost to the New York Mets in the NLCS without their All-Star shortstop.

Concepción rehabbed while playing winter ball in Venezuela. He came back healthy and began a string of four years (1974–77) in which he won a Gold Glove. In 1974 he had his first big offensive season, smacking fourteen home runs and driving in eighty-two runs, while batting mostly sixth or seventh in the lineup. Concepción brought another dimension to the Reds in addition to his offensive and defensive skills. Beginning in 1973 he stole twenty or more bases in six consecutive seasons, pilfering forty-one in 1974.

The Reds finally reached the summit in 1975 and 1976, winning back-to-back World Series. In 1975 Concepción hit .455 in the NLCS against the Pirates but only .179 in the tense and gripping World Series against the Red Sox. The next year he hit .357 in the Series against the Yankees with a triple and three RBIs. On a team filled with All-Stars and future Hall of Famers, Concepción was playing at a high level at the apex of his career. Former Brooklyn Dodgers great Pee Wee Reese, a Hall of Fame shortstop himself, offered a synthesis of Concepción as a shortstop: "Mark Belanger may be a little smoother then Concepcion. Larry Bowa is very quick. Rick Burleson is a leader type. Bill Russell has an accurate arm. But no one does everything as well as Concepcion. It's possible that no one ever has."[7]

Reds third base coach Alex Grammas agreed with Reese's assessment. Grammas had worked with Concepción since he was a rookie, helping him to hone his craft. "There are some mighty good shortstops in the league today," said Grammas. "But Concepcion is a notch ahead of them all in all-around ability because his bat is stronger and his range in the field is greater."[8] Concepción and Grammas had such a solid relationship that Concepción's first son, David Alejandro, takes his middle name from Grammas.

Concepción also famously used Riverfront Stadium's artificial surface to his advantage. He started to develop a pain in his throwing arm and perfected the art of throwing the ball on a bounce off the artificial turf to the first baseman. It was extremely helpful to him on ground balls hit in the hole between shortstop and third base. "I didn't invent that throw," Concepción said. "I saw another fellow do it. I saw Brooks Robinson do it to Lee May here in 1970. Then when my arm hurt, I decided, 'Why not try it?'"[9]

After a couple of second-place finishes, in 1979 the Reds won the NL West to cap off the decade of the 1970s but lost the NLCS to Pittsburgh in a three-game sweep. By that time, many of the cogs in the Big Red Machine had moved on. Pérez was the first to go, in a deal with Montreal. Rose left via free agency in 1978, the same year Anderson was fired. Soon Morgan and Gerónimo would be gone. But Concepción could still play. "The other people move away, and all of a sudden you notice the antique work of art in the corner," Bench said of Concepción.[10] Concepción posted career highs in home runs (sixteen) and RBIs (eighty-four) in 1979. He also claimed his fifth and final Gold Glove Award.

Concepción remained the Reds' regular shortstop through the 1985 season and made the last of his eight All-Star teams in 1982. In that season's All-Star Game, in Montreal's Olympic Stadium, he hit a two-run homer off Boston's Dennis Eckersley and was named the game's Most Valuable Player. Before he hit his second-inning homer, he spoke with All-Star teammate and fellow Venezuelan Manny Trillo of the Philadelphia Phillies: "I told Manny, 'I got a feeling I'm going to hit one out of the ballpark.' He kidded me, but I said, 'I'm gonna do it.'"[11] And he did.

Concepción retired after the 1988 season, having played his entire Major League career with the Reds. His successor at shortstop, Barry Larkin, began his own nineteen-year career in 1986 and eventually was voted into the Baseball Hall of Fame. Concepción was inducted into the Cincinnati Reds Hall of Fame in 2000, and his number 13 was retired by the Reds on August 25, 2007. Said Joe Morgan, "He's the greatest shortstop I've ever played with or I've ever seen."[12]

In retirement, Concepción returned to his native Venezuela and later managed his hometown Aragua Tigers. Later he became an executive in a trucking business.

Concepción continued a fine lineage of shortstops from Venezuela. He grew up idolizing Chico Carrasquel and Luis Aparicio and trying to emulate them in the field. Later, countrymen Ozzie Guillen and Omar Vizquel grew up fantasizing about playing baseball in the Major Leagues like their hero, Dave Concepción. Vizquel paid homage to his boyhood icon by wearing the number 13, saying Concepción was "the one that I liked, the one that I looked up to."[13]

Chapter 31. **Ed Armbrister**

Rory Costello

AGE	G	AB	R	H	2B	3B	HR	TB	RBI	BB	SO	BAV	OBP	SLG	SB	GDP	HBP
26	59	65	9	12	1	0	0	13	2	5	19	.185	.254	.200	3	1	1

The third man from the Bahamas to play in the Major Leagues, Ed Armbrister was a spare part in Cincinnati's Big Red Machine. His career was modest (265 at bats in 224 games), but he won World Series rings in 1975 and 1976. Yet for Boston Red Sox fans, Armbrister was in the wrong place at the wrong time. The outfielder is still best known for his controversial collision with Carlton Fisk in Game Three of the 1975 Series. He was one of the gremlins that wouldn't be cast out until Boston finally became a baseball champion again in 2004.

Even still, some resentment lingers among the old Fenway faithful—but it's hard to find a less likely target. Said Armbrister's manager, Sparky Anderson, "Ed Armbrister is just a nice person. He's a person that anyone would like to be around. He's always smiling, he's happy. I don't think nothin' ever disturbed him. He could run like heck, he was a good outfielder, his offense . . . he wasn't gonna set no records with his bat or anything, but he *was* a great extra man to have. Any club could use a guy like that—a very valuable person to have on your club."[1]

Edison Armbrister Jr. was born on July 4, 1948, in Nassau, the Bahamian capital, on the island of New Providence. He was part of a large family. When his father, Edison Sr., died in June 2009, there were thirteen surviving children. Ed had at least five brothers—one of whom, Jonathan, played briefly in the minors in 1978—and seven sisters.[2]

About 85 percent of the population in the Bahamas is of African descent, and the name Armbrister is prominent among both black and white residents. The story of the Bahamas is colorful and complex, involving the American Revolution, Loy-

A bench player for parts of five seasons with the Reds, Ed Armbrister is most famous for his bunt in Game Three of the 1975 World Series.

alists, plantations, and slavery. The islands were a British crown colony from 1718 until 1964 (when it became an independent nation, a member of the British Commonwealth), so it's no surprise that the main sport, historically, was cricket. Baseball later became visible there, and it took off thanks to former cricketer André Rodgers, who began his professional baseball career in 1954. Later that year the Bahamas Baseball Association (BBA) was formed.

Rodgers made his big league debut in April 1957, when Armbrister was just eight years old. He remained in the Majors through 1967, by which time

Armbrister himself had signed a professional contract. After Rodgers died in December 2004, Armbrister said, "I followed André for a long time, and it was him who inspired me to become a professional ballplayer. André was always a positive guy. He was a strong-minded person, and I always said if I could just be like André I would be successful."[3]

The second Bahamian big leaguer, Tony Curry, signed with the Phillies in 1957. Armbrister also offered memories at Curry's funeral in October 2006:

I never knew Tony Curry the way I did André Rodgers, but I remember when I was small and used to play baseball on the Southern Recreation Grounds, Tony Curry was there, André Rodgers was there, and a lot of these players [also attending Curry's service] were there at the same time. With me being so small—all I knew was, when he went off to play professional baseball he was a good hitter, he was a good player, and he was fast. When he went to play professional baseball, a lot of youngsters said, "Hey—if he can do it, I can do the same thing!" He was someone right from home—he gave a lot of other people in the "backyard" the idea of going to play professional baseball. I was one of them, and "Sudgy" [the late Wil Culmer] was one of them.[4]

Among these other talented men was Vince Ferguson, who signed with the Milwaukee Braves organization in 1961 and reached Triple-A in 1966–67. Another was Ed Moxey, a catcher/outfielder signed by the Giants who tore up lower levels starting in 1962, though he never got past Double-A. Former BBA president Oswald Brown, who later became a prominent journalist, said, "Indeed, in the decade after André Rodgers became the first Bahamian to make it to the major leagues in 1957, baseball had developed to the point where it was unquestionably the most popular sport in the country."[5]

Grassroots support was strong among Bahamian youth. There may not have been much infrastructure, but there was plenty of pickup fun.[6] In 1972

Armbrister recalled that he and his friends "played wherever we found an open space—in streets, vacant lots, and even a cemetery. But we got chased out of there because we were knocking over too many grave markers and crosses. We used any kind of a ball we could find, even tennis balls. For bats we used broomsticks, tree limbs, and boards."[7]

It's likely that Armbrister played at least some cricket too, as did the Ford brothers, Wenty (who pitched for the Atlanta Braves in 1973) and Eddie (who played with Armbrister in their first professional season). Armbrister also enjoyed a variety of other athletic pursuits, including swimming, basketball, and track.

The Bahamas joined the National Baseball Congress (NBC) in 1957, and teams from Nassau went to the NBC tournament in Wichita, Kansas, starting in 1964 and 1965. Armbrister did not make the trip in 1964; though he may have been part of the 1965 squad, he was probably still too young. He was attending Nassau's Western High School, but as he told author Mike Dyer in 1979, "All we had were amateur leagues. I played a little high-school baseball, but there weren't any good baseball facilities and the coaching was poor. I was just lucky."[8] Pro scouts were watching the Bahamas, though, and the eighteen-year-old was signed in late 1966. Armbrister later recalled the circumstances: "I remember I was painting my mother's house during the Christmas and a scout by the name of Paul Florence came by, he was with another gentleman, Bernice Albury, and they asked me to go out to the Sports Centre and do some training."[9] Albury was a member of Nassau's 1964 NBC team. Florence—an old New York Giants catcher who had previously scouted Cuba for Cincinnati—represented the Houston Astros. He had actually been expecting Armbrister for several days, but the young man "didn't know anything about scouts, what they were or what they did, and I didn't show up."[10] It is not known whether the tardiness influenced what was probably a very modest bonus.

Armbrister was not a big man, standing 5 feet 11 and weighing just 160 pounds, but he did have speed. He was also a good bunter, which would be one of his purposes in the Majors. However, Armbrister's first season in the Minors, with Houston's Cocoa team in the Florida State League (Class A), was not auspicious. He hit just .211, with one homer and thirty-two runs batted in. Returning to Cocoa in 1968, Ambre (as his friends also called him) boosted his average (.261-2-32), while stealing thirty-five bases in forty-two tries. He then went to High-A ball in 1969, with Peninsula (Hampton, Virginia) in the Carolina League. Continued improvement was visible, notably some more power (.271-8-30).

Armbrister climbed to Double-A for 1970. *Baseball Digest* issued a prescient scouting report on him that March: "Speed may carry him to majors in two or three years. Can spray hits, but needs work with fielding to get chance."[11] That was an upgrade from the previous year, when the magazine said, "Only glaring weakness is with the glove."[12] Following his typical slow but steady progression, Armbrister spent the 1970 season and the next with Columbus (Georgia) in the Southern League. Although his average dipped to .238 against the stronger competition the first year, he picked up to .298-9-42 in 1971. The Astros also experimented with him at third base during this time.

On November 29, 1971, Houston made a trade with Cincinnati that would work out much better for the Reds. Second baseman Joe Morgan, pitcher Jack Billingham, outfielder César Gerónimo, infielder Denis Menke, and Armbrister left the Astros in return for second baseman Tommy Helms, first baseman Lee May, and utility man Jimmy Stewart. Armbrister, a throw-in, was barely mentioned in the stories about the deal. In 1976 Sparky Anderson remarked, "Hell, Houston gave away Ed Armbrister."[13]

Armbrister took it hard at first. "I was disappointed to think that Houston had given up on me. I thought I had a better chance in the Houston or-

ganization because Cincinnati was an established club with plenty of outfielders. But I just told myself, 'Ed, you're going to have to go extra hard now if you expect to make it with Cincinnati.'"[14]

The diligent Bahamian lifted his game again with the Reds' Triple-A club, Indianapolis. He became a .300 hitter in 1972 and maintained that level in 1973, also hitting ten homers for the first time as a professional baseball player and driving in seventy-two runs. In the outfield with him were George Foster and Ken Griffey Sr. That May Indians manager Vern Rapp said, "These can be the finest three players I've ever managed as far as outfield talent is concerned. They all have excellent speed, good range, and fine arms. This could be the finest outfield, at least defensively, in the minor leagues."[15]

Cincinnati called the entire trio up at roughly the same time in late August. Said author Tom Adelman, "Initially, it struck Pete [Rose] as too much. . . . Griffey was a talent, Rose wouldn't deny that. . . . But Foster was elusive, unreliable, too quiet, too wide-eyed, while Armbrister was not serious enough. Indeed, Armbrister was always exploding with song.[16] Singing in the dugout! By God, it bothered the f*** out of Rose." Adelman went on to explain, though, "In the Bahamas, work means long hours for low pay. To be paid to play a child's game—Armbrister cannot help but giggle."[17]

Armbrister made his big league debut with the Reds on August 31, 1973, beating countryman Wenty Ford to the Majors by ten days. He pinch-ran for Rose, stayed in the game playing left field, and struck out in his first at bat, against Gary Ross of the Padres. Five days later, on September 5, he tripled and later hit his first homer in the Majors, off Houston's Jerry Reuss at the Astrodome. "It's guys like Dan Driessen and Ed Armbrister who are helping us turn the season around," said Rose. (Cincinnati had climbed into first place just two days before.)[18]

A little over a week later, the Braves came to Cincinnati, and there was a Bahamian reunion between Ford and Armbrister. The last time that had

RORY COSTELLO

happened was April 22, 1961, when Rodgers (Chicago Cubs) and Curry (Philadelphia Phillies) both played at Connie Mack Stadium. As of 2012, it has not happened since.

In October Cincinnati dropped the disgruntled Bobby Tolan from its playoff roster, and Armbrister remained. He played in three games and went 1-for-6 with five strikeouts as the New York Mets upset the Reds in the NLCS, three games to two. He even started Game Three in place of lefty-hitting César Gerónimo, since Anderson wanted more right-handers to hit against Jerry Koosman. That game featured the infamous fight near second base between Rose and Mets shortstop Bud Harrelson, with a subsequent bench-clearing brawl. From center field, Armbrister had a close view as the left-field crowd at Shea Stadium heaved bottles, cans, and garbage toward Rose, nearly causing a forfeit.

That off-season the Reds traded for two veteran outfield reserves, Merv Rettenmund and Terry Crowley. Therefore Armbrister spent most of 1974 in Indianapolis, playing only nine games with the big club during September and October. From 1975 through 1977, though, he remained in Cincinnati for the full year. Still technically a rookie in 1975, he got only sixty-five at bats in fifty-nine games, hitting just .185. Yet Armbrister remained assured. "Sooner or later I knew I was going to contribute," said the seldom-used Armbrister. "I've been telling them all year it was going to be my turn in the playoffs."[19]

Indeed, he made his only plate appearance count in the 1975 NLCS. It was the top of the tenth inning in Game Three. Griffey bunted his way on with two strikes and reached third with one out. Then Armbrister, batting for Rawly Eastwick, lifted a sacrifice fly to center. The Reds took the lead and completed their three-game sweep of the Pirates.

In the World Series, against the Red Sox, Armbrister came to the plate four times in four games. The one people still remember came in Game Three at Cincinnati's Riverfront Stadium. Again it was the tenth inning. Gerónimo led off with a single,

and once more Armbrister came on to bat for Eastwick. His job was to sacrifice, but his bunt was not a good one.

"I wanted to push it way out but it took a high bounce right in front of the plate," he explained. "I was standing there and I felt [Fisk] from behind. I saw him make the throw to second. I could see the throw was going to be high. But that's just the way the play went."[20] In 1985 Armbrister said, "I really don't know why I stopped. I still can't tell you that. Carlton Fisk, being experienced, should have known what to do. For some reason, I hesitated and he was out there like a cat. I saw him reaching for the ball, and I decided to make my way down to first base. My right knee hit his left shinguard. He then made a grunt sound, like he wanted to put everything into the throw."[21]

Fisk and Red Sox manager (and former catcher) Darrell Johnson were furious. They thought it was clearly interference. Curt Gowdy and Tony Kubek, calling the game for NBC television, were also vehement. Umpire Larry Barnett, however, said, "I ruled that it was simply a collision . . . simply part of the process of getting to first base."[22]

Johnson's appeal was fruitless, Gerónimo later scored, and Fisk continued to fume—"It's a damn joke"—after the loss. The whole Boston club was in vile temper. Bill "The Spaceman" Lee said, "If it was me out there, I would have bitten [Barnett's] ear off. I'd have Van Goghed him!"[23] Carl Yastrzemski heaped invective on the umpires, who were selected for the postseason via rotation at that time. *Boston Globe* columnist Ray Fitzgerald observed, "I have been in many sullen and snarling locker rooms in the last decade, but none as bitter as the one last night. The Grinch had stolen Christmas from the Red Sox."[24]

On the winning side, Armbrister himself added, "There was no way I was trying to block him. . . . If [Fisk] hit from behind, I would say he interfered with me." This jibed with National League umpire Dick Stello's view on the appeal. Sparky Anderson "ducked that one nicely, with his tongue in his cheek. 'To be honest with you,' he answered, 'I don't see all that well.'" He also said, "We're lucky. . . . The good Lord takes care of us. . . . Thank God I'll never have to decide whether to argue."[25]

There have been many exhaustive postmortems on the play. Johnson could and perhaps should have lodged a protest. Fisk shoved the hesitant Armbrister aside with an empty mitt, but he could simply have tagged him instead of throwing hastily. Barnett and Stello could have interpreted the rulebook better; the issue of intent was nebulous. A shadowy "supplemental instruction" to umpires from Major League Baseball before the Series complicated this aspect still further.[26]

There's still no consensus—except, of course, among Boston supporters—as to whether it was interference. "I still don't know what was right!" said Alex Grammas, Cincinnati's third base coach, in 1999. Even his opposite number for the Red Sox, Don Zimmer, came to say the same thing in his memoirs. The Reds went on to win the Series in seven games. It remains one of the best fall classics ever.

Armbrister appeared in a career-high seventy-three games in 1976, hitting .295 in just seventy-eight at bats. On July 31, in Cincinnati, he enjoyed his peak performance; his four hits included two homers, both off San Diego's Brent Strom. He joked about his playing time in an article on baseball superstition. "Ed Armbrister . . . hails from the Bahamas, where voodoo is feared by many natives. But Armbrister is not among the believers. 'If I believed in it, I'd have some voodoo woman put a hex on somebody and get me in the lineup.'"[27]

In the NLCS that year, Armbrister got into one game with one plate appearance against the Phillies. He did not appear in the World Series—there was little need, as the Reds steamrolled the Yankees in four straight. Armbrister remained in his caddy role in 1977, hitting .256 in seventy-eight at bats in sixty-five games. An off-season operation for a bone spur in his right elbow still hampered his throwing

in the spring of 1978, though.[28] He was sent back to Indianapolis, and Dave Collins became the Reds' spare outfielder. Despite another solid year at Triple-A, Armbrister never resurfaced in the Major Leagues or in U.S. organized baseball. He finished with a career batting average in the majors of .245.

After a season at Indianapolis, two years in the Mexican League then followed. In 1979 Armbrister played for Yucatán and Tampico (.291-13-62). After he hit just .180 in thirty-five games for Nuevo Laredo in 1980, his time as a professional baseball player came to an end.

He returned to the Bahamas. As of 1985, Armbrister was a craps-table croupier at Resorts International's Paradise Island Casino.[29] He later worked for at least one other establishment in the gaming business, a staple of the Bahamian tourist economy.[30] As of 2006, he was with the Local Government and Consumer Affairs agency on Arawak Cay, a popular attraction in the Nassau area. He was married and had three children.[31] In his leisure hours, Armbrister became a notable local softball player.[32]

According to Oswald Brown, "Beginning in the 1980s, baseball was allowed to deteriorate" in the Bahamas.[33] The BBA had become largely dormant. In 1993, however, a new group called the Bahamas Baseball Federation sprang up. The same year, the New Providence Amateur Baseball League started play, and the game regained some momentum in the outer islands as well. The nation still produced a handful of prospects, including Antoan Richardson, who appeared in nine games for the Atlanta Braves in 2011 after battling back from the independent Northern League. Armbrister remained involved, having served as a consultant to the Ministry of Sports on efforts to boost the game in local junior and senior schools. In July 2005 he managed the Bahamian junior national team that beat their Cuban counterparts 7–6.[34]

On March 10, 2007, Armbrister received the honor given to the top sporting figures in the Bahamas, as his picture was added to the Wall of Fame at Lyn-

RORY COSTELLO

den Pindling International Airport. Many local observers felt it was long overdue, but Armbrister took it philosophically, saying, "Better late than never."[35] In October 2008 he became a member of the Bahamas National Hall of Fame.

Armbrister occasionally made it back to Cincinnati for Big Red Machine reunions; the last time was in November 2008. "Armbrister . . . looks like he could still fit into his Reds uniform. 'Eddie,' [formerly thin Dave] Concepción grinned, 'no food in Nassau?'"[36]

At first Armbrister expressed reluctance that one moment should define his career—but over time he came to embrace the idea. In fact, his e-mail address commemorates the notorious bunt play. Still, the greatest measure of this man is his character. In 1999 Sparky Anderson underscored his view: "You would keep him just because you liked him. Everybody liked him. He's a good one." Alex Grammas echoed the feeling: "You couldn't help but like him. That to me is Number One."[37]

Chapter 32. July 1975 Timeline

Mark Miller and Mark Armour

All headlines below are from the next day's edition of the *Springfield (OH) News.*

July 1—REDS WIN 29TH IN LAST 36, NIP ASTROS AGAIN IN 15TH, 8–7—The headline was actually incorrect; they had won thirty of their past thirty-eight games. Nonetheless, the club started July with its fourth extra-inning victory in five days (and its eighth consecutive win in extra-inning contests). The Reds needed a three-run ninth-inning rally to tie the score in regulation, and then patiently waited until Joe Morgan knocked in the winning run with a single in the fifteenth for an 8–7 win. Morgan had homered back in the eighth, and Pat Darcy, the sixth Reds pitcher of the night, picked up the victory. The team's errorless-game streak ended at fifteen games when left fielder Dan Driessen committed an error in the fifth inning.

July 2—FOSTER HITS 480-FOOT HOMER, REDS SWEEP HOUSTON—Speaking of his long home run, George Foster said that he had "hit a golf ball further but not a baseball." The Reds spotted the Astros three runs in the first inning, but Foster's three-run blast in the sixth gave them a 4–3 lead that held up as the final score. Rawly Eastwick relieved Tom Carroll and finished up allowing one hit in four scoreless innings. The Reds finished their home stand with a 6-1 record.

July 3—PADRES' JONES HURLS ONE-HITTER AS REDS LOSE, 2–1—The Reds headed to San Diego for a four-game series and managed just an eighth-inning run-scoring double by Bill Plummer in their 2–1 loss to Randy Jones. Gary Nolan was nearly as sharp, allowing just two hits in eight innings. Will McEnaney relieved in the ninth and allowed two hits before losing the game on an error by right fielder Ed Armbrister.

July 4—BILLINGHAM'S HIT HELPS OVERCOME POOR PITCHING—Jack Billingham did not pitch well (six hits, five walks, and five runs in 5⅓ innings) but picked up the victory thanks in part to his own run-scoring single in the Reds' four-run second inning. The Reds piled up thirteen hits and held on for the 7–6 win. Johnny Bench's seventeenth home run led the attack.

July 5—PADRES' ERRORS HELP REDS TRIUMPH, 6–3—Two San Diego errors led to four unearned runs, allowing the Reds to win their second straight in San Diego, 6–3. Fred Norman collected his fourth win and Rawly Eastwick his third save in combining to give up just seven hits. The hitters were paced by a pinch-hit two-run double by Merv Rettenmund in a three-run seventh inning.

July 6—REDS MAINTAIN EIGHT-GAME LEAD, SWAMP PADRES 13–2—The Reds took three of the four games in San Diego by routing the Padres, 13–2. Clay Kirby pitched five effective innings before Pedro Borbon came in and allowed just one hit in four scoreless innings. Pete Rose (hitting .313) and Joe Morgan (hitting .356) each had three hits while George Foster, Darrel Chaney, and Morgan drove in two runs apiece.

July 7—REDS ROLLING SO SMOOTHLY EVEN SPARKY IS AMAZED—Returning home to Cincinnati, Tony Pérez stroked his eleventh home run and George Foster his fifteenth as the Reds defeated

Steve Carlton and the Phillies, 7–3. Pérez's two-run red-seat (upper-deck) home run was, in his own words, "the best I can hit one." Johnny Bench had three hits for the Reds, winners of four in a row.

July 8—PHILS DOWNGRADE NOLAN'S PITCH-ING, REDS KEEP WINNING—The Reds managed just two runs, but that was enough for Gary Nolan and Rawly Eastwick, who combined on a six hit-ter to beat the Phillies, 2–1. George Foster got four of the Reds' eight hits, including a double that led to their first run. After the game the Phillies den-igrated Nolan's pitching, comparing him to their batting-practice pitcher. Nolan was now 8-5 with a 2.82 ERA.

July 9—"NO WAY WE CAN LOSE NOW," ANDER-SON SAYS—The Reds completed a series sweep of the Phillies in a 9–7 slugfest, their twenty-seventh come-from-behind victory of the season. The Reds trailed 5–4 entering the bottom of the eighth in-ning. Johnny Bench tied the game with his eigh-teenth home run, then watched as his teammates piled on with four more runs. Pedro Borbon pitched two scoreless innings to earn the win, as the Reds survived Mike Schmidt's two-run home run in the ninth off Rawly Eastwick.

July 11—MCENANEY SAVES BOTH ENDS OF SWEEP OVER METS, EIGHTH STRAIGHT UPS REDS LEAD TO 10½—The Reds train roared on, taking two from the Mets at Riverfront Sta-dium. Fred Norman beat Jon Matlack 4–3 in the first game, backed by a double and a home run from Tony Pérez. In the nightcap Johnny Bench got things going with a three-run home run off Randy Tate, and Clay Kirby and the bullpen took things from there, completing a four-hit, 4–1 victory. Pete Rose collected three hits in the doubleheader.

July 12—REDS WIN NINTH STRAIGHT ON 3–2 VICTORY OVER THE METS—The Reds again scored three runs in the first and held on to win 3–2. Pat Darcy started for the Reds, but Sparky

Anderson, in full "Captain Hook" mode, pinch-hit for him with the Reds leading by a run in the second inning. Tom Carroll (3-0) and Rawly East-wick (fifth save) allowed just three hits in the fi-nal seven innings of the game. Merv Rettenmund's two-run single off Jerry Koosman was the big hit in the three-run first.

July 13—REDS 12½ UP, STILL HUNGRY TEAM, NIP METS FOR 10 IN ROW—Pete Rose's two-out, bases-loaded two-run single (one of his three hits in the game) capped a four-run seventh-inning rally, propelling the Reds to a 5–3 victory over the Mets. The victory was the tenth in a row for the Machine and brought them into the All-Star break with a commanding 12½-game lead over the Dodgers in the NL West. They had won a remark-able forty-one of their last fifty games.

July 15—SIGHT OF AL UNIFORMS PRODUCES ANOTHER NL WIN—Four Reds were elected start-ers for the All Star Game, held at County Stadi-um in Milwaukee, and helped the NL to its fourth straight victory. Pete Rose, who had been playing third base for the past two months, led off and played right field; Joe Morgan batted third, John-ny Bench fourth, and Dave Concepción eighth. All four Reds starters had a hit, including Rose, who had two. Rose also drove in a run with a sacrifice fly in the ninth inning. Tony Pérez played the last two innings at first base.

July 17—3–0 LOSS MEANS REDS HAVE WON ONLY 41 OF LAST 51—Beginning the second half in Montreal, the Reds were shut down by the duo of Steve Rogers and Dale Murray, who allowed the Reds seven hits in a 3–0 Expos victory, ending the Reds' winning streak at ten. Pepe Mangual and Pete Mackanin touched Jack Billingham (10-4) for solo home runs in the winning cause.

July 18—PÉREZ GETS CHANCE, BELTS GRAND SLAM HOME RUN—Montreal starter Dennis Blair walked the bases loaded in the third inning, and

Tony Pérez made him pay with a grand slam that put the Reds on the way to their 10–3 victory. Gary Nolan (9-5) gave up three runs in five innings before Rawly Eastwick finished up, allowing one hit in four scoreless innings for his seventh save.

July 19—EXPOS STUN REDS, CINCINNATI LOSES, 4–2—Despite four hits from Johnny Bench and three by Pete Rose (now hitting .321), the Reds dropped the rubber match of the three-game set in Montreal. Joe Morgan's fourteenth home run tied the score in the top of the eighth inning, but Will McEnaney allowed a two-run single by Nate Colbert in the bottom half to break a 2–2 tie. Pedro Borbon was charged with the loss.

July 20—BAD FIELDING HURTS REDS, 11–4 LOSS TO PHILS—Reds starting pitcher Clay Kirby failed to get out of the first inning, allowing just one hit but walking five, and the Reds committed four errors, all helping the team to drop the two-game series opener in Philadelphia 11–4. Mike Schmidt's three-run homer in the second inning put the Phillies up 8–2, and Tom Underwood and Gene Garber coasted from there.

July 21—MORGAN TALKS ABOUT RACES, LIKES PIRATES, REDS—The Reds scored five runs in the second inning and held on for an easy 10–4 victory over the Phillies. Joe Morgan (now batting .347) led the way offensively with three hits, two walks, and a stolen base (his forty-second). Pat Darcy allowed four runs in five innings before turning it over to the bullpen, which once again was brilliant, as Clay Carroll and Rawly Eastwick combined for four scoreless innings.

July 22—KOOSMAN TOUGH FOR REDS, HARD TO HIT AND CATCH—The road trip next headed to New York's Shea Stadium for three games, and the Reds dropped the first game to the Mets, 3–1. Jack Billingham and Pedro Borbon pitched well, but the Reds could do nothing with Mets left-hander Jerry Koosman, who entered the ninth in-

ning with a three-hit shutout but allowed three hit and runs to provide a bit of drama.

July 23—REDS' PLAY PUZZLES SPARKY, BAD DEFENSE, OFFENSE—The Reds dropped their second straight in New York, by a score of 5–2. After a shaky start, Jon Matlack allowed just five hits (including a two-run single by Johnny Bench in the first that gave the Reds a short-lived lead) and the Reds committed three errors. Gary Nolan allowed eight hits in six innings to take the loss.

July 24—DODGERS' ALSTON CALM FOR SHOWDOWN WITH REDS—Though the headline was looking ahead to the next series, the Reds took the time to defeat Tom Seaver and the Mets, 2–1, to salvage a game from their three-game set. The Reds got to Seaver for two runs in the second, and Fred Norman, Will McEnaney, and Rawly Eastwick made the runs stand up. The Reds finished their road trip 3-5 and headed home to face the Dodgers, who were still 12½ games behind in the NL West.

July 25—ROSE RIPS MARSHALL FOR HOMER, SAVES REDS SPLIT—The Reds dropped the first game of a doubleheader, 4–3, to the Dodgers when reliever Clay Carroll allowed two runs in the eighth inning. The Dodgers scored the winning run when Manny Mota laid down a perfect squeeze bunt, and the Reds succumbed to the pitching of Andy Messersmith and Mike Marshall. In game two the Dodgers were leading 3–1 in the seventh when Pete Rose capped a four-run rally with a three-run homer off Marshall, the Dodgers' star reliever and a nemesis of the Reds. George Foster added his sixteenth home run in the eighth inning of the 6–3 win.

July 26—ROSE'S HITTING SPARKS REDS AS DODGERS FALL 13½ BEHIND—In a nationally televised Saturday afternoon affair, the Reds defeated the visiting Dodgers 5–3, with an offense led by four hits and three runs from Pete Rose.

Jack Billingham allowed nine hits and three runs before Rawly Eastwick came on to get the last out of the game.

July 27—LA SPLITS SERIES, FAILS TO CUT LEAD—The Dodgers' 5–3 victory salvaged a split in the four-game series with the Reds, which at this stage of the season is not nearly enough to get back in the NL West race. The Reds managed solo home runs by Joe Morgan (15), Johnny Bench (20), and Tony Pérez (15), but it was not enough against LA's star pitchers Don Sutton and Mike Marshall.

July 28—REDS SET FUTILITY MARK BEAT GIANTS—Pedro Borbon picked up a victory in relief of Gary Nolan in an 8–4 victory over the visiting Giants, as the Reds set a Major League record by using a relief pitcher in forty-four consecutive games. Nolan lasted just 2⅔ innings, allowing only two runs but seven hits and two walks. Dan Driessen's three-run homer in the first inning got the Reds moving, and they led the rest of the way.

July 29—GIANTS NOT CONCEDING TO ANYONE, MOVE CLOSER TO SECOND—San Francisco won the second contest of the four-game series, 4–2. Ken Griffey hit a solo home run in the first inning. For most of the evening the contest was a pitchers' duel between Fred Norman and San Francisco's Jim Barr, but the Giants broke the tie against the Reds' bullpen in the ninth inning. The winning hit was a two-run double by Bobby Murcer off Will McEnaney.

July 30—DARCY'S FIRST COMPLETE GAME ENDS REDS STREAK—Pitcher Pat Darcy broke the Reds' record streak of forty-five games without a complete game in a 6–1 victory over the Giants at Riverfront Stadium. The streak, as much as anything else, led to Sparky Anderson's nickname "Captain Hook." Backing Darcy, Johnny Bench provided three hits and two RBIs, while Tony Pérez added two hits and three RBIs, including a two-run triple.

July 31—REDS MAKE MONTEFUSCO EAT WORDS WITH 11–6 ROUT—Giants starter John Montefusco made a pregame prediction that he would shut out the Reds and strike out Johnny Bench four times. Instead Bench capped a six-run second inning with a three-run home run that drove "The Count" from the mound. Darrel Chaney, in a rare start at second base, hit three doubles, and Clay Kirby and Clay Carroll combined for the victory. The Reds ended July with a 20-9 record.

NL West Standings, July 30, 1975

TEAM	W	L	GB
Cincinnati	69	37	—
Los Angeles	55	52	14.5
San Francisco	52	53	16.5
San Diego	50	56	19.0
Atlanta	46	59	22.5
Houston	38	70	32.0

Chapter 33. Joe Morgan

Charles F. Faber

AGE	G	AB	R	H	2B	3B	HR	TB	RBI	BB	SO	BAV	OBP	SLG	SB	GDP	HBP
31	146	498	107	163	27	6	17	253	94	132	52	.327	.466	.508	67	3	3

Hitting for average and power and stealing bases with aplomb, the diminutive infielder was the star of the Castlemont High School baseball team in Oakland, California. Major League scouts were well aware of the quality of play in the East Bay. Among alumni of Oakland schools were such recent luminaries as Frank Robinson, Vada Pinson, and Curt Flood. Scouts came to Castlemont games not to see a pint-sized infielder but to view the pitching of Rudy May, who eventually signed with the Minnesota Twins for an $8,000 bonus. Regarding the infielder, they felt he was a good little player, with an emphasis on the second of the two adjectives. No one offered him a signing bonus. Who can blame them? At 5 feet 7 and 140 pounds, he did not seem a likely prospect for professional baseball. Who could have guessed that Joe Morgan would go on to become a two-time Most Valuable Player in the National League and a member of the National Baseball Hall of Fame in Cooperstown and to earn almost universal recognition as one of the greatest second basemen in the history of Major League baseball?

Joe Leonard Morgan was born September 19, 1943, in Bonham, Texas, the seat of Fannin County in the Red River Valley, not far from the Oklahoma state line. The oldest of six children born to Ollie and Leonard Morgan, Morgan moved with his family to Oakland when he was five. There his father and several other relatives secured employment with the Pacific Tire and Rubber Company. As a child Morgan enjoyed playing informal games of football, basketball, and baseball, often without using a regulation ball or following the usual rules of the game. His first experience on an organized team

came at the age of thirteen when he won a spot on a team in the local Babe Ruth League. For each of the three years he played Babe Ruth baseball, Morgan made the league's All-Star team.

In high school Morgan ran track and played basketball, but baseball was his best sport. When his team won the championship of the Oakland Athletic League, his friend Rudy May left to play professional baseball, but Morgan's hopes for a similar career were dashed. He was not even offered a baseball scholarship to a four-year college. Instead, in 1961 he enrolled in Oakland City College, a two-year school, where he majored in business and played on the baseball team. The team's second baseman, Morgan was its leading hitter and base stealer and one of the best players in its league. At last he attracted the attention of the bird dogs. The former Major Leaguer Cookie Lavagetto tried unsuccessfully to get the New York Mets to sign Morgan. The youngster heard that the Yankees were interested, but nothing came of that either. Finally, on November 1, 1962, Bill Wright, a scout for the Houston Colt .45s, signed the nineteen-year-old for $500 a month and a $3,000 signing bonus.

After a stint at the Colt .45s' instructional camp in Moultrie, Georgia, Morgan was assigned to the Modesto Colts of the Class A California League for the start of the 1963 season. After playing in forty-five games for Modesto, he was transferred to the Durham Bulls of the Carolina League. In Durham Morgan had his first real exposure to racism. (The players had been shielded from the public in Moultrie.) He was the only black player on the team, and his arrival had been anticipated with some nervousness. Manager Billy Goodman tried to put Morgan

Joe Morgan was an underappreciated star when he joined the Reds in 1972, but he soon became the best player in the game and one of the greatest second basemen ever.

at ease by telling him he would not play in the first game, so he should just relax on the bench. Nevertheless, Morgan could not help hearing hateful words coming from the stands during warmups. By the ninth inning, Morgan was more at ease and he was ready when Goodman called on him to pinch-hit. The Bulls were down by one run with one runner on base. In his first at bat in Durham, Morgan hit a game-winning home run. The complaints about "niggers" were drowned out by cheers. Morgan credited Goodman with having the sensibility to put him into the game at the right time.

Shortly after his Durham debut, Morgan had another rude awakening. In Winston-Salem he was not allowed to stay in the same motel as his white teammates, he saw signs designating segregated water fountains and segregated bathrooms, and worst of all, he saw a section of the right-field stands at the ballpark fenced off like a cage for black fans. He decided to quit, but with Goodman's encouragement he stuck it out. Years later he wrote, "It would be nice to say that I changed my mind because of the

example of earlier black players who had it tougher, like Jackie Robinson. . . . But my decision came from my own sense of shame and embarrassment. When I thought of facing my father and telling him that I had quit—I simply could not go ahead."[1]

Goodman not only helped Morgan feel accepted by the Bulls but he also gave him a valuable tip about hitting, suggesting that he not swing at the first pitch but take pitches to see what kind of stuff the opposing pitcher had. Morgan took this advice to heart and had an outstanding year in Durham, hitting .332 and compiling a .528 slugging percentage. Houston changed its plans for him, bringing him to the Majors sooner than it had anticipated.

When the Major League rosters were expanded in September, Morgan was promoted to the big team. On September 21, 1963, he made his Major League debut just two days after his twentieth birthday. Pinch-hitting in the third inning against Philadelphia starter Dallas Green, Morgan popped out to the second baseman. The next evening he was brought in as a pinch runner in the eighth inning against the Phillies and remained in the game. Houston had tied the game in the bottom of the ninth when Morgan came up with runners on second and third and two outs. With the count 2-0, Philadelphia relief pitcher Johnny Klippstein came inside with a fastball. Morgan grounded a base hit to right, driving in the winning run from third base.

Morgan spent the 1964 season with the San Antonio Bullets of the Double-A Texas League and had a fine season, hitting .323, driving in ninety runs, and stealing forty-seven bases. He was named the Most Valuable Player in the Texas League and earned another late-season promotion to the Majors. This time he was to stay for twenty-two years.

From 1965 through 1971 Morgan was Houston's regular second baseman (except for 1968, when he was sidelined for all but ten games of the season by a torn medial ligament in his left knee). He was a very good one, the best in the league some years, though not at the level he later attained. Early in his time at Houston, Morgan was keeping his back elbow too low when trying to hit. His teammate Nellie Fox suggested that he flap his left elbow like a chicken to keep it up. Morgan took the advice, and his flapping arm became his trademark for the rest of his career. In 1965 he finished second to Jim Lefebvre of the Dodgers in voting for the National League Rookie of the Year. In 1966 and 1970 he made the NL All-Star team. Morgan and his Astros teammate Sonny Jackson earned some fame when they appeared together on the June 6, 1966, cover of *Sports Illustrated*. In his six full seasons with Houston, he ranked among the league's top five in stolen bases four times and in bases on balls all six years. He ranked second in on-base percentage in 1966. He was a fine player.

On April 3, 1967, Morgan married Gloria Stewart, who had been his girlfriend back in his high school days. They established a home in Houston, and Joe became involved in community affairs. He hoped to spend his entire career there. In 1971 he incurred the displeasure of Manager Harry "The Hat" Walker and was placed on the trading block. Morgan believed that the southern-bred Walker was a racist.[2] Walker claimed that Morgan was selfish, moody, and a troublemaker. On November 29, 1971, Morgan was traded along with outfielders Ed Armbrister and César Gerónimo, pitcher Jack Billingham, and infielder Denis Menke to the Cincinnati Reds for second baseman Tommy Helms, first baseman Lee May, and utility man Jimmy Stewart. Morgan was very unhappy at being traded. Gloria was pregnant with their second daughter, Angela. Their first daughter, Lisa, was not quite three years old. Gloria did not accompany Joe to Cincinnati, but she did join him there later. For his baseball career, however, the trade could not have worked out better for Joe. He immediately became one of the biggest stars in the game. In his very first year with the Reds Morgan led the National League in runs scored, bases on balls, and on-base percentage.

Cincinnati fans were not pleased about the trade. Helms and especially the slugging May were among the most popular players on the Reds. "I just want you to know that whatever happened in Houston is over," Manager Sparky Anderson told his new player. "You get a fresh start here."[3] Anderson assigned Morgan the locker right next to Pete Rose, hoping that some of Charlie Hustle's spirit might rub off on the newcomer. Morgan quickly exceeded his manager's expectations. Soon Anderson was saying, "That little man can do everything." He later said that Morgan was the "smartest player I ever coached."[4]

When Morgan joined the Reds, they were not one big, happy family. Pete Rose, playing in his hometown, had long been the favorite of Cincinnati fans. He resented the attention given to neophyte Johnny Bench, the great catcher from Oklahoma. According to Morgan, there were four leaders on the team. He and Rose on one side, Bench and Pérez on the other. Morgan wrote that another player came up to him one day and said, "You can't be Pete's friend and John's friend. . . . On this ball club you can be friends with one but not with both."[5]

Morgan initially thought that Dave Concepción, the shortstop with whom he had to partner on double plays, was not a worthy teammate. Morgan thought the shortstop was not only an inferior player but lackadaisical and sometimes lacking in concentration on the field. Morgan later changed his mind about Concepción and praised him highly in his autobiography.[6] However, he never granted him the star status that the shortstop craved. One reserve player on the team complained that the stars got preferential treatment. Manager Anderson replied, "You're damn right they do and don't expect me to treat you the same. When you contribute to the team what they do, then you'll get the same kind of consideration."[7] Under Anderson's guidance the team pulled itself together, won the National League West, and defeated the Pittsburgh Pirates three games to two during a dramatic NLCS but lost the 1972 World Series to the Oakland Athletics in seven games. Morgan hit .263 with two home runs in the NLCS and batted only .125 in the World Series.

In 1973 the Reds won the most regular-season games of any team in the Major Leagues, but they lost the NLCS in five games to the New York Mets, who had won the East with the lowest winning percentage (.509) ever for a pennant winner. Morgan did not distinguish himself in the postseason, collecting only two hits in twenty times at bat. In 1974 the Reds finished second to the Los Angeles Dodgers in the NL West. Morgan again led the league in on-base percentage and won his first Gold Glove, his third consecutive outstanding season with the Reds. But Cincinnati fans were disgruntled and Sparky Anderson's job was said to be in jeopardy.

The Reds got off to a poor start in 1975. For much of April and part of May they were at .500 or had a losing record, although Morgan was going great. By April 22, he had walked fifteen times in the first fifteen games and was hitting over .400. Of his starting teammates, only Rose was hitting

as high as .300. Going into an afternoon game at Riverfront Stadium against the San Francisco Giants on the twenty-second, the Reds were in fifth place, with a 7-8 record. With the score tied, 4–4, in the bottom of the ninth, Morgan stroked a one-out double, and then Bench was walked intentionally. Still slumping, Pérez struck out. With César Gerónimo at the plate and two outs, San Francisco Giants relief pitcher Charlie Williams threw a pitch in the dirt that got by catcher Marc Hill for a wild pitch. Morgan took off for third but slowed before reaching the bag. Hill tried to throw Morgan out, but his hurried peg went past the third baseman and down the left-field line. Morgan raced home with the winning run. After the game he rubbed salt in the Giants' wounds by telling reporters, "I could have made third easily, but I deliberately held back. . . . I was hoping Hill would do just what he did."[8] The Giants were furious. "If Joe Morgan keeps up his current pace," Anderson said, "He'll be dead in another month."[9] The Giants were not the only players who disliked Morgan. Many baseball people thought he was arrogant.

By June 7, the Reds were in first place to stay. Anderson's risky experiment of moving Rose from left field to third base was paying dividends. The switch enabled George Foster to move to left field, opening up right field for young Ken Griffey. Both Foster and Griffey hit .300 or better that season, but they did not receive much support from Morgan. "George and I both kept waiting for him to take us under his wing, but it didn't happen," Griffey said.[10] In center field Gerónimo was leading the league in put-outs. As summer turned into autumn, the Reds were running away with the NL West. The Big Red Machine cruised to 108 victories, the most by any National League club since the Pirates of 1909. After being a viable candidate for three years, Morgan easily won the Most Valuable Player Award. He hit .327, led the league with an on-base percentage of .466, drew 132 bases on balls, stole sixty-seven bases, and won his third straight Gold Glove. "I have never seen anyone, and I mean anyone, play better than Joe has played this year," gushed Anderson.[11]

The Reds swept Pittsburgh in three straight to take the NLCS. The Boston Red Sox won the American League title, setting the stage for one of the greatest World Series in the history of baseball. Morgan hit just 7-for-27 in the Series and was victimized by a spectacular catch by Dwight Evans in the historic Game Six, but he had two crucial hits: his tenth-inning game-ending single in Game Three, and his game-winning single in the top of the ninth in Game Seven as the Reds won the dramatic Series.

Heading into 1976, most observers thought the Reds and their second baseman were each second to none. The April 12, 1976, issue of *Sports Illustrated* had Morgan on the cover, proclaiming him "The Complete Player." To the surprise of no one, the Reds again rolled to the National League pennant. Their 102 victories were ten more than the Dodgers could win in the West. In the postseason the Reds swept Philadelphia in three games during the NLCS and then swept the New York Yankees in four games during the World Series. They became the first National League team since the 1921 and 1922 New York Giants to win two consecutive World Series. (No National League club has done it since.) They were the only club besides the 1922 Giants and the 1963 Dodgers to sweep the Yankees in a World Series.

Morgan again won the MVP Award, as he remarkably improved on his spectacular 1975 season. He hit .320, led the league in on-base percentage and slugging percentage, hit a career-best twenty-seven home runs, scored 113 runs, batted in 111, walked 114 times, and stole sixty bases. For his fielding, he won his fourth consecutive Gold Glove. It was truly one of the best seasons any player has ever had.

The Reds dealt Pérez after the 1976 season, and the team slowly disintegrated after that. Morgan had a fine year in 1977, .288 with twenty-two home runs and 117 walks, though a bit down from his remarkable 1972–76 stretch. The team finished a distant second to the Dodgers, which they would also do in 1978. Morgan hit just .236 in 1978 and .250 the next year, with his other numbers down as well. After the 1978 season Rose left as a free agent and Anderson was fired. The Reds team that won the 1979 NL West Division bore only a passing resemblance to the Big Red Machine, and the Pirates quickly dispatched them in three games during the NLCS. After the season Morgan, then thirty-six years old, declared for free agency and signed with the Houston Astros, his old team.

After leaving Cincinnati, Morgan played for five more years in the Major Leagues—one season for Houston, two for the Giants, and one each for the Phillies and the Oakland Athletics. He was still a very effective player, if no longer quite a star. In 1982 Morgan was named the NL Comeback Player of the Year and won the Silver Slugger Award for second basemen. In the 1983 World Series Morgan hit two home runs during the Phillies' five-game series loss to Baltimore. He played his last game on September 30, 1984, at the age of forty-one. He went out in style, hitting a first-inning double off Kansas City's Mark Gubicza in his last time at bat. Tony Phillips was sent in to pinch run for Morgan, and Morgan left the field to a large ovation from the Oakland fans.

Following his retirement as a player, Morgan pursued interests in business, broadcasting, and philanthropy. For a time he ran three Wendy's franchises in the Oakland area, then he became a distributor for Coors beer in Northern California. Fulfilling a promise he had made to his mother twenty-seven years earlier, he finished college, earning his bachelor's degree from California State University, Hayward, in 1990.

Morgan started his broadcasting career in 1985 for the Cincinnati Reds. Later he broadcast games for San Francisco and Oakland. In 1988 and 1989 he announced for ABC and from 1994 to 2000 he was with NBC. His best-known stint as an announcer was with ESPN, where he teamed with Jon Miller for twenty-one years on *Sunday Night Baseball* telecasts. Morgan's keen intelligence and vast experience enabled him to be an insightful analyst. Like all announcers, he had his detractors, as some felt he was self-righteous and uninterested in new ways of studying the game.

Morgan's ESPN contract was not renewed after the 2010 season. He accepted a position with the Cincinnati Reds as "special advisor to baseball operations." His duties were primarily in the areas of community outreach and diversity. In 2011 he became host of a syndicated weekly radio program on Sports USA, *The Joe Morgan Show.*

In 2000 Morgan became vice chairman of the board of directors of the National Baseball Hall of Fame. He also joined the boards of a number of other charitable and civic organizations. Among his chief interests was Adventures in Movement, which uses music to help handicapped children experience movement in an enjoyable way. (Morgan is an ardent jazz fan.) He also joined the board of directors of the Baseball Assistance Team (BAT), dedicated to helping former Major League, Minor League, and Negro League players through financial and medical hardships.

On March 15, 1988, while in the Los Angeles International Airport, waiting to make connections for a flight to Phoenix for a charity event, Morgan was detained by two undercover police officers who accused him of being a drug courier. One of the officers pinned Morgan's arms behind him, kneed him in the back, and knocked him to the ground. "Over the next hours, the nightmare deepened, and it was all because I was just another black man. No longer a celebrity, as anonymous as any other black man, I was exposed to whatever fury was going to be meted out," he wrote in his autobiography.[12] After Morgan was taken to the police station, he was able to prove his identity and was released but was not allowed to file a complaint. He filed a suit against the Los Angeles Police Department. In 1993 the Los Angeles City Council settled the suit for $796,000.

In the late 1980s Joe and Gloria drifted apart and divorced. In 1990 he married Theresa Behymer. As Theresa was white, it took some time for both sets of parents to accept the marriage. On February 9, 1991, their twin daughters, Kelly Ann and Ashley Lauren, were born in San Francisco. Both daughters grew up to be college athletes. Kelly played soccer at the University of Southern California, and Ashley became a national-champion gymnast at Stanford.

In 1990, the first year of his eligibility, Morgan was elected to the Baseball Hall of Fame, the highest honor that can come to a baseball player. The good little infielder had proved that he belonged among the game's elite.

Chapter 34. **Doug Flynn**

Gregory H. Wolf

AGE	G	AB	R	H	2B	3B	HR	TB	RBI	BB	SO	BAV	OBP	SLG	SB	GDP	HBP
24	89	127	17	34	7	0	1	44	20	11	13	.268	.324	.346	3	5	0

"This game is tough to play," said eleven-year Major League infielder Doug Flynn in an interview with the author.[1] Progressing through the Cincinnati Reds system in the early 1970s, Flynn was a utility man on the Reds' championship teams in 1975 and 1976 before being traded to the New York Mets in 1977. A Gold Glove winner in 1980, Flynn established a reputation as one of the best-fielding second basemen in the National League. His career batting average in the Major Leagues was just .238. "Hitting never came easy for me on any level," said Flynn, who spent fourteen years in professional baseball. "I figured that if I'm gonna make it, I'm gonna make it with my defense."

Robert Douglas Flynn was born on April 18, 1951, in Lexington, Kentucky, to Robert and Ella (Ritchey) Flynn. His father, who later became a state senator, played for the Hazard (Kentucky) Bombers, a Class D team in the Brooklyn Dodgers' farm system, and for the semipro Lexington Hustlers, the first integrated baseball team in the South.[2] His mother played second base in fast-pitch softball leagues in the late 1940s before giving birth to three children, Doug, Brad, and Melanie.[3] "I had so many influences in my career," said Flynn of growing up with baseball and attending his father's semipro games. "My dad was certainly the most influential." Small but agile, he played shortstop in Little League and in the Pony, Colt, and Thoroughbred Leagues before switching to second base while attending Bryan Station High School in Lexington, where he also played football and excelled in basketball. After graduating in 1969 Flynn played a second year of Connie Mack baseball and then was surprised to be offered a dual basketball-baseball scholarship to the Uni-

A good-field no-hit infielder, Doug Flynn played eleven years with this skill set.

versity of Kentucky. Playing for legendary coach Joe B. Hall on the Wildcats' freshman basketball team, Flynn was an excellent shooter, but at 5 feet 8 and 145 pounds at that time he had a limited future on the hardwood. After an abbreviated and admittedly poor spring with the baseball team, Flynn withdrew from the university, played baseball in the semipro Bluegrass League in Lexington, and matriculated at Somerset Community College in Somerset, Kentucky, which did not field a baseball team.

Flynn's rise from obscurity to the Major Leagues less than four years later had an unusual start: "Some friends woke me up to go to a camp." It was a Cincinnati Reds tryout camp in Somerset in the summer of 1971. "We got to the tryout and we realized, Does anyone have a glove or a pair of spikes? One kid did." The camp was run by Chet Montgomery, the Reds' chief scout, and sorted through six hundred attendees. "I was there in a pair of cutoffs and a tank top," said Flynn, who had grown to 5 feet 11 and 160 pounds during his year away from baseball. After two additional tryout camps (in Frankfort, Kentucky, and at Cincinnati's Riverfront Stadium), Flynn worked out for Montgomery back in Lexington and signed with him as an amateur free agent for a $2,500 bonus in August 1971.

Flynn was assigned to the Reds' Gulf Coast League affiliate in Florida to start spring training in 1972. His willingness to move to third base resulted in a transfer to the Tampa Tarpons, managed by Russ Nixon, in the Class A Florida State League. "For the first batter, [Nixon] yelled, 'Come in,' and for the second, 'Move over, move over,'" Flynn said of his first game at third. "After the third batter he realized that I had never played third before." In fact, Flynn hadn't played much baseball in the previous two years and admitted that he didn't know what to expect. Struggling at the plate (he batted .211 in 349 at bats for Tampa), Flynn recalled that Nixon was patient with him and played him at shortstop, second base, and third base.[4] "Am I wasting my time?" Flynn asked his manager near the end of the season. "Because if I am, I have some scholarship offers and can go back to school and play basketball." Nixon urged Flynn to give it another year.

In the fall of 1972 Flynn played for Ron Plaza, a longtime Reds roving instructor, in the Florida Instructional League. "Ron would wear you out," said Flynn, who took hours of extra fielding practice with the tireless coach. With greater confidence, in the spring of 1973 he was advanced to Trois-Rivieres (Quebec) in the Double-A Eastern League, where "it started becoming fun." Playing for Manager Jim Snyder, Flynn was named to the

league's All-Star team and hit a respectable .258 in five hundred at bats. And he was learning the art of fielding. "My second year I played short in Canada and I felt like I could get to every ball," Flynn said. "I made some stupid plays, but it was good to learn that just because you can get to every ball doesn't mean that you have to throw it to first."

After another session with Plaza in the Florida Instructional League, Flynn was invited as an unofficial participant to the Reds' spring training camp in 1974 and had the opportunity to work out for two weeks with the parent club. Promoted to the Reds' top farm club, the Indianapolis Indians in the International League, managed by Vern Rapp, Flynn teamed with Junior Kennedy at second base and third baseman Ray Knight to form an impressive infield on a team loaded with future Major Leaguers. Named an All-Star for the second consecutive year, Flynn batted .253 and cemented his reputation as a sure-handed middle infielder.

"If you wanted extra work on groundballs, you went to the ballpark and guys like Vern Rapp and Jim Snyder would take you out there and hit as many as you wanted," Flynn said, giving full credit to his managers and coaches for his development as a fielder. Without the natural ability of some other players, Flynn achieved success through hard work and diligence. "My Minor League managers gave me a chance to play," he said.

Named to the Reds' forty-man roster in late 1974, Flynn played winter ball in Venezuela in 1974–75, then was invited to his first official Reds spring training camp in 1975. He recalled, "I was in awe when I walked into the locker room," seeing players he had rooted for as a kid, like Johnny Bench, Joe Morgan, and Pete Rose. Flynn impressed the Reds with his hitting, banging out thirty-two hits in ninety at bats in spring training.[5] Flynn chuckled as he explained how he made the team. "I tricked them. When you were in the lineup with them, they made you feel like you could hit and if you didn't it was embarrassing."

As a valuable utility infielder, the twenty-four-year-old Flynn saw action at shortstop, second base, and third base in his first week in the big leagues. On April 10, against the reigning NL pennant-winning Los Angeles Dodgers, he recorded his first Major League hit and run scored in a 7–6 victory, capping the Reds' sweep of their rivals. With Rose moving from the outfield to play third base in early May and All-Stars Morgan at second and Dave Concepción at short, Flynn had to adjust to a role as a spot starter and late-inning defensive replacement. The Reds had a deep bench, including infielders Darrel Chaney, Terry Crowley, and Dan Driessen. "We knew what our role was, took pride in it, and always tried to be ready when called in," Flynn said.

Flynn credited Chaney with helping him deal with the mental pressures of being a utility player. "Even though I was there and trying to take his job, Darrel would teach me how to prepare for a game," Flynn said. "We'd sit on the bench and talk about ways to stay loose and the mindset you had to have in order not to put pressure on yourself and [to] relax." Though he was batting just .161 in mid-May in a supporting role, Flynn's versatility proved a great advantage and Manager Sparky Anderson had confidence in him. Veteran Reds players were supportive, helped younger ones adjust and find their place on the team, and served as great examples with their timely hitting and fielding. Watching so many good players on the team, "You start expecting [to play well]," Flynn said, "and you say, 'Hey, I'm supposed to hit.'"

Flynn joked that it would have been tough for any manager to replace established stars and big hitters like Bench, Pérez, Morgan, Concepción, and Rose with lighter-hitting role players, but coach George Scherger still prepared his role players to be productive and content. "We had to find out how we fit in to the team and get our work done. Our coaching staff was able to keep everybody happy with the roles we had," Flynn said in his folksy voice. Starting at second base on May 18, Flynn rapped two doubles

in a 6–1 road victory over the Montreal Expos. He belted the first of his seven career home runs three days later in a victory over the New York Mets, and gradually he began to hit more consistently, raising his batting average to .250 just after mid-June.

In third place on May 16 with a record of eighteen wins and nineteen losses, the Reds exploded, winning 90 of their next 125 games, and were on their way to 108 victories, their first World Series championship since 1940, and one of the best seasons in Major League history. "Everybody on that team just pulled together," Flynn said. "It was a unique group of guys. Once we got to the field, we had great chemistry." When Concepción went down for two weeks in mid-August with a slight wrist fracture, both Flynn and Chaney ably replaced him. For the season Flynn batted a surprising .268 in 127 at bats, a higher average than he had in any Minor League season, and knocked in twenty runs. "I knew what my offensive capabilities were," Flynn said. "I watched guys like me, role players and spot starters, because I didn't want to get sent back down. I wanted to see how veterans handled themselves."

Anderson called Flynn one of the most versatile utility men in the Major Leagues, adding, "No matter where I put Doug—second, short or third—he plays as if it's his regular position. He has a great pair of hands and a great arm."[6] With all eight position players healthy, Anderson did not have to juggle his defensive alignments in late innings in the three-game sweep of the Pittsburgh Pirates in the NLCS and against the Boston Red Sox in the World Series. Although he saw no action in the postseason, Flynn concluded his first year in the Major Leagues as a world champion.

Flynn's mentor and rival, Chaney, was traded in the off-season, and after playing winter ball in Venezuela for the second year in a row, Flynn began the 1976 season as the Reds' primary utility infielder. Filling in for an injured Joe Morgan at second base in June, Flynn was batting over .300 and provided the team protection at three positions. "I don't like to see guys on the club get hurt, but I am happy that I'm getting a chance to play," he said.[7] On another pennant-winning team, Flynn finished with a career-high .283 batting average in 219 at bats, though he managed just eight extra-base hits. "I didn't think Flynn would hit as well as he did," said Anderson at season's end.[8]

In the Reds' postseason juggernaut, Flynn saw the only inning of playoff action in his career when he was inserted at second base in the ninth inning of Game One of the NLCS against the Philadelphia Phillies in 1976. With seven consecutive postseason victories, the Reds won their second consecutive World Series, this time over the New York Yankees, and earned the right to call themselves a dynasty. As for Flynn, after championships in his first two seasons, he never again played on a team that finished higher than third place.

Labeled an "untouchable utility man" in the offseason, the twenty-six-year-old Flynn began the 1977 season firmly entrenched behind All-Stars at all three infield positions he played.[9] The Reds were favored to win another pennant. But primarily because of poor pitching, they were seven games behind the Dodgers when they stunned the baseball world on June 15 with a trade that sent Flynn, pitcher Pat Zachry, and outfielders Steve Henderson and Dan Norman to the New York Mets for their disgruntled All-Star pitcher Tom Seaver.

For Flynn, the trade brought mixed emotions. He was leaving the only franchise he ever knew, but as close friend Johnny Bench told him, he had a chance to start and play every day. Traded for Seaver, the Mets' most famous player and face of the franchise, the four young players encountered pressure from fans and the front office to perform. "When we got to New York, it was tough for a while," Flynn said of the never-ending media attention. "The blessing is that once I got there, I had Joe Torre as a manager." Flynn became one of Torre's most prized and favorite players during the course of their four and

a half years together with the Mets through the 1981 season.

A pair of former All-Stars and Gold Glove winners at shortstop and second base, Bud Harrelson and Felix Millan, helped Flynn adjust to his new team. By July he had gradually replaced the thirty-three-year-old Harrelson (who batted just .178 for the season) at shortstop. An ugly incident occurred on August 12 in a game against the Pirates when Flynn fielded a slow grounder hit by Mario Mendoza and flipped it to second baseman Millan, who reacted to catcher Ed Ott's hard slide with a punch to the jaw while clenching the ball. "Ed didn't even move, just picked Felix up and body-slammed him. You could hear his shoulder bust. Knocked him out," said Flynn, who temporarily replaced Millan at second. Millan never played in the Majors again.

Going from a championship team to one that lost ninety-eight games was difficult enough for Flynn, who batted just .191 in 282 at bats with the Mets in 1977; his transition was exacerbated by the unexplained disappearance of his sister earlier that year. "It weighed on me an awful lot," Flynn said somberly of his sister's suspected murder, which was still unsolved as of 2012. Forced to answer questions about his sister from a probing media, Flynn often lashed out at reporters who invaded his privacy. "It took a whole year for me to learn how to deal with that, [but] my faith carried me through," he said.

With a .402 winning percentage (237-352) from 1978 through 1981, the Mets fielded weak-hitting teams with inconsistent pitching. In an annually changing infield, Flynn was one of the few bright spots, winning his only Gold Glove at second base in 1980 and coming in second the other three years. A student of the game, Flynn observed closely how other stellar infielders played and tried to learn from them. "You try to steal a bit from all of them," he said, "and incorporate it into your game without getting too much out of it." In 1978, his first full season with the Mets, the "super glove man" teamed with Tim Foli to create one of the better double play combinations in the National League, finishing second in the league behind the San Diego Padres (with Ozzie Smith).[10] "Flynn has been a dazzler at second base" and provided the young club stability, the *Sporting News* commented.[11] Even though the Mets lost ninety-six games, Manager Torre considered Flynn a "lifesaver" and remarked, "I hesitate to think where we'd be without him."[12]

After another last-place finish in the NL East in 1979, the Mets seemed to come together in 1980 before injuries to Flynn and catcher John Stearns derailed the team in August and September, and they finished in fifth place in the six-team NL East. "I pushed a bunt playing in San Diego," Flynn said. "Mike Ivie was playing first and I was trying to beat it out. At the time I got to the bag, he dove and hit me with a body block. I fell and landed on my wrist." Lacking a star player or even a home run threat (Lee Mazzilli led the team with sixteen), the Mets were scrappy. "The rest of us are just going year to year," the levelheaded Flynn said of his role on the team, "and hoping that we can make a difference and add to the team." This attitude endeared him to Torre and made him a fan favorite. After polling players and media, the *Sporting News* named him to its "All-Hustle Team" in 1980.[13]

Flynn's batting average in his first two years in Cincinnati (.277 for the two seasons) proved to be an aberration; he batted no higher than .255 during the rest of his career. "I was just a lousy hitter," Flynn said honestly but unapologetically; however, it was not from a lack of extra batting practice. "You always want to be better. I always wished I would have been a better hitter. My mechanics were bad in the early days." He worked with Phil Cavarretta, the Mets' batting instructor, to improve his swing. Flynn began his career when light-hitting, slick-fielding middle infielders like the Cardinals' Dal Maxvill, the Orioles' Mark Belanger, and the Mets' Harrelson were de rigueur. "We were told that you just field it and if you get a hit, it'll be a bonus," he said. "Well, that's not true. You want

to be able to hit the ball and make a difference." On August 5, 1980, in a road loss to the Montreal Expos, Flynn tied a post-1900 National League record when he hit three triples in a game during the best week he ever had at the plate. With fourteen hits in thirty-one at bats (.452 average), Flynn was named the National League Player of the Week. Despite occasional hot streaks, Flynn noticed that the game began to change in the early 1980s and successful teams had consistent hitters at second base or shortstop, like the Tigers' Alan Trammell and Lou Whitaker, the Orioles' Cal Ripken Jr., and the Dodgers' Steve Sax.

Before the strike-shortened 1981 season, Flynn signed a five-year, $2.4 million contract with the Mets, negotiated by his agent, Randy Hendricks.[14] With the Mets' horrible start before the strike (just seventeen wins in fifty-one games), General Manager Frank Cashen put pressure on Torre to produce a winner. "I am tired of making excuses," said Flynn, an unofficial spokesman for the team. "We have better players, but we still don't explode. We don't add up to a better team."[15] Though the team played better after the strike, Cashen made wholesale changes in the off-season, firing Torre and trading Flynn and Lee Mazzilli to the Texas Rangers in separate deals. Flynn and pitcher Dan Boitano were dealt for relief pitcher Jim Kern.

"I was absolutely stunned," said Flynn. The trade received mixed reactions in New York (where the Mets already had a top reliever in Neil Allen) and in Arlington, Texas, where Bump Wills had been the starter at second since his rookie year in 1977. Wills was traded before the season to the Chicago Cubs, but Flynn never found a home. He was displaced at second base by Mike Richardt, the Rangers' top prospect (he was the American Association batting champion in 1981), and was moved to shortstop, where he struggled. The Rangers shipped him to the Expos for the standard $40,000 waiver fee in August.[16]

In his 2½ seasons with the Expos, Flynn started at both second base and shortstop. The *Sport-

GREGORY H. WOLF

ing News wrote that he immediately shored up the team's defense. With the double play combination of Flynn and Chris Speier and the hot hitting of Al Oliver, Gary Carter, and Andre Dawson, the Expos made a run at the NL East title. Flynn was excited to be playing for a winning team again, but the Expos faded in September and finished in third place.[17]

Always a team player, Flynn suppressed his own ego for the sake of team success. Among the favorites to win the NL East in 1983, the Expos struggled at the plate. When they acquired Gold Glove–winning second baseman Manny Trillo from the Cleveland Indians in August, Flynn willingly moved to shortstop even though he was leading the league in fielding percentage at second base and could have won his second Gold Glove at the position. The Expos went into first place on September 7 but faltered again down the stretch and again finished third.

In his last season as a starter, the thirty-three-year-old Flynn began the 1984 campaign at shortstop, having been displaced at second base by Bryan Little, but he moved back to his customary position in midseason. Often replaced by a pinch hitter in close games, Flynn had only 382 at bats, his fewest since 1977 (excluding the strike-shortened 1981 season). When the Expos' third skipper in less than half a year, Buck Rodgers, opted for twenty-eight-year-olds Vance Law and Hubie Brooks at second and short to start the 1985 season, Flynn was relegated to the bench. After just six at bats through early June, he was released. He signed as a free agent with the Detroit Tigers later that month and served as a valuable three-position utility infielder for his old Cincinnati manager, Sparky Anderson.

Signed again as a free agent by the Tigers for the 1986 season, Flynn was released during spring training. "You know in your heart when it's time to quit," he said of his decision to end his eleven-year Major League career. He finished with a .238 batting average (918 hits in 3,853 at bats). It's hard to measure Flynn's value just with statistics. He was a hard-nosed player's player who never loafed on the field or in practice. "For someone who was just a .238 lifetime hitter," Flynn said, "I am thankful that people saw enough in me to keep me around the game."

Flynn enjoyed a successful career away from baseball. Blessed with a good voice, he toured with the Oak Ridge Boys, a country music group, during the 1981 strike season and also performed regularly in clubs in New York City while playing for the Mets. Pete Rose introduced him to former Philadelphia Eagles cheerleader Olga Munez, whom he married in 1982. Married for more than thirty years by 2013, they have resided in Lexington since Flynn's retirement. Immediately after his playing days, Flynn led Kentucky's antidrug program for nine years before he was lured back to the Mets and into coaching for two years. He coached at Columbia, South Carolina, in the South Atlantic League in 1996 and at St. Lucie in the Florida State League in 1997 before being promoted in midseason to manage the Gulf Coast League Mets. He left coaching in 1997 when he was offered a job at a bank in his hometown. He remained close to baseball, participating in fantasy camps, hosting golf tournaments, and announcing games for the Reds. "Going from a tryout camp to play eleven years in the big leagues, I was very fortunate," Flynn said. "I'd like to be remembered as a guy who loved the game and played hard. When you got to the ballpark, you got everything that I had. I wished it had been more. It wasn't, but I can't change that."

Chapter 35. **Rawly Eastwick**

Andy Sturgill

AGE	W	L	PCT.	ERA	G	GS	GF	CG	SHO	SV	IP	H	BB	SO	HBP	WP
24	5	3	.625	2.60	58	0	40	0	0	22	90	77	25	61	2	1

In art a painter may create masterpieces on canvas. In baseball the verb *paint* applies to a craft no less skillful. *The Dickson Baseball Dictionary* defines the verb as "to throw pitches over the edges of the plate, which appear to be dark or black because of the contrast of the white rubber plate with the surrounding dirt."[1] The ability to keep the ball away from the middle of the plate and on the edges is crucial to the success of any pitcher. It is truly unusual to find a pitcher for whom the act of putting paint on canvas holds as much meaning as putting a fastball on the outside corner. Rawly Eastwick was an exception, as professionally he painted corners and on the side he painted landscapes.

Rawlins Jackson Eastwick III was born on October 24, 1950, in Camden, New Jersey, and grew up in the upper-middle-class Philadelphia suburb of Haddonfield, New Jersey. He was the youngest child of Rawlins Jackson Eastwick Jr. and Ruth Brown Eastwick. The elder Eastwick worked as an engineer for Bell Telephone, and friends simply called him Bud.[2] While Rawly was given his father's name, he was actually the youngest in his family, arriving after a set of twin brothers, Robert and Richard, a sister, Nancy, and his own twin brother, Ralph. Of his name, the youngest Eastwick said, "[My parents] knew what they wanted to name one of us, but they ran out of names. So they were standing around wondering what to name me, and my father said, 'Give him my name.' I'm glad they didn't name me Walter or Horatio or something like that."[3] At Haddonfield High School, Eastwick earned all-state honors on the diamond and was an honorable mention All-American in 1969. He also excelled as a wrestler, twice winning the district high school championship.[4]

Rawly Eastwick joined the Reds in May 1975 and soon became the ace of their deep bullpen.

Selected by the Reds in the third round of the 1969 amateur draft, the eighteen-year-old Eastwick struggled in his first professional season, posting an earned run average near 5.00 for the Gulf Coast League Reds and allowing almost two base runners an inning. His performance ebbed and flowed over the few seasons before he really asserted himself in Double-A in 1972, when he posted a 2.34 ERA in 119 innings (all in relief) and an Eastern League–leading twenty saves for Trois-Rivieres (Quebec). After two seasons at Triple-A Indianapolis, Eastwick was called up to the Reds in September 1974 and made his debut against the Braves on the twelfth in Cincinnati against the Atlanta Braves. The first batter he faced was Hank Aaron, who earlier in the season had broken Babe Ruth's career home run record. Aaron flied out to center this time. (Eastwick became the answer to a future trivia question in the last game of the season when he surrendered Aaron's 733rd and final National League home run.) In his brief cameo at the end of 1974, Eastwick pitched eight times and earned two saves.

Eastwick pitched well in spring training of 1975 but was sent to Indianapolis when the final cuts were made. Reds pitching coach Larry Shepard encouraged him, saying, "I don't think it'll be long till you're back."[5] Taking Shepard's words and a positive attitude with him, Eastwick was not gone long; he was recalled by the Reds in mid-May. When he arrived in the clubhouse none of his teammates had been expecting him, and he was asked what he was doing there. The rookie matter-of-factly stated, "They told me to come here, so I came."[6] He also brashly asserted, "I've got a job to do. I'm here to help this team win."[7]

When Eastwick was called up, infielder John Vukovich was sent to Indianapolis to clear a roster spot for him. Pete Rose was moved from left field to third base and George Foster was installed in the lineup as the everyday left fielder. After these moves the Reds ripped off a 63-19 run between late May and mid-August that propelled the team from 5 games back in the NL West to 17½ games ahead of the Dodgers, putting the division race away.

Eastwick started out slowly with the Reds; he had a lusty 5.93 ERA on July 1. Veteran starter Don Gullett was on the disabled list at the time, and Shepard challenged Eastwick: "Just who do you suppose is going to be the one to go when Gullett gets healthy? You, that's who. Unless you start throwing the ball. You're trying to guide it, to be too fine. The way you throw, just go ahead and turn it loose."[8]

On July 24, at Shea Stadium, Eastwick got his chance to turn it loose. Entering a 2–1 game against the Mets with runners on first and second and two outs in the ninth inning, he blew away slugger Dave Kingman with three fastballs to end the game. "I stair-stepped him," Eastwick said afterward. "A low fastball, a higher fastball, and a high fastball."[9]

As the 1975 season developed so too did Eastwick's importance to the Reds. The fresh-faced twenty-four-year-old and another rookie reliever, twenty-three-year-old left-hander Will McEnaney, formed the "Kiddie Korps," anchoring the back end of the bullpen for Manager Sparky Anderson, known as baseball's "Captain Hook" because of his reliance on his relief pitchers. Eastwick finished the season with a record of 5-3, twenty-two saves, and a 2.60 ERA in fifty-eight games, including forty games finished. His twenty-two saves tied him with St. Louis's Al Hrabosky for the National League lead, and he finished second to Hrabosky for the National League Fireman of the Year Award.

The 6-foot-3, 185-pound right-hander overflowed with a confidence that could rightly be labeled as arrogance. He claimed to never have a negative thought and believed that this attitude radiated to the hitter.[10] He maintained that he had never been nervous or frightened by anything in his life. Reds second baseman Joe Morgan once ran to the mound during a tense moment in a game and told Rawly, "If you get uptight, step off and take a few breaths." The unmoved Eastwick later said, "Well, I don't really know what he was talking about."[11]

The rookie believed that his regimen for caring for his arm was best. The regimen? Nothing, and no one was allowed to touch his arm.[12] As an eighteen-year-old in the rookie league, he had challenged a teammate from Chicago with reputed Mafia connections to a fight in the woods. Only Eastwick walked out. His cockiness, not surprisingly, carried over to the pitcher's mound. Anderson described him as possessing a "here-it-is-and-now-try-to-hit-it" fastball.[13] Regarding his recall from Indianapolis, Eastwick said, "The bullpen needed a shot in the arm. I think I did it." Bob Hertzel, author of *The Big Red Machine*, where the quote appeared, wrote that Eastwick made his comment without the least bit of modesty.[14]

While Eastwick's self-assurance squared easily with his on-field persona as a fireballing relief ace, it didn't mesh with his off-field interests. Unlike many ballplayers, he enjoyed reading and talking about current events. He was a painter and a sculptor. He collected art and antiques. A painter since he was a boy, as a big leaguer he continued to work with pastels and watercolors, calling himself an expressionist and painting landscapes and still lifes. He gave one of his works to Johnny Bench as a wedding present, Bench pledging to display it in his living room.[15]

In the playoff matchup with the Pirates, Eastwick threw three scoreless innings of relief in the Reds' 6–1 win in Game Two, then relieved McEnaney with a runner on first and one out in the ninth inning of Game Three in Pittsburgh, with the Reds leading 3–2 and only two outs from the pennant. Eastwick gave up a single and two walks, with his second free pass forcing in the tying run. But Cincinnati scored twice in the top of the tenth and the Reds won their third NL pennant in the last six seasons.

For most of the 1975 World Series Eastwick was in line to be the Series MVP. He had pitched in Games Two through Five, allowed one run in seven innings, and picked up two wins and a save as the Reds led the Boston Red Sox three games to two. He was the first rookie to earn a win and a save in the same postseason series.[16] In Game Six, with the Reds leading 6–3 going into the bottom of the eighth inning, sportswriters in the press box voted Eastwick the MVP.[17] Then the first two Red Sox reached base and Eastwick was summoned from the bullpen to relieve Pedro Borbon. He looked untouchable in striking out Dwight Evans and retiring Rick Burleson on a liner to shallow left. With two outs Boston sent up left-hand-hitting Bernie Carbo to pinch-hit. Anderson stuck with Eastwick, and it appeared

he made the right decision as Eastwick worked the count to 2-2. But then he threw a fastball that Carbo launched into the center-field bleachers, tying the score. The Reds' lead and Eastwick's World Series MVP Award evaporated with one pitch.[18] Four innings later Carlton Fisk hit his game-winning home run, and the Red Sox had forced a seventh game. Eastwick didn't pitch in that game as the Reds rallied and won, 4–3, to capture their first title since 1940. In the champagne-soaked clubhouse after the game, Eastwick declared, "I can't believe it. What a year. What a rookie year."[19] Eastwick tied for third in the National League Rookie of the Year voting.

Not content to rest on the success of his rookie season, Eastwick was very direct in his plan for 1976. "I want to win the NL Fireman of the Year Award," he told the *Sporting News*.[20] Toward that end he worked hard in the off-season, running and throwing in the Cincinnati area with McEnaney.

While McEnaney struggled with a severe sophomore slump, Eastwick thrived on his expanded role in his first full Major League season. Pitching in seventy-one games, he compiled an 11-5 record and a 2.09 ERA in 107⅔ innings. He had a league-leading twenty-six saves. He finished fifth in the league's Cy Young voting but did capture the Fireman of the Year Award. The Reds steamrolled through the season, then swept the Phillies in the NLCS and the Yankees in the World Series. Eastwick became the first pitcher to lead the league in saves in his first two Major League seasons since Gordon Maltzberger of the White Sox in 1943–44 (before saves were an official statistic).[21]

Before the 1977 season Eastwick made headlines for his unhappiness with the Reds organization. After the team traded Tony Pérez and McEnaney to the Montreal Expos, Eastwick referred to the deal as "stupidity."[22] He also complained that his $29,000 salary in 1976 left him underpaid.

Unable to come to terms on a contract for 1977, Eastwick determined to play out his option year and become a free agent. He suggested that Reds management had decided to use him less than he was needed because of his contract situation. In early June the Reds informed him that they were looking to move him by the June 15 trade deadline, and he was almost included in the deal that brought Tom Seaver to the Reds; the Mets were scared off by his contract situation.[23] The same day the Reds got Seaver, Eastwick was sent to the St. Louis Cardinals for Minor League pitcher Doug Capilla. His stay in St. Louis was short and uneventful (3-7, 4.70 ERA, four saves in forty-one games), aside from his continued insistence on becoming a free agent at the end of the season and for his return to Cincinnati in an enemy uniform, when he was booed loudly.[24]

After the season Eastwick hit the free-agent market, one of the prized clients of 1970s super-agent Jerry Kapstein. During the winter meetings in Hawaii, they struck a deal with the Yankees for $1.1 million over five years.

The deal was curious from both sides. From Eastwick's perspective, he was a relief pitcher who voluntarily signed with a club that had reliever Sparky Lyle, the 1977 American League Cy Young Award winner, and had just signed another premier reliever, Goose Gossage (another Kapstein client). Yankees owner George Steinbrenner had been warned before the signing that Eastwick was not throwing well, and there was concern that his arm was dead. Ever the involved owner, Steinbrenner met with Eastwick and Kapstein and decided to sign him anyway.[25]

Eastwick's signing with the Yankees proved to be one of the earliest busts in the era of free agency. He made only eight appearances for the Yankees, mostly in garbage time. On June 14, barely six months after signing with the Yankees, he was traded to the Philadelphia Phillies for outfielders Bobby Brown and Jay Johnstone. Eastwick's status as one of Steinbrenner's favorites likely kept Manager Billy Martin from ever embracing him.[26]

Eastwick expressed excitement about his arrival in Philadelphia, just across the Delaware River

from his hometown of Haddonfield. He talked of living and dying with the Phillies as a boy and expressed regret that he had not signed with them before the 1978 season.[27] Despite the good feelings, little changed in Eastwick's career arc in Philadelphia. He pitched in seventy-three games for the team in 1978 and 1979, recording six saves and a 4.61 ERA. He was never counted on too heavily in a bullpen that featured veterans Tug McGraw and Ron Reed. The highlight of his Phillies career came on a blustery day at Wrigley Field in May 1979 when he threw two perfect innings to secure a 23–22 win over the Cubs. Before that day he had given up nine runs in his previous 5⅓ innings. But in the ninth inning he retired the side in order to send the game to extra innings at 22–22, then did it again in the bottom of the tenth after Mike Schmidt hit a home run in the top of the inning. Eleven pitchers were used by the two teams that day, with Eastwick being the only hurler of the game not to give up a hit. Eastwick's Phillies career ended in spring training of 1980, when no-nonsense manager Dallas Green cut him, along with Bud Harrelson, Doug Bird, and Mike Anderson, players the manager felt carried attitude and acted as though they were entitled to a spot on a Major League roster.[28]

Eastwick signed as a free agent with Kansas City in June 1980 and spent a month at Omaha of the American Association before being recalled to the Royals. He pitched in fourteen games before he was released in late August. The Cubs invited him to spring training on a Minor League deal in 1981. He made the club and threw well as a middle reliever, posting a 2.28 ERA in thirty games. He was released at the end of spring training in 1982, and his professional baseball career was over. Made a millionaire by the Yankees at the age of twenty-seven, Eastwick threw his last professional pitch a full year before the Yankees contract was even set to expire. He had been released three times in the interim.

What happened to Rawly Eastwick? Was he blown out by overuse early in his career with the

Reds? While Eastwick asserted that he pitched better with more work, the evidence shows that he never even got close to the level of success he attained during his first two seasons in the Majors, when he pitched 232⅓ innings, including playoffs and a stint in the Minors. While Sparky Anderson acknowledged that it would be unwise to run Eastwick out to the mound every night, he appeared to do just that in 1975 and 1976.

After his playing career ended, Eastwick embarked on a career in commercial real estate in New England. In 2011 he resided with his wife, Sandra, in West Newbury, Massachusetts.

Chapter 36. **Gary Nolan**

Richard Miller

AGE	W	L	PCT.	ERA	G	GS	GF	CG	SHO	SV	IP	H	BB	SO	HBP	WP
27	15	9	.625	3.16	32	32	0	5	1	0	210.2	202	29	74	1	1

Eighteen-year-old Cincinnati Reds pitcher Gary Nolan, in his first Major League start, defeated the Houston Astros 7–3 at Cincinnati's Crosley Field on April 15, 1967. In the first inning he faced four batters and struck out Sonny Jackson, Jim Landis, and Jimmy Wynn en route to a 7–3 victory. Later in the season, on June 7, during a scoreless game and with two runners on in the sixth inning against the San Francisco Giants, Nolan used his fireball pitches to strike out Willie Mays, Willie McCovey, and Jim Ray Hart. At game's end he had struck out Mays four times. "Nobody's ever done that to me before," Mays said.[1] By the end of his stellar first Major League season Nolan had set modern-day records for a pitcher who began the season at the age of eighteen or younger, with a 14-8 win-loss record, a 2.58 earned run average, four shutouts, and 206 strikeouts in 226⅔ innings.

The Reds had expected Nolan to succeed. And Nolan knew he would succeed. A Northern Californian, he was born on May 27, 1948, in Herlong, California, on the border with Nevada. Later the family moved to Oroville, an old gold rush town in the foothills of the Sierra Nevada. At the age of ten, Gary sat next to his father, Ray, a switchman for the Union Pacific Railroad, listening to Russ Hodges broadcast a San Francisco Giants game. Ray did not care for baseball, but it was obvious that Gary planned to play Major League baseball. In high school he became such a good pitcher that baseball scouts, sometimes twenty-five of them, would drive to Oroville to see the new boy wonder.

Nolan was the Reds' number-one choice (thirteenth pick overall) in the 1966 amateur draft, and the team sent its top negotiator, Jim McLaughlin, to

Gary Nolan came back from missing two seasons to have two excellent seasons for the Reds World Series winners.

Oroville to cut a deal with Gary's father. Ray said, "Talk to Gary. He's a grown man."[2] Gary negotiated his own deal and signed for $40,000.

The Reds assigned Nolan to their Sioux Falls (South Dakota) short-season Northern League club for his first professional season in 1966. There he fulfilled his predicted success, pitching in twelve games and going 7-3 with a 1.82 ERA. His fastball was overpowering. In 104 innings he struck out 163. Above all, he had that best gift of all: control. He walked only thirty batters. The next season, 1967, Nolan was in the Reds' pitching rotation at the age of eighteen, and he proceeded to have several exemplary seasons as a starter with the Reds before being undone by arm problems.

Standing 6 feet 3 inches and weighing 190 pounds, the handsome Nolan was an immediate favorite of Reds fans, especially the young women. Alas, Nolan had married his high school sweetheart, Carole Widener, in February 1965. He became a father at seventeen. The family grew to six with Gary Jr., Tim, Mark, and Kathy.

Hopes were high for another strong year for Nolan in 1968, but at spring training dark clouds began forming. Nolan strained his shoulder and walked off the mound after throwing two pitches in the second inning of his first start in an exhibition game. It was a cold, blustery day, and Nolan apparently had extended himself too fast, too soon for a first outing.

Nolan was shocked when he heard General Manager Bob Howsam observe, "We just may send him to the minors to get in shape."[3] No mention of the pain Nolan was suffering, just the implication that he was out of shape and just a kid who didn't know about pain.

A week later Nolan was indeed in the Minor Leagues, with Tampa in the Class A Florida State League. His sore arm remained as he attempted to pitch five innings in two games. Tampa manager George Scherger called the Reds' home office to report that Nolan was completely demoralized. Ironically, it was after his great game against the Giants the previous season that Giants pitching coach Larry Jansen remarked, "With his motion he's sure to hurt his arm."[4]

The Reds, however, needed pitching help, still had visions of Nolan's strong 1967 season, and recalled him from Tampa in mid-May. On May 31 he pitched five innings in an exhibition game and five days later lasted only five minutes pitching batting practice. "I wouldn't say I'm disgusted," Nolan remarked. "The word is impatient. Either that or I'm fouled up."[5]

Despite the sore arm, Nolan continued to pitch.

He rebounded with a seven-game winning streak and finished the season at 9-4, with a team-leading 2.40 ERA. His best game was a 5–0 shutout over San Francisco at Candlestick Park on June 29; he helped himself with his only Major League home run, a three-run shot with two outs in the seventh inning off Ray Sadecki. Unfortunately for Nolan, his sore-arm problems would plague him throughout a career that ended before his reached his thirtieth birthday.

The Reds' Opening Day pitcher in 1969, Nolan struck out twelve Dodgers but lost 3–2. In his next start, at Atlanta, he pulled a muscle in his right forearm while delivering a pitch to Henry Aaron in the sixth inning. He was the winning pitcher, but the injury eventually cost him three months of Major League action.

Those three months with the Reds' Minor League club in Indianapolis turned out to be a blessing for Nolan. Under the tutelage of Indianapolis manager Vern Rapp and Reds Minor League instructor Scott Breeden, he developed an outstanding off-speed pitch. After his recall by the Reds in early August 1969, Nolan finished the season with seven games won in twelve starts, helped by his new change-up pitch.

Under Manager Dave Bristol, the Reds of the late 1960s were competitive but couldn't make it to the top. In an interview, Nolan recalled, "With guys like Johnny Bench, Tony Perez, and Pete Rose we obviously had the talent. Injuries and bad breaks kept us from winning consistently. We all knew there would be a change of managers after 1969."[6]

The new manager was the unknown Sparky Anderson, under whom the team had immediate success in the 1970s, with Nolan an important cog in what became the Big Red Machine. Meanwhile, his family, now with two children, moved back to Oroville, where he worked hard physically to get a good start for 1970.

In 1970 Nolan posted his best win-loss record ever, winning eighteen games and losing only seven with 181 strikeouts and a 3.27 ERA, helping the Reds to the NL pennant. He pitched even better than his record indicates. In one stretch during eight starts between July 16 and August 15 he allowed no more than three runs in any one contest but had only four wins. During the second half of the season, in twenty starts Nolan was 10-3 with a 2.65 ERA.

On September 16 Nolan beat the Houston Astros in a 3–2 game, clinching a tie for the NL West crown. At Pittsburgh in Game One of the NLCS, he pitched nine innings of shutout ball. The Reds didn't score until a three-run tenth inning, but Nolan still won the contest and reliever Clay Carroll got the save. The Reds won the NL pennant in a three-game sweep.

Along with the entire Reds team, Nolan did not perform as well in the World Series, won by the Baltimore Orioles in five games. After being staked to a 3–0 lead, he lost Game One to Jim Palmer, allowing four runs on three home runs in 6⅔ innings and was relieved in Game Four in the third inning with the Reds behind 3–2. The Reds rallied to win the game 6–5 on the back of Lee May's three-run homer in the eighth inning.

After a disappointing 12-15 record (but with a slightly better ERA of 3.16 and a career-best nine complete games) in 1971, Nolan posted thirteen victories before the 1972 All-Star Game. Selected for the NL team, he was withdrawn from the team when Reds manager Sparky Anderson called NL All-Star team manager Danny Murtaugh without telling Nolan. Suffering from neck and shoulder pains, Nolan went on the disabled list. When he returned to the team, he finished the season with a 15-5 record and a 1.99 ERA, leading the league in winning percentage (.750), his ERA just behind Steve Carlton's league-best 1.97. Nolan pitched six strong innings during Game Three of the NLCS. He left with a 2–1 lead, but the Pirates scored twice in the late innings to come back and win the game. However, Cincinnati took the next two games to win the NL pennant. Then, once again, the home run "bug"

bit Nolan during Game One of the World Series as Oakland's catcher Gene Tenace connected off him twice for a 3–2 Athletics' win in Cincinnati. After having trouble getting loose the day before, Nolan was scratched as the starter by Anderson for Game Five. Nolan then started Game Six but was relieved by Ross Grimsley with two outs in the fifth inning just after Oakland hit three consecutive deep drives to the outfield with one of them going for a double to tie the score. The Reds eventually won this game, 8–1, but then they dropped Game Seven the next afternoon.

Nolan appeared only twice for the Reds in 1973 and missed the entire 1974 season after the surgical removal of a calcium spur from his right shoulder by Dr. Frank Jobe, who told him, "I have no idea how you pitched in that sort of pain. You must have been in agony."[7] Someone believed him. Jobe was also seeing Dodgers pitcher Tommy John and had a long-shot idea. He replaced John's damaged ligament with a ligament taken from another part of his body. Tommy John did pitch again, and "Tommy John surgery" would save countless pitchers' careers.

Nolan recalled, "The hardest part was that many people, including some of my teammates, didn't think there was anything the matter with me. That was one of the reasons I moved out of Cincinnati and sold our home after the 1972 season. Back in Oroville, people didn't doubt my word."[8] Manager Anderson, for one, had told him constantly, "Pitchers have to throw in pain. Bob Gibson says every pitch he's ever thrown cut through him like a knife. You gotta pitch with pain, kid."[9]

Nolan reported back to Indianapolis near the end of the 1974 season, hurled six innings in two games, and found that his pain had disappeared. For the remainder of his career, his great off-speed pitch compensated for the loss of velocity on his fastball. He never lost his excellent control.

After the 1974 season, Nolan went to the Instructional League and pitched forty-five innings, which helped build up his shoulder so that he was ready to try the big leagues again. He returned to the Reds in 1975 in good form with a new attitude. He had inwardly turned to God as a practicing Christian and developed a sense of humor and a new philosophy that reflected the inner turmoil he had survived.

On May 3 Nolan beat the Atlanta Braves, 6–1, in a complete game, his first regular-season victory in thirty-one months. For the year he was 15-9 with a 3.16 ERA. He zipped through the season, walking only twenty-nine batters, and led the club in innings pitched with 210⅔. With his on-the-road roommate Don Gullett, Nolan spent many days going over the other club's hitters, a probing that helped both pitchers.

The Reds again won the NL pennant in 1975, defeating the Pittsburgh Pirates in a three-game sweep of the NLCS. Nolan was the starting pitcher for Game Three, pitching the first six innings and allowing two runs and five hits with five strikeouts. He struck out Willie Stargell twice, and with two runners on base in the fifth inning got pinch hitter Ed Kirkpatrick on a harmless pop-up and then struck out pitcher John Candelaria. "You're pitching your ass off," Pete Rose shouted happily.[10] After his stint, the Reds came back from a 2–1 Pittsburgh lead to win the game, scoring two runs in the tenth inning for a 5–3 victory. Relief pitcher Rawly Eastwick got the win.

The 1975 World Series against the Boston Red Sox is long remembered for Game Six, when Boston's Carlton Fisk "waved" his twelfth-inning drive for the game-winning home run that struck the left-field foul pole. Nolan started that game and left after two innings with the Red Sox ahead 3–0. His start in Game Three had been better; he gave up one run in four innings but had to leave with a stiff neck. (The Reds won the game, 6–5 in ten innings.)

After the season Nolan received the Hutch Award, voted by Major League broadcasters and players to a player who had overcome major adversity. The award was named in honor of the late Fred Hutchinson, manager of the Reds from 1959 to 1964, the year he died of cancer. Nolan brought his family back to Ohio and purchased a new home.

He duplicated his 15-9 record in 1976 and finally got his first World Series victory, beating the New York Yankees in the last game of a four-game Reds sweep. Nolan held the Yankees to two runs in 6⅔ innings to earn the 7–2 victory.

While sipping his victory champagne, Nolan told reporter Hal McCoy of the *Dayton (OH) Daily News*, "We've got an underrated pitching staff, no Tom Seaver or Cy Young, but we get the job done. This was my first World Series victory and I'm glad I got it in the house that Ruth built. I didn't set the world on fire out there but I got them out. Some day when I'm telling my grandson about tonight, I might stretch things a bit."[11] While Nolan was with the team and healthy, the Reds won NL West titles in 1970, 1972, 1973, 1975, and 1976 to go with world championships in 1975 and 1976.

Nolan's arm problems returned with a vengeance in 1977, and he was traded to the California Angels on June 15 for Minor League pitcher Craig Hendrickson. With the Angels he made only five appearances, compiled a 0-3 record, and was placed once more on the disabled list. He was released by the Angels in January 1978. He recalled, "I saw Dr. Frank Jobe while out [in California], but I pretty much knew I was done. All of a sudden my career was over."[12]

Nolan found a second career as a blackjack dealer at the Golden Nugget in Las Vegas in 1978. In 1989 he became executive casino host at the Mirage, where he left any interest in baseball behind him. He wanted nothing to do with the Reds, never wore his championship rings, and even snubbed the team when he was elected to the Reds Hall of Fame in 1983.

Cincinnati sportswriter John Erardi went to Las Vegas in 1986 to interview Nolan. When asked if his memories with the Reds were fond ones, Nolan answered that he did enjoy pitching and the relationships he formed with his teammates and the people of Cincinnati. Then he added, "The Reds organization left a bad taste in my mouth by not believing my arm was hurt and thinking it was probably in my head. I know they did and they know I did."[13]

Nolan continued, "I was blessed. I played in the big leagues, I was fortunate. But I have learned to separate my baseball life and my life in Las Vegas. Most people in the casino probably don't even know I played ball."[14]

Nolan was visiting Cincinnati in 2006 and decided to visit the Reds Hall of Fame and Museum. The building was closed because it was a Monday, but museum curator Chris Eckes was there, welcomed Nolan, and guided him through the building to the Hall of Fame room with Nolan's Hall of Fame plaque. The result was a new relationship with the Reds organization and Nolan's subsequent return to several Reds Hall of Fame annual induction ceremonies.

Over his ten-year career, Nolan was 110-70 with a stellar 3.08 ERA. He struck out 1,039 batters and gave up only 413 walks in 1,674⅔ innings pitched. Subtracting his time lost to arm injuries, his career was more like six years.

As of 2012 Nolan resided in Oroville, where a sign on the highway proclaims it the hometown of Gary Nolan. Also, as part of the Feather River Recreation and Park District, Oroville is home to the Gary Nolan Baseball Complex. Nolan has kept his hand in the game by coaching and preparing the Oroville High School pitchers for college ball.

Chapter 37. **Darrel Chaney**

Derek Norin

AGE	G	AB	R	H	2B	3B	HR	TB	RBI	BB	SO	BAV	OBP	SLG	SB	GDP	HBP
27	71	160	18	35	6	0	2	47	26	14	38	.219	.280	.294	3	3	0

An eleven-year Major League infielder, Darrel Chaney stayed in the game due largely to his versatility and positive attitude. After a career that included appearances in three World Series, Chaney became a successful announcer, businessman, and motivational speaker.

Darrel Lee Chaney was born on March 9, 1948, in Hammond, Indiana, the second of Carlos and Eleanore Chaney's three children. His brother, Larry, was older by a year, while his sister, Mary Kay, was seven years younger. Chaney played football, baseball, and basketball while growing up in Hammond. In baseball he was a gifted switch-hitting shortstop whose hero was Chicago Cubs star Ernie Banks. When he was twelve Chaney met Banks at a Little League banquet in Hammond. Chaney's friends sent him up to the podium to talk to Banks. Banks signed his autograph, "To Darrel Chaney: I'll see you in the big leagues."[1]

In football at Morton High School, Chaney was a 1965 *Parade* High School All-American quarterback. "Back in the day, they ran a running offense—single T, split T formation."[2] Chaney was especially known for his ability to carry out fakes, keeping and running the ball himself. He received thirty-five scholarship offers, including academic-athletic scholarship combinations from the University of Washington and the Air Force Academy. As a two-way player, Chaney intercepted twenty-seven passes in three seasons. He was heavily recruited by Notre Dame, whose coach, Ara Parseghian, wanted him to play safety (with Terry Hanratty and Coley O'Brien already at quarterback). Chaney turned down a chance to visit Notre Dame because he already had scheduled a visit with coach Duffy Daugh-

Once considered the shortstop of the future for the Reds, Darrel Chaney ended up backing up Dave Concepción for a few years.

erty at Michigan State, and his commitments to his high school basketball team limited his time. Notre Dame never called back.

Chaney was a five-tool prospect as a baseball player. "You have to be, in order to get drafted that high," he said. (The Reds drafted him in the second round of the June 1966 draft, number thirty-three overall.) "I could hit for power, I could hit for a high average, I could throw, and I could run some."[3] The Reds sent an official to make an offer, giving Chaney a day to deliberate with his family. Chaney discussed it with his father and decided to accept the Reds' offer because he had always dreamed of becoming a Major League ballplayer.

The eighteen-year-old spent his first professional summer with Sioux Falls (South Dakota) in the Class A Northern League, hitting just .206. He then spent most of a year in the Army Reserve, playing just twenty-six games with Knoxville (Tennessee) of the Double-A Southern League in 1967 and hitting .189. Back from the service, Chaney broke through in 1968 with Double-A Asheville (North Carolina), hitting just .231 but with twenty-three home runs, good for second in the league. After the season the Reds traded their starting shortstop, Leo Cardenas, to the Minnesota Twins, partly because they felt Chaney was ready.[4]

Chaney was the Reds' regular shortstop for most of the first half of the 1969 season, though poor hitting eventually cost him the job and veteran Woody Woodward took over. On his first trip to Chicago, in June, Chaney met up with Ernie Banks, his old hero, and doubled and singled with his parents in the stands. Banks had read about Chaney in the paper that morning and warmly greeted him as he took first: "Welcome to the big leagues, kid. I knew you would make it. It's a long way from that banquet hall in Hammond, Indiana." Chaney recalled, "One of my greatest thrills was seeing my mom and dad, sitting behind the dugout in Chicago when I first came up the leagues, knowing how much it meant to them, especially my dad, who had been my coach."[5]

After hitting just .191 with no home runs in his rookie year of 1969, Chaney realized he was never going to be a power hitter. "I have to forget about the home run completely," he said in retrospect. "If I'm going to hit for any kind of respectable average, I have to shorten my swing, use a heavy bat, choke it, and swing down on the ball."[6]

While playing that winter in Puerto Rico, Chaney and his wife, Cynthia, were driving on a four-lane highway when a car sideswiped their rented Volkswagen on the passenger side. "It didn't hit us at a sharp angle or else it would have been tragic," Chaney recalled. The four men in the other car were all drunk, and one of them clubbed Chaney over the head when he was getting a pen to write down their license-plate number. Chaney's eyes were still leaky four days later. He did get their plate number, and the perpetrators were caught and jailed. "It was a traumatic experience for a young couple with a wife who was seven months pregnant at the time," Chaney recalled.[7]

Back in Hammond, Chaney worked for the city engineer as a city inspector before reporting for spring training in late February 1970. "I know I had troubles at the plate last year, but I'm going to spring training with the idea of making the club," he said before the season.[8] He made the club as a utility infielder, playing shortstop, second, and third and hitting .232 in 101 plate appearances. He did get his first Major League home run, on September 7 off the San Francisco Giants' Juan Marichal. He played in three games in the World Series against the Baltimore Orioles as a late-inning replacement at shortstop, striking out in his only plate appearance.

Besides Woodward, by 1971 Chaney had been passed on the shortstop depth chart by rookie Dave Concepción, and that spring Chaney was sent to Triple-A Indianapolis. He played the entire International League season, batting .277 in 120 games. His good year earned a September recall to the Majors, where he hit .125 in twenty-four at bats. After the season Woodward retired, clearing the path for Chaney to assume his role as the top utility infielder. He even went to work in the off-season for Woodward, his ex-roommate, who had become an executive with Winewood, Inc., a Florida land-development firm. "Woody had just retired, and then I started working for his golf course development in Tallahassee," Chaney said. "I bought a lot and built a house on it. We kept the house until I got traded."[9]

During the summer of 1972, when the Reds were on the road in St. Louis, Chaney got a call from his brother, telling him their mother had cancer. "I suddenly realized there are so many things over which I have no control, and which I can't fix. I can't do anything about my playing time. Sparky Anderson made the lineup card. That very night, I went back to my hotel room [at the Chase Park Plaza Hotel], got down on my knees, and asked Jesus into my life," Chaney recalled.[10]

Chaney saw plenty of action over the next few seasons. In 1972 he played in eighty-three games, including fifty-four starting assignments, and hit a respectable .250 with eleven extra-base hits and a fine .345 on-base percentage. The Reds returned to the postseason and Chaney played in nine games, batting 3-for-16 in the NLCS win over the Pittsburgh Pirates, then 0-for-7 in the World Series loss to the Oakland Athletics. Despite his increased playing time, the Reds did not see the twenty-four-year-old as a regular player. "It's our belief," said General Manager Bob Howsam, "that Chaney's future in the major leagues is limited to the role of a utilityman."[11] Concepción emerged as a star in 1973, making his first All-Star Game, but his broken leg in July made a regular out of Chaney for the last eight weeks of the season. Chaney ended up playing in 105 games but hit just .181 in 227 at bats. Late in the season he stopped switch-hitting, hitting just left-handed for a couple of years before reverting back.

Chaney spent the winter of 1973 working with former Cincinnati first baseman Gordy Coleman, who headed the Reds' speakers bureau. "He's doing a good job," said Coleman at the time. "We've received a lot of letters complimenting him from the organizations he's talked to." Chaney reported, "What surprises me is that despite all the banquets I've attended, I'm still only two pounds over my reporting weight."[12] Reds broadcaster Al Michaels also helped Chaney get a third-class operator's license through the Columbia School of Broad-

casting. "I didn't have the credentials to become a broadcaster through my playing career alone," Chaney recalled.[13]

Chaney played in 117 games in 1974, but most of them were as a late-inning defensive replacement at third base, a role he assumed seventy-nine times. He hit just .200 in 135 at bats but did have one memorable hit, the only grand slam of his career, against the Cardinals during the second game of a doubleheader. "I still remember the date and time. It was July 7, 1974, at 4:20 p.m. Sparky Anderson had told me to stop switch-hitting. I got up to bat with the bases loaded in the second inning. Rich Folkers left one out over the plate."[14] Chaney hit his homer from the left side against the left-handed-throwing Folkers.

The switch of Pete Rose to third base in 1975 gave the Reds All-Stars at all four infield positions. Chaney remained the primary backup infielder, hitting .219 in 160 at bats. "It was a thrill to be a part of a world championship team," he recalled. "I considered myself the twenty-fifth-best player on a twenty-five-man team, but being able to wear a world championship ring around Cincinnati was unbelievable. I was the only member of the team that played for Sparky Anderson at Double-A Asheville. I went to Sparky's office to ask for more playing time, but Sparky explained that while we had Hall of Famers at almost every position, I had a role to play. I was a defensive replacement for Pete Rose at third, while no one turned the double play better than me at second and short." The lessons Chaney took from his time on the Big Red Machine, which he always shared as a public speaker, were to recognize and believe in your own significance, always tell the truth, and no matter what position you have, remember that you are a valuable part of your organization.[15]

"My first manager with the Reds, Dave Bristol, told me that he would try to trade for me if he had the opportunity," said Chaney.[16] With Bristol now managing in Atlanta, Chaney was traded to

DEREK NORIN

the Braves for outfielder Mike Lum on December 12, 1975. For the first time in his career he was the regular shortstop for an entire season, and he responded by hitting .252 with one home run and fifty RBIs. He struggled in the field, however, making a league-leading thirty-seven errors.

After the 1976 season the Braves returned Chaney to his utility infielder role, and he hit .201, .224, and .162 in that role over the next three seasons. On May 17, 1978, Chaney was ejected for arguing after being called out on a play at home plate. He recalled the incident: "Bobby Cox will stand up for his players whether you are Chipper Jones or David Justice or whether it's people like me. There was a play at the plate in New York. I slid in under the catcher's tag and kicked up dirt when I got up. The home plate umpire was Ed Montague, and he ejected me for kicking up dirt. Bobby took up the argument. Bobby destroyed the toilet with a bare hand after that."[17]

Support or not, Cox, near the end of the 1979 season, had some truth to impart. "They're not renewing your contract," Cox told Chaney. "They're gonna release you. But I'll play you as much as I can these last two weeks, so other clubs can see you." Chaney hit .333 (9-for-27) for the Braves in what turned out to be the final two weeks of his career.[18] It didn't work out well: "I didn't retire. I was released. I would have liked to continue my career, but I couldn't. Most of us don't retire."[19]

Unable to hook on with another big league team, Chaney joined the Braves' broadcast crew in 1980, teaming with Ernie Johnson, Skip Caray, and Pete Van Wieren for three seasons. His many years of speaking for the Reds had prepared him for the new role. "I didn't retire from the broadcast booth, either. I was naïve then. After the Braves lost to the Cardinals in the 1982 playoffs, I was brought into the office of the Braves senior vice president to discuss the improvements they were going to make. I asked, 'What are we going to do?' 'We're going to replace you.' It was Halloween, late in October, and everybody had filled their vacancies. I was a couple of weeks late, or I may have had an opportunity with the Reds."[20]

Chaney spent nearly three decades in corporate reality before retiring. He had married the former Cynthia Pajak, a fellow Hammond native, on February 17, 1968. The couple raised a son, Keith, who eventually gave them three grandsons. Darrel and Cindy settled in the Atlanta area when he was traded there, and after he retired they moved to Sautee, in White County, Georgia, two hours north of Atlanta. "I moved to the mountains. I make appearances as a public speaker, but I live off Social Security and my Major League pension," he said.[21] He also spent many years working with the Major League Baseball Alumni Association.

Chaney also got involved in charitable work in White County. "The United Way White County Celebrity Golf Tournament started with a fundraiser to play a round of golf with me. I didn't think anybody would want to buy a round of golf with me but someone paid $800. Then I called my MLB friends, and I called my NFL friends. The golf tournament is now the biggest fundraiser the United Way has in White County," Chaney said proudly.[22]

Chapter 38. **August 1975 Timeline**

Mark Miller and Mark Armour

All headlines below are from the next day's edition of the *Springfield (OH) News.*

August 1—CEY'S 10TH INNING HOMER GIVES LA WILD VICTORY—Starting their West Coast trip in Los Angeles, Johnny Bench gave the Reds a 3–0 lead with his two-run home run in the sixth, but the Dodgers chipped away and finally won it, 5–3, on Ron Cey's two-run homer in the bottom of the tenth. Pete Rose had five hits, only to be left stranded four times.

August 2—FOSTER'S CLOUT NIPS DODGERS—Second-year starter Tom Carroll and veteran reliever Clay Carroll (unrelated) combined to beat Dodgers ace Andy Messersmith, 1–0, in Los Angeles. George Foster provided the Reds' offense with a home run in the fifth inning.

August 3—REDS BUILD LEAD, 15½ BULGE—In another stellar pitching performance, this time a seven-hitter by Pat Darcy and Rawly Eastwick, the Reds defeated the Dodgers, 3–1, in the finale of their series in Dodger Stadium. The Reds managed only five well-timed hits themselves, including a seventh-inning home run by Dave Concepción off Dodgers starter Doug Rau.

August 4—REDS TOP GIANTS WITH NINTH-INNING RALLY—George Foster's eighth-inning grand slam off Randy Moffitt gave the Reds a temporary lead, and two runs in the ninth sealed the deal in the opener of their three-game series with the Giants in Candlestick Park. Tony Pérez and Johnny Bench were given the night off, and the Reds' pitchers had to overcome three errors in the 7–5 victory.

August 5—REDS REMAIN SAME, EVEN WITHOUT SLUGGERS—Joe Morgan joined Johnny Bench and Tony Pérez on the bench, and the Reds kept rolling along, defeating the Giants again, 6–3. Ken Griffey and César Gerónimo provided six of the Reds' thirteen hits, backing the solid pitching of Clay Kirby, Pedro Borbon (who ran his record to 7-3), and Will McEnaney.

August 6—REDS KEEPING EVERYONE HAPPY ON WAY TO CROWN—The Reds finished off a three-game sweep of the Giants, 12–5, with twenty hits, including three each by Pete Rose, Dan Driessen, and Darrel Chaney (subbing for the resting Dave Concepción). Jack Billingham allowed ten hits and three runs in 6⅔ innings but cruised to his twelfth victory. The Reds won five of six games on their West Coast trip.

August 8—FRYMAN ENDS TORMENT, FINALLY WHIPS REDS—Returning home, the Reds thought they had this one in hand when they entered the ninth inning with a 7–5 lead. Unfortunately, the Expos rallied for four hits and three runs off Pedro Borbon and prevailed, 8–7. The winning pitcher for the Expos in relief was Woody Fryman, who entered the game with a 1-10 lifetime record against the Reds.

August 9—REDS WALK PAST EXPOS—The Reds amassed eleven hits (all singles) and, more importantly, ten walks against Montreal pitching and ran away with a 9–1 victory. Gary Nolan, who had missed almost all of the previous two seasons, ran his record to 10-6 with the victory.

August 10—SPARKY REVEALS SECRET OF REDS HITTING—Sparky Anderson's secret, he suggested after the Reds' 11–3 win, was having three hot hitters in the lineup at the same time. Of course, Anderson had several, including Johnny Bench and Tony Pérez (who each had three hits), Joe Morgan (who had two), and George Foster (who hit his nineteenth home run). Fred Norman and Rawly Eastwick were the night's beneficiaries.

August 11—REDS FIND FANCY FOOTWORK LEADS TO VICTORY—George Foster went 5-for-5 with a double as the Reds crushed the Cubs 9–3 in the opener of a three-game series at Riverfront Stadium. In the fifth inning, the Reds were trailing 3–2 but were sparked by Johnny Bench, who caught the Cubs napping on his own infield ground ball. The Cubs thought he was out at first and left the field, only to have Bench storm all the way to third base. He scored the tying run on a Tony Pérez double. Jack Billingham went the distance to run his record to 13-5.

August 12—REDS CAPTURE SLUGFEST—Pat Darcy was knocked out of the box in the first inning after giving up five hits and four runs to the visiting Cubs, but the Reds stormed back for a 12–8 victory. The Reds' eighteen-hit attack was led by Tony Pérez, who had four hits, and Joe Morgan and George Foster, who had three each. Clay Kirby, Pedro Borbon, and Rawly Eastwick pitched the final 8⅔ innings, during which the Reds' bats came alive. The Reds were now 78-39, getting their winning percentage up to .667.

August 14—SAGGING BUCS GET NO RESPECT; FOSTER, NOLAN KEY REDS WIN—George Foster drove in five runs on his twentieth and twenty-first home runs while Gary Nolan allowed only four hits in eight innings as the Reds defeated the Pirates 6–1 in the start of a four-game series in Cincinnati between the two NL division leaders. Nolan was working on a two-hit shutout with one

out in the eighth before Manny Sanguillen touched him for a solo home run.

August 15—PRESSURE SHOWING ON BUCS, REDS TOPPLE EAST LEADERS—The Reds scored six runs in the first inning and rode them to an easy 8–3 victory over the reeling Pirates. Johnny Bench got things going with a three-run home run in the first, and a few batters later, starter Jim Rooker was finished. Fred Norman (8-3) went all the way for the win and added two singles and two RBIS to his cause.

August 16—REDS TRIM BUCS, 5–3, FOR SEVENTH STRAIGHT—John Candelaria and Jack Billingham were locked in a 2-2 duel into the eighth inning, but Tony Pérez's two-run shot in the bottom of the eighth gave the Reds the lead and they held on to win 5–3, as César Gerónimo also added a solo home run. George Foster extended his hitting streak to fourteen games, and Billingham won his team-leading fourteenth game.

August 17—REDS VERSION OF "JAWS" CHEWS UP PIRATES—For the second straight game more than fifty thousand fans were on hand at Riverfront Stadium and they saw Pete Rose collect his twenty-five hundredth hit in a 3–1 victory over Bruce Kison and the Pirates. Pat Darcy allowed just three hits and a run in 7⅓ innings, and three relievers finished the job. After being swept in the four-game series, the Pirates' division lead over the Phillies was down to a half game. The Reds wrapped up their home stand with an 8-1 record.

August 18—NINTH STRAIGHT FOR REDS, CAPTAIN HOOK AT BEST—After more than two months out of action with his broken thumb, Don Gullett pitched five shutout innings in the Reds' 3–2 victory in St. Louis. Sparky Anderson then did what he did best, calling upon four of his excellent relievers to finish the job. Rookie Rawly Eastwick picked up his fifteenth save.

August 19—FOUR-HITTER STOPS REDS—Cardinals pitcher Lynn McGlothen stopped the Reds on four hits and Gary Nolan was the hard-luck loser in a 2–1 loss in St. Louis. McGlothen allowed his run in the first inning but dominated after that, striking out ten and walking just one. The Reds were still 16½ games ahead of the Dodgers in the NL West.

August 20—MCBRIDE'S HOMERS SPARKS CARDS; REDS LOSE AGAIN, 4–0—Cardinals outfielder Bake McBride homered twice to pace the Redbirds to a 4–0 victory. For the second game in a row the Reds managed just four hits, this time being stymied by Ron Reed, who pitched the shutout.

August 22—REDS LOSSES CONTINUE AFTER DROPPING TWO TO BUCS, 7–2 AND 4–2—The Reds' losing streak grew to four as they dropped both games of a doubleheader, getting only eleven hits in the eighteen innings. In the first game Richie Zisk reached Jack Billingham for two home runs in a relatively easy 7–2 victory. The second game was scoreless through seven innings before Tony Pérez hit a two-run home run off John Candelaria to give the Reds a 2–0 lead in the top of the eighth. In the bottom half the Pirates scored four times, including back-to-back home runs by Dave Parker and Richie Hebner off Will McEnaney to score a 4–2 win.

August 23—REDS POUND PIRATES 12–7—After they had scored just five runs in their last four games and fell behind 4–0 in this one, the Reds' bats broke through with an eight-run fifth inning and held on. Johnny Bench's twenty-fourth home run, a three-run shot in the eighth, helped put the 12–7 victory away.

August 24—REDS, BUCS BREAK EVEN IN SEASON SERIES—Jerry Reuss pitched a complete game to lead the Pirates to a 5–1 victory. The Pirates managed just five hits, led by Al Oliver's triple, home run, and three RBIs. The victory evened the season series between the likely NLCS foes at six games apiece, with each team having a 4-2 record at home. During their regular-season games each team scored fifty-five runs.

August 25—CUBS UPSET AFTER DEFEAT; REDS, CONCEPCIÓN BLASTED—The Reds thumped the Cubs 11–4 at Wrigley Field. The Cubs were upset at Dave Concepción for tagging up and advancing from second to third with a 10-4 lead in the ninth inning and for his hard slide that forced third baseman Bill Madlock from the game with an injury. The Reds put together nineteen hits, including six doubles and Darrel Chaney's first home run of the year, a three-run blast. Fred Norman won his ninth, helped immeasurably by Clay Carroll's 3⅔-inning, one-hit relief stint.

August 26—REDS HUSTLE TO 6–5 WIN, RALLY IN NINTH FOR VICTORY—With the Reds trailing 5–4 with two out and the bases empty in the ninth inning, pinch hitter Terry Crowley singled to ignite a two-run rally and a Reds 6–5 victory. Once again the bullpen was the star, as Jack Billingham allowed all five runs in 4⅓ innings before yielding to Pedro Borbon, Rawly Eastwick, and Will McEnaney, who combined to allow two hits and no runs the rest of the way. Johnny Bench hit his twenty-fifth home run to help the offense.

August 27—CATCH PLEASES GRIFFEY, MORE THAN FOUR HITS—Ken Griffey had a leaping first-inning catch into Wrigley Field's right-field ivy to rob Rick Monday and added four singles, two RBIs, and a stolen base as the Reds defeated the Cubs 6–5. The Reds had fifteen hits in the game, all singles. This completed a three-game sweep and gave the Reds an 11-1 season record against the Cubs, outscoring Chicago 99–51 in the process.

August 28—GULLETT IN FIVE-HIT WIN, CHANEY HOMERS AGAIN—Don Gullett tossed a five-hit shutout against the visiting Cardinals in a 4–0 Reds victory. The Reds managed only five hits themselves, including Darrel Chaney's second homer in four games.

August 29—SLUMP ENDED BY GERÓNIMO, REDS DOWN CARDINALS—Gary Nolan won his twelfth game and center fielder César Gerónimo hit a three-run home run to propel the Reds to a 6–2 win over St. Louis. Will McEnaney was brilliant in relief, allowing one hit over the final 2⅔ innings to notch his thirteenth save.

August 30—REDS NIP CARDS IN 10TH FOR SIXTH VICTORY IN A ROW—The Reds beat the Cardinals, 3–2, on Johnny Bench's ground ball out in the bottom of the tenth inning. With one out, Ken Griffey singled, then advanced to third when a pickoff throw by Mike Garman sailed into right field. Garman intentionally walked Joe Morgan and Tony Pérez before Bench hit a slow grounder past the mound that St. Louis shortstop Mike Tyson fielded but could only throw to first base, as Griffey had already crossed the plate with the winning run. Fred Norman pitched into the ninth and allowed just two runs, and Rawly Eastwick got the relief victory.

August 31—CARDS RASMUSSEN BEATS BILLINGHAM—Rookie Harry Rasmussen allowed nine hits and three runs in 7⅔ innings, but it was enough to stop the Reds' six-game winning streak in a 5–3 loss and to drop Jack Billingham's record to 14-7. Ken Griffey had three hits for the Reds, who finished August with a 21-8 record.

NL West Standings, August 31, 1975

TEAM	W	L	GB
Cincinnati	90	45	—
Los Angeles	72	64	18.5
San Francisco	67	68	23.0
San Diego	61	75	29.5
Atlanta	59	77	31.5
Houston	52	85	39.0

Chapter 39. **Tony Pérez**

Philip A. Cola

AGE	G	AB	R	H	2B	3B	HR	TB	RBI	BB	SO	BAV	OBP	SLG	SB	GDP	HBP
33	137	511	74	144	28	3	20	238	109	54	101	.282	.350	.466	1	12	3

It was Wednesday evening, October 22, 1975, Game Seven of the greatest World Series ever played. The Big Red Machine from Cincinnati faced the Boston Red Sox the night after an amazing Game Six marathon won by the Red Sox in dramatic fashion on Carlton Fisk's home run leading off the bottom of the twelfth inning. The Reds were heavily favored, as they had been in the 1970 and 1972 World Series, as well as the 1973 NLCS, each of which ended in a loss. The Reds were the team of the 1970s, but by the middle of the decade they had yet to win a World Series. The pressure was on the city, the organization, and the players. For Game Seven the Red Sox had all the momentum and it appeared that the Reds were going to lose in the postseason for the fourth time in five years.

Boston took a 3–0 lead in the bottom of the third against the Reds' ace, Don Gullett. Bill "Spaceman" Lee was still shutting out the Reds with two outs in the top of the sixth inning when Tony Pérez stepped to the plate. He was 0-for-2 and had struggled throughout the Series. He had started the Series 0-for-15 with seven strikeouts up to his second at bat in Game Five. However, he kept smiling despite friendly ridicule by his manager and teammates, who knew him as Mr. Clutch for the Reds throughout his twelve-year career. Pérez faced Lee with Johnny Bench on second base by virtue of a hit, a force play, and a throwing error. The count on Pérez was 1-0 and Lee, hoping to catch Pérez off guard, threw a slow overhand curveball (nicknamed the "Leephus"). But Pérez double-clutched before he connected and the ball soared into the night over the left-field wall. The Reds now trailed

The veteran leader of the Reds, Tony Pérez contributed humor and an annual ninety RBIS to the cause. NBL Doug McWilliams.

by only a run, and suddenly the momentum had shifted. The Reds tied the game in the seventh and won it with a run in the ninth for Cincinnati's first world championship in thirty-five years. The team of the 1970s had made their mark and their future Hall of Fame first baseman had turned the tide in their favor with a big swing of the bat.

Atanasio "Tony" Pérez Rigal was born on May 14, 1942, in the town of Ciego de Ávila in Camagüey Province, Cuba. As a teenager he worked with his father in a sugar factory, putting stamps on packages, but he described his life in those days as being about "school, work, and baseball, and baseball was what you lived for." He had one sister and one brother and his family teased him about becoming a professional baseball player, telling him he was too skinny (nicknaming him Flaco, Spanish for skinny) and saying he would spend his life working in the factory like his father and brother. He played shortstop for the factory team, batted and threw right-handed, and stood 6 feet 2 and weighed 155 pounds.

Despite his family's jibes, in 1960 the teenage Pérez signed with the Havana Sugar Kings of the International League. The team was owned by a prominent businessman, Bobby Maduro (the "sugar king" of Havana). Havana had a working agreement with the Reds, who became interested in Pérez. He left Cuba for the United States just before Fidel Castro restricted the ability to travel out of the country. Pérez was criticized for leaving his country to play baseball, but the political climate caused tremendous additional anxieties for young players, and Pérez's love of baseball forced the tough decision to leave his family and his home, knowing that he might not ever be allowed to return to Cuba. He was inspired by Minnie Miñoso, a fellow Cuban who had a successful Major League career between 1949 and 1964 (with cameo appearances in 1976 and 1980). The Reds signed Pérez without a signing bonus and just for the price of a plane ticket and a $2.50 exit visa. During his first few off-seasons he went home to Cuba, but it was becoming more and more difficult to leave the country on time for spring training, so by 1963 Pérez began spending the off-season in the United States and eventually in Puerto Rico, not returning to Cuba again until 1972 to visit his parents.

Pérez broke in with the Reds as a third baseman, but his throwing was erratic (thirty-one, forty-two, and thirty errors in his first three Minor League seasons), and eventually the Reds moved him to first base. His professional baseball career started with Geneva in the Class D New York–Pennsylvania League in 1960, and fielding problems aside, it was clear that he had great ability. In 1961, just nineteen, he returned to Geneva and broke out as a hitter (.348, twenty-seven home runs, 132 RBIs, 110 runs scored). Pérez moved up to Class B Rocky Mount (Carolina League) in 1962 and was hitting .292 with eighteen home runs when he broke his leg and missed the last several weeks of the season. In 1963 he was moved up to Macon (Georgia) of the Double-A Sally League and hit .309 in sixty-nine games, though his home run total fell to eleven. He spent the end of the season with Triple-A San Diego, where his manager, Dave Bristol, urged him to gain weight in the off-season. Pérez picked up more than forty pounds, returned to San Diego in 1964, and batted .304 with thirty-four home runs and 107 RBIs, earning him the Pacific Coast League's Most Valuable Player Award as well as a call-up to the Reds in late July. He made his Major League debut on July 26, 1964, against the Pittsburgh Pirates at Cincinnati (he walked in his first at bat and went 0-for-2). Pérez went on to appear in twelve games, playing first base in six of them and pinch-hitting in the rest. He was just 2-for-25 but was in the big leagues to stay.

During the next two seasons Pérez platooned at first base with Gordy Coleman. He showed some power and clutch production. He was moved to third base in 1967 to make room for a first base prospect named Lee May, and much to Pérez's surprise Los Angeles Dodgers manager Walter Alston named him to the National League squad for the All-Star Game in Anaheim. Pérez entered the game in the tenth inning, struck out in his first at bat in the twelfth, and then, in the fifteenth inning, he hit a one-out home run off Catfish Hunter to give the National League a 2–1 victory. Pérez was voted the game's Most Valuable Player. (In an article in *Baseball Digest* in 1974—before he hit his shot against the Red Sox—Pérez named this "the game I'll never forget.") Pérez wound up 1967 hitting .290 with twenty-six home runs and 102 RBIs in 156 games.

His 102 RBIS began a string of eleven seasons in which he drove in at least ninety runs, and his All-Star Game appearance was the first of seven.

In 1968 Pérez batted .282 with eighteen home runs and ninety-two RBIS and in 1969 he batted .294 and blossomed as a power hitter with thirty-seven home runs and 122 RBIS. Pérez was now an established star in the prime of his career, playing for an emerging powerhouse of a team that would soon take the baseball world by storm.

After the 1969 season the Reds had hired an obscure Minor League manager named George "Sparky" Anderson, and under Anderson the 1970 team got off to one of the best starts in the history of baseball. After one hundred games the team's record was 70-30. Pérez and Johnny Bench were leading the way in this historic season. Pérez topped his previous year's figures with a .317 batting average, forty home runs, and 129 runs batted in. On July 16 Pérez hit the first home run at Pittsburgh's new Three Rivers Stadium. He finished third in the National League in the voting for the Most Valuable Player behind his superstar teammate Bench and the Cubs' Billy Williams. After their sensational start the Reds played just over .500 ball the rest of the way but won 102 games and defeated the Pirates in the NLCS to capture the pennant. Then they lost the World Series in five games to the Baltimore Orioles, with their dominant pitching (Pérez was 1-for-18 and failed to hit a home run or drive in a run) and the amazing defensive play of Orioles third baseman Brooks Robinson. The expectations for Pérez and his teammates were now extremely high. Perhaps not surprisingly, the Reds finished tied for fourth in the National League West in 1971, as several of the stars were injured at points during the season. Pérez was solid, if unspectacular, hitting .269 with twenty-five home runs and ninety-one RBIS.

Pérez moved back to first base in 1972 after the Reds traded the slugging May in the off-season and acquired infielder Denis Menke from Houston in the deal that also got them second baseman Joe Morgan, pitcher Jack Billingham, and outfielders César Gerónimo and Ed Armbrister. Pérez remained a first baseman or a designated hitter for the rest of his career. Bench won his second MVP Award and Pérez hit .283 with twenty-one home runs and ninety RBIS in 1972. The Reds won the NLCS over the Pirates for the second time in three seasons but disappointingly lost the World Series in seven games to the Oakland Athletics. Pérez hit .435 in the World Series (10-for-23) but again failed to hit a home run and drove in only two runs.

The Reds won the National League West again in 1973 (Pérez batted .314 with twenty-seven home runs and 101 RBIS) but fell to the New York Mets in the NLCS. Pérez struggled again in the postseason, going 2-for-22 (.091), but one of his hits was a home run. The team now had a great mix of speed and power but did not seem to have the depth of pitching that the Orioles, Athletics, and Mets trotted out in stifling the Big Red Machine in three of the last four postseasons. And in 1974 another pitching-rich team, the Dodgers, beat out the Reds by four games for the NL West title. Pérez's batting average dipped to .265, but he hit twenty-eight home runs and drove in 101 runs while making his first All Star Game in four years as a reserve. Despite his clutch play and power, there was discussion of trading Pérez. Still, despite the trade talk, Pérez's teammates considered him a leader of the team, referring to him as Big Dog or Doggie.

In 1975 the Reds got off to a slow start and stood at 19-19 in mid-May. Critics said they did not have the pitching to win a World Series, Pérez was past his prime, Bench could not continue to catch nearly every game, Morgan was good but not great, Anderson pulled his pitchers too soon and could not lead this team of stars to the ultimate goal, and the team did not have a skilled third baseman. Eventually Anderson moved Pete Rose to third base to make room for a young power-hitting outfielder named George Foster, and something magical happened as the Reds dominated the rest of the league on their way to a final record of 108-54, beating out the Dodgers by an amazing twenty games in the N L West. Morgan became a superstar, winning the National League M V P (making him the fourth Red to win the award in the past six seasons); Rose was a star at his fourth position; Bench continued to star; the pitching turned out to be very good after all as Gullett, Billingham, Gary Nolan, Rawly Eastwick, Clay Carroll, and others emerged as a cohesive staff; the gold gloves of Bench, Morgan, Dave Concepción, and Gerónimo up the middle were unprecedented; Anderson was a genius after all; and Pérez was consistent on and off the field, as always.

The teammates did not always get along; there was some jealousy among them as to who were the best of the best. But Pérez kept them all together and loose. He was an agitator and made fun of his star teammates as relentlessly as he drove in runners in scoring position. Concepción and Gerónimo looked up to him as a great Latino player, while the others looked to him for veteran leadership. Pérez related to both the star and nonstar players and made them all feel part of the team. On the field he was the same consistent offensive force. He hit .282 with twenty home runs and 109 R B I s.

In 1976 the Reds swept another good Pirates team in the N L C S. Pérez had his best N L C S, batting .417 with a home run and four R B I s as the team roared to the World Series. A fellow Cuban emerged as the early star of the Series as Luis Tiant shut out the Reds in Game One. Was it to be another disappointing Series, with the other team's pitching dominating the Reds' All-Star lineup? The offense sputtered in Games Two and Three but managed to pull out a one-run victory in each before Tiant beat them again in Game Four, throwing an amazing 163 pitches. At this point Pérez appeared washed up after failing to get a hit in the first four games and striking out seven times. However, in Game Five he homered twice and drove in four runs as the Reds took the lead, three games to two. The epic Game Six went to the Red Sox in extra innings on Carl-

ton Fisk's walk-off home run. Then Pérez emerged again with his uplifting home run in Game Seven, and the Reds wound up winning the decisive game. Pérez was the leader, the key to the Machine running smoothly, the venerable veteran who finally had a World Series ring. Though he hit only .179 in the Series, he showed clutch hitting at its finest by driving in seven runs.

For an encore, the 1976 Reds won 102 games to take the N L West by ten games over the Dodgers, then they swept the postseason—the Philadelphia Phillies in three games in the N L C S and the Yankees in four games in the World Series. Pérez came through in a big way against Catfish Hunter as his two-out ninth-inning single to left field drove in Ken Griffey to win Game Two. It was the first time a team had won every postseason game since the introduction of the extra round of playoffs in 1969. Pérez, by now thirty-four years old, continued to be the off-the-field leader and consistent on the field. During the regular season, he hit .260 with nineteen home runs and ninety-one R B I s. Morgan won his second M V P Award, while Bench, Rose, Griffey, Concepción, Gerónimo, and Foster all continued to play at superstar levels. As a group they became known as the "Great Eight."

General Manager Bob Howsam believed the Reds were so great that they no longer needed the heart and soul of the team. He shipped Pérez to the Montreal Expos on December 16, 1976, along with relief pitcher Will McEnaney for pitchers Woodie Fryman and Dale Murray. "The Mayor of Riverfront," as fellow players and fans had dubbed Pérez, was gone in a stunning trade. Howsam underestimated the intangibles Pérez brought to the club. He thought they would be even better with Dan Driessen, who was nine years younger and much cheaper, playing first base, along with some additional pitching. The Reds finished second to the Dodgers in each of the next two seasons and the Big Red Machine would never reach the World Series again. (They appeared in only one more N L C S, losing to the Pirates in 1979.)

Pérez played for the Expos from 1977 through 1979. For the three seasons he hit .281, with forty-six home runs and 242 RBIs. He left the Expos as a free agent after the 1979 season and signed with the Boston Red Sox, the team he had helped conquer in 1975. He hit .275 with twenty-five home runs and 105 RBIs in 1980 but he struck out ninety-three times and grounded into a league-leading twenty-five double plays. That year he received the Lou Gehrig Memorial Award from the Phi Delta Theta fraternity (Gehrig's fraternity at Columbia University) for integrity on and off the field. The 1980 season was the last in which Pérez appeared in more than one hundred games. He played with the Red Sox for two more seasons, frequently as a designated hitter, before being released in November 1982. Pérez signed with Philadelphia in January 1983 in time to be part of the Phillies' pennant win, being reunited with former teammates Rose and Morgan. Pérez batted .241 with six home runs in ninety-one games. He started two World Series games as the Phillies lost the Series to Baltimore in five games.

After the season Pérez came full circle—the Phillies sold him to the Reds. By now in his forties, he was a bench player for the Reds for the next three years. The team was long past its Big Red Machine days. Pérez was reunited with Rose again in August 1984 when Rose returned as a player-manager. Pérez played in just over seventy games each of his three seasons. Two of the seasons were mediocre, but in 1985 he hit .328 with six home runs and thirty-three RBIs. Pérez retired as a player after the 1986 season. His career batting average was .279 with 2,732 hits and 379 home runs. He played in five World Series and was a seven-time All-Star.

In 2000 Pérez was inducted into the Baseball Hall of Fame. (He had been inducted into the Reds Hall of Fame in 1998 and his number 24 was retired by the Reds in 2000.) Though he will always be first remembered as a Cincinnati Red, he was the first player elected to the Hall of Fame who had played for the Montreal Expos.

Pérez was a coach for the Reds from 1987 to 1992. He started coaching under Rose and continued during Lou Piniella's tenure as manager that included the 1990 world championship season. In 1993 Pérez was named the manager of the Reds but was inexplicably fired after forty-four games with a record of 20-24 and replaced by Davey Johnson. The Reds were in fifth place in the National League West when he was fired and remained in fifth under Johnson. In late May 2001 he succeeded the fired John Boles as manager of the Florida Marlins as they finished fourth in the National League East. Jeff Torborg succeeded him in 2002 and Pérez became the assistant to the general manager.

As of 2012 Pérez had been married to his wife, Petuka, for almost fifty years. Both of their sons, Victor and Eduardo, played professional baseball. Eduardo played for the Angels, Reds, Cardinals, Devil Rays, Indians, and Mariners from 1993 to 2006 except for a season in Japan in 2001. He also was a baseball analyst on ESPN and was the hitting coach for the Marlins in 2011. Victor played in 1990 for the Reds' Billings (Montana) farm team in the Pioneer League.

Chapter 40. **Jack Billingham**

Bill Nowlin

AGE	W	L	PCT.	ERA	G	GS	GF	CG	SHO	SV	IP	H	BB	SO	HBP	WP
32	15	10	.600	4.11	33	32	0	5	0	0	208	222	76	79	9	8

Although the 1970s Reds were famous for their great offense, a pitcher holds one of the team's—and baseball's—most impressive records. Jack Billingham has the lowest earned run average in World Series play, 0.36. He allowed just one earned run in 25⅓ innings spread over three different World Series for the Reds. In addition to his two Series wins, his 145 regular-season wins make a strong case that some of those Reds could pitch a little, too.

John Eugene Billingham, of English and Swedish descent, was born on February 21, 1943, in Orlando, Florida. He believes that he is a distant cousin of Christy Mathewson; the exact relationship is not known. He, his older sister, Judy, and his younger brother, Richie, were raised in Winter Park, Florida, where their father, Jack, ran a Standard Oil service station. His mother, Dorothy Newton Billingham, came from Minnesota. Young Jack played Little League baseball from around the time he was ten or eleven years old. After he got a little older, Billingham worked on weekends at the service station. "I was a car washer," he remembered. "I would check the oil and wash the windshield and fill up the gas tank. I worked there when I could."[1] There were some good athletes in the family, including an uncle in Winter Park, his father, and an uncle in Minnesota who played baseball and fast-pitch softball for many years.

Billingham signed with Los Angeles Dodgers scouts George Pfister and Leon Hamilton on June 12, 1961. "The Yankees wanted to sign me; there was an older scout who wanted to send me to the Appalachian League," he recalled. "My high school coach knew somebody over in Orlando with the

The winner of 145 big league games, Jack Billingham allowed just one earned run in 25.1 World Series innings (an 0.36 ERA).

Dodgers, and I'd go over there a couple of times and throw batting practice after baseball season was over with. My future in college didn't look too good. I wasn't a student necessarily."[2]

After signing, Billingham spent seven years in the Dodgers' Minor League system, beginning with the Orlando Dodgers in the Class D Florida State League. He started nine out of his twelve games, throwing fifty-six innings with a 4.50 earned run average, with a hardly impressive record of 1-6.

The next year he moved to St. Petersburg and had similar results: 1-5 and a 5.16 ERA in sixty-eight innings. In 1963 all of the Class B, C, and D Minor Leagues were redesignated as Single-A, and the twenty-year-old Billingham pitched for the Salisbury Dodgers in the Western Carolinas League. He got a lot of work and pitched well, throwing 142 innings with a 3.49 ERA and a 9-6 record. The tall (6 feet 4) right-hander weighed less in those days than the 195 pounds he would attain. In fact, his frame earned him nicknames like Blade and Bone.

When the Dodgers assigned Billingham for the 1964 season to Single-A Santa Barbara of the California League, three thousand miles from his Florida home and his fiancée, Jolene Suslar, he reported for duty but his financial reality weighed on him. He wanted to marry but didn't see how he could afford to on $450 a month. He contemplated quitting the game. "Even the newest rookies on the club were making $500, and many of them had received big bonuses, but I decided to risk a call to Fresco Thompson, in charge of the farm system."[3] A few days after the call, Thompson came through, boosting Billingham's pay to $500 and transferring him back to St. Petersburg a few weeks into the 1964 season.

Billingham said he knows how fortunate he was. "My first year was with Orlando and then the next year I went to St. Pete. I was a young, immature kid who hadn't been away from home much. That was a good start, to break into the pro baseball program and have Mom still able to cook me dinner."[4] With St. Petersburg in 1964 he was 7-3 with an eye-catching 1.03 ERA over 105 innings. On October 9 Jack and Jolene married, and three days later the newlyweds were off to Nicaragua, where Jack played winter ball. Later trips took him to the Dominican Republic and Venezuela. "My wife and I, fortunately, we've been blessed," he recalled in 2011. "We've been together forty-six years, and she's traveled with me wherever I go."[5]

The couple spent most of 1965 with Double-A Albuquerque, where Billingham finished 7-3 with a 1.78 ERA, which earned a call-up to Triple-A Spokane at the end of the season. By this time he was used entirely as a relief pitcher. Billingham pitched all of the 1966 and 1967 seasons for Spokane, both years under Manager Roy Hartsfield. He was 6-9 (in fifty games, with just two starts) and 7-4 (fifty-one games, two starts), with ERAs of 3.82 and 3.00. During the off-seasons, he returned to Winter Park. "In the Minor Leagues, when you're making $350 a month, I'd come home and I drove delivery trucks for a big electrical supply company, and then I got into driving fuel oil trucks in the wintertime. Running through backyards with a hose over my shoulder. Down here in Florida, they don't have 275-gallon tanks. They have 55-gallon tanks. After my first year that I did that, I actually came home and looked for the same jobs for like three years. I felt that it really kept me in shape. It was hard work, but I was young and it didn't bother me back then."[6]

After attending the Arizona Instructional League late in 1967 and working on an overhand curve, Billingham made the Dodgers out of spring training in 1968 and stayed all year. It was the first time he'd laid eyes on Dodger Stadium. The first of his fifty appearances came on April 11 in a home game the Dodgers were losing to the New York Mets, 3–0. He came in with one out in the top of the eighth and a runner on second and got a groundout and a strikeout. A pinch hitter took his place in the order. Billingham was the team's closer in each of his next six appearances, earning a splash headline in the *Los Angeles Times* when he saved both games of a Shea Stadium doubleheader against the Mets: "Billingham Saves the Day." Pitching coach Lefty Phillips said, "He started out the day a rookie and emerged a man."[7] He didn't give up his first run until his seventh game. His first win came in Atlanta in a twelve-inning, 1–0 game, and Billingham was quickly anointed with headlines such as that in the *Chicago Tribune*: "Dodgers' Billingham Takes Over as Bullpen Ace: Inherits Mantle of Perranoski and Regan."[8]

Billingham finished the season 3-0 with a 2.14 earned run average. The one start he was given (on three hours' notice) came on August 5 at Dodger Stadium. He shut out the Pirates through eight innings, allowing five hits and walking two before being lifted for a pinch hitter. The game went into extra innings, and the Dodgers won, 1–0, in the tenth.

Despite this great start, the Dodgers did not protect Billingham in that fall's expansion draft, and the brand-new Montreal Expos selected him as the tenth overall pick. In January 1969 Montreal traded Donn Clendenon to Houston for Rusty Staub, but Clendenon refused to report to Houston, and in early April Commissioner Bowie Kuhn ordered Montreal to send cash and a couple of players instead. Billingham was one of the players sent to the Astros.

For Manager Harry Walker, Billingham was 6-7 and pitched 82⅔ innings in fifty-two games, though with an inflated 4.25 ERA. His struggles may have been partly due to family concerns: his daughter was born prematurely early in the season and nearly died.

In 1970 Billingham changed his motion somewhat to more of a side-arm delivery. "I'm a sinkerball pitcher," he said, "and run into trouble if my pitches come up."[9] After beginning the year in his typical bullpen role, Billingham joined the rotation in midsummer and remained a starter for several years. "I started out as a reliever in the big leagues, and I enjoyed that role because I could throw every day. But I didn't know if I had the makeup to be a reliever, which is to be an aggressive, growling person," he said. "I'm more of a laid-back type. I was traded to Houston as a reliever, and was semi-successful for a year and a month. Then Harry [Walker] asked me in 1970 if I could start, and I said yes."[10]

Billingham was 13-9 in 1970 and 10-16 in 1971, on a team with a deep and talented pitching staff but not much hitting. But he enjoyed pitching in the Astrodome and credited his fielders on defense.

I just loved going there. . . . When you got loose, you stayed that way with your jacket on. One of the most disappointing things for any pitcher is when it starts raining, and you don't know if you're going to play. If you've built yourself up, it's easy to lose that edge while you wait. You don't have that problem in a domed stadium. . . . [Although people said the Astroturf surface] would hinder my pitching ability because balls would go shooting through the infield for base hits, it ended up helping me because I had good infielders. They played back a few steps more than usual, and they knew there'd be no bad hops.[11]

He also admitted enjoying the way the scoreboard lit up when an Astro hit a home run.

Jolene and Jack, by then parents of John Jr. and Jennifer, were looking for a house in Houston when they learned he'd been traded to Cincinnati. In November 1971 the Reds sent Tommy Helms, Lee May, and Jimmy Stewart to Houston and received Joe Morgan, Denis Menke, César Gerónimo, Ed Armbrister, and Billingham. Billingham played the next six seasons for Cincinnati and Manager Sparky Anderson. He said, "I was very fortunate I was in the right place at the right time."[12]

In 1972, his first season with the Reds, Billingham's ERA dropped to 3.18 and he was 12-12. The following year he won nineteen games and lost ten, lowered his ERA for the fourth year in a row, to 3.04, and led the National League in starts, innings pitched, and shutouts (seven, a Reds record). It was the first of back-to-back nineteen-win seasons, and it earned Billingham a trip to his only All-Star Game. He attributed his improvement in 1973 to the confidence that came from his Series start and from Roberto Clemente telling him that with the stuff he had, he should never be a .500 pitcher.[13]

Billingham pitched in four games in the 1972 postseason, including three starts. In Game Three of the World Series, against Oakland, he threw eight innings of three-hit, three-walk, shutout baseball in a 1–0 win. He also pitched the first five innings of the deciding Game Seven. When he was taken out for a pinch hitter, he had given up one unearned first-inning run on two hits. The Athletics scored the decisive runs off his successor, Pedro Borbon. The next October he started two games in the National League Championship Series and took the loss in the deciding Game Five to the New York Mets.

Billingham won nineteen games again in 1974 and the Reds won ninety-eight games but finished four games behind the Dodgers. On Opening Day he gave up a historic home run, the 714th of Hank Aaron's career. Billingham's ERA climbed to 3.94, reflecting a nagging shoulder problem that had developed for the first time in his career. That winter he worked as customer service manager for Westwood Chrysler-Plymouth in Cincinnati.

Billingham finished 15-10 for the great 1975 Reds team that won 108 games. His victory total tied Gary Nolan's (15-9) and Don Gullett's (15-4) to lead the Reds, but his 4.11 ERA was the worst among the Reds' main starters. Billingham didn't appear in the NLCS, but he got into three games in the World Series against the Red Sox, starting and pitching 5⅔ innings of two-run ball (one earned) in Game Two, then throwing crucial middle relief in Games Six and Seven, allowing no runs in 3⅓ innings.

For the 1976 club, Billingham won twelve games and was no longer near the top of the rotation. He pitched just once in the postseason but was again outstanding—pitching 2⅔ innings of shutout ball to win Game Two of the Reds' four-game sweep over the Yankees. Billingham had two World Series rings and he had played a crucial role in both Series.

The thirty-four-year-old Billingham regressed significantly in 1977, with a 10-10 record and a career-high 5.23 ERA as the Reds dropped to second place. The Reds dealt him to the Detroit Tigers during 1978 spring training. Bob Hertzel of the *Cincinnati Enquirer* wrote, "With Billingham goes a little bit of the class that was the Cincinnati Reds." He acknowledged that Billingham had become "the man Cincinnati fans loved to boo" and agreed that the time was right for the trade, with as

many as ten pitchers ahead of Billingham, but was wistful about the loss of his quiet clubhouse presence and what he'd brought to the team. The Tigers gave up relatively little: Minor Leaguers John Valle and George Cappuzzello. Sparky Anderson told Hertzel, "A manager may not be supposed to have favorite people but Jack Billingham was one of my favorites. He is a tremendous guy and a super person."[14]

In 1978 Billingham enjoyed a rebound year (15-8, with ten complete games and a 3.88 earned run average), resulting in headlines such as "Tigers Hit Jackpot on Longshot Billingham."[15] Detroit manager Ralph Houk was pleased. He had expected Billingham to work in long relief and start occasionally. As it worked out, Billingham worked exclusively as a starter—and was effective both on the field and in the clubhouse. Speaking of his influence on the younger pitchers, Houk said, "He's a great model for the rest of them. If they don't learn from him, I don't know who they can learn from."[16]

Billingham was said to have a dry sense of humor and a self-effacing style, but he was simply being candid when he took a moment to reflect on his season: "I'm no Cy Young Award winner. I leave things like that to Jim Palmer and Tom Seaver, guys who can reach back and throw the ball by people. When I reach back, there ain't nothing extra there. What you see is what you get. I've never considered myself a strikeout pitcher. I've never considered myself a complete-game pitcher or a shutout pitcher, either."[17]

In 1979 the Tigers moved Billingham to a mixed role—nineteen starts and sixteen relief stints—and he finished his tenth consecutive season of ten or more wins, with a 3.30 ERA in 158 innings. His old boss Sparky Anderson had taken over as manager about a third of the way into the season.

There was little room for Billingham on the 1980 Tigers. At the start of the season he appeared in 7⅓ largely unsuccessful innings, giving up six earned runs. Detroit traded him to the Boston Red Sox

BILL NOWLIN

in early May. With the Red Sox, the thirty-seven-year-old Billingham endured a little friendly hazing, with teammates continually taping photographs of Sparky Anderson over his locker; Anderson had, after all, twice ushered him out of town, once with the Reds and then with the Tigers. And it was known that Billingham might have grumbled aloud about what he considered his underutilization in Detroit. For the Red Sox he appeared in seven games, winning his first start and losing the next three, giving up thirty earned runs in 24⅓ innings. He was released by the Red Sox on June 21, and his professional career was at an end.

After baseball, Billingham operated a sporting-goods store named The Pass in Casselberry, Florida.

I came home and watched my kids grow up. My son was in junior high and my daughter was in sixth grade, and I just wanted to see them grow up. Professional Athletic Service Stores—it was a franchise. A friend of mine that I'd played sports with in high school, who played in the Minor Leagues, Ronnie Cayll, he was in the sporting-goods business and he asked myself and another friend I played ball with in high school, Terry Williams. We were all buddies. Winter Park was a small town. Terry had just retired from Shell Oil Company. He was a bookkeeper, and Ronnie was a salesman, and I was kind of just a guy who stood around and sold stuff in the store. Seven years. We actually bought Ronnie out after a couple of years.

I was out of baseball from '80 to '87, and then my daughter was a senior in high school and I had a job offer from Houston. My wife and I and my daughter talked about it and I decided that I wanted to try to get back into baseball.

When I got back in baseball, after one year, I realized that I didn't want to run a store and coach baseball. I had coaches calling me up in the morning. I'd get home at one or two o'clock in the morning from a road trip, and they're wanting to meet me at six or six-thirty at the school. I realized I wanted to stay in coaching as long as possible, so Terry and I sold the store.[18]

Once again, Billingham had lucked out geographically.

I was a Minor League coach in Kissimmee, Florida, which was about a half-hour, forty-five minutes from Winter Park. I had a great job. For fourteen years, I drove to the ballpark and when we were at home, I came home every night and slept in my own bed. Then the last four years, I stayed in Florida until June—until after the draft—and then I went up to the Appalachian League. Three years in Martinsville, Virginia, and one year in Greeneville, Tennessee. I spent eighteen years as a pitching coach for Houston. When I got [to age] sixty-two, I said thanks to baseball. I had a couple of pensions coming in and I decided I'd lead a retired life and watch my grandkids grow up.[19]

In 1984 Jack Billingham was inducted into the Reds Hall of Fame at the 1984 Ballplayers of Yesterday dinner.

Chapter 41. **Clay Kirby**

Charles F. Faber

AGE	W	L	PCT.	ERA	G	GS	GF	CG	SHO	SV	IP	H	BB	SO	HBP	WP
27	10	6	.625	4.72	26	19	3	1	0	0	110.2	113	54	48	5	12

In his Major League career Clay Kirby won seventy-five games, yet he is best remembered for one of his losses. On July 21, 1970, Kirby, on the mound for the San Diego Padres, pitched eight innings of no-hit ball against the New York Mets before Manager Preston Gomez removed him for a pinch hitter. Kirby had given up one run in the first inning on a walk, two stolen bases, and an infield out. The Padres were trailing 1–0 with two out and nobody on in the eighth inning, when Kirby was due to bat. Gomez sent Clarence Gaston to the plate. Gaston struck out. The Mets scored two runs on three hits and a walk against a relief pitcher in the ninth inning and won the game, 3–0. Many Padres fans, irate that Gomez had deprived the youngster a chance of a no-hitter by removing him from the game, booed long and loud. The manager's decision became a matter of intense controversy. Was Kirby treated unfairly by being removed from a potential no-hitter? Was Gomez fulfilling the manager's responsibility by making the move that he thought gave his team its best shot at a victory?

A ten-game winner for the 1975 Reds, Clay Kirby did not pitch in the postseason.

Clayton Laws Kirby Jr. was born in Washington DC on June 25, 1948, the only son of Gloria Deener and Clayton L. Kirby. Clay and his sister, Carolyn, both grew up in suburban Arlington, Virginia. Clay started playing Little League baseball at the age of seven and went on to play baseball, basketball, and football at Washington and Lee High School. In one high school contest he pitched a perfect game while striking out nineteen batters. Kirby was selected by the St. Louis Cardinals in the third round of the June 1966 amateur draft. He was signed to a contract by St. Louis scout Charles "Tim" Thomp-

son and assigned to the Sarasota (Florida) Cardinals of the rookie Gulf Coast League and soon earned a promotion to St. Petersburg of the Florida State League, where he won his three starts, giving up only nine hits in twenty innings. He spent 1967 with Modesto of the California League. During his first two off-seasons he attended Old Dominion University in Norfolk, Virginia, and Benjamin Franklin University in Washington DC, respectively. He started the 1968 season with the Arkansas Travelers of the Double-A Texas League and then advanced to Tulsa in the Triple-A Pacific Coast League, winning twelve games as a starting pitcher for the two teams. At the end of the 1968 season the twenty-year-old right-hander was chosen by the new San Diego Padres in the expansion draft. Kirby was the sixth player taken by the Padres.

Kirby made the Padres squad in spring training and the 6-foot-3, 175-pound right-hander made his Major League debut on April 11, 1969, against the San Francisco Giants. Giving up four runs in four innings, he was the losing pitcher. His teammates dubbed the fuzzy-cheeked youngster "The Kid." In his rookie season Kirby led the National League in losses with twenty, but the Padres were not discouraged. Pitching coach Roger Craig said, "The Kid has a lot of Drysdale's competitive drive. When he was 20 in his rookie year, he wasn't afraid. And when he lost 20, it didn't get him down. I told him he had to be a pretty good pitcher to lose 20 games, because it means he was getting the ball every four days."[1] Gomez said he thought Kirby and fellow rookie Al Santorini were both potential twenty-game winners. "They both have great arms and all they need to become complete pitchers in the major leagues is experience," the skipper said.[2] Kirby shared his manager's confidence in his ability. One of his teammates, pitcher Steve Arlin, said of him, "Clay was cocky, brash, arrogant, and still very popular. He was a young kid who did not back down from anything or anybody. He could beat the world and he knew it."[3] But with the woeful Padres behind him he could not beat the majority of Major League clubs he faced. In five years with San Diego he had only one winning season and won fifty-two games while losing eighty-one for a less-than-stellar .391 winning percentage.

However, Kirby did have some outstanding games. In fact, he almost pitched three no-hitters for the Padres. The season after the game in which Gomez lifted him for a pinch hitter, Kirby pitched no-hit ball at Houston for 7⅓ innings on September 13, 1971, before Johnny Edwards broke it up with a double. Kirby lost the game 3–2, as the Pa-

dres committed two infield errors in the ninth inning, allowing the winning run to score. In his next start, at San Francisco on September 18, Kirby set down the first twenty-one Giants to face him and was in pursuit of a perfect game until Willie McCovey started the bottom of the eighth inning with a home run. It was the only hit Kirby gave up in the game as the Padres won, 2–1.[1]

Kirby caught what at first appeared to be a good break when he was traded to the Cincinnati Reds after the 1973 season for outfielder Bobby Tolan and pitcher Dave Tomlin. After five years of laboring for a team that finished in last place every season, he was now with a contender. The trade caught the pitcher by surprise, coming the day after he and his wife, the former Susan Gantt, had purchased a house in San Diego County. The Kirbys had married quite young and already had a six-year-old daughter, Theresa, and a three-year-old son, Clayton. Cincinnati manager Sparky Anderson said he was pleased to acquire Kirby. "This kid is a real competitor," said Anderson, who had managed Kirby at St. Petersburg and Modesto in the Cardinals' farm system. "I'm counting on him being a regular starter for us. He wants the ball all the time. He wants to get out there and beat you. He believes he can win and never seems to lose that feeling."[4]

Some of the Reds knew that Kirby got in hot water with the Padres by questioning Manager Don Zimmer when he approached the mound to remove the pitcher one day in 1973. "What do you want?" Kirby asked. "I don't want much," replied Zimmer, "I just want the ball." The pitcher mumbled something, and the irate manager angrily said, "If you don't like the way I'm running the club, then go home."[5] Anderson, like Zimmer, wanted no questions from faltering pitchers. "Once the ole boy bounces out of the dugout, don't get excited because you're gone," pitching coach Larry Shepard told Kirby. "There are no ifs, ands, or buts about it."[6] Anderson reinforced his coach's advice. "When I go to the mound," said Sparky, "nothing is said unless I say it or ask for it.

That's my role on this club, and the pitchers who don't know it will soon learn it."[7]

When he joined the Reds, Kirby asked for uniform number 31. "That's the opposite of 13. Maybe it will change my luck," he said.[8] In his third start for the Reds, in Cincinnati on April 16, Kirby retired sixteen of the first seventeen Los Angeles Dodgers batters he faced and was working on a one-hit shutout when pitcher Andy Messersmith hit a home run in the sixth. Kirby left the game with a stiff back after seven innings, and the Reds lost the game in extra innings. He fared better in a game against Houston on May 12, when he carried a one-hitter into the ninth and survived a home run to win a two-hitter. But despite having the powerful Big Red Machine behind him, Kirby never became the twenty-game winner he aspired to be. In 1974 he won twelve games. In 1975 his victory total fell to ten. In 1974 he ranked fourth on the Reds in wins behind Don Gullett, Jack Billingham, and Fred Norman. The return of Gary Nolan, who had missed almost two full seasons with shoulder trouble, and the arrival of Pat Darcy in 1975 further reduced Kirby's opportunities, and he became a spot starter and an occasional reliever. In his two seasons with the Reds Kirby won twenty-two games against fifteen losses for a respectable .595 winning percentage. To his dismay, he did not get into a single postseason game after Cincinnati won the 1975 National League pennant. Newspapers reported that if the World Series went beyond five games, the "baby-faced" hurler would get a start against the Boston Red Sox. The Series went the full seven games, but Kirby never got his shot. After the season was over, a Cincinnati newspaper conducted a poll of fans to see which Reds players they would most like to see traded away. Kirby collected the most votes.

Not that the poll had anything to do with it, but in December the Reds traded Kirby to the Montreal Expos for infielder Bob Bailey. In January 1976 Kirby was stricken with a long bout of pneumonia

before he joined the Expos in Florida for spring training. He was still weak and had a sore shoulder when the season opened. He got off to a miserable start and never recovered. He won only one game for the Expos, lost eight, and posted a 5.72 earned run average, while walking sixty-three batters in 78⅔ innings. After all the Major League clubs passed on Kirby in the off-season, Montreal released him on December 2, 1976. In January 1977 the Padres decided to give their former pitcher another chance. They invited him to their spring training camp in Yuma, Arizona. Kirby's string of bad luck continued when he incurred a knee injury in the final week of spring training. His comeback try was delayed for almost two months. The Padres sent him to their Pacific Coast League farm club in Hawaii. He won his first game for the Islanders on June 18 but never won another. His record for the season was one win, seven losses, and an earned run average of 7.95.

After San Diego gave up on Kirby, he tried out with the Minnesota Twins during spring training in 1978. He lasted only two weeks before he was released. Kirby's career in organized baseball was over before his thirtieth birthday. His family continued to live in San Diego County until 1983, when they returned to Virginia. Kirby became a self-employed financial securities broker. For several years he was tournament chairman for the Major League Baseball Players alumni in golfing events to benefit the American Lung Association.

Although Kirby once listed his hobby as building miniature racing cars, his main recreational activities were hunting and fishing. "I started to fish and hunt when I was 7," he said. "I was 12 when I was allowed to carry my first gun, and I got my first deer the same year."[9] Kirby acquired his love of hunting and fishing from his father, who in partnership with two friends had bought three hundred acres in the Shenandoah Mountains just so they could hunt and fish on the land. The morning after Kirby lost his chance for a no-hitter when Preston Go-

CHARLES F. FABER

mez removed him from the game, Kirby and his father went fishing. Afterward someone asked if they talked about the game. "We talked only about fishing," Kirby replied.[10]

On July 19, 1991, Kirby underwent a coronary atherectomy to open a blockage in an artery just above his heart. After the procedure he was advised that he had suffered a silent heart attack. The Kirbys had been living with his mother in Arlington. His sister said they thought Kirby was recuperating nicely, but she later learned from friends that he had been complaining about chest discomfort and numbness in his arm. He died of a heart attack on October 11, 1991, at the age of forty-three. His wife found him about eleven o'clock in the morning in his easy chair. It appeared that he had fallen asleep while reading and then suffered the fatal attack. He was survived by his wife, Susan; his mother, Gloria; his sister, Carolyn Twyman; his son, Clayton; his daughter, Theresa Schoengold; and two grandchildren, Derek and Brandon Schoengold. He was buried in National Memorial Park in Falls Church, Virginia.

Chapter 42. **Don Werner**

Malcolm Allen

AGE	G	AB	R	H	2B	3B	HR	TB	RBI	BB	SO	BAV	OBP	SLG	SB	GDP	HBP
22	7	8	0	1	0	0	0	1	0	0	0	.125	.222	.125	0	0	1

Don Werner played eighteen seasons of professional baseball and appeared in 118 Major League games, backing up one Hall of Famer and catching the only no-hitter pitched by another. Though he batted just .176 during limited opportunities in the Major Leagues, Werner grasped enough of the finer points of the art of catching to stay employed in the game for more than two decades when his playing days ended, passing on what he'd learned to younger players.

Donald Paul Werner was born on March 8, 1953, in Appleton, Wisconsin. His father played softball, and Werner tagged along as a youngster, serving as the team's batboy and generally soaking up the game. Even when his dad was dead tired, Werner recalled, he would summon the energy to throw or hit the ball to his young son. Werner wasn't certain that his mother particularly cared for baseball, but she always supported his interest in the game and attended all his games when he started playing himself.

Werner grew up rooting for the Chicago Cubs, especially their classy All-Star shortstop Ernie Banks. As Werner developed into a full-time catcher on the diamond, he looked up to Cubs backstop Randy Hundley, Tim McCarver of the Cardinals, and later, Reds standout Johnny Bench. Scouts took note of Werner's strong throwing arm when they saw him playing American Legion ball as a teen, and he was an All-State and All-City selection for baseball (as well as All-City for basketball) by 1971, when he graduated from Appleton East High School. He wanted to get drafted and play professional baseball, and his dream came true when Bench's Cincinnati Reds selected him in the fifth round of the

Don Werner had the misfortune of breaking into the Majors as a catcher with the Reds during the prime of Johnny Bench but managed to stay in the game for another four decades.

amateur draft that June. Through 2012, Werner remained the only big leaguer to come out of his high school.

Werner signed quickly and debuted with the Bradenton (Florida) Reds of the Gulf Coast Rookie League that summer, batting .333 in ten games. He slipped to .172 in thirty-six contests with the Single-A Tampa Tarpons after a promotion, but gained valuable experience playing with more than a half-dozen future big leaguers under Manager Russ Nixon, who himself had been a big league catcher for more than a decade. Back with Tampa in 1972, Werner earned Florida State League All-Star honors after batting .257 with a .352 on-base percentage and leading the circuit's catchers in fielding percentage. He also connected on his first professional home run.

Moving up to Double-A in 1973 proved challenging for the twenty-year-old, and Werner hit just .201 for the Trois-Rivieres (Quebec) Aigles of the Eastern League. The following year the Reds returned him to Tampa, where, despite a .232 average, he walked more than he struck out and established professional bests up to that point in doubles, runs scored, and RBIS. Werner also earned his first defensive mention in the *Sporting News* for making a barehanded catch of a foul pop-up in the season opener after tossing away his mask and glove while in pursuit.

Werner was invited to Major League spring training with the Reds in 1975 before heading to the Triple-A Indianapolis Indians to platoon with Minor League veteran Sonny Ruberto. Playing for another former catcher, Vern Rapp, Werner thrived offensively to the tune of a .281 batting average, .397 on-base percentage, and .491 slugging average, showing the power within his 6-foot-1, 185-pound frame with nine homers in 228 at bats. The Reds brought him to the big leagues in September, and he was hit by a pitch from the San Diego Padres' Dave Freisleben as a pinch hitter in his debut. Werner got his first start in the second game of a doubleheader on September 14 at Candlestick Park and delivered his first Major League hit, a single off Giants right-hander Greg Minton. Though Werner got just eight at bats in seven games that month, the Reds voted him a $500 partial World Series share. Werner ended the year on Cincinnati's forty-man roster.

Most of Werner's playing time in 1976 came in Richmond, Virginia, with the Atlanta Braves' Triple-A affiliate. When Joe Nolan, a catcher in the Braves chain, went down with a knee injury, the Reds loaned Werner to Richmond from the first week of May until mid-July. He logged a .405 on-base per-

centage but mostly struggled after returning to Indianapolis and hit a light .240 overall. Nevertheless, the Reds made Werner their only immediate call-up when rosters expanded in September. He batted only four times in three games during the month but did record his first big league RBI with a double off Doug Rau at Dodger Stadium. The Reds won the World Series again and this time voted Werner a larger share, $750. "The Reds have been giving Don Werner, a young catcher, a big buildup," wrote Earl Lawson in the *Sporting News*. "One can't help but gather that, in doing so, they're paving the way for [catcher Bill] Plummer's departure."

Plummer was still backing up Johnny Bench in Cincinnati in 1977, however, so Werner returned to Indianapolis. He started slowly, tore ligaments in his left thumb on a play at the plate in early May, had surgery, and missed a couple of months of action. Foreshadowing his future coaching career, he was chosen to comanage the club (with first baseman Dave Revering) when skipper Roy Majtyka missed time with an intestinal disorder. On the field Werner homered in his first game back in the lineup and launched five homers in ninety-four at bats before a third straight September call-up by the Reds. On September 18 in San Francisco, he threw out two Giants trying to steal and hit his first Major League homer, off southpaw Bob Knepper to break a scoreless tie in the seventh. (Cincinnati ended up losing, 3–2.) Two days later Werner went deep again in San Diego to cap the scoring in Tom Seaver's two-hit, 4–0 shutout of the Padres. After catching every pitch, Werner asked "Tom Terrific" to autograph his game ball. The home run was his last in the Major Leagues.

Werner finally made the Reds' Opening Day roster in 1978, taking over as the primary backup for Bench. By late May the future Hall of Famer was battling a stiff back, and Werner spent a few weeks as the only healthy catcher on the team, starting twenty-five consecutive games at one point. (The Reds went 15-10.) On June 16 at Riverfront Stadium, Werner caught the only no-hitter ever pitched in the illustrious career of the 311-game-winner Seaver, in a 4–0 blanking of the Cardinals. "Here you are, only a half-year in the majors, and you catch a no-hitter," teased Seaver with a smile. "I'll be damned."

Though Werner observed, "I've found that when you're the backup catcher, it's more important to do your job defensively than offensively," the .152 batting average with just three extra-base hits he produced in forty-eight games through July 2 was not enough to keep him in the big leagues. Seventeen days after catching Seaver's no-no, Werner was sent back to Indianapolis. Later he called it a "crushing blow." Reds hitting instructor Ted Kluszewski, a four-time All-Star who had smacked 279 career home runs, scolded Werner for changing stances too often and summed up his struggles thusly: "Werner's biggest problem as a hitter is that he's too eager and swings at pitches off his front foot, which makes him easy to fool and robs him of power."

Werner wore contact lenses and lifted weights but acknowledged that he'd been a bad hitter. What stung him back in Triple-A was the knowledge that a minor neck injury he'd suffered in Houston early in 1978 impaired his throwing and got him "tagged as a catcher who couldn't throw," as he put it, adding, "I felt it was a bad rap because I was originally signed because of my strong arm." He contributed as Indianapolis reached the American Association championship series, and helped them to their only series win with a three-run homer, but got into only a couple of games after another September call-up to the Reds. In 1979 the twenty-six-year-old Werner lost a spring training battle to thirty-three-year-old veteran Vic Correll for the right to back up Bench, and he never got into a Reds game that season. After the season Cincinnati sent Werner outright to Triple-A. Any other team could have drafted him, but none did. "I thought that of all available catchers, I was the best," Werner said. "I felt sure one club would feel it was a good gamble for $25,000."

Werner went to spring training in 1980 just hoping to impress another club enough that it would make a deal for him. Then Correll went down with an injured Achilles tendon and Werner was on Cincinnati's Opening Day roster for the second time in three years. "I'll have an opportunity, and if I can't take advantage of it, I'll have only myself to blame," he responded.

Werner overcame minor knee surgery late in the spring to make nineteen starts backing up Bench early in the year for the Reds, but he was hitting a punchless .172 and opponents stole twenty-nine bases in thirty-three tries against him. When Cincinnati signed free agent Joe Nolan—the player Werner had filled in for in Richmond four years before—Werner was sent back to Triple-A to back up highly rated 1978 second-round pick Dave Van Gorder. Though he hit a solid .274 in sixty-five games, Werner's eight years with the Reds came to an end when he was traded to the Texas Rangers after the season.

After six straight seasons spent at least partially in Indianapolis, Werner played for three different Rangers Triple-A affiliates (Wichita, Denver, and Oklahoma City) from 1981 through 1983. The Rangers had perennial Gold Glove winner Jim Sundberg catching for them, so opportunities were few, and Werner's only big league action in 1981 was a couple of starts as designated hitter late in the year. Early in the following year Werner suffered a chipped bone in his left index finger on an opponent's swing, but he found himself back in the big leagues by late May, batting .203 in twenty-two games. Seven years to the day after his Major League debut, he hit safely for the final time as a big leaguer with an RBI single off the White Sox's Britt Burns at Comiskey Park on September 2. Seventeen days later he played his final Major League game, at Seattle's Kingdome, wrapping up his career with a .176 average and two homers in 118 games and 279 at bats.

The Rangers released Werner after the 1983 season, and he signed with the Kansas City Royals before the 1984 campaign but was traded to the Chicago Cubs three days before Opening Day. The Cubs had their catcher position covered with Jody Davis and Steve Lake, so Werner went to Iowa of the American Association and played mostly in the outfield. Surprisingly, he blasted eleven home runs in his first forty-six at bats en route to a career-high twenty-five homers to go with seventy-seven RBIS and a .283 batting average. Thirteen years into his professional career, he had learned to go deep on breaking pitches in addition to fastballs, keeping the top half of his body behind his front leg. Werner was thirty-one years old, though, and a return call to the big leagues never came.

He bounced around the Minors in 1985 without much success before returning to Oklahoma City from 1986 through 1988, the last two seasons as a player-coach. Werner wrapped up his nineteen-season Minor League career with a .252 batting average, .338 on-base percentage, and a .378 slugging average, with eighty-eight home runs. After a rumored spot on Bobby Valentine's Major League coaching staff with the Rangers did not pan out, Werner commenced his post-playing career managing the Single-A short-season New York–Penn League Jamestown Expos to a first-place finish in the Stedler Division in 1989, before they slipped to second the following year.

Werner moved on to the Pittsburgh Pirates organization in the 1990s, managing Minor League affiliates and serving as a roving hitting instructor at various times. He secured his reputation as a teacher starting in 1996 with a successful five-year run managing the San Diego Padres' Pioneer League rookie club in Idaho Falls. The club finished first in three straight seasons (1998–2000), and in 1999 Werner earned the franchise's Jack Krol Award, presented to the organization's top player development person.

Werner joined the Baltimore Orioles organization in 2003 After a few years coaching and managing in the Minors, he was named the organi-

zation's roving catching instructor following the 2006 season. Perhaps it's no coincidence that Orioles catcher Matt Wieters won consecutive Gold Glove Awards in his first two full seasons. "Wieters makes a catching instructor look really smart," Werner quipped.

Looking back on more than four decades in professional baseball, Werner said he considered himself fortunate to have come of baseball age in a "great organization" with "great instruction," noting that many of the managers he played for in the Reds chain were catchers like himself. He said the people he worked with in the game were his greatest asset in coaching young players, citing among them "Sparky [Anderson], Zim [Don Zimmer], Jim Leyland, Buck Rodgers, Felipe Alou, and Buck [Showalter]."

In 2013 Werner lived with his wife, Cynthia, in Arlington, Texas. They have a son together, Ryan, and Werner is the stepfather of Richard and Troy.

Chapter 43. **Will McEnaney**

Mark Miller

AGE	W	L	PCT.	ERA	G	GS	GF	CG	SHO	SV	IP	H	BB	SO	HBP	WP
23	5	2	.714	2.47	70	0	38	0	0	15	91	92	23	48	2	1

In his youth, Will McEnaney was a mischief maker. In his adulthood, mischief became roistering, somewhat to the detriment of McEnaney's career as a National League pitcher. Still, he posted a few achievements, including sterling performances as a reliever for the Reds in the 1975 and 1976 World Series.

William Henry McEnaney was born, with his twin brother Michael, on February 14, 1952, in Springfield, Ohio, one of five children (four boys and one girl) born to Bill and Eleanor McEnaney. Bill worked at International Harvester and Eleanor was a hospital nursing supervisor.

The mirror twins were constant companions. They were identical in every way except that Will was left-handed and Mike right-handed. Their Springfield North High baseball coach, Don Henderson, said he could tell them apart by their mannerisms. Mike was more serious, Will was a little "loosey-goosey."[1]

Through youth leagues Will was usually on the mound, and although Mike did pitch, he was usually behind the plate. They played in the Babe Ruth League, were selected to its All-Star teams, and won the fifteen-year-old state championship.

The mischievous twins often exchanged identities. In school they frequently attended each other's classes. One time Mike had to answer questions in Spanish (Will didn't take Spanish) to prove his identity. In a baseball game Will was scheduled to pitch four innings and Mike three, so they persuaded Coach Henderson to allow them to swap jerseys. The opposition thought they were facing an ambidextrous pitcher. They were known to exchange identities when with female companions,

Will McEnaney was on the mound when the Reds won both the 1975 and 1976 World Series.

even changing clothes in a restroom during a double date.

Because of his behavior, Will's high school baseball career was limited to his sophomore season, when he finished 8-2 with a 0.91 ERA and 122 strikeouts in 69⅓ innings. Then, as a junior, he was caught drinking at a drive-in movie and the next year was involved in an altercation at a school basketball game that led to the discovery that he had been drinking. He was suspended athletically both years. Henderson recalled, "Will was a joy to coach. He loved baseball, worked hard and played hard. But off the field he was as ornery as cat dirt."[2]

During his high school years McEnaney played for a summer traveling team. Scouts took notice of McEnaney's abilities. A call to Reds scout Cliff Alexander from umpire and scouting bird dog Warren Barnett brought Alexander to town for a closer look. That night McEnaney pitched five no-hit innings against an adult team, striking out thirteen. Suitably impressed, the Reds selected him in the eighth round of the June 1970 amateur draft, held the same day as his high school graduation. "I was out all night with my buddies. The next morning I came home and the morning paper had already come and my mom is saying, 'You got drafted.' Hell, I thought she meant the Army."[3]

Though his traveling-team coach tried to convince him that he might do better financially in the January secondary phase draft, McEnaney signed with the Reds for a $3,500 bonus. "Growing up I would follow guys like Frank Robinson, Vada Pinson, Jim O'Toole, Jim Maloney," McEnaney recalled. "I thought there would be nothing greater than to play for them one day."[4]

Harvey Haddix, the Reds' pitching coach in 1969, was a local resident. Bill McEnaney took his son to Haddix's farm for some advice. Harvey's advice: "Will, don't get married until after you finish playing ball. It will distract you."[5] A week later McEnaney left for the Reds' rookie camp.

"I almost quit in Florida," McEnaney remembered. "Ron Plaza, an instructor, drill-sergeant kind of guy, and Russ Nixon ran the camp. All we did was run. Florida in June. I wasn't used to it, the discipline, constantly being schooled on baseball situations. We would drill, then practice, practice, practice. We didn't play any games. Just practice and run. I had no idea that it would be like that. I was miserable and homesick, but my dad said, 'Stick it out.'" Reds scout George Zuraw told him, "You're just flakey enough to make it to the major leagues."[6] At the end of the camp, McEnaney was sent to the Sioux Falls (South Dakota) Packers, but he was ineffective, leading the Northern League in losses, hits, and earned runs. His record was 3-10 with a 5.17 ERA in eighty-seven innings.

That fall in the Instructional League, McEnaney began to flourish, posting a 1-0 record and 0.82 ERA in twenty-two innings. He followed with a breakthrough 1971 season with the Tampa Tarpons of the Florida State League, finishing 14-5 with a 2.44 ERA in 181 innings. "I've learned two things this year," he told a sportswriter back home. "To have patience with my teammates and to throw a strike when I need it."[7] Another fine season followed with the Double-A Trois-Rivieres (Quebec) Aigles, in which he recorded an 11-6 record and 2.80 ERA in 138 innings and made the Eastern League All-Star team.

He was assigned to the Triple-A Indianapolis Indians in 1973. Manager Vern Rapp taught him to throw a slider. He also learned to control his temper. Once a poor performance meant a quick shower. In the locker room he destroyed benches and lockers. Rapp, also known for having a temper, told McEnaney, "There are other pitchers who would like the opportunity to pitch in the American Association." "I got the message," McEnaney recalled. "I decided to curb my temper for fear of hurting my wallet and physical well-being."[8]

But he continued to frustrate Rapp with other clowning, like walking an invisible dog around the stadium. After a tough loss, the manager yelled, "McEnaney, get that damn dog out of here." He was the life of every party. Rapp once caught him with a woman in the hotel past curfew and threatened to fine him. He also gave McEnaney some advice: "Get married. . . . Settle down," contradicting Haddix's advice.[9]

McEnaney's 1973 statistics were disappointing (9-9 with a 3.92 ERA), though he earned a victory in the league All-Star game. The following spring the Reds determined that he would be better suited as a reliever. His fastball and slider were ready, but his curveball was below average. Relieving suited him, as he collected two wins and five saves in twenty-nine appearances for Indianapolis in 1974. McEnaney was called up by the Reds on July 2. "Vern Rapp had a bigger smile on his face when he told me than I did," he said.[10]

The rookie was nervous his first time in the Reds' clubhouse, having heard stories about rookie hazing. But a teammate reassured him. Remembered McEnaney, "My shoes were really horrible, all scuffed up, and the cleats were all worn down." Scolded Peter Rose, "Hey, you can't wear those. Can you fit into a 9½?" Inside Rose's locker were thirty pairs of shoes. "Pick out a couple of pair," Rose said. "Good luck, have fun up here."[11]

"A day after I got to Cincinnati they put me in against the Dodgers," McEnaney recalled. "I was never more nervous in my life. . . . I was scared to walk out on the field. The crowd noise was awesome and when I got on the mound and looked around, it was scary. It so happens the first batter I faced was the Dodger pitcher, Tommy John. My first pitch I threw between his legs."[12] McEnaney retired the first three hitters he faced on infield pop-ups and held the Dodgers scoreless on one infield single in two innings pitched. His first save came on July 7 against the Cardinals and he got his first win ten days later in a twelve-inning victory in St. Louis.

Although McEnaney was disappointed with the amount of work he received (twenty-seven innings), pitching coach Larry Shepard was encouraged. "He does a creditable job for us," said Shepard. "But he is not comfortable on the mound yet. Will must learn to change speeds on all his pitches."[13]

McEnaney continued to live the night life to its fullest. Fellow Reds pitcher Pat Darcy remembered, "Sparky called Will McEnaney and me in his office at . . . spring training. We were roommates. He told us to behave . . . reminded us about curfew. Merv Rettenmund would call our room and imitate Sparky. . . . One night we went out, got some beer and some pizza and went back to the room and the phone rang and we thought it was Retten-

mund. McEnaney picked it up but it was Sparky. McEnaney said some things. . . . All I could hear was Sparky yelling!"[14]

McEnaney got off to an excellent start in 1975. The other left-handed relief pitcher on the club, Tom Hall, was traded in April. By May 6 McEnaney was the only Reds reliever with a save.

"I can't say enough about McEnaney," said Anderson. "He has really done a job for us . . . has tremendous courage. He is an unusual young man."[15] McEnaney ended the season with ninety-one innings of relief, five wins, fifteen saves, and a 2.47 ERA.

On October 9, two days before the World Series, he and his wife, Lynne, became parents for the first time with the birth of their daughter, Faith. He pitched in five World Series games against the Boston Red Sox. The most memorable moments were in the final two games. In the ninth inning of Game Six, with the game tied, runners on second and third, and no outs, McEnaney came in and intentionally walked Carlton Fisk to load the bases, then got Fred Lynn to fly out into a double play and retired Rico Petrocelli on a ground ball. The next evening he was called upon to pitch the final inning of the Reds' 4–3 victory in Game Seven, retiring the Red Sox one-two-three. McEnaney jumped into catcher Johnny Bench's arms, creating a memorable photo that appeared on the cover of *Sports Illustrated*.

That winter McEnaney was in demand on the banquet circuit, and he made so many speeches that his teammates nicknamed him Face. He had another contract dispute before the 1976 season. "Had I not been so selfish, I would still be in the majors today," McEnaney said in 1985. "I wanted a $6,000 raise, and they wanted to give me $1,000."[16]

The Reds had another great year but the same couldn't be said for their erstwhile ace reliever. As he struggled, his role diminished. "Last year I had to learn to adjust to success. This year I have had to learn to handle defeat," McEnaney said.[17] His 4.85 ERA was the worst on the staff, but he turned it around against the Yankees in the World Series with

MARK MILLER

saves in Games Three and Four of the Reds' sweep, allowing no runs in 4⅔ innings. With the Game Four save, he became the first National League pitcher to finish consecutive World Series on the mound.

In December the Reds traded McEnaney and first baseman Tony Pérez to the Montreal Expos for pitchers Woodie Fryman and Dale Murray. Devastated by the deal, the death of his mother, and a painful divorce, McEnaney was soon drinking frequently and experimenting with drugs. "I chose to do it," he said. "I was not a heavy user, but every time you do drugs you abuse yourself."[18]

McEnaney's pitching improved a bit in 1977, as he posted a 3.95 ERA in sixty-nine games, but not enough to impress Expos manager Dick Williams, who commented, "We did not get anything from our bullpen, especially the left side."[19] Near the end of spring training of 1978, Montreal sent him to the Pittsburgh Pirates for pitcher Timothy Jones. In June he had pitched just 8⅔ innings and had a 10.38 ERA, prompting his demotion to Triple-A Columbus. Legend has it that his brother Mike even dressed for a game and sat in the Clippers' bullpen, not endearing Will to the Pirates further. At the end of the season, after putting up a 6.24 ERA, McEnaney was released.

In December 1978, while driving drunk, McEnaney crashed his car into a house and almost died. Realizing that his life was spinning out of control, he moved to Fort Lauderdale, Florida, to be with his sister, Kathy. There he met the woman who was to become his second wife, Cindy, who introduced him to a psychologist. With Cindy's support, he said, he became clean and sober. "She constantly told me, 'You're better than this. You're smarter than this,'" he said.[20] The therapist helped him regain the aggressiveness he needed to be a successful athlete. He signed with the St. Louis Cardinals, and after spring training in 1979 he was sent to their Triple-A team in Springfield, Illinois. He was recalled by the Cardinals a month into the season and pitched in forty-five games out of the bullpen

with a 2.95 ERA. But he was released at the end of spring training in 1980, ending his big league career. He hooked on with Nashville of the Southern League and posted a 1.44 ERA in twenty-two games. McEnaney went to spring training in 1981 with the Detroit Tigers but did not make the club. That season he pitched with Tabasco of the Mexican League, then spent 1982 with Tulsa and Denver in the Texas Rangers system.

"Finally Cindy and I decided to chuck it all and get on with our lives," McEnaney recalled. "I didn't want to hang on and become an embarrassment to myself or my family. . . . It was time to look at the facts. I chased dreams that no longer brought in money to support them. I sold cars for a while but that wasn't me. Then I got into broadcasting"[21]

McEnaney attended broadcasting school and got a job covering covered the University of Miami Hurricanes for WGBS, a Miami radio station, in 1984. He also became a successful painting contractor.

The allure of playing baseball hit McEnaney twice more. When the Miami Marlins of the Florida State League began playing without a Major League affiliation in 1985, he and thirteen other former big leaguers gave baseball another try. He pitched in thirty-nine games. Four years later, in 1989, he signed to pitch for his old Montreal manager, Dick Williams, with the West Palm Beach Tropics in the Senior Professional Baseball Association but spent the entire season on the disabled list.

Later McEnaney owned a bathtub refurbishing business until the economy caused the building industry to decline. Still living in the Palm Beach area with Cindy as of 2012, he worked for Dick's Sporting Goods and signed on as the scoreboard operator for the Jupiter Hammerheads of the Florida State League. He has three children, Faith, Weston, and Alex.

Chapter 44. September 1975 Timeline

Mark Miller and Mark Armour

All headlines below are from the next day's edition of the *Springfield (OH) News*.

September 1—JONES LIKES SCREWBALL, AFTER BEATING REDS, 2–1—The Reds had their chances, with nine hits, but San Diego's Randy Jones spread them out to defeat the Reds, 2–1, notching his eighteenth victory. Pedro Borbon allowed one run over the final five innings but earned the loss to drop to 8-5.

September 2—SPARKY INSISTS GULLETT O.K.—The Reds used a seven-run fifth inning to defeat the Padres 10–4. Don Gullett allowed four runs in seven innings to bring his record to 12-3, despite having missed two months of action. Tony Pérez collected career RBI number 1,010 to pass Frank Robinson as the Reds' all-time leader.

September 3—REDS DRIVING DODGERS BATTY, MAGIC NUMBER CUT TO FIVE—The Reds scorched the Dodgers for ten runs in the fourth inning to defeat the visitors 13–2. The Reds had just nine hits but took advantage of the eleven walks issued by Dodger pitchers. Gary Nolan coasted to his thirteenth victory.

September 4—DODGERS FIND PITCHER—Dodger hurler Doug Rau allowed just four hits, one of which was George Foster's twenty-second home run, and defeated the Reds 3–2. All the Dodgers' run scoring was accounted for by the game's first three batters—a single by Davey Lopes, followed by an errant pickoff throw from Clay Kirby allowing Lopes to go to third, a run-scoring single by Lee Lacy, and a two-run home run by Willie Crawford. Kirby settled down after that, but the Reds could not overcome the early deficit.

September 5—REDS SET RECORD, 58TH HOME WIN—César Gerónimo's ninth-inning single drove in the winning run in a 4–3 Reds victory over the Giants, the club's best-ever and fifty-eighth home victory. A seventh-inning two-run home run by Pete Rose gave the Reds a 3–0 lead, but the Giants finally broke through in the eighth with three runs off Fred Norman to tie the score. Gerónimo's two-out single, his third hit of the game, scored pinch runner Ed Armbrister and sent the crowd home happy.

September 6—REDS MAGIC NUMBER REDUCED TO 3—César Gerónimo drilled three hits for the second straight game, and the Reds defeated the Giants, 3–2. Jack Billingham (6⅔ innings) won his fifteenth and Will McEnaney (2⅓ innings) recorded his fourteenth save.

September 7—REDS CELEBRATE EARLIEST CLINCHING—The Reds swept the three-game series as they defeated the Giants 8–4, extending their divisional lead to 20½ games and clinching first place in the NL West, the earliest clinching in NL history. George Foster led the way with four hits and four RBIs, while Don Gullett won his thirteenth game with less than his best stuff—nine hits, four walks, and four runs allowed.

September 8—REDS RALLY, BEAT PADRES—Johnny Bench's two-run eighth-inning homer gave the Reds a come-from-behind 3–2 victory over the Padres on their last visit to the West Coast of the season. Gary Nolan pitched six solid innings, while Clay Carroll earned the victory in relief.

September 9—PLAYOFFS WORRY SPARKY—The Padres defeated the Reds 11–2, clobbering Clay Kirby and Tom Carroll. Journeyman Rich Folkers (6-9) cruised, allowing a Johnny Bench two-run home run only after leading 11–0. The Reds' win-loss record in road games is just 36-32, a cause for concern for Sparky Anderson, looking ahead to the NLCS.

September 10—REDS CAN'T CONVINCE LA—The Dodgers took a 9–8 advantage in the season series by defeating the Reds 3–2 at Dodger Stadium. Burt Hooton pitched a four-hitter for the Dodgers, who won on Leron Lee's pinch-hit run-scoring double in the bottom of the ninth off Rawly Eastwick.

September 11—REDS TO BE TOUGH IN '76, SAYS SPARKY—The Reds dropped their third straight game, and their second to the Dodgers, 5–2. Los Angeles broke out to a 5–0 lead through five innings, and Rick Rhoden held on for the complete-game victory. Pete Rose hit a late home run, but Jack Billingham was ineffective in dropping to 15-8. The Dodgers took the season series from the Reds, ten games to eight.

September 12—REDS WIN—Fred Norman won his tenth game as the visiting Reds defeated the Giants 6–3. Pete Rose had three hits, singling and scoring in the first and hitting a run-scoring single in the second. Doug Flynn, starting at short-stop, had two RBIS. Rawly Eastwick came on for his nineteenth save.

September 13—GIANTS END LOSSES WITH REDS, 9–2—San Francisco erupted for seven runs off Don Gullett in the fifth to break open a tight game and propel them to a 9–2 win. Dave Concepción had three hits, including a triple, but the rest of the team provided only four hits to the cause.

September 14—GIANTS AND REDS SPLIT—The Reds wrapped up a 4-5 road trip with a double-header split in San Francisco. In the seventh inning of the first game, Dave Rader and Steve Ontiveros homered on consecutive Gary Nolan pitches, boosting the Giants to a 4–2 victory. Dave Concepción had four hits, while the Reds' Joe Morgan had four stolen bases, including the front end of a triple steal in the sixth. Terry Crowley's three-run homer and two-run hits by Dan Driessen and Darrel Chaney brought the Reds back in the nightcap, 8–3, behind ten-game winner Pat Darcy.

September 16—BILLINGHAM IN DOGHOUSE—The Reds returned home for a two-game series with the Astros, losing 5–1. Jack Billingham continued his recent struggles, allowing ten hits and four runs in five innings. Larry Dierker threw a five-hitter for his fourteenth win.

September 17—SPARKY PRAISES NORMAN'S WORK—The Reds put up fourteen hits to back Fred Norman (11-4) to a 10–1 win against the Astros. Tony Pérez hit his nineteenth home run, while Dave Concepción had three more hits and Joe Morgan three more steals (giving him sixty-three) along with three RBIS.

September 18—HOMER SPARKS REDS, REDS FANS LINE UP FOR TICKETS—Bill Plummer's two-out run-scoring single in the tenth inning carried the Reds to a 4–3 win over the hometown Braves. In regulation, the Reds' runs had come courtesy of solo home runs by Dan Driessen, Tony Pérez, and George Foster.

September 19—REDS TOP BRAVES—A solo homer by Dave Concepción and a three-run double by Terry Crowley keyed a five-run Cincinnati fifth inning and lifted them over Atlanta, 7–6. Starting pitcher Pat Darcy picked up his eleventh win, aided by Will McEnaney's three-inning save, his fifteenth.

September 20—REDS EQUAL TEAM RECORD—The Reds recorded their 102nd victory of the season, a team record, with a 9–2 victory over the Braves. Pete Rose's ninth-inning single was his two hundredth hit of the season. Dan Driessen replaced Tony Pérez at first base in midgame and later hit a three-run home run, backing Gary Nolan's fourteenth win.

September 21—GULLETT DISPLAYS GREAT STUFF—Don Gullett pitched seven innings allowing two hits and Rawly Eastwick was perfect in relief as the Reds beat Phil Niekro and the Braves, 3–0. Dave May and Larvell Blanks provided the two singles for Atlanta, while the Reds got all the runs they needed on a Ken Griffey two-run home run in the first inning.

September 22—CEDENO AND JOHNSON ROCKETS LIFT ASTROS—Houston's César Cédeño hit a three-run home run off Jack Billingham in the bottom of the first, leading the Astros to a 5–1 win. Joe Niekro had a two-hit shutout heading into the ninth before being touched for a run. Niekro's win was the first for the Niekro brothers against the Reds this season, following eight losses.

September 23—REDS EDGE HOUSTON 5–3—Fred Norman allowed only four hits and the Reds defeated the Astros, 5–3. Rawly Eastwick picked up another save. The Reds' offense was spurred by Ken Griffey, who had three of the club's ten hits. The Astros scored their runs on home runs off Norman in the second and the third, by Cliff Johnson and Larry Milbourne.

September 24—KIRBY GETS 10TH IN HOUSTON—Clay Kirby notched his tenth win of the season, the sixth Reds starter to reach the milestone, as the Reds beat the Astros 6–4. Joe Morgan collected his sixteenth home run, and Rawly Eastwick gained his twenty-second save.

September 26—REDS PICKING UP SPEED, SET MARK FOR HOME WINS—The Reds defeated Braves ace Phil Niekro, 12–5, beating him for the sixth time in six starts this season and setting a Major League record with sixty-two home victories in a season. The Reds had thirteen hits, including three from Tony Pérez, to back Gary Nolan (15-9).

September 27—MORGAN, REDS SET, TIE MARKS IN WIN—In the Reds' 7–6 win, Joe Morgan's two-run homer was the fifteen hundredth hit of his career and allowed him to set a team record with ninety-four RBIS as a second baseman. Johnny Bench also homered, his twenty-eighth. With their 107th win, the Reds became the winningest NL team since the 1909 Pittsburgh Pirates.

September 28—REDS DENY PLAYOFF JINX—In their regular-season finale, the Reds defeated the Braves 7–6 on César Gerónimo's infield single in the bottom of the ninth. Pete Rose had two hits, giving him 210 for the season, while Dave Concepción added three. Joe Morgan stole his sixty-seventh base.

NL West Standings, FINAL, 1975

TEAM	W	L	GB
Cincinnati	108	54	—
Los Angeles	88	74	20.0
San Francisco	80	81	27.5
San Diego	71	91	37.0
Atlanta	67	94	40.5
Houston	64	97	43.5

Chapter 45. **Marty Brennaman**

Matt Bohn

On July 23, 2000, Marty Brennaman, radio voice of the Cincinnati Reds since 1974, was honored by the Baseball Hall of Fame with the Ford C. Frick Award, the highest award bestowed on a baseball broadcaster. (Honored with Hall of Fame induction that day were former Reds manager Sparky Anderson and former Reds first baseman Tony Pérez.) No stranger to controversy, Brennaman had already indicated that in his acceptance speech he would make a statement in support of Pete Rose's reinstatement to baseball. Bob Feller and Ralph Kiner had announced that if Brennaman made such comments in support of Rose, they and other Hall of Famers were prepared to walk out on his speech. As the assembled crowd listened anxiously, Brennaman thanked several of the players from the 1975 and 1976 World Champion Reds teams and then paid tribute to those "who should be here," ending the list "and yes, by God, Peter Edward Rose."[1] None of the Hall of Famers left the stage. When he returned to his seat after his speech, Brennaman recalled that Feller turned to him and said, "I don't agree with you but I respect the fact that you said what you had to say."[2] The incident was emblematic of a key facet of Brennaman's career, which continued past the first decade of the twenty-first century: he has been known not only for his accurate and entertaining play-by-play but also for being unafraid to express his opinions.

The longtime Reds broadcaster was born Franchester Martin Brennaman Jr. in Portsmouth, Virginia, on July 28, 1942. He was the son of Franchester "Chet" Brennaman Sr. and Lillian (Skipwith) Brennaman. Growing up in Portsmouth, Brennaman was a right fielder for his Little League

Marty Brennaman was just starting out when he was the voice of the Big Red Machine, but he would become a legend in Cincinnati.

team and played high school basketball. Though Brennaman enjoyed baseball (growing up listening to broadcasts of Nat Allbright doing re-creations of Brooklyn Dodgers games), sports were not the primary focus of his early life. Attending Woodrow Wilson High School in Portsmouth, Brennaman aspired to be an actor. After his high school graduation, he studied at Randolph-Macon College in Ashland, Virginia, and at the University of North Carolina.

Though Brennaman participated in the University of North Carolina drama program and performed in summer stock, by the time of his graduation in 1965, he had put acting aside. By this time Brennaman had a wife, Brenda, and two children, Thom and Dawn. Shortly after graduation, Brennaman was hired by a High Point, North Carolina, television station to work on the morning news show and occasionally substitute for the sports anchor. Six months later Brennaman left the television station to work at radio station WSTP in Salisbury, North Carolina.

It was at WSTP that Brennaman got his first taste of sports play-by-play when he broadcast a high school football game in Spencer, North Carolina. Broadcasting football games on Friday nights, Brennaman also became the voice of the Catawba College Indians football and basketball broadcasts. He also began his baseball broadcasting career, describing Rowan County American Legion games. "I did as much play-by-play as any human could conceivably do," Brennaman said later. "I did 25 high-school and college football games, and I did over 80 basketball games a year and American Legion Baseball."[3] Brennaman credited the experience with helping to develop his talents: "Everything that's happened for me happened because of Salisbury."[4]

After five years of broadcasting in Salisbury, Brennaman was hired by radio station WTAR in Norfolk, Virginia. While there he provided play-by-play for the American Basketball Association Virginia Squires. Norfolk also provided Brennaman with his first opportunity to do Minor League baseball play-by-play, as he became the voice of the Triple-A Tidewater Tides, beginning in 1971. "It was against my better judgment to give a guy a job at the Triple-A level who'd never worked a full season of baseball," Tides general manager Dave Rosenfield said later of hiring Brennaman. However, "his approach and desire were top-notch."[5] After just three seasons of broadcasting at the Minor League level, Brennaman was recommended by Rosenfield for the Major Leagues.

The Cincinnati Reds were looking for a new play-by-play radio broadcaster as the 1974 season approached. Al Michaels, who had covered the team for three seasons, had taken a job broadcasting for the San Francisco Giants. During winter baseball meetings in Houston, Rosenfield approached Dick Wagner, then assistant to Reds general manager Bob Howsam. "I'd heard Dick was looking for an announcer," Rosenfield said. "I said, 'I've got the best damn broadcaster around. If there's a tape on your desk when you get back, will you listen to it?' He said he would. I called Marty and told him to get that tape on Dick's desk."[6] One of 220 applicants for the job, Brennaman was hired as the voice of the Reds.

Brennaman took the job knowing "Al Michaels is a tough act to follow."[7] Years later he recalled, "I remember the situation then was not ideal. Number one, I was succeeding a guy who was eminently popular in Al Michaels. Number two, I was broadcasting for fans who knew more about team history than I'll ever know."[8] Brennaman did his first spring training game from Bradenton, Florida, against the Pirates and felt that it went well enough that "the ghost of Al Michaels had disappeared." The second spring training broadcast was from Al Lopez Field in Tampa and Brennaman inadvertently began the broadcast by welcoming listeners to "Al Michaels Field." Brennaman recalled, "I was embarrassed almost to tears." Broadcast partner Joe Nuxhall turned to him during the commercial break and said, "I'll be damned—we haven't even begun the regular season and I already have material for the banquet circuit next fall."[9]

The chemistry between Marty and former Reds pitcher Joe Nuxhall was evident from the start. Meeting for the first time in a Dayton, Ohio, photo studio for publicity shots before the season began, Bren-

MATT BOHN

naman greeted Nuxhall by saying, "I have your baseball card." Brennaman later reflected, "From that moment on we developed a one-of-a-kind relationship."[10] Working together for the next three decades, "Marty and Joe" became an institution in Cincinnati. In between pitches, the pair might chat about their tomato plants, their golf games, or anything else that might come to mind. "I think our success has to do with two things," Brennaman explained. "First, we genuinely like each other. Second, we talk about stuff outside of baseball that people can relate to. We make fun of ourselves and we don't take ourselves too seriously. I don't know if our act would fly outside of Cincinnati."[11] The two became so closely linked in the minds of Reds fans that when Brennaman stopped into a grocery store near his home early one morning, a fan approached him to ask, "Where's Joe?" Marty and Joe worked together until Joe's retirement after the 2004 season. The two remained close friends until Nuxhall's death in 2007.

In Brennaman's first inning of regular-season play-by-play, Henry Aaron hit his 714th home run to tie Babe Ruth on the career list. During the commercial break, Nuxhall turned to him and said, "What the hell do you do for an encore?"[12] Early that season, Brennaman would spontaneously utter what would become his signature call of a Reds win: "This one belongs to the Reds!" It was a phrase he said often during the early years, as the Reds won the World Series in 1975 and 1976. Assigned to cover the World Series each of those years for NBC radio and TV, Brennaman would not fully appreciate the team's talent and accomplishments until years later: "I agree with what Bob Howsam said in the clubhouse at Yankee Stadium after the fourth and final game of the 1976 World Series. He said that in our lifetime we'll never see another team the equal of this one."[13]

Brennaman's style evolved over the years. At the beginning he was, in his own words, an "unmitigated homer."[14] In 2000 he admitted, "When I hear tapes from back then, it's the most embarrassing thing in the world."[15] Originally referring to the Reds as "we" and "our side," Brennaman dropped the references to "we" after a player asked him how many hits he had had that day. Eventually Brennaman became known for his blunt assessments of the play in front of him. "I'm like a bull in a china shop. If a guy doesn't run out a groundball or loafs going after a ball hit in the gap, I'll say it," he said.[16] His candor wasn't always appreciated by the players. In 1985 Dave Concepción threatened to punch Brennaman in the nose for criticizing him. In 2000 Ken Griffey Jr. took issue when Brennaman accused the outfielder of loafing during his first year with the Reds. "I am just not concerned about what they think," Brennaman commented. "I know there are guys down there that don't like me. That's fine with me. There are a lot of guys down there I don't like."[17] For Brennaman, maintaining his credibility with the fans was most important. "I'm probably more critical than any other baseball play-by-play announcer in the business, and I think that when I walk away from this job, the only thing I will have is a measure of credibility."[18]

One person who didn't appreciate the broadcaster's candid approach was Reds general manager Dick Wagner. By the early 1980s, with the Big Red Machine largely dismantled, Wagner objected to Brennaman's criticism of the team and added a third broadcaster to the radio booth. "In 1980, he put Dick Carlson with Joe and me for a few games to make it a three-man booth," Brennaman said. "It was done because I was critical of the club and that was Wagner's way of warning me."[19] Brennaman was so angered that he "spent three days trying to get fired" and "called Dick Wagner everything known to man to every writer who covered the club."[20] In early 1983 Brennaman asked Wagner for a contract extension and was refused. Brennaman was sure that he would be fired by the end of the season. Instead, Wagner was fired in July. Brennaman stayed with the team and never again had an issue with team management objecting to what he said on the air.

Though team management would no longer object to Brennaman's criticism, commentary by Marty and Joe got the attention of National League president Bart Giamatti in 1988. On April 30, during a game against the Mets at Riverfront Stadium, Manager Pete Rose argued with first base umpire Dave Pallone about a delayed call at the bag with two outs in the top of the ninth inning, which allowed New York to score the game's winning run. After Rose was ejected, the heated exchange between the manager and umpire continued. Rose shoved Pallone twice and subsequently earned a $10,000 fine along with a one-month suspension for his part in the incident. On the air Brennaman called Pallone "incompetent" and a "horrible" umpire while Nuxhall, recalling Pallone's work during a 1979 umpire strike, called him a "scab." Fans, reacting to the umpire's call and the ensuing altercation, threw radios, golf balls, and other objects onto the field. Pallone was forced to leave the game before it ended. Giamatti blamed Brennaman and Nuxhall for "inciting the unacceptable behavior of some fans." Days later, the broadcasters met with Giamatti and Commissioner Peter Ueberroth for a meeting about the incident. "There was no indication they were trying to censure us. It was a discussion of what they felt was improper," Brennaman said after the meeting. In retrospect he characterized some of their on-air statements during the game as "inappropriate," but years later, he insisted, "They accused us of inciting a riot. I don't think we did then and I don't think we did now."[21]

Admittedly a "college basketball freak," by the late 1980s Brennaman was spending his winters broadcasting college basketball.[22] He provided play-by-play for Atlantic Coast Conference games and covered NCAA tournaments for CBS radio. He partnered with Larry Conley to work on telecasts of University of Kentucky basketball from 1987 to 1990.

In the course of his career, Brennaman has cov-

ered many historic moments in Cincinnati baseball history, including the Reds' 1990 World Series win, Tom Browning's perfect game in 1988, no-hitters by Tom Seaver in 1977 and Homer Bailey in 2012 and 2013, and Ken Griffey Jr.'s five hundredth home run in 2004 and six hundredth in 2008. However, Brennaman's "single most exciting moment" in the game came on September 11, 1985, when Pete Rose broke Ty Cobb's record to become the all-time base-hit leader. "Everybody knew it was just a matter of time. But when it happened it was just overwhelming," Brennaman recalled.[23] When Rose was banned from baseball for betting on games in 1989, Brennaman insisted that he still deserved recognition by the Baseball Hall of Fame. Brennaman's support of Rose's reinstatement never wavered. In 2011 Brennaman said, "He bet on baseball. . . . There's no question about that. He admitted it in a book a few years ago. But, if they're going to allow these guys who are either confirmed, or alleged, druggies . . . steroid guys . . . just to be on the Hall of Fame ballot, which they are . . . then damn it, Pete needs to be on there too."[24]

Though Brennaman and his wife, Brenda, divorced shortly after his arrival in Cincinnati, their son, Thom, recalls having a "terrific childhood."[25] Unlike most children, when Thom went to visit his father at work, he also got to meet such stars as Pete Rose, Johnny Bench, and Joe Morgan. Marty later remarried. He and his second wife, Sherri, had a daughter, Ashley. Reflecting on it, Marty said he felt he was a "much better father" to Ashley than he had been able to be to Thom and Dawn during the more hectic early years of his career.[26] Though Thom understood how difficult the travel and long absences could be for a broadcaster and his family, he chose to follow his father's career path.

Thom Brennaman made his Major League broadcasting debut in 1989 providing play-by-play on Reds telecasts. In 1990 he moved to the Chicago Cubs booth and eventually went on to provide play-by-play for the Arizona Diamondbacks and for Fox

Sports. In 2007 Thom returned to Cincinnati to work with his father on Reds radio. Thrilled with the working arrangement, Marty said that working with his son was "a dream fulfilled."[27] That year Thom and Marty worked about ninety games together on radio (with Thom moving to TV duties on Fox Sports Ohio for many of the remaining games.) They are the only father-and-son baseball broadcasters to have each broadcast a perfect game (Marty called Tom Browning's, Thom broadcast Randy Johnson's in 2004), a world championship team (Thom broadcast for the 2001 Arizona Diamondbacks), and a twenty-strikeout game (both were broadcasting when Randy Johnson struck out twenty Reds batters in 2001).

"After three years I expected Marty to move on because of his expertise and the way he handled things," Joe Nuxhall once admitted.[28] Though Brennaman had several offers from other teams in larger markets over the years, he preferred to stay in Cincinnati and became just as identified with the team as Sparky Anderson, Johnny Bench, or Joe Nuxhall. Recognizing what an institution the broadcaster had become in Cincinnati, the Reds symbolically retired his microphone (similar to retiring a player's uniform number) in a 2007 ceremony. By that year, Brennaman (at the advice of his friend Vin Scully) had cut back on his schedule, taking off twenty games during the season. In 2010 Brennaman said that he could "conceivably work indefinitely, as long as my health permits."[29]

Chapter 46. **Postseason**

Mark Armour

The 1975 NL West regular-season race, which was supposed to be a tight struggle between two great teams, turned out to be no race at all. Sitting with a 20-20 record on May 20, the Reds won seven in a row and never really let up. They took over first place on June 8, and five weeks later, at the All-Star break, they led by 12½ games. Their final margin, twenty games over the Los Angeles Dodgers, was the largest in baseball history. While there was little question that the Reds were baseball's best team, there was still the matter of winning two postseason series. The Reds lost the 1972 World Series and the 1973 NLCS to teams considered their inferior by most observers, and neither Sparky Anderson nor his veteran stars were satisfied with what they had thus far accomplished.

In the best-of-five NLCS, the Reds faced the Pittsburgh Pirates, winners of their fifth NL East title in six years. Although Pittsburgh did not have the top-flight stars that the Reds had, their offense featured a well-balanced group, including right fielder Dave Parker (25 home runs, .308 average), first baseman Willie Stargell (22, .295), center fielder Al Oliver (18, .280), left fielder Richie Zisk (20, .290), and catcher Manny Sanguillen (.328). Their three scheduled playoff starters—Jerry Reuss (18-11, 2.54), Jim Rooker (13-11, 2.97), and twenty-one-year-old rookie John Candelaria (8-6, 2.76)—matched up well with the Reds group. In the regular season the clubs had split twelve games.

The clubs finished their seasons on Sunday, September 28, and opened their series in Cincinnati six days later, on Saturday, October 4, with Don Gullett matching up against Reuss. The Pittsburgh left-hander had won three of his four starts versus

the Reds in 1975, along with posting a 2.40 ERA in those games. The Pirates got on the board first with two in the top of the second, but the lead was temporary. Down 2–1 in the bottom of the third, Joe Morgan led off with a walk and then stole second and third bases on consecutive pitches—he had earlier walked and stolen second in the first but had been left stranded. This time, Reuss crumbled. He walked Johnny Bench and gave up a run-scoring single to Tony Pérez and, two outs later, a two-run double to Ken Griffey. Just like that, Reuss was out of the game and the Pirates never got back in it. To cap a four-run inning in the bottom of the fifth Gullett hit a two-run home run off Larry Demery, the first round-tripper of Gullett's professional career. The Reds' ace went the distance and prevailed, 8–3.

On Sunday the Reds again ran roughshod on Sanguillen, stealing seven bases in their easy 6–1 win. The Reds stole bases not merely to move their base runners along but also to break down the psyche of the opposing pitcher. In the sixth inning Griffey led off with a single off reliever Kent Tekulve and quickly stole second base (his second swipe of the day) before César Gerónimo walked. After pinch hitter Ed Armbrister missed a bunt, Sanguillen threw down to second, easily trapping Griffey off the base. Griffey raced instead for third, sliding in safely. After a change of pitchers, Griffey trotted home when Ken Brett balked attempting to pick Gerónimo off first base. Pérez's first-inning home run, which had given the Reds a 2–0 lead, was forgotten after all the dramatic baserunning.

After an off day, the series resumed on Tuesday three hundred miles to the northeast, where the

The passion and joy of Pete Rose, the MVP of the 1975 World Series, came to personify the team.

Pirates could win the pennant by capturing three straight games at Three Rivers Stadium. For most of the evening, the story was the pitching of the 6-foot-7 Candelaria, who through seven innings had surrendered just one hit, a second-inning home run by Concepción, had struck out twelve, and led 2–1. In the top of seventh he fanned Griffey and Gerónimo, giving him fourteen Ks, before he finally ran out of gas. After pinch hitter Merv Rettenmund walked, Pete Rose homered to give the Reds the lead, Morgan doubled, and Candelaria was done. The Pirates did not go quietly, as they rallied to tie the game in the bottom of the ninth on a bases-loaded walk.

In the top of the tenth, the Reds won the game the way they had won the first two games—with their legs. Griffey reached on a bunt single, moved to second on a balk, to third on a ground ball, and home on a fly ball. The Reds added an insurance run on another Morgan double after Rose had singled, and Pedro Borbon finished off the 5–3 win. The Reds had won their third pennant in six seasons.

That same day, the Boston Red Sox completed their ALCS sweep of the Oakland A's, winners of the previous three World Series. The AL champs had been led by the dynamic rookie duo of Fred Lynn (twenty-one home runs, .331) and Jim Rice (twenty-two home runs, .309), along with catcher Carlton Fisk (.331, after missing the first half of the season with a broken arm). Unfortunately for the Red Sox, Rice suffered a broken hand when he was hit by a late-season pitch, and he missed the entire postseason. The Red Sox pitching staff was led by veteran Luis Tiant (18-14), who struggled most of the season before enjoying a strong September and a brilliant victory in Game One of the ALCS. Bill Lee (seventeen wins) and Rick Wise (nineteen) were their other big winners.

The Series began on October 11, a rainy Saturday afternoon at Boston's Fenway Park. Going into the Series, there had been much talk about the Reds' running game and how it would affect Fisk and the Boston pitchers. "I guess if they steal 12 times on me," lamented Fisk, "no matter whether it's my fault or the pitchers or to the credit of great baserunners like Morgan and Concepcion, I'll be the goat."[1] After Tiant retired the first ten Reds batters, Morgan singled to center field. Tiant threw over to first base three times before first base umpire Nick Colosi called a balk, delighting Morgan and the Reds, who had spent the past few days claiming that Tiant's move to first was illegal. That Colosi was a National League umpire, unfamiliar with Tiant, further enraged the pitcher and his manager, Darrell Johnson.

Morgan's gamesmanship was all too familiar to NL observers, who now sat back and waited for the inevitable onslaught. Instead, Tiant retired Bench and Pérez to get out of the jam, and the game remained scoreless into the bottom of the seventh inning. Tiant led off with a single to start a six-run rally and then retired the final six Reds batters. Far from being ruffled by the balk, Tiant pitched a masterful five-hit shutout. For a Reds club that had been beaten by great pitching in the 1972 World Series and the 1973 NLCS, this was an eerie beginning. "You open the door and they score runs," lamented Bench in admiration.[2]

On Sunday the Reds were nearly shut down again, this time by Bill Lee. Through eight innings the Red Sox had scratched out a 2–1 lead and Lee had a four-hitter going. Bench led off the ninth inning with a double, and Lee was replaced by Dick Drago. After a ground ball, a short fly ball out, a run-scoring infield single by Dave Concepción, a stolen base, and a Griffey double, the Reds had a 3–2 lead, and Rawly Eastwick held it in the bottom of the ninth. Conceding that his team had its ugly moments, Sparky Anderson nonetheless declared, "Over the course of a year, you won't see a better baseball team than the Cincinnati Reds."[3] The Series was tied and headed to Cincinnati.

After an off day, the Series resumed on Tuesday, October 14, when Rick Wise faced off against Gary Nolan. The Red Sox struck first on Fisk's second-inning home run, but the Reds countered with a two-out two-run shot by Bench in the fourth and solo blasts from Concepción and Gerónimo to start the fifth. A triple by Rose chased Wise, and Rose soon scored on a fly ball, making the score 5–1 Cincinnati after five innings, a lead generally sufficient for Anderson's great bullpen. But after Boston scratched out a run (without a hit) off Pat Darcy in the sixth, former Red Bernie Carbo launched a pinch-hit home run off Clay Carroll in the seventh, making the score 5–3.

Remarkably, in the top of the ninth Dwight Evans hit a dramatic two-run home run off Rawly Eastwick to make the score 5–5, where it remained into the bottom of the tenth. After Gerónimo led off with a single, pinch hitter Ed Armbrister had the most controversial plate appearance of the Series. When he tried to sacrifice, his bunt hit the artificial surface right in front of the plate and bounced straight up. Fisk reached out to field it but collided with Armbrister, who had been moving from the right-hand batter's box toward first base but suddenly stopped in his tracks. After the collision Fisk managed to field the ball and then shoved Armbrister away with his glove hand, but his throw to second sailed into center field. The Reds now had runners on second and third with no one out. Fisk and the Red Sox claimed interference, but American League umpire Larry Barnett disagreed. After an intentional walk and a strikeout, Morgan singled to center off Roger Moret to end the game. "It's a damn shame to lose a ballgame like that," said Fisk later.[4]

For Game Four, Red Sox manager Darrell Johnson elected to bring back Tiant on three days' rest, while Anderson went with Fred Norman. The Reds struck first, with long run-scoring doubles by Griffey and Bench in the first. The Red Sox chased Norman with five runs in the fourth, keyed by a game-tying triple to deep right by Evans. The Reds came right back with two in the bottom of the inning, and a triple by Gerónimo made the score 5–4. Tiant had allowed six hits and four runs before getting out of the fourth, and he seemed completely spent. "When

MARK ARMOUR

he walked Rose in the fifth inning," said Fisk, his catcher, "his first two pitches were fastballs and I motioned to Johnson that he had nothing."[5] Remarkably, the proud Tiant forged on and completed the game without allowing another run, despite several more base runners and hard-hit balls. On the evening, the Reds had nine hits, four for extra bases, and walked four times. When Joe Morgan popped out with two on and two out in the ninth, Tiant had his 5–4 victory, on a staggering 163 pitches.

Heading into Game Five, the Reds had to feel fortunate to be even in the Series—with a couple of breaks the Red Sox might have won all four games. The Reds now put together their best game of the Series, with the strong pitching of Gullett and two home runs by Pérez enough for a 6–2 victory. Pérez had been 0-for-15 for the Series. "I have played this game too long to get down on myself," he said later.[6] Still, the Red Sox did not make it easy—Gullett was just one out away from a 6–1 two-hitter when he allowed two singles and a Fred Lynn double. With the tying run in the on-deck circle, Eastwick came on to strike out Rico Petrocelli, to put the Reds up three games to two.

After a travel day, Game Six was scheduled for Saturday the eighteenth at Fenway Park, but heavy rains postponed events for three days. What baseball fans eventually got, on Tuesday the twenty-first, was a game for the ages. Lynn put the Red Sox up with a three-run home run off Nolan in the first, forcing the Reds, once again, to try to break through against Tiant, who was going for his third victory. This time they finally did, tying things with three runs in the fifth, keyed by Griffey's two-run triple. After taking the lead on Foster's two-run double in the seventh, they chased the valiant Tiant on Gerónimo's lead-off home run in the eighth. Heading into the bottom of the frame, the Reds had a 6–3 lead, six outs from winning the Series.

A single and a walk brought Anderson out to replace Borbon, but Eastwick struck out Evans and retired Rick Burleson. That brought up pinch hitter Bernie Carbo, who had homered in Game Three in the same role. Anderson considered bringing in McEnaney to face the left-handed-swinging Carbo but ultimately chose to stick with Eastwick. Remarkably, after looking very bad on a couple of two-strike foul balls, Carbo came through again, crushing a booming drive to the bleachers in straightaway center field, soaring around the bases, and tying the score of this amazing game, six runs apiece.

After the Reds went down meekly against Drago in the top of the ninth, the Red Sox looked as though they would end things in the bottom half, loading the bases with none out. Facing McEnaney, Lynn flied out down the line in short left, and Foster gunned down Denny Doyle at home plate. Third base coach Don Zimmer had tried to hold Doyle at third, but the runner misunderstood the instruction and was an easy out. A ground ball ended the threat. In the tenth Drago retired the Reds again, while Darcy, the eighth Reds pitcher of the game, did the same with the Red Sox.

When Rose led off the top of the eleventh, he turned to Fisk, squatting behind the plate, and raved, "This is some kind of game, isn't it?"[7] Drago hit Rose with a pitch, but Fisk fielded Griffey's bunt and gunned Rose down at second—a play that he had not been able to make in the tenth inning of Game Three. With one out now, Morgan crushed a towering line drive to deep right field, a shot remarkably hauled down by a leaping Evans near the three-and-a-half-foot wall. Evans turned and threw the ball back toward first base, doubling Griffey off the bag. The game continued.

Darcy baffled the Red Sox again in the eleventh, making it six batters in row. Wise relieved Drago in the twelfth and allowed two singles but no more, striking out Gerónimo to end the threat. Darcy, who had looked sharp in his two innings, came back out for the twelfth. The first batter was Fisk, the great Red Sox leader. After taking the first pitch for a ball, the catcher then hit one of history's most famous home runs, down the left-field line where it struck the foul pole, finally winning this epic, historic battle. It was after midnight in Boston, more than four hours since the game had begun.

After all of that, the teams still had to go back out and play a seventh game, Gullett vs. Lee. This contest, under ordinary circumstances, would be remembered for its own remarkable moments, but it was not able to live up to the previous game. But really, how could it? The Red Sox struck first, getting three runs in the third on two singles and three walks. Lee made this lead stand up until the top of the sixth, when Pérez hit a two-out two-run home run way over Fenway Park's left-field screen to bring the Reds to within a run. A Rose single off Moret tied the score in the seventh, and this great Series remained knotted, appropriately, and headed to the ninth.

Rookie Jim Burton came on to pitch the top half for the Red Sox. After walking Griffey on a 3-2 pitch, Burton induced a sacrifice bunt and a ground ball, moving Griffey to third with two outs. Burton pitched carefully to Rose, issuing another full-count walk, which brought Morgan, baseball's best player, to the plate. Burton got ahead 1-2, then threw a tailing fastball low and away that Morgan blooped into shallow center field for the 4–3 lead. "A couple of years ago I would have struck out on that pitch," Morgan admitted after the game.[8] In the bottom the ninth inning McEnaney came on to retire two pinch hitters before getting Carl Yastrzemski to fly out to Gerónimo in left-center field. The Reds had won their first world championship in thirty-five years.

The 1975 Cincinnati Reds had demolished the NL West and won the NLCS in a breeze. The Red Sox, comparatively young and inexperienced, gave them all they could handle and joined with the Reds to give us all an epic seven games. "We're the best team in baseball," Anderson repeated after the seventh game in Boston. "But not by much."[9] Although both teams produced memorable moments, the Reds ul-

timately accomplished what they needed to accomplish. A case could be made that they had been the best team in the game for the past four years, but history is not always kind to teams that do not finish the job. This time, they finished it.

Chapter 47. **The Reds of Summer**

Steve Treder

They were a ball club well-known then and well-remembered today not just for their victories and championships but also—indeed, more so—for the manner in which those victories and championships were achieved. The team presented a gallery of stars displaying an exceptional breadth of athleticism and skill, who did not defeat opponents so much as overwhelm them. Observers were typically struck with not so much admiration as awe.

Yet for all this ball club's profound ability, there was for many seasons a sense of underachievement about them. Though reliably among the close contenders, multiple times the team fell short in crucial title-deciding confrontations. For year after frustrating year, the failure to win that final big one—that fourth "bad boy" victory during the World Series—rendered the sterling reputation slightly hollow.

Pundits at the time pointed to a structural explanation for this team's inability to close the deal. Yes, their offense was an explosive brew of speed and power rarely sniffed in history. And yes, their team defense was extraordinary as well, presenting multiple fielders widely regarded as the best at their position. But the pitching staff never measured up.

The health and durability of their starters was a nagging issue, and the team struggled for years to develop a dominant ace, an anchor for the pitchers to be tethered around. As a result, the staff never seemed quite settled, and they relied on the bullpen to a degree unusual for winning teams of the era. Without elite-level starting pitching, they struggled to achieve in tight October contests what they had routinely done against lesser opponents over the long spring and summer schedules.

Thus when that ultimate champagne-popping moment finally arrived for this team, it represented more than just your garden-variety World Series victory. It brought with it a particularly keen sense of vindication, a sigh of relief along with the whoop of joy.

We are speaking, of course, of the Brooklyn Dodgers of 1949–56, the charismatic and robustly talented ball club christened "The Boys of Summer" by Roger Kahn in his iconic 1972 remembrance. You were expecting maybe, what, the Big Red Machine of 1970–76?

Perception of the similarity between these celebrated dynasties is hardly original, and hardly new. Bill James, in the 1982 *Baseball Abstract*—the first nationally distributed abstract—put it this way:

> There is a parallel between the Cincinnati Reds of today and the Brooklyn/Los Angeles Dodgers of 20 years ago . . . which gives no hint of breaking. . . . The Dodgers won the National League pennant in 1952, 1953, 1955, 1956, and 1959. The Reds won the National League West in 1972, 1973, 1975, 1976, and 1979. Both teams had won one previous title, the Reds in 1970 and the Dodgers in 1949; both teams got progressively better, and progressively older, throughout the decade. The 1976 Reds had the oldest starting lineup of any National League champion since the 1956 Dodgers.
>
> . . . Beyond the coincidental pattern of years, there are profound similarities in the two teams. Both the Dodgers of the midfifties and the Reds of the midseventies featured awesome 8-man lineups with adequate pitching. At many positions, they

match up beautifully. There is probably no player in the history of the game as much like Johnny Bench as Roy Campanella. Both were superb catchers and RBI men, MVPs; both had the same strong on-year/off-year pattern throughout much of their careers. Was Tony Perez's career a lot like Gil Hodges's? Is Wyoming quite a bit like Montana? Joe Morgan and Jackie Robinson, Pee Wee Reese and Dave Concepcion—these are very, very similar types of players. It is my opinion that the 1975–76 Reds had the greatest 8-man lineup ever assembled, but they weren't much ahead of the Brooklyn 8.[1]

These points are worth exploring in some detail.

Campy and Johnny

Of all the player parallels, this is the very strongest. It truly borders on the eerie: In terms of role and impact on the field of play—and what a phenomenal impact it was—Bench was essentially Campanella's clone, with the amazing rifle arm, the free-swinging, dead-pulling, right-handed power bat, and the vulnerability to the hitting slump.

And more than that: as personalities, as characters within the clubhouse drama, Campy and Johnny took comparable roles. Despite mastering the central responsibilities inherent in the catcher position, neither assumed primary leadership of the ball club; that was handled by more veteran and more assertive stars. Campanella's persona was genial, a bit playful, and Bench—who, lest we forget, was exceptionally young when he arrived in the Majors—appeared content to retain his polite, slightly deferential public posture even as a multi-MVP-awarded superstar.

Gil and Doggie

Pérez is in the Hall of Fame, and Hodges is not. The general consensus in the sabermetric community is that this inconsistency is an error: these two durable, dependable right-handed first basemen are so comparable in value that it is wrong for one to be enshrined in Cooperstown and the other not. That consensus, moreover, is that neither belongs; outstanding as both performers were, neither was a superstar, and they deserve prominent placement only in the Hall of Very Good.

They were not identical players. Hodges was a standout defensive first baseman, while Pérez was just average with the glove, and Pérez's career was 25 percent longer. But they were remarkably similar nonetheless, steadily providing the RBIs, month after month and year after year, in a quietly determined, workmanlike manner.

It was in the quiet-but-strong force of personality that Gil and Doggie demonstrated the most striking similarity. Neither was a big talker or a rah-rah guy. Yet both, even early in their careers, were widely respected leaders, men's men whom everyone in the clubhouse looked up to as models of professionalism, dignity, and strength. Nobody ever dared mess with either of these guys. Both would become Major League managers (though, to be sure, Hodges enjoyed far greater success in that role).

Jackie and Joe (and Pete)

James makes the unavoidable connection between Robinson and Morgan, two second basemen who delivered dazzling breadth of capability, all-time great ballplayers excelling in every conceivable phase of the game.

Yet there is an additional angle worth considering. Robinson, of course, was shifted away from the second-base position following the 1952 season, and he spent the remaining four years of his Dodger career playing mostly third base and left field, adaptively filling the team's evolving needs as a supersub, while remaining an on-base machine. The Reds had a certain ballplayer named Pete Rose whom they shifted away from second base in mid-career and moved around from position to position, first in the outfield and then, significantly and decisively, to third base in early 1975: adaptively filling the team's evolving needs as a moveable, every-day starter, while remaining an on-base machine.

There might be a further parallel between Robinson and Rose. For very different reasons and in obviously different ways, Robinson and Rose were both outsized as national celebrities beyond their pure status as ballplayers. Each was the key focus of media attention on his ball club, holding a status of public prominence shared by no teammate.

And in their ball field manner, Robinson and Rose were interestingly alike. Both were aggressively big talkers and rah-rah guys (which, of course, renders Robinson's success at keeping himself bottled up in his first couple of years in the league all the more remarkable), loud and flashy and demonstrative, profoundly fearless, seeking and ruthlessly grabbing every possible tiny advantage, strutting around (in Rose's case, sprinting around) the yard with an in-your-face what-are-you-going-to-do-about-it chip on the shoulder. Leo Durocher, as only he could, said in sheer admiration of Robinson, "This guy didn't just come to play. He came to beat ya. He came to stuff the goddamn bat right up your ass."[2] Such was utterly true of Rose as well.

Pee Wee and Davey

The parallel between the shortstops is not perfect, but it is strong. Reese was the better player, but not dramatically so (he is deservedly in the Hall of Fame, and Concepción deservedly not quite). Both were highly regarded fielders known especially for their strong and accurate throwing arms. Both dependably put up a batting average between .270 and .300, with more pop than most shortstops, and both ran the bases extremely well.

In the off-field realm, they part ways. Concepción, younger even than Bench and not a full-season regular until 1974, did not assume a leadership role on the ball club until later in his career, after Pérez, Rose, and Morgan had departed. Reese, in contrast, the first-string Brooklyn shortstop since 1940, was the elder statesman among Dodger regulars, older

even than Robinson. Reese was the team captain, both officially and unofficially, in every sense.

Reese's on-field gesture of walking over and putting his arm around Robinson during an ugly incident early in 1947 is recognized as one the most powerful demonstrations of team leadership in the history of sports. Reese's model as a southerner openly and unwaveringly accepting and supporting Robinson's presence was crucial to the successful integration of the Dodgers, and baseball generally.

Okay, but . . .

The similarities between the ball clubs do not extend much to the outfield. It is the case that Carl Furillo and César Gerónimo were tremendous defensive stars, but the former was a strong-hitting right fielder and the latter a so-so-hitting center fielder. Each outfield housed a prodigiously powerful middle-of-the-order slugger (well, for the Reds, only from 1975 forward), but beyond that there is not a lot in common between the left-handed-batting, all-around-superstar center fielder Duke Snider and the right-handed-batting, walk-resistant left fielder George Foster. And the Dodgers did not have anyone to match up with speedy Reds outfielders Bobby Tolan and Ken Griffey.

Then There's the Pitching

As James put it, on the mound both teams were "adequate." They shared a frustrating pattern of introducing impressive young pitchers (for the Dodgers, from the farm system, for the Reds, often via trade), only to see them struggle to one degree or another after promising beginnings, with sore arms a chronic, seemingly contagious complaint. In Brooklyn it was Rex Barney, Erv Palica, Ralph Branca, Billy Loes, and Karl Spooner, and in Cincinnati it was Wayne Simpson, Jim Merritt, Roger Nelson, Tom Hall, Tom Carroll, and Clay Kirby.

Even the best pitchers both organizations developed, the closest either team came to a top-tier ace—for the Dodgers, Carl Erskine and Don Newcombe, and for the Reds, Gary Nolan and Don Gullett—all grappled with recurrent issues of health, durability, and consistency.

Both teams adapted to the circumstance of an unreliable starting rotation by making groundbreaking liberal use of the bullpen, blazing staff-deployment trails others would soon follow. Neither team featured dominant relief stars, but Jim Hughes, Clem Labine, and Ed Roebuck for the Dodgers and Wayne Granger, Clay Carroll, Pedro Borbon, Will McEnaney, and Rawly Eastwick for the Reds pulled heavy loads and emerged among the more durable and reliably solid firemen of their day.

The First Dance

The Boys of Summer coalesced as a unit in 1949, winning the pennant behind a monster offense that led the league in runs, home runs, total bases, and stolen bases. For the Reds, the analogous season was 1970, when their wire-to-wire division runaway brought them national renown as the Big Red Machine, leading the league in home runs, total bases, and slugging while stealing the most bases (115) of any Cincinnati ball club since 1929. Both teams got spanked in five games in the World Series (Brooklyn by the Yankees, Cincinnati by the Orioles), and while that outcome was obviously disappointing, it was not heartbreaking, given that neither upstart had been expected to get to the Series.

The Years in the Desert

But following that, expectations were sensibly high, and the tension began to mount. The Dodgers fell achingly short of the National League pennant in both 1950 and 1951 (with the latter carrying the devastating double exclamation point of the huge blown lead and the Bobby Thomson home run to end the playoff). They succeeded in winning the pennant in both 1952 and 1953 but lost the World Series, again to the Yankees, both times (despite coming into the latter as the favorite

with a blistering 105-49 runaway regular season). And in 1954 they fell back to second place, losing out again to the Giants.

That excruciating roller-coaster ride to nowhere was echoed by the Reds twenty years later. They slumped badly in 1971, then were defeated in an epic seven-game World Series battle with the Oakland A's in 1972, then in 1973 suffered the humiliation of dropping the NLCS to a laughably inferior New York Mets outfit. In 1974 the Reds rolled out a ninety-eight-win season in predictably machinelike fashion yet wound up second in the division behind an exceptionally strong Dodgers team.

The Summit at Last

It was in that year ending in 5 that both teams finally grasped the Holy Grail, a pleasure no doubt all the sweeter for its elusiveness. For both teams, doing so required prevailing in a close Game Seven, on the road, in memorable form. For the Dodgers, unheralded supporting players came up huge, as platoon left fielder Sandy Amoros turned in a sensational sixth-inning catch-and-throw double play to support just-turned-twenty-three-year-old southpaw Johnny Podres's complete-game 2–0 shutout of the dreaded Yankees. The Reds methodically fought back from a three-run deficit in the late innings and carefully manufactured (yes, just like a machine) the winning run in the top of the ninth with a walk to Griffey, a sacrifice bunt by Gerónimo, a base-advancing ground ball, and a two-out dying-quail single by Morgan.

And Yet There's More

In that 1982 abstract James marveled at how the parallel pattern just would not quit:

Both teams began to break apart in '7, the Dodgers in 1957, and the Reds in 1977. Both won another flag in '9, and in both cases they did so with unusually low winning percentages (.564, .559) for first-place teams. Both of those were titles won from weak races with teams in transition. The 1959 Dodgers won by combining the remnants of the great Brooklyn team (Duke Snider, Gil Hodges) with the core of their great speed-and-pitching teams of the sixties (Maury Wills, Sandy Koufax, Don Drysdale, John Roseboro), a couple of players who spanned the gap (Jim Gilliam, Johnny Podres), and a few spare parts just rustled up for the occasion (Charlie Neal, Wally Moon, Don Demeter, Roger Craig).

What is intriguing about the parallel is wondering whether it will break before 1983, wondering if the 1979 Reds were, also, the parts of two champions. For it is quite apparent, if there is another champion in the making here, what the strength of that champion will be. The young pitching, while no one should be compared to Koufax or Drysdale . . . is imposing. Is there something inevitable about this form, some reason why a champion which is strong in every department except pitching should yield gradually to a champion which is based on pitching?[3]

Alas, the parallel did indeed break before 1983, as the seemingly up-and-coming Reds team suffered a cringe-worthy face-plant by losing 101 games in 1982. Mario Soto would prove to be the real deal, but the rest of the potentially imposing young Cincinnati pitching staff never got it together. The long spell of similarity between the generation-apart franchises was cast away at last.

Actions and Consequences

James did not seem entirely serious about his "is there something inevitable about the form?" pondering—two teams, no matter how similar, can hardly provide evidence for the inevitability of anything—but it remains genuinely intriguing that these two followed such a uniquely detailed path of development, decline, and rebuilding over such an extended period. While the dual transformation from hitting-centric to pitching-centric orientation is probably just a coincidence, perhaps there is something to the notion that both organizations, enduring season after season of pitching headaches, became particularly focused on identifying and developing superior young arms.

In any case, an attribute shared by both franchises was extremely sound management, from the top down. The Dodgers' foundation had been laid, of course, by none other than Branch Rickey. By the time the Mahatma departed Brooklyn in late 1950, nearly all of the key Boys of Summer were already on the big league roster, and moreover Rickey had put in place a state-of-the-art farm system and a unified organizational model of instruction and development. His successor as general manager, young Buzzie Bavasi, was a Rickey protégé promoted from within.

If it is fair to say that Bavasi's challenge was to execute against Rickey's master plan rather than design one himself, it is equally fair to say that Bavasi met that challenge with remarkable skill. Bavasi would remain in place as one of the sport's mostly widely respected GMs through 1968, and the field manager he hired after the 1953 season—another rookie, promoted from within the system—was named Walt Alston, and he would remain in place for more than two decades (indeed, he was managing the Dodgers team that outplayed the Big Red Machine in the 1974 NL West), on his way to the Hall of Fame.

The designing architect of the Big Red Machine, GM Bob Howsam, was, you guessed it, also a protégé of Rickey, going back to the late 1950s and continuing into the St. Louis Cardinals organization in the mid-1960s. That the team Howsam would eventually field in Cincinnati bore dramatic structural parallels with the Rickey-Bavasi Dodgers was likely coincidental, but that Howsam's meticulously orchestrated organizational approach was reminiscent of the Dodgers was not.

Howsam had clear and strong ideas about what he wanted to accomplish, and there is no doubt he was inspired by the principles so successfully set down by Rickey and Bavasi. The field manager Howsam would hire in October 1969—a rookie, promoted from within the Reds system—was named Sparky Anderson, and he would remain a highly celebrated big league manager for a quarter century, on his way to the Hall of Fame. And, you guessed it: Anderson had spent the first six years of his playing career—his formative phase in professional baseball—in the 1950s Dodgers organization.

Chapter 48. **1976 and Beyond**

Anthony Giacalone

The Big Red Machine reached its destiny when César Gerónimo closed his glove around Carl Yastrzemski's fly ball on October 22, 1975, at Fenway Park to end the World Series. In that moment of ecstasy and exhaustion the Cincinnati Reds became world champions, finally grasping the ring that had eluded their reach in the first half of the decade. On a cold October night in Yankee Stadium nearly one year later, after another brilliant campaign, they successfully defended the title. But then it was over. And while the Reds empire didn't exactly fall in the second half of the 1970s, it did stumble. There are several reasons why the Reds failed to reach the summit again after 1976. First, the contenders for the crown were very powerful. Additionally, some the team's old warriors were sent away or allowed to leave, while age and injury dulled the skills of some who remained. Finally, the Reds failed to modernize, allowing their opponents to strengthen their legions while the Cincinnatians grew weaker. So, despite six years of valiant battling, by 1982 the Reds dynasty lay in ruins, a victim of miscalculation and cruel fate.

Having built the Reds into champions, the team's longtime general manager, Bob Howsam, looked to improve his world champion squad. In an effort to give the team more vitality and versatility, after the 1975 season, Howsam dealt away former All-Star reliever Clay Carroll and starter Clay Kirby, along with bench players Darrel Chaney, Merv Rettenmund, and Terry Crowley, and replaced them with veterans and talented players from the Reds' Minor League organization. Bob Bailey and Mike Lum, who had played a combined twenty-one full Major League seasons, were acquired to reinforce

the bench, while Howsam turned to a pair of hard-throwing homegrown pitchers, Pat Zachry and Santo Alcala, to supplement the pitching staff. With these changes, Reds management believed that they had improved an already great club. "Our front line is the best eight men in either league," Howsam declared, "and our bench is now as good as anybody has in baseball."[1]

For now, the changing economics of the game did not affect the Reds. Within a year, the players' newly won right to become free agents if they played a season without a signed contract would overturn baseball's hidebound economic structure, but Howsam and the Reds dealt with it well during the 1975–76 off-season. Despite an owners' lockout during spring training, by Opening Day the Reds had signed all of their players except one, although they had to give some, like Joe Morgan and Pete Rose, significant raises to do so. Only the headstrong Don Gullett, the team's best starting pitcher, was playing with an unsigned contract. Reds management, it seemed, was willing to adapt to the game's new economic uncertainties. After all, as Morgan summarized, "The players realized it long ago. It's a business."[2]

Though they entered the 1976 season as the overwhelming choice to defend their division title and were 2-to-1 favorites to repeat as world champions, the Reds were just 12-10 on May 6 and still trailed the Los Angeles Dodgers by 2½ games on May 23. Only a few players struggled with injuries in 1976, notably Johnny Bench, whose "strange spasms of pain" compromised his production, but the rest of the team's hitters compensated for their catcher's relative decline. As for the pitchers, injuries pushed Gullett's first start back to April 25, but, like the team's hitters, their pitchers also picked up the slack. By the All-Star break, the Reds were 53-33 and in front of the second-place Dodgers by six games.[3]

And no one in the NL West really challenged the Reds during the second half of the season. The Dodgers managed to sneak to within seven games of Cincinnati in early September, but the Reds then won seven of eight games to widen the lead back to eleven games and finished the campaign ten games in front of the Dodgers. They were an excellent team. In fact, it is arguable that the 1976 Reds, despite a poorer overall record and a lesser margin of victory in their division, were the equal of Cincinnati's more celebrated 1975 squad. Unlike the 1975 team, the 1976 group never slipped below .500, and while the 1975 Reds padded their gaudy win-loss record by beating the league's worst teams, the 1976 squad won a remarkable 61.1 percent of the time against the best teams in the National League.[4]

The 1976 Reds burnished their reputation with remarkable play during the NLCS and in the World Series. With Gullett and Zachry on the mound, the Reds dominated the 101-win Philadelphia Phillies in the first two games of the best-of-five NLCS and then rallied for three runs in the bottom of the ninth inning of Game Three to complete the sweep and return to the World Series. There the Reds dismantled the AL champion New York Yankees in all facets of the game, crushing them in a four-game sweep during an "utterly one-sided and almost passionless World Series." Having won back-to-back titles and gone undefeated in the 1976 postseason, the Reds cemented their reputation as one of the better teams in baseball history. For Joe Morgan, the Reds' place in history seemed obvious: "How can you have a much better team than this one?"[5]

But big changes were ahead for the Reds. For one, it was nearly certain that Gullett would opt to become a free agent and leave the team, which he did, less than a month later, by signing a six-year, $2 million deal with the Yankees. Further, even as Howsam watched Tony Pérez win Game Two of the

World Series for the Reds with a ninth-inning single off Catfish Hunter, he knew that the popular Cuban-born slugger would not be with the 1977 team. Faced with the dilemma of either turning first base over to Dan Driessen, one of the World Series's batting heroes, or losing the young and promising player to free agency after the 1977 season, Howsam traded Pérez and reliever Will McEnaney to the Montreal Expos for thirty-seven-year-old left-handed starter Woody Fryman, who was coming off a terrific bounce-back season, and hard-throwing twenty-seven-year-old reliever Dale Murray. In the years to come, as the Reds were unable to reach the heights they scaled in 1975 and 1976, Sparky Anderson, many of the team's players, and even Howsam himself pointed to the loss of Pérez's clubhouse presence as the turning point in the team's fortunes. And while that conclusion is credible, it's difficult to see how Howsam could have rationally opted to keep the thirty-four-year-old Pérez over the twenty-six-year-old Driessen.[6]

Having won four of the last five NL West titles, including the two most recent campaigns by a combined thirty games over the second-place Dodgers, the Reds expected to continue their winning ways in 1977, even without Pérez and Gullett. The Dodgers and their new manager, Tommy Lasorda, had other ideas. Under outgoing manager Walter Alston, the Dodgers had spent most of the first half of the 1970s as bridesmaids for the Reds, having finished in second place six times in the previous seven years. But Lasorda knew the Dodger squad well and they responded to his infectious positivism. "The players were ready, the pitchers were ready," remembered veteran Dodgers pitcher Tommy John, "and we started off '77 like a house afire. Boom." Boom, indeed. Los Angeles leapt from the gate in 1977, winning 17 of its first 20 games and running up a 13½-game lead on the Reds by May 27.[7]

Meanwhile, the Reds started slowly. So much so that at the end of May, the two-time defending champions were still a game under .500. Injuries

ANTHONY GIACALONE

slowed the team's offense, while the Gullett-less rotation struggled so badly that one observer declared that there was "only one word for Reds' hurlers—horrible." The team's offense stumbled too, failing to display the energy of previous seasons. It was obvious to all, including Sparky Anderson, that the Reds "weren't the world champions [they] were supposed to be."[8]

Still, the Reds were nothing if not resilient. They were tested, they were supremely confident, and they had little respect for the Dodgers' staying power. "They just keep grinding it out," noted a former teammate. So no one was terribly surprised when the Reds started gaining ground in early June. Facing "virtual elimination," Cincinnati beat the Dodger aces, Don Sutton and Rick Rhoden, and then won 16 of 20 games to close to within 6½ games of the Dodgers on June 18. Bob Howsam, at least, believed that the Reds were poised to win the division again.[9]

So Howsam reconstituted the Reds in a flurry of moves at the June 15 trading deadline. First he traded discontented ace reliever Rawly Eastwick and then dumped veteran pitchers Gary Nolan and Mike Caldwell while adding infielder Rick Auerbach. But those deals were all just a prelude to the biggest news of the trade deadline. Outbidding the Phillies, Howsam acquired ace starting pitcher Tom Seaver from the New York Mets for Zachry, slick infielder Doug Flynn, and two promising hitting prospects. Howsam realized that he had given up a lot for Seaver but was also aware that "you can't give ashes for coal." In making these deals, the Reds' GM walked a difficult line between putting the best possible team on the field in 1977 and getting a return for players who were determined to become free agents after the season, like Eastwick and Nolan.[10]

Seaver shut out the Expos in Montreal in his first start for the Reds, but that ultimately proved to be the team's high-water mark. Six days later Seaver lost a 3–2 home contest to Tommy John and the Dodg-ers in what one close observer called the "biggest setback of the season." And then things got much worse. Beginning on July 10, the Reds careened through a three-week losing skid that saw them drop sixteen of twenty games, including eight games in a row, fall back under .500, and slip to fourteen games behind Los Angeles. By the time Cincinnati rallied in late August to cut the Dodgers' NL West lead to 8½ games, it was too little and too late. The 1977 Reds won eighty-eight games and even posted a winning record against the Dodgers but still finished ten games behind Los Angeles.[11]

It was a team that prided itself on its group accomplishments but could only point to personal accolades in 1977. For example, Pete Rose and Johnny Bench each set records that year. No one, however, had a better year than George Foster. A "walking evangelist" who preached "brotherly love, clean living, and a love of God," Foster wielded his ebony-stained bat (the "Black Death") like an avenging angel that season, smiting NL pitchers with a .320 average, fifty-two home runs, and 149 runs batted in en route to the Most Valuable Player Award.[12]

After finishing a season that left him feeling never "more disappointed in my life," Bob Howsam turned over the general manager's job to Dick Wagner, his longtime assistant and "hatchet man." On principle, Wagner and the Reds eschewed free agency, the new way to accrue talent, and so turned to the trade market. He traded for sinkerballer Bill Bonham, purchased infielder Junior Kennedy, acquired speedy outfielder Dave Collins, and added relievers Doug Bair and Dave Tomlin. Then, for the second time in six months, the Reds shocked the game. Hoping to ensure that the Reds had the best pitching in baseball, Wagner dealt Minor League first baseman Dave Revering and $1.75 million to the Oakland A's for former Cy Young Award winner Vida Blue, who was widely regarded as one of the better pitchers in the game. "People have said all we needed was pitching," said Rose. "With Blue and Bill Bonham joining us, we got it now."[13]

But just as they seemed to be back on top, Commissioner Bowie Kuhn dashed the Reds' hopes by nullifying the Vida Blue trade on January 30, 1978. After a hearing that was "more like an inquisition than the fact-finding procedure," Kuhn reaffirmed his earlier ruling that invalidated trades involving the exchange of more than $400,000. Reds president Howsam raged at Kuhn's "kangaroo court" decision and Sparky Anderson declared, "If I hear [Kuhn] say just once more he's doing something for the betterment of baseball, I'm going to throw up." Yet there was more than a touch of insincerity in Howsam's position. After all, the Reds owners were one of a majority of owners who had urged Kuhn to cancel Oakland's sales (of Blue, Joe Rudi, and Rollie Fingers) the previous year, and Howsam had testified on Kuhn's behalf in the subsequent court battle over the decision. It was evident to many at the time that Howsam's fit was an illustration of the rule that the "only time an owner squeals is when his own ox is gored."[14]

Another cloud also hung over the 1978 Reds. After an acrimonious negotiation with the team, Rose was playing on a two-year contract that allowed him to be a free agent after the season. Yet if this was to be Rose's last year with his hometown Reds, then he was determined to prove that he could still play. After becoming the player to accumulate three thousand hits most quickly on May 5, Rose added to his lore in June and July. He was hitting just .267 on June 14 but grounded two singles into center field that day and then, back in Cincinnati two days later, Rose doubled and singled in support of Tom Seaver's only no-hitter. He had officially begun the longest hitting streak in NL history. By mid-July, Rose had hit in thirty consecutive games and was a national phenomenon. Good fortune allowed him to extend the streak on July 19, so that on July 25 he broke Tommy Holmes's twenty-three-year-old NL record and a week later tied Wee Willie Keeler's nineteenth-century record by hitting in his forty-fourth consecutive game. Just twelve games shy of Joe DiMaggio's famed fifty-six-game record, Rose's streak ended the following evening when the Braves' soft-tossers held him hitless.

The end of Rose's streak began the Reds' worst month of the 1978 season. Cincinnati had surged from the gate, winning seven of its first eight games, but the Dodgers and the surprising San Francisco Giants, their rotation augmented by a sanctioned trade for Vida Blue, remained in a dogfight with the Reds for most of the year. By August 1 Cincinnati trailed the front-running Giants by just a half game, but they slumped through August and found themselves seven games behind the division-leading Dodgers by the beginning of September. For all intents and purposes, the Reds' season was over. They righted the ship a bit in early September and finished the 1978 campaign just 2½ games behind Los Angeles, but that figure is highly misleading, since after the Dodgers clinched the division the Reds won their final six games while the Dodgers lost five of their last six meaningless contests. So the Reds were 20-8 down the stretch in 1978 but it was just "cosmetic improvement" and there was no pennant race in the final year of the Big Red Machine.[15]

November brought the final days of the Big Red Machine. After another protracted but this time fruitless contract negotiation with the Reds, Pete Rose filed for free agency after his record-setting 1978 season and signed with the powerhouse Phillies. Rose's departure had been anticipated, if not expected, but the Reds' firing of Sparky Anderson on November 28, 1978, shocked the baseball world. Rose's stunned "What the hell's going on?" was a typical reaction. While General Manager Wagner had squabbled in the past with the fiercely loyal Anderson about the team's coaching staff, he and Sparky were close friends and the general manager had given Anderson a resounding vote of confidence late in the season. "Sparky is in absolutely no jeopardy," Wagner had said and then showed Anderson the article, proclaiming, "That is exactly the way I feel about you." Further, Wagner had not suggested anything about a change during the rest of the season, nor on the Reds' recently completed four-week tour of Japan. However, upon reflection Wagner decided that Sparky had not been stern enough at the helm, which led to the team's not being "an aggressive ballclub in the field." Believing that "the situation today calls for a new approach," Wagner concluded that he couldn't "just can't sit back and let the ballclub go downhill."[16] Now, without Rose and Anderson, the Reds were the Big Red Machine only in metaphor.

However, the Reds did not fall apart after the departures of Rose and Anderson. Wagner's Reds would eventually slide into irrelevance because of the team's dogmatic refusal to partake in the modern economics of the game. Still, reinforced by a strong farm system, new manager John McNamara's Reds performed quite well into the early 1980s. The Reds replaced Rose at third base with Ray Knight and put youngster Mike LaCoss into the rotation, but McNamara basically used the same squad that Anderson had fielded in 1978 and won the 1979 NL West title. After the Reds' NLCS loss during a three-game sweep by the "We-Are-Family" Pirates, two more vital cogs of the Big Red Machine, Joe Morgan and Fred Norman, left the team as free agents. Scorning the free-agent market themselves, the Reds continued to fill holes from within, giving starting jobs to Dave Collins, Ron Oester, Mario Soto, Frank Pastore, and Joe Price. McNamara's 1980 Reds started well, finished well, and won eighty-nine games but ended the season in third place, 3½ games behind Morgan's new team, the Houston Astros. Then Rose and the eventual world champion Phillies bested Morgan and the Astros during the NLCS in one of baseball's greatest playoff series. An aging Johnny Bench caught only seven games in 1981 and split time at first base with Dan Driessen during an injury-plagued season, but powered by George Foster and Tom Seaver, the Reds played very well during both halves of the strike-ravaged campaign. In fact, the Reds compiled the best record in baseball that year

but missed the expanded postseason after finishing a half game behind the Dodgers in the first part of the season and a game and a half behind the Astros during the season's second act.

After the immense disappointments of 1981, Wagner dismantled the remnants of the old Big Red Machine by trading away Griffey and Foster. While Morgan, Rose, and Pérez would play together again on the 1983 Phillies' Wheeze Kids squad, only Bench, now playing an awkward third base to save his aching knees, and Dave Concepción remained on the Reds. And both they and their Reds, who lost 101 games in 1982, cast but a faint shadow of the team's faded glory.

Epilogue

The Big Red Machine can be said to broadly refer to the Reds of 1970 through 1976, who won four NL pennants, and more narrowly to the 1975 and 1976 clubs, who won back-to-back World Series titles. After years of knocking on the door, the 1975 Reds finally finished the job.

This club has been well respected by baseball analysts and historians, who usually rank them comfortably in the top ten of all-time baseball teams. They might have had the best eight-man lineup ever put together, the Great Eight, and only the lack of a true, healthy ace pitcher keeps them from being considered as the best team ever.

Two players on this club are contenders for being the greatest player ever at his position: catcher Johnny Bench and second baseman Joe Morgan. Only the 1920s Yankees, with Babe Ruth and Lou Gehrig, could make a claim to have two players on baseball's all-time first team.

A third player on these Reds has been enshrined in baseball's Hall of Fame: first baseman Tony Pérez. A fourth player would be a cinch to have made the Hall years ago had he not gotten into trouble after his playing career was over: third baseman Pete Rose. Shortstop Dave Concepción is often mentioned as a candidate for the Hall of Fame, though he has not gotten close to election.

In addition, the team's manager, Sparky Anderson, is in the Hall of Fame. As of 2013 he was baseball's sixth all-time winningest manager. The architect of the team, Bob Howsam, has been a candidate of late for the Hall of Fame and highly deserves the honor.

The Reds were the last great team prior to the onset of free agency. After 1976 wealthier teams had the opportunity to purchase ready-made talent to act as the last piece or pieces to a championship club. The Reds were not able, or least not willing, to participate in this new marketplace, and Howsam saw his great team wither away after his second championship.

But the Big Red Machine will never be forgotten.

Notes and References

This section first lists a number of key sources that were consulted repeatedly while researching this book, followed with chapter-by-chapter notes and bibliographies.

General References

Anderson, Sparky, and Si Burick. *The Main Spark: Sparky Anderson and the Cincinnati Reds.* Garden City NY: Doubleday, 1978.

Bench, Johnny, and William Brashler. *Catch You Later.* New York: Harper and Row, 1979.

Bjarkman, Peter C. *Baseball's Great Dynasties: The Reds.* New York: Gallery Books, 1991.

Bradley, Richard. *The Greatest Game.* New York: Free Press, 2009.

Feldmann, Doug. *The 1976 Cincinnati Reds: Last Hurrah for the Big Red Machine.* Jefferson NC: McFarland, 2009.

Frost, Mark. *Game Six: Cincinnati, Boston, and the 1975 World Series: The Triumph of America's Pastime.* New York: Hyperion, 2009.

Hertzel, Bob. *The Big Red Machine.* Englewood Cliffs NJ: Prentice-Hall, 1976.

Johnson, Lloyd, and Miles Wolff. *The Encyclopedia of Minor League Baseball.* 2nd ed. Durham NC: Baseball America, 1997.

Lawson, Earl. *Cincinnati Seasons: My 34 Years with the Reds.* South Bend IN: Diamond Communications, 1987.

McCoy, Hal. *The Relentless Reds.* Shelbyville KY: Press-Co, 1976.

Morgan, Joe, and David Falkner. *Joe Morgan: A Life in Baseball.* New York: W. W. Norton, 1993.

Posnanski, Joe. *The Machine: A Hot Team, a Legendary Season, and a Heart-Stopping World Series; The Story of the 1975 Cincinnati Reds.* New York: William Morrow, 2009.

Rhodes, Greg, and John Erardi. *Big Red Dynasty: How Bob Howsam and Sparky Anderson Built the Big Red Machine.* Cincinnati: Road West Publishing, 1997.

Rhodes, Greg, and John Snyder. *Redleg Journal: Year by Year and Day by Day with the Cincinnati Reds since 1866.* Cincinnati: Road West Publishing, 2000.

Smith, Darryl, and Lee May. *Making the Big Red Machine: Bob Howsam and the Cincinnati Reds of the 1970s.* Jefferson NC: McFarland, 2009.

Spatz, Lyle, ed. *The SABR Baseball List & Record Book.* New York: Scribner, 2007.

Thorn, John, Phil Birnbaum, and Bill Deane. *Total Baseball: The Ultimate Baseball Encyclopedia.* 8th ed. Toronto: Sport Media Publishing, 2004.

Walker, Robert Harris. *Cincinnati and the Big Red Machine.* Bloomington: Indiana University Press, 1988.

Cincinnati Reds Yearbook, 1968–77.
Cincinnati Reds Media Guides, 1968–77.

Baseball-Reference.com
Retrosheet.org
Ancestry.com
Baseball-almanac.com

National Baseball Hall of Fame Library, Cooperstown NY, player files.

1. Bob Howsam

Golenbock, Peter. *The Spirit of St. Louis.* New York: William Morrow, 2000.

Howsam, Bob, with Bob Jones. *My Life In Sports.* Self-published, 1999.

Smith, Daryl, and Lee May. *Making the Big Red Machine: Bob Howsam and the Cincinnati Reds of the 1970s.* Jefferson NC: McFarland, 2009.

2. Scouting and Player Development

SABR Scouts Committee's databases

3. Sparky Anderson

1. Sparky Anderson and Si Burick, *The Main Spark: Sparky Anderson and the Cincinnati Reds* (Garden City NY: Doubleday, 1978), 41.

2. Anderson and Burick, *Main Spark*, 48.

3. Anderson and Burick, *Main Spark*, 49.

4. Anderson and Burick, *Main Spark*, 55.

5. Anderson and Burick, *Main Spark*, 84.

6. Anderson and Burick, *Main Spark*, 98.

7. Anderson and Burick, *Main Spark*, 90.

8. Anderson and Burick, *Main Spark*, 120.

9. Anderson and Burick, *Main Spark*, 181.

10. Sparky Anderson with Dan Ewald, *They Call Me Sparky* (Chelsea MI: Sleeping Bear Press, 1998), 99.

11. Anderson and Ewald, *They Call Me Sparky*, 235.

12. Anderson and Burick, *Main Spark*, 198.

13. Anderson and Ewald, *They Call Me Sparky*, 142.

14. Anderson and Ewald, *They Call Me Sparky*, 164.

15. Anderson and Ewald, *They Call Me Sparky*, 169.

16. Sparky Anderson and Dan Ewald, *Bless You Boys: Diary of the Detroit Tigers' 1984 Season* (Chicago: Contemporary Books, 1984), 214.

17. Anderson and Ewald, *Bless You Boys*, 214.

18. Anderson and Ewald, *They Call Me Sparky*, 185.

19. Anderson and Ewald, *They Call Me Sparky*, 186.

20. Anderson and Ewald, *They Call Me Sparky*, 188.

21. Anderson and Ewald, *They Call Me Sparky*, 197.

22. Mark Pattison, "CNS Newsmaker Interview with Sparky Anderson," Catholic News Service, August 29, 1996.

23. John Erardi, "Sparky Anderson, Reds Great, Dies," Cincinnati.com, November 4, 2010.

4. George Scherger

1. *Robesonian* (Lumberton NC), August 19, 1979, 12.

2. Tom Loomis, "Rose at Center Stage with Candor, Charm," *Toledo Blade*, August 17, 1984, 19.

3. "Former College Librarian Mozelle Scherger Dies," *Charlotte Observer*, May 30, 1993, 4B.

4. Kim Rogers, "Veteran Scherger Top Pilot," *Sporting News*, December 12, 1982, 48.

5. *Sporting News*, July 16, 1947; *Sporting News*, July 4, 1951.

6. *Sporting News*, October 20, 1973.

7. Ritter Collett, *The Men of the Machine* (Dayton OH: Landfall Press, 1977), 96.

8. *Bluefield (WV) Daily Telegraph*, June 2, 1976, 6.

9. *Sporting News*, March 24, 1973.

10. Collett, *Men of the Machine*, 97.

11. Collett, *Men of the Machine*, 96.

12. *Sporting News*, December 9, 1978.

13. Rogers, "Veteran Scherger Top Pilot," 48.

14. Rogers, "Veteran Scherger Top Pilot," 48.

15. Earl Lawson, "Rose Returns to Run Show," *Sporting News*, August 27, 1984, 37.

16. Paul Attner, "Pete Rose, Manager," *Sporting News*, May 18, 1987, 10–11.

17. "Former College Librarian Mozelle Scherger Dies," 4B.

5. Alex Grammas

Thanks to Matt Bohn, George Demetriou, Alex Grammas, Tula Grammas, Merle Harmon, Aaron Honoré, Thomas Karn, Randy Messel, Larry Moffi, and Al Yellon.

Aaron, Hank, and Lonnie Wheeler. *I Had a Hammer: The Hank Aaron Story.* New York: Harper Collins, 1991.

Berger, Jack H., ed. *Pittsburgh Pirates 1969 Media Guide.* Pittsburgh: Pittsburgh Pirates, 1969.

Dewey, Donald, and Nicholas Acocella. *Total Ballclubs: The Ultimate Book of Baseball Teams.* Toronto: Sport Media Publishing, 2005.

Eisenbath, Mike. *The Cardinals Encyclopedia.* Philadelphia: Temple University Press, 1999.

Fehler, Gene. *Tales From Baseball's Golden Age.* Champaign IL: Sports Publishing, 2000.

Finoli, David, and Bill Ranier. *The Pittsburgh Pirates Encyclopedia.* Champaign IL: Sports Publishing, 2003.

Honoré, Aaron J. *Beards: On Men, On Women, On Gods and More—How Facial Hair Serves as Both a Means to an End and an End of Communication.* New York: Fordham University, 2005.

Mishler, Todd. *Baseball in Beertown.* Neenah WI: Big Earth Publishing, 2005.

Preston, Joseph G. *Major League Baseball in the 1970s: A Modern Game Emerges.* Jefferson NC: McFarland, 2004.

Swirsky, Seth. *Every Pitcher Tells a Story: Letters Gathered by a Devoted Baseball Fan.* New York: Crown Publishing Group, 1999.

Zervos, Diamantis. *Baseball's Golden Greeks: The First Forty Years, 1934–1974.* Canton MA: Aegean Books International, 1998.

Stone, Larry. "Little Fanfare Surrounds Aaron's HR No. 755," *Seattle Times*, July 22, 2007.

Halofan, Rev. "The 100 Greatest Angels: Frank Tanana." HalosHeaven.com. February 13, 2006. Accessed February 21, 2009. http://www.halosheaven.com/story/2006/2/14/23549/1427.

6. Larry Shepard

1. Daryl Smith and Lee May, *Making the Big Red Machine: Bob Howsam and the Cincinnati Reds of the 1970s* (Jefferson NC: McFarland, 2009), 64.

2. Eddie Fisher, "Darkhorse Jets Copped Int Flag without .300 Hitter," *Sporting News*, September 20, 1961.

3. Les Biederman, "Shepard Given Task of Putting Some 'Lion' into Lamby Bucs," *Sporting News*, October 28, 1967.

4. Les Biederman, "Optimist Brown Tells Buc Fans of '68 Dreams," *Sporting News*, December, 16, 1967.

5. Biederman, "Shepard Given Task."

6. Les Biederman, "Shepard Shoots for Flag in Bow as Bucs Skipper," *Sporting News*, February 24, 1968.

7. Les Biederman, "Shepard Learns the Hard Way; All Pilot Glitter Is Not Gold," *Sporting News*, April 27, 1968.

8. Les Biederman, "Why Do Managers Get Gray? Shepard Knows the Answer," *Sporting News*, August 3, 1968.

9. Bill Christine, "Bucs Leaving Ailing Shepard Behind," *Pittsburgh Press*, July 14, 1969.

10. Ritter Collett, *Men of the Machine* (Cincinnati: Landfall Press, 1977), 93.

11. Smith and May, *Making the Big Red Machine*, 191–92.

12. Greg Rhodes and John Erardi, *Big Red Dynasty: How Bob Howsam and Sparky Anderson Built the Big Red Machine* (Cincinnati: Road West Publishing, 1997), 82–85.

13. Rhodes and Erardi, *Big Red Dynasty*, 85.

14. Collett, *Men of the Machine*, 93–94.

15. Rhodes and Erardi, *Big Red Dynasty*, 198–99.

16. Bob Hertzel, *The Big Red Machine* (Englewood Cliffs NJ: Prentice-Hall, 1976), 96.

17. Mark Frost, *Game Six: Cincinnati, Boston, and the 1975 World Series: The Triumph of America's Pastime* (New York: Hyperion, 2009), 41.

18. Rhodes and Erardi, *Big Red Dynasty*, 198.

19. Bill Brink, "Obituary: Lawrence W. Shepard," *Pittsburgh Post-Gazette*, April 8, 2011.

20. Collett, *Men of the Machine*, 94.

21. Rhodes and Erardi, *Big Red Dynasty*, 199.

22. Rhodes and Erardi, *Big Red Dynasty*, 199.

7. Ted Kluszewski

1. Billy Pierce, interview with author, August 2008.

2. Pierce, interview.

3. Bill Skowron, interview with author, August 2008.

4. John Kuenster, interview with author, September 2008.

5. Pierce, interview.

6. Pierce, interview.

7. Pierce, interview.

8. Pierce, interview.

9. Kuenster, interview.

8. Preseason Outlook

1. Ross Newhan, "Phillies Top East after 24-Year Drought; Dodgers to Repeat in West," *Street and Smith's Official Yearbook* (1975): 43.

2. Zander Hollander, *The Complete Handbook of Baseball* (New York: New American Library, 1975); Cord Communications Corporation, *Major League Baseball 1975* (New York: Pocket Books, 1975).

3. C. C. Johnson Spink, "Spink Sees Yankees Back on Throne, *Sporting News*, April 12, 1975, 3.

4. Roy Blount Jr., "NL West," *Sports Illustrated*, April 7, 1975, 56–57.

9. Pete Rose

1. David Jordan, *Pete Rose: A Biography* (Chicago: Greenwood, 2004), 3–4.

2. Joe Posnanski, *The Machine: A Hot Team, a Legendary Season, and a Heart-Stopping World Series; The Story of the 1975 Cincinnati Reds* (New York: William Morrow, 2009), 129.

3. Jordan, *Pete Rose*, 5.

4. Jordan, *Pete Rose*, 7.

5. Greg Rhodes and John Erardi, *Big Red Dynasty: How Bob Howsam and Sparky Anderson Built the Big Red Machine* (Cincinnati: Road West Publishing, 1997), 23–24.

6. Jordan, *Pete Rose*, 26.

7. Joe Morgan and David Falkner, *Joe Morgan: A Life in Baseball* (New York: W. W. Norton, 1993), 285.

8. Rich Westcott and Frank Bilovsky, *The Phillies Encyclopedia*, 3rd ed. (Philadelphia: Temple University Press, 2004), 244.

9. Westcott and Bilovsky, *Phillies Encyclopedia*, 244.

10. Pete Rose and Roger Kahn, *Pete Rose: My Story* (New York: Macmillan, 1989), 9.

11. Mark Frost, *Game Six: Cincinnati, Boston, and the 1975 World Series: The Triumph of America's Pastime* (New York: Hyperion, 2009), 59.

12. Bob Molinaro, telephone interview with author, May 27, 2011.

13. Posnanski, *The Machine*, 91–95.

14. Robert Harris Walker, *Cincinnati and the Big Red Machine* (Bloomington: Indiana University Press, 1988), 68.

15. Rob Neyer and Eddie Epstein, *Baseball Dynasties* (New York: W. W. Norton, 2000), 314.

16. Posnanski, *The Machine*, 3.

17. Rhodes and Erardi, *Big Red Dynasty*, 216.

18. Frost, *Game Six*, 265.

19. Rose and Kahn, *Pete Rose*, 180–85.

20. Rhodes and Erardi, *Big Red Dynasty*, 280.

21. Rhodes and Erardi, *Big Red Dynasty*, 286.

22. Bill Giles with Doug Myers, *Pouring Six Beers at a Time* (Chicago: Triumph Books, 2007), 131–32.

23. Giles, *Pouring Six Beers at a Time*, 121.

24. Giles, *Pouring Six Beers at a Time*, 133.

25. Frank Fitzpatrick, *You Can't Lose 'Em All* (Boulder CO: Taylor Trade Publishing, 2001), 74.

26. Posnanski, *The Machine*, 266–75.

10. Tom Hall

1. Earl Lawson, "Reds Forecast 150 Runs for Galloping Morgan," *Sporting News*, July 1, 1972, 5.

2. Tom Hall, interview with twinstrivia.com, August 2009.

3. Bob Fowler, "Twins Shave Enemy Bats with Razor-Sharp Blade," *Sporting News*, June 20, 1970.

4. Hall, interview.

5. Mel Derrick, "Hall Puts Hitters on a Skimpy Diet," *Sporting News*, June 15, 1968, 35.

6. Hall, interview.

7. Fowler, "Twins Shave Enemy Bats with Razor-Sharp Blade."

8. Fowler, "Twins Shave Enemy Bats with Razor-Sharp Blade."

9. Ed Rumill, "Hall's Elastic Arm Puts the Snap in Reds," *Baseball Digest*, December 1972, 48.

10. "Tom Hall Key Factor in Reds' Flag Drive," *Utica (NY) Press*, June 23, 1972.

11. Charley Feeney, "Pirates and Reds Engage in Swap of Opportunities," *Sporting News*, October 21, 1972, 21.

12. Unattributed clipping, May 4, 1974, in Hall's clippings file, National Baseball Hall of Fame Library, Cooperstown NY; "Reds Ex-Pitcher Sues Stadium over Injury," *Pittsburgh Post-Gazette*, September 16, 1976.

13. Steve Cady, "Mets Get Lift from New Hurler," *New York Times*, April 17, 1975.

14. Hall, interview.

11. Bill Plummer

1. Bob Finnigan, "Plum Truthful—Mariner Manager Bill Plummer Is Direct, Straightforward," *Seattle Times*, April 2, 1992.

2. Scouting Report on Cubs system, *Baseball Digest*, March 1968, 80.

3. Scouting Report on Reds system, *Baseball Digest*, March 1972, 62.

4. Barry McDermott, "Few Things Come to Him Who Waits: The Reds' Bill Plummer Plays behind the Finest Catcher in Baseball—At Times," *Sports Illustrated*, July 18, 1977.

5. Hal McCoy, *Baseball Digest*, September 1974, 43.

6. Bob Hertzel, "The Bullpen Where Characters and Oddball Capers Abound," *Baseball Digest*, July 1976, 81.

7. Bill James, *The New Bill James Historical Baseball Abstract* (New York: Free Press, 2001).

8. McDermott, "Few Things Come to Him Who Waits."

9. McDermott, "Few Things Come to Him Who Waits."

10. Finnigan, "Plum Truthful."

11. McDermott, "Few Things Come to Him Who Waits."

12. Finnigan, "Plum Truthful."

13. Finnigan, "Plum Truthful."

14. Finnigan, "Plum Truthful."

15. Finnigan, "Plum Truthful."

16. *Baseball Digest*, June 2000, 48.

17. Jim Street, "Seattle Mariners," *Sporting News*, August 3, 2012.

18. Mel Antonen, "Seattle Fires Plummer After Last-Place Finish," *USA Today*, October 14, 1992.

12. Don Gullett

1. *USA Today*, October 24, 2000.

2. *Mansfield (OH) News Journal*, March 4, 1970.

3. *Cincinnati Post*, May 22, 1971.

4. *Newark (OH) Advocate*, April 17, 1970.

5. *Cincinnati Post*, September 19, 1970.

6. *Cincinnati Post*, July 22, 1974.

7. *Cincinnati Post*, July 22, 1974.

8. *Cincinnati Post*, September 6, 1975.

9. *Billings (MT) Gazette*, October 3, 1975.

10. George Vecsey, "Don Gullett Is Supposed to Go Straight from the Holler to the Hall of Fame," *Sport*, April 1976.

11. Vecsey, "Don Gullett."

12. *Cincinnati Post*, April 17, 1976.

13. *New York Daily News*, February 6, 1986.

13. Tom Carroll

1. Tom Carroll, interview with author, June 1, 2012. The author would like to express his gratitude to Tom, who also provided additional information via e-mail.

2. Carroll, interview.

3. Carroll, interview.

4. Carroll, interview.

5. Carroll, interview.

6. Carroll, interview.

7. Carroll, interview.

8. Carroll, interview.

9. *Sporting News*, November 27, 1971, 51.

10. Carroll, interview.

11. Carroll, interview.

12. Carroll, interview.

13. *Sporting News*, June 28, 1973, 45.

14. Carroll, interview.

15. *Sporting News*, September 1, 1973, 30.

16. Carroll, interview.

17. *Sporting News*, October 13, 1973, 28.

18. *Sporting News*, November 17, 1973, 39.

19. Carroll, interview.

20. Carroll, interview.

21. *Sporting News*, June 8, 1974, 34.

22. Carroll, interview.

23. Associated Press, "Studies Wait for Reds' Tom Carroll," *Bangor (ME) Daily News*, August 7, 1974, 26.

24. *Sporting News*, August 17, 1974, 29.

25. *Sporting News*, August 31, 1974, 24.

26. Associated Press, "Studies Wait for Reds' Tom Carroll."

27. Carroll, interview.

28. Carroll, interview.

29. Carroll, interview.

30. Carroll, interview.

31. Carroll, interview.

32. *Sporting News*, December 25, 1976, 35.

33. Brodie Snyder, "Expos Take Draft Gamble on Young Pitcher," *Montreal Gazette*, December 7, 1976, 4.

34. Carroll, interview.

35. Carroll, interview.

36. Carroll, interview.

37. Carroll, interview.

38. Syllabus, STIA-475, Information Technology and International Security, spring 2010–11, http://courses.georgetown.edu/index.cfm?Action=View&CourseID=STIA-475&AcademicYear=2010&AcademicTerm=FallSpring.

15. Ken Griffey

1. Joe Posnanski, *The Machine: A Hot Team, a Legendary Season, and a Heart-Stopping World Series; The Story of the 1975 Cincinnati Reds* (New York: William Morrow, 2009), 151–53. Posnanski also wrote that Griffey could not hit a lick in high school. That statement stands in stark contrast to accounts in area newspapers at the time crediting Griffey with game-winning home runs and triples, among other hits.

2. Joe Morgan and David Falkner, *Joe Morgan: A Life in Baseball* (New York: W. W. Norton, 1993), 195.

3. Posnanski, *The Machine*, 154.

4. Posnanski, *The Machine*, 210.

5. Bob Sherwin, "Griffey Gap: Model Father Bitter at Own Dad—Ken Sr. Can't Forget Abandonment," *Seattle Times*, October 7, 1990.

6. Sherwin, "Griffey Gap."

16. Fred Norman

1. *Sporting News*, July 14, 1973.
2. Bill Baucher, "Fred Norman's Long Search for Major League Stardom," *Baseball Digest*, June 1975.
3. *Cincinnati Reds Yearbook*, 1975.
4. Baucher, "Fred Norman's Long Search."
5. Associated Press, "Fred Norman Disagrees with Anderson's Logic," *Tuscaloosa (AL) News*, October 10, 1975.
6. Joe Frohlinger, "Sharp Norman Proves Sparky was 'Dummy,'" United Press International, *Sarasota (FL) Journal*, July 27, 1976.
7. *Sporting News*, September 4, 1976.
8. Jim Murray, syndicated column, *Modesto (CA) Bee*, October 19, 1976.

17. Rose to Third

1. Joe Posnanski, "The Hit King's Lament," *Cincinnati*, July 2009, 71.
2. Earl Lawson, "Howsam Sees Safety in Numbers at Hot Sack," *Sporting News*, December 14, 1974, 54.
3. Earl Lawson, "Hot Corner Will Be Crowded When Reds Open Camp," *Sporting News*, January 4, 1975, 43.
4. Earl Lawson, "Sparky to Give Reds Refresher in Fundamentals," *Sporting News*, February 8, 1975, 36.
5. Joe Posnanski, *The Machine: A Hot Team, a Legendary Season, and a Heart-Stopping World Series; The Story of the 1975 Cincinnati Reds* (New York: Harper-Collins, 2009), 26–28.
6. Posnanski, *The Machine*, 75, 89.
7. Greg Rhodes and John Erardi, *Big Red Dynasty: How Bob Howsam and Sparky Anderson Built the Big Red Machine* (Cincinnati: Road West Publishing, 1997).
8. United Press International, "Pete Rose Hot at Third Base," July 20, 1975.
9. United Press International, "Pete Rose Hot at Third Base."
10. United Press International, "Pete Rose Hot at Third Base."
11. William A. Cook, *Pete Rose: Baseball's All-Time Hit King* (Jefferson NC: McFarland, 2004), 46–47.

18. Clay Carroll

1. Earl Lawson, "Reds Have Hawk Who's Sudden Death to Hitters," *Sporting News*, June 24, 1972, 11.
2. Ritter Collett, *The Men of the Machine* (Dayton OH: Landfall Press, 1977), 243.
3. Clay Carroll, as told to George Vass, "The Game I'll Never Forget," *Baseball Digest*, June 1981, 69.
4. John W. Chace, "Baseball Gave Clay Carroll His Ticket to a Better Life," *Tuscaloosa (AL) News*, September 17, 1972, 13.
5. Frank Haraway, "Country Boy Carroll Tabbed by Tepee as $1,000 Hill Bargain," *Sporting News*, May 25, 1963, 27.
6. Carroll, "Game I'll Never Forget," 69.
7. Haraway, "Country Boy Carroll Tabbed," 27.
8. Haraway, "Country Boy Carroll Tabbed," 27.
9. Wayne Minshew, "Country Boy Carroll Turns Out to Be City Slicker on Tepee Hill," *Sporting News*, September 17, 1966, 7.
10. Minshew, "Country Boy Carroll Turns Out to Be City Slicker," 7.
11. Wayne Minshew, "Carroll Pedals Bike and Sheds Excess Pounds," *Sporting News*, November 25, 1967, 37.
12. "Carroll, Who Balked at Trip to Minors, Returns, Wins," *Sporting News*, August 19, 1967, 19.
13. Earl Lawson, "With Clay in Bullpen, Reds Sigh with Relief," *Sporting News*, September 7, 1968, 5.
14. Earl Lawson, "A Story-Book Clout by Carroll," *Sporting News*, June 14, 1969, 8.
15. Earl Lawson, "Hitters Just Putty in Hands of Clay, Reds' Rescue Ace," *Sporting News*, August 1, 1970, 19.
16. Lawson, "Reds Have Hawk."

19. Merv Rettenmund

1. Brian Hiro, "Hitters Warming Up to Rettenmund's Advice," *North County Times* (Escondido CA), June 24, 2006.
2. U.S. Census, via Ancestry.com and RootsWeb.com, accessed December 16, 2008.
3. Merv Rettenmund, interview with author, January 12, 2009.
4. Robert Markus, "Rettenmund So Wrong, He's Right," *Chicago Tribune*, October 10, 1971.
5. Rettenmund, interview.
6. Dan Nilsen, "1961 Buick Colts Baseball Team," *Flint (MI) Journal*, http://blog.mlive.com/flintjournal/sports/2007/11/1961_buick_colts_baseball_team.html, accessed December 23, 2008.

7. Rettenmund, interview; John Ginter, "Baseball at Ball State," Ball State University Alumni Association, http://bsu.edu/alumni/march2003/sportsfeature/, accessed December 9, 2008.

8. Ed Rumill, "Rookie Balks at No. 4 Idea," *Christian Science Monitor*, March 31, 1969; Doug Brown, "Orioles Find a Place for Rookie Merv's Mighty Bat," *Sporting News*, September 28, 1968, 11.

9. Brown, "Orioles Find a Place."

10. Rettenmund, interview; Shaun O'Neill, "Padres Inside Pitch," *North County Times* (Escondido CA), April 27, 1997.

11. "Bunker, Rookie Help Orioles Sweep A's," *Chicago Tribune*, August 28, 1968; "Orioles Beat A's 5–3 in First Game," *Hartford (CT) Courant*, August 28, 1968.

12. Rettenmund, interview.

13. Rettenmund, interview.

14. Rettenmund, interview.

15. Ron Fimrite, "Well, He's That Kind of Guy," *Sports Illustrated*, October 4, 1971.

16. Doug Brown, "Birds' Slump-Ridden Merv Making Mark as Prankster," *Sporting News*, August 18, 1973.

17. Mark Heisler, "Homecoming for the Anaheim Chapter of the Oriole Alumni," *Los Angeles Times*, September 28, 1979; Rettenmund, interview.

18. Rettenmund, interview.

19. Phil Collier, "Rettenmund Chants a Hymn of Thanks for Padre Trade," *Sporting News*, June 5, 1976, 11; Rettenmund, interview.

20. Rettenmund, interview; David Porter and Joe Naiman, *The San Diego Padres Encyclopedia* (Champaign IL: Sports Publishing, 2002), 49.

21. Rettenmund, interview.

22. Rettenmund, interview.

23. Ross Newhan, "Angels Get 'Tough' with Blue Jays," *Los Angeles Times*, June 9, 1982.

24. Rettenmund, interview.

25. Rettenmund, interview.

26. Chris Jenkins, "An Eye on the Ball," *Baseball Digest*, September 2002.

27. Rettenmund, interview.

28. Shaun O'Neill, "Rettenmund Decides to Head South," *North County Times* (Escondido CA), November 9, 1999; Rettenmund, interview.

29. Rettenmund, interview.

30. Rettenmund, interview.

31. Rettenmund, interview.

21. Johnny Bench

1. Roy Blount Jr., "The Big Zinger from Binger," *Sports Illustrated*, March 31, 1969.

2. Johnny Bench and William Brashler, *Catch You Later* (New York: Harper and Row, 1979), 1–16.

3. Bench and Brashler, *Catch You Later*, 20.

4. Bench and Brashler, *Catch You Later*, 26.

5. *Sports Illustrated*, March 11, 1968.

6. Blount, "Big Zinger from Binger."

7. Blount, "Big Zinger from Binger."

8. Al Stump, "Johnny Bench Is Another . . . ," *Sport*, January 1969, 52.

9. Stump, "Johnny Bench Is Another," 68.

10. Bench and Brashler, *Catch You Later*, 61.

11. "There'll Be No Second Season: Johnny and Vicki Bench Find Love Is a Many-Splintered Thing," *People*, March 29, 1976.

12. Bench and Brashler, *Catch You Later*, 203.

13. "Johnny Bench Talks Bryce Harper, the Decision Not to Catch and Replacement Hips," *USA Today*, July 9, 2010.

22. Pat Darcy

1. John Erardi, "Catching Up with Pat Darcy," Cincinnati.com, November 3, 2011, http://news.cincinnati.com/article/20111103/COL19/311030150/Catching-up-Pat-Darcy.

2. Corky Simpson, " Ex-Big Red Machine Hurler Darcy Makes Pitch for Mayor," TucsonCitizen.com, June 30, 1999, http://tucsoncitizen.com/morgue2/1999/06/30/136409-simpson-column/.

3. All Minor League statistics have been verified on Baseball-Reference.com (www.baseball-reference.com). All Major League statistics have been verified on Baseball-Reference.com and Retrosheet.org (www.retrosheet.org).

4. *Sporting News*, September 1, 1973, 30.

5. John Ring, "Pat Darcy and the Reds 1975 World Series," Reds Report, http://www.theredsreport.com/2011/01/14/pat-darcy-and-the-reds-1975-world-series/ (site discontinued), accessed January 14, 2011.

6. Ring, "Pat Darcy and the Reds."

7. Ring, "Pat Darcy and the Reds."

8. *Sporting News*, April 26, 1975, 10.

9. Norm Clark, "Darcy Goes the Distance in Reds Win," Associated Press, *Kentucky New Era* (Hopkinsville KY), July 22, 1975, 99.

10. *Sporting News*, October 25, 1975, 3.

11. Ron Berler, "The Reds on the Road," *Cincinnati*, July 1976, 26.

12. *Sporting News*, August, 23, 1975, 13.

13. Erardi, "Catching Up with Pat Darcy."

14. Erardi, "Catching Up with Pat Darcy."

15. Norm Clark, "Pete Rose Calls Game Greatest He Ever Saw," Associated Press, *Lewiston (ME) Evening Journal*, October 22, 1975, 12.

16. Erardi, "Catching Up with Pat Darcy."

17. *Sporting News*, July 3, 1976, 13.

18. *Sporting News*, September 10, 1977, 41.

19. Ring, "Pat Darcy and the Reds."

20. David Haugh, "The Wrong End of Fame," *Baseball Digest*, December 2006, 55.

23. Dan Driessen

1. Tony Ferulla, "Driessen Confident Reds Can Win," *Charleston (SC) News and Courier*, July 15, 1978, 40.

2. Ferulla, "Driessen Confident."

3. Bob Speak, "The Quiet Star: Dan Driessen's Express Ride to the Majors Had a Humble Beginning in Hilton Head," TheState.com, July 20, 2004.

4. Speak, "Quiet Star."

5. Bob Hertzel, "The Bargain Bonus Boys," *Baseball Digest*, June 1974, 42.

6. All Minor League statistics have been verified on Baseball-Reference.com (www.baseball-reference.com).

7. Hertzel, "Bargain Bonus Boys," 43.

8. *Sporting News*, June 30, 1973, 17.

9. William C. Smith, "Dan Driessen: Best Young Hitter in the N.L." *Baseball Digest*, November 1973, 46.

10. *Sporting News*, November 11, 1972, 44.

11. *Sporting News*, June 23, 1973, 38.

12. William Leggett, "Reds' Rookie Is a Tough Cookie." *Sports Illustrated*, September 27, 1973.

13. All Major League statistics have been verified on Baseball-Reference.com (www.baseball-reference.com) and Retrosheet.org (www.retrosheet.org).

14. Speak, "Quiet Star."

15. *Sporting News*, June 30, 1973, 17.

16. *Sporting News*, October 6, 1973, 9.

17. Leggett, "Reds' Rookie Is a Tough Cookie."

18. Smith, "Dan Driessen," 46.

19. *Sporting News*, April 26, 1975, 10.

20. *Sporting News*, May 31, 1975, 9.

21. *Sporting News*, July 24, 1976, 10.

22. *Sporting News*, August 25, 1976, 25.

23. *Sporting News*, October 30, 1976, 10.

24. *Sporting News*, January 15, 1977, 53.

25. *Sporting News*, November 5, 1977, 4.

26. Associated Press, "Will Driessen Be Best Hitter?" *Florence (SC) Morning News*, March 3, 1977, 17.

27. *Sporting News*, August 29, 1981, 3.

28. *Sporting News*, September 19, 1981, 16.

29. *Sporting News*, October 18, 1982, 34.

30. *Sporting News*, August 6, 1984, 21.

31. Paul Meyer, "Cards' Durable Dan Driessen Having One Long Last Laugh," *Pittsburgh Post-Gazette*, October 9, 1987, 11

32. Meyer, "Cards' Durable Dan Driessen."

33. *Sporting News*, September 29, 1987.

34. Ben Walker, "Driessen Has Major Role in Cards' Win," *Bowling Green (KY) Daily News*, October 7, 1987, 11.

35. Associated Press, "Driessen Finally Eludes Post-Season Woes," *Milwaukee Journal*, October 7, 1987, 76.

36. Mark Sheldon, "Trio Elected to Reds Hall of Fame," Reds.com, November 28, 2011.

37. Ferulla, "Driessen Confident," 40.

24. César Gerónimo

1. Ritter Collett, *Men of the Machine: An Inside Look at Baseball's Team of the 1970s* (Dayton OH: Landfall Press, 1977), 210.

2. See "Cesar Geronimo," *SABR Encyclopedia of Baseball*, http://sabrpedia.org/w/index.php?title=Cesar_Geronimo(2980)&printable=yes; "Cesar Geronimo," BaseballLibrary.com, http://www.baseballlibrary.com/ballplayers/player.php?name=Cesar_Geronimo_1948&page=chronology; "César Gerónimo," Baseball-Reference.com, http://www.baseball-reference.com/players/g/geronce01.shtml; "1967 Johnson City Yankees," Baseball-Reference.com, http://www.baseball-reference.com/minors/team.cgi?id=e61345f5; "1968 Fort Lauderdale Yankees," Baseball-Reference.com,

http://www.baseball-reference.com/minors/team.cgi?id=cd503102.

3. Jim Ogle, "Inside Pitch: Light Hitting Geronimo Provided Yank Surprises," April 10, 1971, in César Gerónimo file, National Baseball Hall of Fame Library, Cooperstown NY; Stan Isle, "Hurlers Are Hottest Items in Majors' Draft," *Sporting News*, December 14, 1968, 33–34.

4. *Sporting News*, March 27, 1971, 39–40.

5. John Wilson, "Astros Toughen 6 Arms on Florida Pad," *Sporting News*, November 15, 1969, 53; "Astros Beat War Drums for Geronimo," *Sporting News*, March 27, 1971, 39–40; "Dodgers Learn Geronimo Boasts Rifle for an Arm," *Sporting News*, April 17, 1971, 8; "Farmhands Fuel Strongest Astro Drive of Season," *Sporting News*, October 2, 1971, 22.

6. Earl Lawson, "Menke Eager to Show Reds Made Wise Deal," *Sporting News*, February 12, 1972, 39; "Reds to Test Speedy Geronimo's Bat," *Sporting News*, April 1, 1972.

7. Earl Lawson, "Sure Hands Cesar Wins Cincy Salute," *Sporting News*, April 15, 1972, 21, 28.

8. Mark Purdy, "Mild Mannered Cesar Often Misunderstood during 9 Years as Red," *Cincinnati Enquirer*, January 18, 1981, in César Gerónimo file, National Baseball Hall of Fame Library, Cooperstown NY.

9. Robert L. Burnes, "Baseball's Lasting Charm Is Its Unpredictability," *St. Louis Globe Democrat*, July 9, 1980; Earl Lawson, "Griffey, Blue-Streak Rookie, Makes Reds Think of Rose," *Sporting News*, March 10, 1973, 36; "Reds Snoozing Swingers Baffle Pilot Sparky," *Sporting News*, June 16, 1973, 11; "Foster's Hot Bat Lights Torch in Red Garden," *Sporting News*, April 13, 1974, 9; "Geronimo! Cesar Recovers, Adds Fire to Reds," *Sporting News*, June 22, 1974, 7; "Geronimo Surprises Reds with Torrid Swatting Pace," *Sporting News*, August 17, 1974, 29; "Reds Nip at Dodgers' Heels with Six-Game Win Spree," *Sporting News*, June 14, 1975, 16; "Reds Rule N.L.'s Top Defensive Unit—Concepcion, Bench, Geronimo, Morgan" *Sporting News*, November 29, 1975, 38; Lowell Reidenbaugh, "Late-Inning Red Lightning Shocks Hunter and Yanks," *Sporting News*, October 30, 1976, 8; "Hot Dispute Marks Vital Play in Reds' Triumph," *Sporting News*, November 1, 1975, 7.

10. Earl Lawson, "'No Way We'll Trade Geronimo,' Howsam Insists," *Sporting News*, October 22, 1977, 26;

"Confident Geronimo Eager to Atone for 1978 Slump," *Sporting News*, March 31, 1979, 46; Mike Fish, "Royals Praise Cesar's Glove," *Sporting News*, February 7, 1981, 38. Mike McKenzie, "Geronimo a Terror as Fill-In for Royals," *Sporting News*, May 17, 1982, 33; Ron Fimrite, "The Reds Are Singing the Blues," *Sports Illustrated*, August 22, 1977, http://sportsillustrated.cnn.com/vault/article/magazine/MAG1092724/index.htm.;E. M. Swift, "Say Hi to the Little Red Machine," *Sports Illustrated*, September 3, 1979, http://sportsillustrated.cnn.com/vault/article/magazine/MAG1095308/index.htm; "Cesar Geronimo," SABR *Encyclopedia of Baseball*; "Cesar Geronimo," BaseballLibrary.com; "César Gerónimo," Baseball-Reference.com.

11. César Gerónimo pages, Cincinnati Reds Media Guide, 1980, 36, 37.

12. "The Champs of '75," *Sports Illustrated*, July 31, 2000; Alan M. Klein, *Sugarball: The American Game, the Dominican Dream* (New Haven CT: Yale University Press, 1991), 41, 55; Mark Kurlansky, *The Eastern Stars: How Baseball Changed the Dominican Town of San Pedro de Macoris* (New York: Riverhead Books, 2010), 197. For more information on the Dominican Republic Sports and Education Academy (DRSEA), visit the organization's website at www.drsea.org. There you can also download copies of their publication DRSEA *Informer*. For more information on the Hiroshima Toyo Carp, see "Hiroshima Toyo Carp," Bob Bavasi's Guide to Japanese Baseball, www.japanball.com/carp.htm.

13. "Cesar Geronimo," Cincinnati Reds Hall of Fame and Museum, Member Directory, http://mlb.mlb.com/cin/hof/hof/directory.jsp?hof_id=114723.

25. John Vukovich

1. Paul Hagen, "He Changed People's Lives," *Philadelphia Daily News*, March 9, 2007.

2. Ken Mandel, "Vukovich Passes Away at 59," Phillies.com, March 8, 2007.

3. Larry Whiteside, "Spear-Carrier Vukovich Becomes Brewer Kingpin," *Sporting News*, May 5, 1973.

4. Whiteside, "Spear-Carrier Vukovich."

5. Earl Lawson, "Sparky to Give Reds Refresher in Fundamentals," *Sporting News*, February 8, 1975.

6. Joe Posnanski, *The Machine: A Hot Team, a Legendary Season, and a Heart-Stopping World Series; The*

Story of the 1975 Cincinnati Reds (New York: William Morrow, 2009), 72–78.

7. Posnanski, *The Machine.*

8. Mandel, "Vukovich Passes Away."

9. John W. Smith, "Vukovich with Reading Again," *Reading (PA) Eagle*, April 8, 1977.

10. William Kashatus, *Almost a Dynasty* (Philadelphia: University of Pennsylvania Press, 2008), 184.

11. Hal Bodley, "Spare-Part Vukovich Plugs Phil Defense," *Sporting News*, July 26, 1980.

12. Frank Dolson, "Vukovich Set to Join Phils," *Philadelphia Inquirer*, November 3, 1987.

13. Jim Salisbury, "Vukovich Was a Man of Lasting Friendships," *Philadelphia Inquirer*, March 9, 2007.

14. Doug Glanville, "A Tribute to 'Vuk,'" Phillies.com, March 15, 2007.

15. Hagen, "He Changed People's Lives."

16. Todd Zolecki, "Loyal Soldier Out of Uniform," *Philadelphia Inquirer*, February 28, 2005.

17. Paul Hagen, "Major League Turnout to Pay Final Respects," *Philadelphia Daily News*, March 14, 2007.

18. Hagen, "He Changed People's Lives."

27. George Foster

1. Thomas Boswell, column, *Washington Post*, August 18, 1976.

2. *Cincinnati Reds Yearbook*, 1973, 34.

3. Malka Drucker with George Foster, *The George Foster Story* (New York: Holiday House, 1979), 55–56.

4. Drucker with Foster, *George Foster Story*, 58.

5. Drucker with Foster, *George Foster Story*, 61.

6. Drucker with Foster, *George Foster Story*, 75.

7. Drucker with Foster, *George Foster Story*, 87–88.

8. Drucker with Foster, *George Foster Story*, 94.

9. Gannett Westchester-Rockland (NY) Newspapers, August 7, 1986.

10. Joseph Durso, "Mets to Drop Foster amid Racial Controversy," *New York Times*, August 7, 1986.

11. Drucker with Foster, *George Foster Story*, 72–73.

28. Terry Crowley

The epigraph is from Jim Henneman, "Crowley Fattens Up as Orioles Cinch In Pinch," *Sporting News*, August 5, 1978, 13.

1. Terry Crowley, interview with author, May 17, 2008.

2. Crowley, interview.

3. Crowley, interview.

4. Crowley, interview.

5. Doug Brown, "Orioles Chirp-Chirp over Fledgling Flyhawk Baylor," *Sporting News*, November 30, 1968.

6. Crowley, interview.

7. Louis Berney, *Tales from the Orioles Dugout* (Champaign IL: Sports Publishing, 2004), 102.

8. Crowley, interview.

9. Crowley, interview.

10. Phil Jackman, "Crowley in Boxing Form for O's Job," *Sporting News*, March 11, 1972, 30.

11. Berney, *Tales from the Orioles Dugout*, 104.

12. Lou Hatter, "Baylor, Grich, Crowley: Orioles Jewels," *Sporting News*, June 24, 1972, 3.

13. "Crowley's Confident," *Sporting News*, March 30, 1974, 55.

14. Crowley, interview.

15. "Crowley Doesn't Belong in International League," *Sporting News*, August 13, 1977, 33.

16. "Crowley Doesn't Belong," 33.

17. "Crowley Doesn't Belong," 33.

18. Crowley, interview.

19. Ken Nigro, "Crowley Gives O's Punch in a Pinch," *Sporting News*, June 21, 1980, 35.

20. Ken Nigro, "'Deep Depth' Cited for Oriole Sky Course," *Sporting News*, July 21, 1979, 12.

21. Henneman, "Crowley Fattens Up," 13.

22. Crowley, interview.

23. Ken Nigro, "Pinch-Hitter Deluxe Crowley Is a Victim of His Own Talent," *Sporting News*, April 4, 1981, 50.

24. Nigro, "Pinch-Hitter Deluxe Crowley."

25. Jim Henneman, "Crowley Shocked by Orioles Release," *Sporting News*, April 18, 1983, 24.

26. Crowley, interview.

27. Crowley, interview.

28. "Crowley Takes Over as Batting Coach," *Sporting News*, November 26, 1990, 41.

29. Crowley, interview.

30. Crowley, interview.

29. Pedro Borbon

1. John Wiebusch, "What a Miracle This Is! Dead Angels Walk Again," *Sporting News*, September 13, 1969, 19; "Tatum Angels' Bullpen King," *Sporting News*, No-

vember 15, 1969, 48; "Angels Get Sock in Alex Johnson," *Sporting News*, December 6, 1969, 56; Earl Lawson, "Shoppers and Swappers Check Maloney Showcase," *Sporting News*, December 13, 1969, 38; "83 Percent Red Turnover in 3 Year Howsam Reign," *Sporting News*, January 24, 1970, 41.

2. John Wiebusch, "Kuhn Fines Two for 'Inexcusable Conduct' in D.R.," *Sporting News*, February 21, 1970, 47.

3. Earl Lawson, "Reds Thank Angels as McGlothlin Flies High," *Sporting News*, June 6, 1970, 15; "Pilot Sparky Rates Dodgers No. 1 Threat to His Reds," *Sporting News*, April 17, 1971, 17; "Deals of the Week," *Sporting News*, September 25, 1971, 12; Miguel Frau, "Licey Romps to Caribbean Championship," *Sporting News*, February 27, 1971, 31; "D.R. Data," *Sporting News*, December 11, 1971, 55.

4. Earl Lawson, "Reds Forecast 150 Runs for Galloping Morgan," *Sporting News*, July 1, 1972, 5.

5. Earl Lawson, "Reds Copy A's Plan with Fist Fight," *Sporting News*, August 16, 1975, 40; Earl Lawson, "Caught on the Fly" *Sporting News*, December 31, 1977, 62; Jeff Meron, "Put Up Your Dukes," ESPN Page 2, http://espn.go.com/page2/s/list/basebrawl.html; "Pedro Borbon," Cincinnati Reds Hall of Fame and Museum, Member Directory, http://mlb.mlb.com/cin/hof/hof/directory.jsp?hof_id=111227.

6. Earl Lawson, "Only One Word for Reds' Hurlers—Horrible," *Sporting News*, July 16, 1977, 5; "Don't Blame Pitching Staff for Reds' Pratfall," *Sporting News*, August 27, 1977, 17; Nick Peters, "Swap Shocks Giants' Players," *Sporting News*, July 14, 1979, 18; "Curtis Sizzles as Giant Fireman," *Sporting News*, July 21, 1979, 18; "Giants' Trouble Spots Remain Unchanged," *Sporting News*, March 8, 1980, 30; Rick Hummel, "Redbirds Turn to Greybeards to Liven Up Their Bullpen," *Sporting News*, May 17, 1980, 35; Salo Otero, "Ex-Major Leaguers Hold On in Mexico," *Sporting News*, May 9, 1981, 41.

7. Stacy Y. China, "After Up and Down Times, Bronx's Borbon Jr. Up Again," *Newsday*, October 26, 1995, A74; Karen Crouse, "Adversity Makes Borbon Better," *Daily News*, 1999, accessed through http://www.thefree library.com, July 29, 2011.

8. "Pedro Borbon Dead at 65," *Cincinnati News*, June 4, 2012.

30. Dave Concepción

1. George Vass, "The Game I'll Never Forget," *Baseball Digest*, December 1987, 86.

2. Earl Lawson, "Reds' Phenom Bears Out Latin Raves," *Sporting News*, March 28, 1970, 11.

3. Lawson, "Reds' Phenom."

4. Earl Lawson, "McCrae-Carbo Bat Platoon Is Cincy's Assault Force," *Sporting News*, May 23, 1970, 7.

5. Si Burick, "The Making of Dave Concepcion," *Baseball Digest*, August 1974, 40–42.

6. Jim Brosnan, "Dave Concepcion: Best in the Business," *Boys' Life*, September 1975, 20–23.

7. Dick Peebles, "Dave Concepcion: Best All-Around Shortstop in the Majors," *Baseball Digest*, December 1979, 50–51.

8. Earl Lawson, "Concepcion Almost Immaculate at Shortstop." *Sporting News*, April 26, 1975, 3.

9. Doug Feldmann, *The 1976 Cincinnati Reds: Last Hurrah for the Big Red Machine* (Jefferson NC: McFarland, 2009), 41.

10. Ivan Maisel, "An All-Star Comes to Light," *Sports Illustrated*, July 25, 1982, 46.

11. Maisel, "All-Star Comes to Light," 46.

12. Kevin Kelly, "No Shorting Concepcion on This Night," *Cincinnati Enquirer*, August 26, 2007.

13. Tim Wendel, *The New Face of Baseball* (New York: Harper Collins, 2003), 76.

31. Ed Armbrister

1. Sparky Anderson, telephone interview with author, September 21, 1999.

2. Funeral announcement, *Nassau (Bahamas) Guardian*, June 18, 2009. This story printed Ed Sr.'s middle name as Rosander, though baseball references show it as Rosanda for Ed Jr. Further family information, including the name of Ed's mother and whether he had other siblings, is available as of the time of this writing.

3. Sheldon Longley, "Rodgers Gets a Sporting Salute!" *Nassau (Bahamas) Guardian*, December 21, 2004.

4. Denez Jones, "A Final Tribute Is Paid to Local Baseball Icon," *Nassau (Bahamas) Guardian*, October 26, 2006, C1.

5. Oswald Brown, "BBF Has Saved Baseball in the Bahamas," *Freeport (Bahamas) News*, October 19, 2007.

6. The *Williamsport (PA) Sun-Gazette*, October 6,

1973, stated that Armbrister played Little League ball, which conflicts with his own description of his childhood.

7. Les Koelling, "'Throw-in' Armbrister Bidding for Batting Crown with Indy," *Sporting News*, August 12, 1972.

8. Mike Dyer, *Getting into Pro Baseball* (New York: Franklin Watts, 1979), 6.

9. Barbara Walkin, "Ed Armbrister—A Bahamian Hero," *Freeport (Bahamas) News*, June 8, 2006.

10. Koelling, "'Throw-in' Armbrister Bidding for Batting Crown,"

11. "Scouting Reports on 1970 Major League Rookies," *Baseball Digest*, March 1970, 67.

12. "Official Scouting Reports on 1969 Major League Rookies," *Baseball Digest*, March 1969, 24.

13. "Staying on Top," *Cincinnati*, October 1976, 40.

14. Koelling, "'Throw-in' Armbrister Bidding for Batting Crown."

15. Brian Herman, "Here and There," *Valley Independent* (Monessen PA), May 1, 1973, 10.

16. One of Armbrister's cousins is Colyn "Mo" Grant, drummer for the Baha Men, who gained fame for the ballpark anthem "Who Let the Dogs Out?" See Lance Gould, "'Dogs' Anthem Is the Cat's Meow," *New York Daily News*, October 25, 2000.

17. Tom Adelman, *The Long Ball: The Summer of '75—Spaceman, Catfish, Charlie Hustle, and the Greatest World Series Ever Played* (Boston: Back Bay Books, 2004), 102.

18. Associated Press, September 6, 1973.

19. Associated Press, "Double Shockn," October 8, 1975.

20. United Press International, "Armbrister: 'There Was No Way I Was Trying to Block Him," October 15, 1975.

21. Ira Winderman, "Recalling the Greatest World Series Ever: Boston, Cincinnati's Classic 1975 Matchup," *South Florida Sun-Sentinel*, October 15, 1985.

22. United Press International, "Armbrister: 'There Was No Way."

23. Roger Angell, *Five Seasons: A Baseball Companion* (New York: Simon and Schuster, 1977), 300. This quote has since appeared in many anthologies.

24. Glenn Stout and Richard A. Johnson, *Red Sox Century* (New York: Houghton Mifflin Harcourt, 2004), 360.

25. Bill Gilbert, *The Seasons* (New York: Citadel Press, 2004), 203.

26. Angell, *Five Seasons*, 299; Doug Hornig, *The Boys of October* (New York: McGraw-Hill, 2003), 111.

27. Norm Clarke, "Of Rabbit's Feet and Witch Doctors," Associated Press, August 13, 1976.

28. *Sporting News*, May 27, 1978, 39.

29. Winderman, "Recalling the Greatest World Series Ever."

30. John Erardi, "Big Red Machine Reassembled," *Cincinnati Enquirer*, November 23, 1996.

31. Walkin, "Ed Armbrister—A Bahamian Hero." Names of family members are unavailable.

32. Eric Rose, "Sports Minister Lauds Hall of Fame Inductees," *Bahamas Post*, October 29, 2008.

33. Brown, "BBF Has Saved Baseball."

34. Fred Sturrup, "Victory over Cuba A Big Boost for Local Baseball Programme," *Bahama Journal*, July 27, 2005.

35. Gerrino Saunders, "Wall of Fame Fanfare," *Bahama Journal*, March 19, 2007.

36. Rick McCrabb, "'Big Red Machine' Players Batting Memories Around," *Dayton (OH) Daily News*, November 22, 2008.

37. Anderson, interview; Alex Grammas, telephone interview with author, October 1999.

National Baseball Congress, *Official Baseball Annual*, 1965

Treto Cisneros, Pedro, ed. *Enciclopedia del béisbol mexicano*. Mexico City: Revistas Deportivas, 1998.

This Is Baseball Bahamas. http://www.baseballbahamas .net.

Anderson, Sparky. Telephone interview with author. September 21, 1999.

Grammas, Alex. Telephone interview with author. October 1999.

Kemp, Craig (president, Bahamas Baseball Federation). Several e-mails with author, 1999.

33. Joe Morgan

1. Joe Morgan and David Falkner, *Joe Morgan: A Life in Baseball* (New York: W. W. Norton, 1993), 52–53.

2. Walker, along with his brother Dixie, had been among the leaders of the attempted boycott of Jackie Robinson back in 1947.

3. Joe Posnanski, *The Machine: A Hot Team, a Legendary Season, and a Heart-Stopping World Series; The Story of the 1975 Cincinnati Reds* (New York: William Morrow, 2009), 42.

4. Posnanski, *The Machine*, 42, 43.

5. Morgan and Falkner, *Joe Morgan*, 142.

6. Morgan and Falkner, *Joe Morgan*, 156–58.

7. Morgan and Falkner, *Joe Morgan*, 162.

8. Posnanski, *The Machine*, 84.

9. Posnanski, *The Machine*, 84.

10. Posnanski, *The Machine*, 132.

11. Posnanski, *The Machine*, 190.

12. Morgan and Falkner, *Joe Morgan*, 98–99.

34. Doug Flynn

1. The author would like to express his gratitude to Doug Flynn, who was interviewed on June 6, 2012. Unless otherwise cited, all quotations originate from this interview.

2. "Baseball in Black and White. The Lexington Hustlers," *Kentucky Life*, Kentucky Educational Television, http://www.ket.org/kentuckylife/900s/kylife907.html.

3. Don Collins, "With Help from Parents Doug Flynn Makes the Major Leagues," *Bowling Green (KY) Daily News*, August 4, 1976, 51.

4. All Minor League statistics have been verified on Baseball-Reference.com (www.baseball-reference.com); all Major League statistics have been verified on Baseball-Reference.com and Retrosheet.org (www.retrosheet.org).

5. *Sporting News*, April 19, 1975, 12.

6. *Sporting News*, November 1, 1975, 22.

7. *Sporting News*, July 17, 1976, 15.

8. *Sporting News*, October 23, 1976, 3.

9. *Sporting News*, December 25, 1976, 50.

10. *Sporting News*, April 8, 1978, 20.

11. *Sporting News*, May 13, 1978, 18.

12. *Sporting News*, July 15, 1978, 24.

13. *Sporting News*, October 4, 1980, 3.

14. *Sporting News*, January 31, 1981, 46.

15. *Sporting News*, May 23, 1981, 22.

16. *Sporting News*, August 2, 1982, 23.

17. United Press International, "Expos Could Be in Like Flynn with Doug," *Pittsburgh Press*, August 14, 1982, 4.

35. Rawly Eastwick

1. Paul Dickson, *The Dickson Baseball Dictionary* (New York: Facts on File, 1989), 291.

2. *New York Times*, October 19, 1975.

3. *New York Times*, October 19, 1975.

4. Philadelphia Phillies Media Guide, 1980.

5. *Portsmouth (OH) Times*, October 18, 1975.

6. *Portsmouth (OH) Times*, October 18, 1975.

7. Joe Posnanski, *The Machine: A Hot Team, a Legendary Season, and a Heart-Stopping World Series; The Story of the 1975 Cincinnati Reds* (New York: William Morrow, 2009), 115.

8. *Anchorage (AK) Daily News*, July 25, 1975.

9. Bob Hertzel, *The Big Red Machine* (Englewood Cliffs NJ: Prentice-Hall, 1976), 101.

10. Mark Frost, *Game Six: Cincinnati, Boston, and the 1975 World Series: The Triumph of America's Pastime* (New York: Hyperion, 2009), 231.

11. *Sports Illustrated*, November 3, 1975.

12. Hertzel, *Big Red Machine*, 102.

13. *Sporting News*, October 16, 1976.

14. Hertzel, *Big Red Machine*, 100.

15. Posnanski, *The Machine*, 166.

16. Tim Wendell, *High Heat* (Boston: Da Capo Press, 2010), 53.

17. Darryl Smith and Lee May, *Making the Big Red Machine: Bob Howsam and the Cincinnati Reds of the 1970s* (Jefferson NC: McFarland, 2009), 209.

18. Frost, *Game Six*, 242.

19. Hertzel, *Big Red Machine*, 21.

20. *Sporting News*, January 24, 1976.

21. Dave Zeman and David Nemec, *The Baseball Rookies Encyclopedia* (Dulles VA: Potomac, 2004).

22. *Miami News*, January 25, 1977.

23. Smith and May, *Making the Big Red Machine*, 264.

24. *Deseret News* (Salt Lake City), August 1, 1977.

25. *Sporting News*, May 20, 1978.

26. Richard Bradley, *The Greatest Game* (New York: Free Press, 2009), 139.

27. *Sporting News*, March 31, 1979.

28. William C. Kashatus, *Almost a Dynasty: The Rise and Fall of the 1980 Phillies* (Philadelphia: University of Pennsylvania Press, 2008), 166.

36. Gary Nolan

1. Bob Hertzel, *The Big Red Machine* (Englewood Cliffs NJ: Prentice Hall, 1976), 114.
2. Joe Posnanski, *The Machine: A Hot Team, a Legendary Season, and a Heart-Stopping World Series; The Story of the 1975 Cincinnati Reds* (New York: William Morrow, 2009), 35.
3. Hertzel, *Big Red Machine*, 118.
4. Hertzel, *Big Red Machine*, 118.
5. Hertzel, *Big Red Machine*, 118.
6. John Erardi, "Nolan Buries His Baseball Past," *Cincinnati Enquirer*, August 13, 1986.
7. Posnanski, *The Machine*, 40.
8. Ritter Collett, *Men of the Machine* (Dayton OH: Landfall Press, 1977), 108.
9. Posnanski, *The Machine*, 37.
10. Posnanski, *The Machine*, 214.
11. Hal McCoy, *The Relentless Reds* (Louisville KY: PressCo., 1976), 181.
12. Erardi, "Nolan Buries His Baseball Past."
13. Erardi, "Nolan Buries His Baseball Past."
14. Erardi, "Nolan Buries His Baseball Past."

Miller, Richard D. "Gary Lynn Nolan." In *Biographical Dictionary of American Sports: Baseball*, edited by David L. Porter, 1127–28. Westport CT: Greenwood Press, 2000.

37. Darrel Chaney

1. Darrel Chaney, interview with author, August 2012.
2. Chaney, interview.
3. Chaney, interview.
4. Earl Lawson, "Draft Blows Fog over Cardenas' Future," *Sporting News*, November 2, 1968, 34.
5. Chaney, interview.
6. Chaney, interview.
7. Chaney, interview.
8. Earl Lawson, "'Forget Homers,' Chaney Tells Himself," *Sporting News*, February 14, 1970, 40.
9. Chaney, interview.
10. Chaney, interview.
11. Earl Lawson, "Who's Playing Shortstop? Reds Win with Juggle Act," *Sporting News*, January 20, 1973, 35.
12. Earl Lawson, "Cincy's Chaney Drenched in Sunny Hawaii," *Sporting News*, December 29, 1973.

13. Chaney, interview.
14. Chaney, interview.
15. Chaney, interview.
16. Chaney, interview.
17. Chaney, interview.
18. Thomas Lake, "Thumbing His Way Back Home," *Sports Illustrated*, July 26, 2010.
19. Chaney, interview.
20. Chaney, interview.
21. Chaney, interview.
22. Chaney, interview.

39. Tony Pérez

Perez, Tony, and George Vass. "The Game I'll Never Forget." *Baseball Digest*, August 1974.

"Atanasio 'Tony' Pérez Regal." Latino Legends in Sports. http://latinosportslegends.com/tonyperez .htm. Accessed February 21, 2011.

40. Jack Billingham

1. Jack Billingham, interview with author, February 21, 2011.
2. Billingham, interview.
3. *Sporting News*, August 24, 1968.
4. Billingham, interview.
5. Billingham, interview.
6. Billingham, interview.
7. "Billingham Saves the Day," *Los Angeles Times*, April 22, 1968.
8. "Dodgers' Billingham Takes Over as Bullpen Ace: Inherits Mantle of Perranoski and Regan," *Chicago Tribune*, May 8, 1968.
9. *Sporting News*, November 4, 1972.
10. *Sports Collectors Digest*, August 5, 1994.
11. *Sports Collectors Digest*, August 5, 1994.
12. Billingham, interview.
13. *Columbia (SC) State*, July 27, 1973.
14. *Cincinnati Enquirer*, March 7, 1978.
15. "Tigers Hit Jackpot on Longshot Billingham," *Sporting News*, August 12, 1978.
16. "Tigers Hit Jackpot on Longshot Billingham," *Sporting News*, August 12, 1978.
17. "Tigers Hit Jackpot on Longshot Billingham," *Sporting News*, August 12, 1978. Billingham had actu-

ally come in fourth in the Cy Young voting in 1973 and sixth in 1974.

18. Billingham, interview.

19. Billingham, interview.

41. Clay Kirby

1. *Sporting News*, July 3, 1971.

2. *Sporting News*, August 30, 1969.

3. *San Diego Union*, October 17, 1991.

4. Cincinnati Reds, "Reds Get Clay Kirby from San Diego," news release, November 9, 1973.

5. *Sporting News*, August 18, 1973.

6. *Cincinnati Post*, May 18, 1974.

7. *Cincinnati Post*, May 18, 1974.

8. *Cincinnati Post*, May 18, 1974.

9. San Diego Padres, "Padre Close Up," news release, June 19, 1971.

10. San Diego Padres, "Padre Close Up."

Faber, Charles F. *Major League Careers Cut Short: Leading Players Gone by 30*. Jefferson NC: McFarland, 2011.

42. Don Werner

Lawson, Earl. "After Five Brushoffs, Fortune Kisses Seaver." *Sporting News*, July 1, 1978, 40.

Lawson, Earl. "Mishap to Correll Is Break for Werner." *Sporting News*, March 29, 1980, 46.

"Iowa Cubs' Werner Enjoys New Power." *Spencer (IA) Daily Reporter*, May 9, 1984, 9.

Salter, Stephanie. "Bench's Backup on Spot." *San Francisco Examiner*, June 22, 1978.

Werner, Don. Telephone interview. September 18, 2012.

43. Will McEnaney

1. Don Henderson, interview with author, January 26, 2011.

2. Henderson, interview.

3. Greg Rhodes and John Erardi, *Big Red Dynasty: How Bob Howsam and Sparky Anderson Built the Big Red Machine* (Cincinnati: Road West Publishing, 1997), 173.

4. Tim Archdeacon, "Inside Moves: A New Coat of Paint for Opening Day," *Miami News*, April 7, 1986, http://www2.palmbeachpost.com/archives.

5. Joe Posnanski, *Joe's Blog*, August 2009, http://joeposnanski.blogspot.com.

6. Rhodes and Erardi, *Big Red Dynasty*, 176.

7. *Springfield (OH) Sun*, August 13, 1971.

8. Posnanski, *Joe's Blog*.

9. Posnanski, *Joe's Blog*.

10. *Springfield (OH) Daily News*, July 2, 1974.

11. Rhodes and Erardi, *Big Red Dynasty*, 201.

12. Archdeacon, "Inside Moves."

13. John Ring, "Pat Darcy on Sparky, the Big Red Machine and the Ball," Reds Report, http://www.thedsreport.com (site discontinued), accessed January 15, 2011.

14. Ring, "Pat Darcy on Sparky."

15. *Springfield (OH) Sun*, May 6, 1975.

16. Dean Chang, "When Will McEnaney Left Baseball, He Left the Only Life He Knew; Now He's Back for One Last Shot; Reincarnation of a Reliever," *Fort Lauderdale Sun-Sentinel*, July 1, 1985.

17. Chang, "When Will McEnaney Left Baseball."

18. Rhodes and Erardi, *Big Red Dynasty*, 266.

19. Rhodes and Erardi, *Big Red Dynasty*, 266.

20. Camille Bersamin, "Will McEnaney," *Sports Illustrated*, July 17, 2000.

21. Archdeacon, "Inside Moves."

45. Marty Brennaman

1. Marc Katz, "Spat Splits Marty, Johnny," *Dayton (OH) Daily News*, July 28, 2000.

2. Bill Koch, "Brennaman Emotional at Hall Ceremonies," *Cincinnati Post*, July 24, 2000.

3. Greg Paeth, "The Voices of the Reds—Baseball's 'Odd Couple' Marty and Joe," *Cincinnati Post*, October 2, 1990.

4. "NSSA Weekend: Marty Brennaman Comes Back to Salisbury," *Salisbury (NC) Post*, May 1, 2005.

5. Rich Radford, "Brennaman Named to Baseball Hall of Fame," *Norfolk Virginian-Pilot*, February 4, 2000.

6. Tom Robinson, "Brennaman Talks His Way into Fame; Reds Radio Announcer from Portsmouth Goes into Baseball Hall of Fame Today," *Norfolk Virginian-Pilot*, July 23, 2000.

7. Bill Smith, "Brennaman, Reds' 'Voice,' Young, Enthusiastic, Good," *Charleston (WV) Daily Mail*, January 31, 1974.

8. Duane Schuman, "Marty and Joe Keep Livin' on the Air in Cincinnati," *Fort Wayne (IN) News-Sentinel*, October 1, 1993.

9. Marty Brennaman and Lonnie Wheeler, "Marty's Story," *Cincinnati Post*, July 22, 2000.

10. Hal McCoy, "Marty on Joe: 'People Genuinely Loved Him'—Brennaman Says His Longtime Radio Partner Was the No. 1 Figure in Cincinnati Reds History," *Dayton (OH) Daily News*, November 17, 2007.

11. Jeff Horrigan, "Running Gag," *Cincinnati Post*, March 30, 1998.

12. Doug Fernandes, "Brennaman, McCoy Covered Reds since Early '70s," *Sarasota (FL) Herald-Tribune*, March 22, 2009.

13. Brennaman and Wheeler, "Marty's Story."

14. Robinson, "Brennaman Talks His Way into Fame."

15. Robinson, "Brennaman Talks His Way into Fame."

16. Brennaman and Wheeler, "Marty's Story."

17. Robinson, "Brennaman Talks His Way into Fame."

18. Brennaman and Wheeler, "Marty's Story."

19. Brennaman and Wheeler, "Marty's Story."

20. Robinson, "Brennaman Talks His Way into Fame."

21. Associated Press, "Reds' Broadcasters Apologize for Remarks about Ump," *Cleveland Plain Dealer*, May 4, 1988; Associated Press, "And This Honor Belongs to Marty," *Charleston (WV) Daily Mail*, February 4, 2000.

22. Jerry Tipton, "'This One Belong to Cats'? Brennaman Says It's Taken," *Lexington (KY) Herald-Leader*, October 25, 1987.

23. Bill Leffler, "Announcer Recalls that First Major Mistake; The Reds' Voice Remembers that Al Michaels Was Always on His Mind during a Big Game," *Norfolk Virginian-Pilot*, February 21, 1993.

24. Rich Stevens, "Brennaman Not Afraid to Speak His Mind," *Charleston (WV) Daily Mail* online, February 7, 2011, http://www.dailymail.com/Sports/RichStevens/201102070063.

25. Robinson, "Brennaman Talks His Way Into Fame."

26. Robinson, "Brennaman Talks His Way into Fame."

27. Associated Press, "Brennamans Will Team up in Cincinnati," *Lexington (KY) Herald-Leader*, October 5, 2006.

28. C. Trent Rosecrans, "Mike's Retired, but Not Marty," *Cincinnati Post*, June 11, 2007.

29. Jack Bogaczyk, "Brennaman Sees Potential This Season for the Reds; Announcer Says He Has Never Been as Optimistic about Any Other Year," *Charleston (WV) Daily Mail*, April 9, 2010.

Silvia, Tony. *Fathers and Sons in Baseball Broadcasting: The Carays, Brennamans, Bucks and Kalases* (Jefferson NC: McFarland, 2009).

Associated Press. "And This Honor Belongs to Marty." *Charleston (WV) Daily Mail*, February 4, 2000.

———. "Brennamans Will Team up in Cincinnati." *Lexington (KY) Herald-Leader*, October 5, 2006.

———. "Concepcion Threatens Broadcaster." *San Jose Mercury News*, September 8, 1985.

———. "Marty Brennaman Signs 3-Year Contract Extension." *Lima (OH) News*, August 10, 2007.

———. "Reds' Broadcasters Apologize for Remarks about Ump." *Cleveland Plain Dealer*, May 4, 1988.

"Bench Resigns from Radio Show with Brennaman." *Lexington (KY) Herald Leader*, July 28, 2000.

Bogaczyk, Jack. "Brennaman Sees Potential This Season for the Reds; Announcer Says He Has Never Been as Optimistic about Any Other Year." *Charleston (WV) Daily Mail*, April 9, 2010.

"Brennaman, Franchester Sr." (obituary). *Norfolk Virginian-Pilot*, March 29, 1993.

Brennaman, Marty, and Lonnie Wheeler. "Marty's Story." *Cincinnati Post*, July 22, 2000.

Clay, John. "No Identity Crisis in Reds' Radio; Duo Wants to Be Called Just Marty and Joe, and You Can Leave Off Brennaman, Nuxhall." *Lexington (KY) Herald-Leader*, July 7, 1990.

Fernandes, Doug. "Brennaman, McCoy Covered Reds Since Early '70s." *Sarasota (FL) Herald-Tribune*, March 22, 2009.

Goldblatt, Abe. "Reds' Brennaman Calls Bonds 'a First-Class Jerk.'" *Norfolk Virginian-Pilot*, November 9, 1993.

Horrigan, Jeff. "Running Gag." *Cincinnati Post*, March 30, 1998.

Hunter, Bob. "Reds Resolve TV Woes." *Columbus (OH) Dispatch*, January 9, 1987.

Jones, David. "Reds Fans Call 'Foul' at Announcers' Split." *Columbus (OH) Dispatch*, April 10, 1986.

Katz, Marc. "Spat Splits Marty, Johnny." *Dayton (OH) Daily News*, July 28, 2000.

Koch, Bill. "Brennaman Emotional at Hall Ceremonies." *Cincinnati Post*, July 24, 2000.

Lancaster, Marc. "Marty Ad-Libbed Call." *Cincinnati Post*, June 21, 2004.

Leffler, Bill. "Announcer Recalls That First Major Mistake; The Reds' Voice Remembers That Al Michaels Was Always on His Mind during a Big Game." *Norfolk Virginian-Pilot*, February 21, 1993.

"Lillian E. Brennaman" (obituary). *Norfolk Virginian-Pilot*, May 16, 2003.

McCoy, Hal. "Brennamans a Pair of 'Perfect' Announcers." *Dayton (OH) Daily News*, May 21, 2004.

———. "Marty on Joe: 'People Genuinely Loved Him' Brennaman Says His Longtime Radio Partner Was the No. 1 Figure in Cincinnati Reds History." *Dayton (OH) Daily News*, November 17, 2007.

———. "Nervous Marty Signs on with His Son." *Dayton (OH) Daily News*, March 2, 2007.

"NSSA Weekend: Marty Brennaman Comes Back to Salisbury." *Salisbury (NC) Post*, May 1, 2005.

Paeth, Greg. "Brennaman May Return to Reds' TV Broadcasts." *Cincinnati Post*, November 30, 1993.

———. "The Voices of the Reds—Baseball's 'Odd Couple' Marty and Joe." *Cincinnati Post*, October 2, 1990.

Peterson, Bill. "Twenty-Five Years of Marty and Joe." *Cincinnati Post*, June 6, 1998.

Radford, Rich. "Brennaman Named to Baseball Hall of Fame." *Norfolk Virginian-Pilot*, February 4, 2000.

Raissman, Bob. "From the Booth to the Hall." *New York Daily News*, July 18, 2000.

Reed, Billy. "Brennaman to Become Cats' TV Play-by-Play Man." *Lexington (KY) Herald-Leader*, July 28, 1987.

———. "Marty and Joe Blend Together Like Beer, Brat." *Lexington (KY) Herald-Leader*, March 31, 1998.

Robinson, Tom. "Brennaman Appreciates Life with the Reds." *Norfolk Virginian-Pilot*, October 13, 1990.

Robinson, Tom. "Brennaman Talks His Way into Fame; Reds Radio Announcer from Portsmouth Goes into Baseball Hall of Fame Today," *Norfolk Virginian-Pilot*, July 23, 2000.

Rosecrans, C. Trent. "Father to Son to Fans—Now It's 'Dad' and Thom, and a New Tradition." *Cincinnati Post*, March 2, 2007.

———. "Mike's Retired, but Not Marty." *Cincinnati Post*, June 11, 2007.

Schuman, Duane. "Marty and Joe Keep Livin' on the Air in Cincinnati." *Fort Wayne (IN) News-Sentinel*, October 1, 1993.

Smith, Bill. "Brennaman, Reds' 'Voice,' Young, Enthusiastic, Good." *Charleston (WV) Daily Mail*, January 31, 1974.

Stein, Ray. "Brennaman's First Choice: Remain in Reds Country." *Columbus (OH) Dispatch*, March 11, 1988.

Stevens, Rich. "Brennaman Not Afraid to Speak His Mind." *Charleston (WV) Daily Mail* online, February 7, 2011, http://www.dailymail.com/Sports/Rich Stevens/201102070063.

Strauss, Joe. "Duncan Calls Remarks Classless; Notebook: Pitching Coach Was Reacting to Comments by Reds Broadcaster Brennaman." *St. Louis Post-Dispatch*, May 18, 2011.

Tipton, Jerry. "'This One Belong to Cats'? Brennaman Says It's Taken." *Lexington (KY) Herald-Leader*, October 25, 1987.

Tolliver, Lee. "A Hero's Welcome; Reds Broadcaster Brennaman Is Deeply Touched as He Is Honored at the Portsmouth Jamboree." *Norfolk Virginian-Pilot*, February 9, 2001.

Williams, Marty. "'Understanding Each Other' Is the Key—The Two Have Broadcast More Than 4,000 Reds Games over the Last 24 Years." *Dayton (OH) Daily News*, April 1, 1997.

Woody, Paul. "Game Announcers Can Speak Freely—Up to a Point." *Richmond (VA) Times-Dispatch*, May 5, 1988.

46. Postseason

1. Peter Gammons, "Fisk Clutch Bat Bosox' Key Weapon," *Sporting News*, October 26, 1975, 18.

2. Ron Fimrite, "Reaching Out for the Series," *Sports Illustrated*, October 20, 1975, 14.

3. Fimrite, "Reaching Out for the Series," 17.

4. Ron Fimrite, "Stormy Days for the Series," *Sports Illustrated*, October 27, 1975, 22.

5. Fimrite, "Stormy Days for the Series," 22.

6. Fimrite, "Stormy Days for the Series," 23.

7. Ron Fimrite, "Everything Came Up Reds," *Sports Illustrated*, November 3, 1975, 27.

8. Hal McCoy, *The Relentless Reds* (Shelbyville KY: PressCo, 1976), 136.

9. Fimrite, "Everything Came Up Reds," 22.

47. The Reds of Summer

1. Bill James, *The Bill James Baseball Abstract, 1982* (New York: Ballantine, 1982), 105.

2. Jules Tygiel, *Baseball's Great Experiment—Jackie Robinson and his Legacy* (New York: Oxford University Press, 1983), 190.

3. James, *Bill James Baseball Abstract*, 106.

48. 1976 and Beyond

1. Other trades may have presented themselves under the right circumstances. As Mets star pitcher Tom Seaver haggled with management, rumors suggested that lefty Jerry Koosman might be on his way to the Reds. Doug Feldmann, *The 1976 Cincinnati Reds: Last Hurrah for the Big Red Machine* (Jefferson NC: McFarland, 2009), e-book, chap. 3-4.

2. Feldmann, *1976 Cincinnati Reds*, e-book, chap. 4.

3. Feldmann, *1976 Cincinnati Reds*, e-book, chap. 4.

4. The 1975 team posted a .744 winning percentage against the five worst teams in the league (teams with a composite .436 winning percentage) but just .561 against the five best teams in the NL (those with a combined .531 record). In contrast, the 1976 Reds were "only" .628 against the worst NL teams (combined .425) but were a phenomenal .611 against the league's best teams (combined .557).

5. Roger Angell, *Five Seasons: A Baseball Companion* (New York: Simon and Schuster, 1977), 377. For discussions of the Reds' "greatness," see Ray Fitzgerald, "These Reds Don't Overwhelm You but Baby, They're Tough," *Boston Globe*, October 20, 1976, 69; Ulish Carter, "Reds Great in Any Era, No Cinch Next Season," *New Pittsburgh Courier*, October 30, 1976, 25; Lowell Reidenbaugh, "Reds Tinged with Greatness, Says Sparky," *Sporting News*, November 6, 1976, 3; Art Spander, "Yanks Mere Shell of Old Days," *Sporting News*, November 6, 1976, 14; Joe Falls, "Baseball's Ten Best Teams," *Sporting News*, November 13, 1976, 13.

6. On Howsam having already decided to trade Pérez, see John Erardi and Greg Rhodes, "Reds Put the Kibosh on Martin's Chutzpah," Cinicnnati.com, http://reds.enquirer.com/bigred/bigred3.html (excerpt from Rhodes and Erardi, *Big Red Dynasty: How Bob Howsam and Sparky Anderson Built the Big Red Machine* (Cincinnati: Road West Publishing, 1997). Nearly all the Reds echoed what Howsam said later, "Losing Tony took so much of the chemistry away. He had more of an effect on our team—on and off the field—than I ever realized." Dan Epstein, *Big Hair and Plastic Grass: A Funky Ride through Baseball and America in the Swinging '70s* (New York: Thomas Dunne Books, 2010), 210. There remains the question of whether Howsam could have engineered a better deal for Pérez. The Cleveland Indians needed a hard-hitting first baseman, were rumored to be interested in Pérez, and allegedly were willing to part with pitchers Pat Dobson, Jim Bibby, and/or young outfielder George Hendrick, but the Reds balked when the Indians asked for hard-throwing reliever Jim Kern "and a prospect." The Yankees, too, were interested in acquiring Pérez but felt that Howsam "wanted too much." After Pérez was traded to the Expos, the Yankees were "perplexed" because they felt they had offered the Reds more than the Reds received from Montreal. Russell Schneider, "Indians Get Back Carty, Tribe's '76 Man of the Year," *Sporting News*, December 18, 1976, 50; Russell Schneider, "Indians Stronger on Mound, but Attack Looks Anemic," *Sporting News*, December 25, 1976, 44; Phil Pepe, "Yanks See Trade Shutout as Sign of Strength," *Sporting News*, December 25, 1976, 53; Phil Pepe, "Yanks Reward Cox's Faithful Service," *Sporting News*, January 8, 1977, 35.

7. Earl Lawson, "Reds Confident of Success with Driessen and Fryman," *Sporting News*, March 5, 1977, 31; Earl Lawson, "Reds Blueprint Third Title, Admit It Won't Be Easy," *Sporting News*, April 9, 1977, 22; Phil Pepe, *Talkin' Baseball: An Oral History of Baseball in the 1970s* (New York: Ballantine Books, 1998), 274.

8. Earl Lawson, "Only One Word for Reds' Hurlers—Horrible," *Sporting News*, July 16, 1977, 5; Earl Lawson, "Fast-Starting Morgan Shooting for Lofty 30–30," *Sporting News*, April 29, 1978, 10.

9. Most of the Reds, including Pete Rose, Gary Nolan, and Sparky Anderson, believed that the Reds were better than the Dodgers. Rose told Reds beat reporter Earl Lawson, "We've been out to L.A. and seen . . . that we're a better ballclub than they are." For Nolan, see Dick Miller, "Angels See Nolan, Brett Deals as Flag Coup," *Sporting News*, July 2, 1977, 11. Well into midsummer Sparky Anderson believed that the Reds would "win our 95 games. If the Dodgers win 105, they'll beat us. But they aren't that good." Epstein, *Big Hair and*

Plastic Grass, 208. Earl Lawson, "Red Confidence Soars Again after a Visit to Dodger Den," *Sporting News*, June 18, 1977, 19; Bench quoted in "N.L. Flashes," *Sporting News*, June 18, 1977, 32. On the Reds' lack of respect for the Dodgers and the feeling that LA would collapse in 1977: Sparky felt that the acquisition of Seaver would cause panic among the Dodgers. And even in August, Joe Morgan believed that the Dodgers might collapse: "The key to overtaking the Dodgers is pulling to within five games of them—and quick." Then the Dodgers would hear footsteps "and those guys have rabbit ears." See Earl Lawson, "Tom Terrific Caps Impossible Dream of Reds," *Sporting News*, July 2, 1977, 16; and Earl Lawson, "Reds Weary, Resting on Fat Pay, Bench Thinks," *Sporting News*, September 3, 1977, 9. Further, the Reds just didn't care much for many of the Dodgers and the feeling started at the top, as Sparky had publicly called Lasorda "Walking Eagle" because "he's so full of it he can't fly." Epstein, *Big Hair and Plastic Grass*, 208.

10. Eastwick was originally supposed to go to the Mets instead of Zachry, but they refused to take him after Eastwick made it clear that he intended to enter the free agent reentry draft at season's end. Ray Kelly, "Bake Sale Leaves Some Sour Tastes in Philly," *Sporting News*, July 2, 1977, 8; Randy Galloway, "Rangers Set for Twin Bills—Ellis No. 6 Starter," *Sporting News*, July 2, 1977, 12. For Eastwick's conflicts with the Reds, see Earl Lawson, "Tom Terrific Caps Impossible Dream," 16. Seaver never forgave Mets owner M. Donald Grant. "Grant called me a Communist," Seaver claimed later. "That was a plantation mentality that was going on there. Willie Stargell came over and he said, 'They're putting the big N on you. He's putting the big nigger on you.' Stargell was exactly right." Pepe, *Talkin' Baseball*, 280. Ultimately, Seaver's dispute with the Mets led to a series of trades even as far away as California, where Angels general manager Harry Dalton said of his team's series of deadline trades, "Seaver caused this whole thing by being unhappy." Miller, "Angels See Nolan, Brett Deals," 11. Anderson's reaction from Pepe, *Talkin' Baseball*, 377; Dick Young, "Young Ideas," *Sporting News*, July 2, 1977, 15.

11. *Sporting News Official Baseball Guide, 1978* (St. Louis: Sporting News, 1978), 151.

12. The prospect the Reds originally wanted instead of Foster was outfielder Bernie Williams, no relation to the Yankees All-Star of the same name, who later hurt his arm and finished his career playing in Japan. Foster's physique was so impressive that Joe Morgan believed only Willie Mays's surpassed it and Pete Rose believed that Foster was "too strong to be playing baseball. He should be hunting bears with switches." Earl Lawson, "Reds Relish Tom's Humor as Well as His Hurling," *Sporting News*, July 30, 1977, 14. "I thought he might be a guy who batted .280 and hit 15 to 20 homers a season," Morgan remembered of his first impressions of Foster, "but this . . ." Earl Lawson, "Foster Uses Long-Distance in Cincy for All It's Worth," *Sporting News*, August 20, 1977, 12. Likewise, Foster's close friend Willie McCovey admitted, "If I said that I thought he'd blossom into the star that he is today, I'd be lying." Earl Lawson, "Foster's Homers Stir Reds' Disappointed Fans," *Sporting News*, September 24, 1977, 18; Earl Lawson, "Foster Promises He Won't Be Confused Again," *Sporting News*, July 9, 1977, 5; Earl Lawson, "Foster's 'Black Death' Pumps New Life into Reds," *Sporting News*, April 1, 1978, 56.

13. Earl Lawson, "Reds Bench Warmers Face Up to Minor Spectre," *Sporting News*, March 25, 1978, 43; Earl Lawson, "Reds Map Out Short Relief Role for a Delighted Tomlin," *Sporting News*, April 15, 1978, 22. As in the Seaver trade, Wagner actually engineered a better trade than the one that was finalized. The Cubs had agreed to take Jack Billingham and Fryman for Bonham but Billingham vetoed the trade, saying, "I just don't think that Wrigley Field is a fair park in which to pitch." So the Reds yielded future Major League closer Bill Caudill instead. Earl Lawson, "Reds Satisfy All Regulars; Bench Signs Five-Year Pact," *Sporting News*, November 26, 1977, 56; "Reds: 'At Last We Have Pitching,'" *Hartford (CT) Courant*, December 11, 1977, 3C; Lawson, "Reds Bench Warmers," 43. There were other rumors as well that offseason, like the one, quickly denied by Howsam, that had the Reds moving Dave Revering, Billingham, and César Gerónimo to the Giants for John "The Count" Montefusco. Earl Lawson, "'No Way We'll Trade Geronimo,' Howsam Insists," *Sporting News*, October 22, 1977, 26; "Bunts and Boots," *Sporting News*, April 1, 1978, 56.

14. For example, the respected Jerome Holtzman related a "typical" story of two general managers who hoped for Kuhn's removal. Kuhn's talk of competitive balance was nonsense, said Holtzman, since it was compe-

tition that assured the integrity of the game and nobody "should be allowed to rig the race" and establish himself as an "almighty seer." Allegedly, the owners' consortium urged Kuhn's veto of Oakland's 1976 sales so that the players would not be made aware of their value on the open market. And then the owners misrepresented themselves in support of Kuhn's legal defense of the decision because of the damages that each would incur if Finley proved successful. "Sure we didn't tell the whole truth," admitted one candid owner. "What were we supposed to do? If Kuhn loses, it would've cost each club about $170,000." Jerome Holtzman, "Kuhn's Legal Bills Irk Owners," *Sporting News*, March 4, 1978, 30. For the Reds' reaction to the trade, see Earl Lawson, "Reds Infuriated over Blue Decision," *Sporting News*, February 18, 1978, 46. Anderson quoted in "Insiders Say," *Sporting News*, March 4, 1978, 4.

15. Red Smith, "The End of Sparky's Affair," *New York Times*, November 29, 1978, B10.

16. Rose felt a bit betrayed by the way the Reds handled his contract. "This is the best place to play baseball," he said. "I have business interests here. Because of that the Reds could offer me less." But a few weeks later he had concluded, "It seems to me the way the Reds are negotiating this whole contract, they are saying between the lines, 'We don't want you no more.'" Dan Hafner, "Rose Says He'll Go Out Swinging," *Los Angeles Times*, October 1, 1978, C16; "Rose Says He's Free Agent and 12 Clubs Can Draft Him," *Los Angeles Times*, October 19, 1978, E4; "Miscellany: Rose Tells Reds 'No,'" *Boston Globe*, November 27, 1978, 32. For Anderson's side of the firing, see Dick Young, "Sparky Was Hurt, Stunned When Ax Fell," *Hartford (CT) Courant*, November 30, 1978, 71A; Red Smith, "The End of Sparky's Affair," *New York Times*, November 29, 1978, B10; *Los Angeles Times*, November 29, 1978, E1.

Contributors

MALCOLM ALLEN is a lifelong Baltimore Orioles fan and the coeditor of *Pitching, Defense, and Three-Run Homers: The 1970 Baltimore Orioles* (University of Nebraska Press, 2012).

MARK ARMOUR is the founder and director of SABR's Baseball Biography Project and the author or editor of five books on baseball, including *Joe Cronin—A Life in Baseball* (University of Nebraska Press, 2010). He lives in Oregon's Willamette Valley with Jane, Maya, and Drew.

As of this writing, MATT BOHN lives in the Portland, Oregon, area. Originally from Hemlock, Michigan, he grew up a Tigers fan enjoying the play-by-play of Ernie Harwell.

PHILIP A. COLA is vice president, research and technology, at University Hospitals Case Medical Center and an adjunct assistant professor at the Case Western Reserve University (CWRU) School of Medicine. He is a doctoral candidate at the Weatherhead School of Management, CWRU. He wishes to thank his wife, Diane, for her patience as well as his children, Adam and Sami, for being Reds fans too.

RORY COSTELLO grew up as a Mets fan in Connecticut. He first gained deeper appreciation of the Big Red Machine's strength in 1973, when the Mets managed to upset the heavily favored Reds in the National League Championship Series. He lives in Brooklyn, New York, with his wife, Noriko, and son, Kai.

CHARLES F. FABER is a historian living in Lexington, Kentucky. His most recent book, with coau-thor Richard B. Faber, is *The American Presidents Ranked by Performance*, 2nd ed. (McFarland, 2012.) Among his baseball books, all published by McFarland, are: *Baseball Pioneers* (1997); *Spitballers* (2006); *Baseball Ratings*, 3rd ed. (2008); and *Major League Careers Cut Short* (2011). He is currently writing a book on the leading baseball prodigies who reached the majors before their twenty-first birthday.

MICHAEL FALLON is a longtime writer on arts and culture. Born and raised in Southern California in the 1970s, he grew up with a near-constant soundtrack of Beach Boys music and Vin Scully play-by-play. Now a resident of the Twin Cities, Michael runs a community media center in Minneapolis and is, by necessity, selective about his writing projects. To wit, he is currently completing, for the University of Nebraska Press, his first book on baseball, tentatively titled "All Tom's Boys," about the great Dodger teams of 1977 and 1978 and the unfulfilled promise of the California Dream.

ANTHONY GIACALONE is an independent historian specializing in twentieth-century politics and popular culture. He has presented numerous research papers to SABR's annual meetings and has contributed articles to Baseball Think Factory and the *Hardball Times*. He is currently writing a book on baseball in the 1960s and 1970s.

JORGE IBER, PhD, is a professor of history at Texas Tech University and his research focuses on the role of Latinos/Latinas in U.S. sports. His most recent coauthored work is *Latinos in U.S. Sport: A History of Isolation, Cultural Identity, and Ac-*

ceptance (Human Kinetics, 2011), and he will also have a new anthology (tentatively titled "More Than Just Peloteros") from Texas Tech University Press appearing in late 2013. He is currently working on a manuscript on the life and career of Mexican American pitching great Mike Torrez.

MAXWELL KATES is a chartered accountant based in Toronto. He is a member of both the Society for American Baseball Research and the Mayo Smith Society, and his biography of Alex Grammas has previously appeared in *1984 Detroit Tigers: What a Start! What a Finish!* He claims to have seen Cincinnati Reds home games in person, albeit situated in two different states—in the bleachers at the Great American Ballpark (Ohio) and the next day while standing on the Roebling Bridge (Kentucky).

PAUL LADEWSKI, a native Chicagoan, has covered Major League Baseball for various newspapers, magazines, and websites for more than three decades. He is a lifetime member of the Baseball Writers' Association of America and takes part in the Hall of Fame election annually. He currently resides in Orland Park, Illinois.

RUSS LAKE lives in Champaign, Illinois, and is a retired college professor. He was raised in Belleville, Illinois, which is located on the "other side of the river" from downtown St. Louis. The 1964 Cardinals remain his favorite team, and he was distressed to see Sportsman's Park (aka Busch Stadium I) being demolished not long after he had attended the last game there on May 8, 1966. His wife, Carol, deserves an MVP Award for watching all of a fourteen-inning ball game in Cincinnati with Russ in 1971—during their honeymoon. In 1994 he was an editor for David Halberstam's book *October 1964*.

LEN LEVIN, a retired newspaper editor and an unretired Boston Red Sox fan, cheered for the losing side in the 1975 World Series but agrees that the Reds had a great team. He has been an editor

on most of SABR's recent book projects and hopes to be the editor for many more. Len lives with his wife, a university professor, in Providence, Rhode Island.

MARK MILLER is a retired recreation department director in Springfield, Ohio, where he lives with his wife, Connie. A high school baseball coach for twenty-two years, he is currently the president of the Springfield/Clark County Baseball Hall of Fame. His research, speaking, and writing are related to local baseball topics.

RICHARD MILLER is a longtime Ohio resident who knows this team well.

DEREK NORIN is a freelance journalist based in Washington DC.

BILL NOWLIN has been vice president of SABR since 1994 and has been very active in editing a number of books for SABR, such as *Can He Play?: A Look at Baseball Scouts and Their Profession*, as well as nearly a dozen team books. Cofounder of Rounder Records, he's a lifelong Red Sox fan and was at Fenway Park for both Game Six and Game Seven of the 1975 World Series.

JACOB POMRENKE is SABR's web content editor/producer. He lives in Scottsdale, Arizona, with his wife, Tracy Greer, and their cat, Nixey Callahan.

JIM SANDOVAL is a history teacher, writer, and associate scout for the Minnesota Twins. He is the coeditor of *Can He Play?: A Look at Baseball Scouts and Their Profession*. He currently lives in Harvest, Alabama.

ANDY STURGILL is a college administrator and avid reader of books about baseball, football, and presidents. A lifelong Phillies fan, he lives in suburban Philadelphia with his wife, Carrie.

CINDY THOMSON is a freelance writer and coauthor of *Three Finger: The Mordecai Brown Story*, the biography of a Cubs Hall of Famer who also pitched one season in Cincinnati. The first in her new historical fiction series releases in 2013. A lifelong Reds fan, she writes full-time from her home in central Ohio, where she and her husband, Tom, raised three sons to root for Cincinnati. She also mentors writers through the Jerry B. Jenkins Christian Writers Guild. Visit her online at www.cindyswriting.com.

STEVE TREDER attended his first SABR meetings in 1985 and has been a frequent contributor and presenter in the decades since. He has been a writer for the *Hardball Times* since its founding in 2004.

JOSEPH WANCHO lives in Westlake, Ohio, and is a lifelong Cleveland Indians fan. Working at AT&T since 1994 as a process/development manager, he has been a SABR member since 2005. He is the co-chair of SABR's Minor Leagues Research Committee.

DOUG WILSON is the author of *Fred Hutchinson and the 1964 Cincinnati Reds* (McFarland, 2010), *The Bird: The Life and Legacy of Mark Fidrych* (Thomas Dunne Books/St. Martin's Press, 2013), and *Brooks Robinson: The Biography of a Baseball Icon* (2014). He lives with his wife and three children in Columbus, Indiana.

A lifelong Pirates fan, GREGORY H. WOLF was born in Pittsburgh but now resides in the Chicago-land area with his wife, Margaret, and daughter, Gabriela. A professor of German and holder of the Dennis and Jean Bauman endowed chair of the humanities at North Central College in Naperville, Illinois, he has published articles on baseball history at the *Hardball Times*, regularly contributes to SABR projects, including the BioProject, and is currently editing a SABR book on the 1957 Milwaukee Braves.

In the Memorable Teams in Baseball History series

The Great Eight: The 1975 Cincinnati Reds
edited by Mark Armour

Pitching, Defense, and Three-Run Homers:
The 1970 Baltimore Orioles
edited by Mark Armour and Malcolm Allen

Bridging Two Dynasties: The 1947 New York
Yankees
edited by Lyle Spatz
associate editors: Maurice Bouchard and
Leonard Levin

The Team That Forever Changed Baseball and
America: The 1947 Brooklyn Dodgers
edited by Lyle Spatz
associate editors: Maurice Bouchard and
Leonard Levin

Drama and Pride in the Gateway City:
The 1964 St. Louis Cardinals
edited by John Harry Stahl and Bill Nowlin
associate editors: Tom Heinlein, Russell Lake,
and Leonard Levin

Pitching to the Pennant: The 1954 Cleveland Indians
edited by Joseph Wancho
associate editors: Rick Huhn, Leonard Levin,
Bill Nowlin, and Steve Johnson

To order or obtain more information on these or other
University of Nebraska Press titles, visit nebraskapress
.unl.edu.